Ethics and Global Politics

Series Editors: Tom Lansford and Patrick Hayden

Since the end of the Cold War, explorations of ethical considerations within global politics and on the development of foreign policy have assumed a growing importance in the fields of politics and international studies. New theories, policies, institutions, and actors are called for to address difficult normative questions arising from the conduct of international affairs in a rapidly changing world. This series provides an exciting new forum for creative research that engages both the theory and practice of contemporary world politics, in light of the challenges and dilemmas of the evolving international order.

Also in the series

Cosmopolitan Global Politics
Patrick Hayden
ISBN 0 7546 4276 3

Understanding Human Rights Violations
New Systematic Studies
Edited by Sabine C. Carey and Steven C. Poe
ISBN 0 7546 4026 4

International Environmental Justice
A North-South Dimension
Ruchi Anand
ISBN 0 7546 3824 3

In War We Trust

The Bush Doctrine and the Pursuit of Just War

CHRIS J. DOLAN
University of Central Florida, USA

ASHGATE

Published by
Ashgate Publishing Limited
Gower House
Croft Road
Aldershot
Hampshire GU11 3HR
England

Ashgate Publishing Company
Suite 420
101 Cherry Street
Burlington, VT 05401-4405
USA

Ashgate website: http://www.ashgate.com

British Library Cataloguing in Publication Data
Dolan, Chris J.
   In war we trust : the Bush doctrine and the pursuit of just
   war. - (Ethics and global politics)
   1.War on Terrorism, 2001- - Moral and ethical aspects
   2.Just war doctrine 3.United States - Foreign relations -
   2001-
   I.Title
   973.9'31

Library of Congress Cataloging-in-Publication Data
Dolan, Chris J.
   In war we trust : the Bush doctrine and the pursuit of just war / by Chris Dolan.
      p. cm. -- (Ethics and global politics)
   Includes bibliographical references and index.
   ISNB 0-7546-4234-8
  1. United States--Military policy--Moral and ethical aspects. 2. Just war doctrine.
3. War on Terrorism, 2001---Moral and ethical aspects. 4. United States--Foreign
relations--2001- I. Title. II. Series.

   UA23.D5983 2005
   172'.42--dc22

                                                              2004030882

ISBN 0 7546 4234 8

Printed and bound in Great Britain by MPG Books Ltd, Bodmin, Cornwall

Contents

For Holly Gonyea Dolan and Braiden Gonyea Dolan

List of Abbreviations

CBU	Cluster Bomb Units
CENTCOM	Central Command
CFR	Council on Foreign Relations
DPG	Defense Planning Guidance
EU	European Union
FAO	Food and Agriculture Organization
GAO	General Accounting Office
HRW	Human Rights Watch
HVT	High Value Target
IAEA	International Atomic Energy Agency
ICC	International Criminal Court
ICJ	International Court of Justice
INC	Iraqi National Congress
MLRS	Multiple Launch Rocket System
NAFTA	North American Free Trade Agreement
NATO	North Atlantic Treaty Organization
NPR	Nuclear Posture Review
NPT	Non Proliferation Treaty
NSS	National Security Strategy
OPEC	Organization of Petroleum Exporting Countries
PNAC	Project for a New American Century
QDR	Quadrennial Defense Review
TST	Time Sensitive Target
UNHCR	United Nations High Commission on Refugees
UNICEF	United Nations Children's Fund
UNMOVIC	UN Monitoring, Verification, and Inspection Commission
UNSCOM	United Nations Special Commission in Iraq
WMD	Weapons of Mass Destruction

Acknowledgements

My motivation to research and write this book would not have been possible without the support of several important individuals. Above all, I want to thank my wife Holly for her unending love and support. Holly and I were blessed on 3 November 2004 when our son Braiden was born. I also want to thank our families for their support during the very busy year of 2004. In addition, Ms. Kirstin Howgate was especially helpful in her role of helping to bring this book to completion. The editors of the series in which this book appears, Dr. Tom Lansford and Dr. Patrick Hayden, supplied productive commentary that strengthened the overall presentation. Finally, I would like to acknowledge the outside reviewers who provided valuable insight into key elements of the book.

Chapter 1

September 11th and Offensive Warfare

Introduction

Among the most consequential decisions for any government involves the decision to use military force. Such decisions tap the moral fabric of society, since violence, death, and suffering are the defining features of war. In general, it is reputed that what is meant by morality is a notion of an acceptable code of ethical conduct in international politics, of a national belief in a set of criteria for right and wrong behavior in the global setting, and the idea of conforming to a certain standard of uprightness and justice. These suppositions often conflict with the advancement of political interests, which are sometimes placed above moral and ethical concerns. For Americans, the nexus between morality and politics is manifest in the Declaration of Independence, which inscribes "We hold these truths to be self-evident, that all men are created equal, that they are endowed by their Creator with certain unalienable rights that among these are life, liberty and the pursuit of happiness."[1] But do these words represent the bedrock of America's moral and political vision or its fixation on unethical expansionism?

When terrorists attacked the US on 11 September 2001 (9/11), many believed that President George W. Bush was left with no choice but to use offensive military force against the Al-Qaida terrorist network and the Taliban in Afghanistan in order to obviate future attacks from that country. The news footage of Flights 11 and 175 crashing into the twin towers of the World Trade Center in New York, the image of Flight 77 ripping a hole in the Pentagon, and the story of United Airlines Flight 93 scattered throughout a field in western Pennsylvania struck a far-reaching emotional and psychological chord with the world and challenged America's sense of invulnerability. Then, throughout the fall 2001, traces of anthrax were detected all over the country including the offices of the US Senate, resulting in thirteen infections and five deaths. War had been delivered to the US.

By late November 2001, after six weeks of punishing US air attacks and the deployment of special operations forces working in tandem with the Afghani Northern Alliance, the Taliban collapsed and Al-Qaida terrorists were dispersed. The rapid and ongoing military force and the quick fall of enemy strongholds amazed the world. President Bush was beloved by Americans, the US was praised on the world stage, and America's traditional allies rushed to its side to support what many believed was a justifiable and ethical response to prevent additional terrorist attacks. At the moment, it appeared that America had a clear and unique opportunity to forge a new era of international politics, build on its multilateral achievements, and to bring the nations of the world, including it former enemies and emerging challengers, closer to the norms and rules of international law, the principles of which had been constructed by the US and its allies during the Cold War.

But the moment seemed to come and go. Beginning in early 2002, Bush began making a series of dramatic leaps in America's global war on terrorism. First, the president claimed the US possesses the moral and political right to wage offensive wars with preemptive military force and preventive war against states it believes are harboring terrorists and/or pursuing weapons of mass destruction (WMD). The right to offensive force could even be waged against so-called rogue regimes not directly implicated in the 9/11 attacks. The president went on to identify the most dangerous of these governments by proclaiming Iraq, Iran, and North Korea as members of an axis of evil. Even more, Bush has asserted that the US has the broader right to forcefully reshape the international political system and retains the power to act unilaterally in order to maintain its self-proclaimed status as the world's preeminent global power.

After America had used force in Afghanistan to prevent further terror attacks by Al-Qaida under the military protection of the Taliban, Bush applied his offensive strategy in Iraq. His administration spent 2002 and 2003 building a domestic and global case for war against what the president believed was a "grave and gathering danger" that had the intent and capability of carrying out a "sudden and catastrophic attack" with WMD. In fact, the president even suggested:

> We must not ignore the threat gathering against us. Facing clear evidence of peril, we cannot wait for the final proof - the smoking gun - that could come in the form of a mushroom cloud ... We have every reason to assume the worst, and we have an urgent duty to prevent the worst from occurring.[2]

However, as the US began more actively projecting its moral and political might onto the world stage via its ultimate invasion of Iraq in March 2003, concerns arose over what many believed was the Bush Administration taking advantage of a post cold war world in which there appeared to be no counterweight to American global power. One important question emerged: is the application of offensive military force morally and politically acceptable as it has been framed by the Bush Administration?

Since the 9/11 attacks, the Bush Administration has decided to make Afghanistan and Iraq the centerpieces in what it perceives to be a broader just war against terrorists and rogue states. The goal of this book is to address the hotly debated issue of whether or not the use of offensive military force against Afghanistan to obviate future terrorist attacks and against Iraq in order to prevent rogue states from pursuing WMD meets the necessary moral and political requirements set forth by just war principles. A cursory overview of each chapter is in order. This chapter (Chapter 1) introduces the reader to the moral and political components of the Bush Administration's doctrine of striking first and assesses its consistency in the history of American foreign policy. It explains why the doctrine places such high a premium on targeting so-called rogue states that are thought to pursue WMD and allegedly align themselves with terrorist groups. The examination also focuses on the moral foundation of the strategy: the right of self-defense. It then engages in an historical analysis of US offensive force and American interventionism, and in doing so, argues that the Bush Doctrine of striking first is not an innovative national security strategy. Then, it dissects the power of Democratic Moralism in the Bush presidency.

Chapter 2 turns to an investigation of the empirical research and theory in international relations dealing with notions of just war theory and political power. In doing so, it put forth a review of war along the lines of *jus ad bellum* (justification for going to war), *jus in bello* (conduct of justifiable acts in wartime), and *jus post bellum* (the justifiable imposition of peace once major combat has ceased) requirements. It also identifies power as an important factor in just war theory by identifying key political factors that complement notions of just war. Realism helps us to explain the relationship between justice and power in international politics and foreign policy.

Jus as bellum principles shall be assessed in Chapters 3 to 7. Chapter 3 will seek to address the issue of whether or not the application of the Bush Doctrine to Afghanistan and Iraq are defensible from the perspective of just cause. Throughout the chapter, the notion of Just Cause is interpreted as "punishing injustice" and "responding to aggression." In Chapter 4, we will apply the requirement of Right Intention to waging offensive war. While the goal is not to advance ethical purity, we will assess the America's diversity of intentions against the notion that the goals of just cause must be realized. Chapter 5 will apply the just war principle of Legitimate Authority in order to determine the consistency of US offensive military actions with particular international legal constraints the US itself adheres to. Then, in Chapter 6, the idea that the decision to go to war should always be arrived at as a Last Resort will be the major focus. The notion that fear can sometimes produce hasty and ill-conceived results that push the war option to the forefront of national security decision-making is of particular concern. The Bush Administration's definition of success in the wars against terrorism and rogue states sponsoring terrorism and seeking WMD will be the subject of interest in Chapter 7 on the Likelihood of Success.

Chapter 8 and 9 shift the just war analysis to *jus in bello* principles that place constraints on how a just offensive war must be waged in order to be considered just and moral. The principle of Proportionality is examined in Chapter 8. Here we are most concerned with the use of weapons that minimize the destructive capacity of war and targets that are relevant to the prosecution of a just war. Chapter 9 puts forth the idea that warring parties must safeguard the just war principle of Non-Combatant Immunity. Although this requirement imposes significant prohibitions on attacks against non-combatant civilians or civilian objects, the toll that war takes on non-combatant life will be emphasized.

Jus Post Bellum requirements will be the subject of Chapter 10, which argues that warring parties recognize that the goal of war should be the moral attainment of a state of peace. The establishment of a just peace in both Afghanistan and Iraq will be dissected according to four key principles: Just Cause for Termination, Right Intention, Discrimination, and the Likelihood of a Lasting Peace. A just peace is more than a simple end to major hostilities; it also includes reconciliation, reconstruction, goodwill, and the creation of particular conditions that lead to a persistent state of peace.

Just war analysis has some difficulties from the standpoint of its critics. However, however, mean that just war criteria are useless. Just war theory demonstrates that ethical questions are never clear-cut and that there will always be gray areas where well intentioned people will not necessarily agree. The criteria are helpful in that they provide a sense of where wars can "go wrong," assuming that they are not inherently wrong to begin with. Although they may not define absolute boundaries, at the very least they do describe what nations must strive towards or what they must move away from in order for their actions to be judged reasonable and justified.

The Bush Doctrine of Striking First

Political Premise: Targeting Rogue States

The 9/11 terrorist attacks provided the US with the political opportunity to transform America's strategic national security strategy away from what some perceived as a Cold War-era policy of containment and deterrence toward one that emphasizes offensive warfare against terrorists and so-called rogue states. For one observer, 9/11 represented a "long-standing call for the US to develop a comprehensive strategy that finally spoke to the challenges of the Post-Cold War era."[3] National Security Adviser Condoleezza Rice described the political opportunities for strategic alteration of US national security policy by comparing 9/11 to the immediate post-WW II period that provided fertile ground for the assertion of the Truman Doctrine:

> I really think this period is analogous to 1945 to 1947 - that is, the period when the containment doctrine took shape - in that the events so clearly demonstrated that there is a big global threat, and that it's a big global threat to a lot of countries that you would not have normally thought of as being in the coalition. That has started shifting the tectonic plates in international politics. And it's important to try to seize on that and position American interests and institutions and all of that before they harden again.[4]

President Bush decided immediately to build his doctrine on a foundation that included the targeting of states. In a speech on 12 September 2001, the president stated "we will make no distinction between the terrorists who committed these acts and those who harbor them."[5] Bush also added, that the attacks "were more than acts of terror, they were acts of war." Thus, unlike any other attack on American targets by terrorists, 9/11 would not be interpreted by Bush as merely an isolated crime, but the beginning of a war against states and non-states.

But how the US should respond, with what means and, most importantly, where? Some in the administration saw 9/11 as an opportunity to attack Iraq, but other believed the president had to target only those terrorists and states directly implicated in the attacks on the US, namely Al-Qaida and the Taliban in Afghanistan. Leading the charge to influence the president to target states was Deputy Secretary of Defense Paul Wolfowtiz who stated: "I think one has to say it is not just simply a matter of capturing people and holding them accountable, but removing the sanctuaries, removing the support systems, ending states who sponsor terrorism. And that is why it has to be a broad and sustained campaign."[6]

The attacks of 9/11 allowed the Bush Administration to expand the military response to include terrorists and state sponsors of terrorism in a world that for Bush was clearly defined. In other words, the president retained the option of overthrowing states that supported terrorism or pursued weapons of mass destruction that could be supplied to terrorists. He contended:

> And we will pursue nations that provide aid or safe haven to terrorism ... Every nation, in every region, now has a decision to make. Either you are with us, or you are with the terrorists. From this day forward, any nation that continues to harbor or support terrorism will be regarded by the United States as a hostile regime ...[7]

Bush also expanded the war on terrorism to include preemptive and preventive action against states that both sponsor terrorism and/or pursue WMD. In his 2002 State of the Union, Bush stated, "First, we will shut down terrorist camps, disrupt terrorist plans and bring terrorists to justice. And second, we must prevent the terrorists and regimes who seek chemical, biological or nuclear weapons from threatening the United States and the world." [8] Bush also labeled North Korea, Iran, and Iraq as rogue states and hinted at US action against Iraq.

> North Korea is a regime arming with missiles and weapons of mass destruction, while starving its citizens. Iran aggressively pursues these weapons and exports terror, while an unelected few repress the Iranian people's hope for freedom. Iraq continues to flaunt its hostility toward America and to support terror. The Iraqi regime has plotted to develop anthrax and nerve gas and nuclear weapons for over a decade. This is a regime that has already used poison gas to murder thousands of its own citizens, leaving the bodies of mothers huddled over their dead children. This is a regime that agreed to international inspections then kicked out the inspectors. This is a regime that has something to hide from the civilized world.[9]

Bush also made a case that all three states served as imminent threats to the US:

> States like these, and their terrorist allies, constitute an axis of evil, arming to threaten the peace of the world. By seeking weapons of mass destruction, these regimes pose a grave and growing danger. They could provide these arms to terrorists, giving them the means to match their hatred. They could attack our allies or attempt to blackmail the United States. In any of these cases, the price of indifference would be catastrophic.[10]

Bush made his most forceful public case for striking first on 1 June 2002 in his graduation speech to Army cadets at West Point. He stated that "our security will require all Americans to be forward-looking and resolute, to be ready for preemptive action when necessary ..."[11]

The publication of the 2002 *National Security Strategy* (NSS) cemented these ideas into a formal presidential doctrine. It states, "today, our enemies will use weapons of mass destruction as weapons of choice ... We cannot let our enemies strike first." It also goes on to justify the need for preemption based on the concept of self-protection:

> we will not hesitate to act alone, if necessary, to exercise our right of self-defense by acting preemptively against such terrorists; to prevent them from doing harm against our people and our country ... nations need not suffer an attack before they can lawfully take action to defend themselves against forces that present an imminent danger of attack.[12]

The NSS also claims the power to engage in preventive war:

> The greater the threat, the greater the risk of inaction – and the more compelling the case for taking anticipatory action to defend ourselves, even if uncertainty remains as to the time and place of the enemy's attack.[13]

Furthermore, it asserts US global primacy by stating that "our forces will be strong enough to dissuade potential adversaries from pursuing a military build-up in hopes of surpassing, or equaling, the power of the United States."[14]

Bush's embrace of preemption and preventive war became known as the "first strike doctrine."[15] Preemptive military force or preemption involves striking first at an imminent and ominous threat, believing that an attack is going to occur. Preventive war is the use of force against non-imminent threats in the hope of preventing against future attacks. This highly controversial method of using force places considerable faith in predicting the future intentions of states and non-states. Both preemption and preventive war are premised on the belief that terrorists which combine suicidal attacks with other deadly tactics and states that support terrorism and pursue WMD cannot be contained and deterred.

Preemption and preventive war strategies reflect what many international relations scholars perceive as a US foreign policy fluctuating and vacillating between multilateralism and unilateralism.[16] Proponents of multilateralism recommend greater US reliance on international laws, institutions, and organizations to manage global issues and promote international cooperation.[17] Advocates of unilateralism maintain that the US should use its power to reshape the global system in accordance with its national interests.[18]

The Moral Premise: The Right of Self-Defense

The moral premise of Bush's doctrine of striking first rests on the traditional right of self-defense. Article 51, Chapter VII of the United Nations Charter preserves for member states the right of self-defense: "Nothing in the present Charter shall impair the inherent right of individual or collective self-defense an armed attack occurs against a Member of the United Nations, until the Security Council has taken measures necessary to maintain international peace and security."[19] Like any legal text, the exact meaning and scope of what constitutes legitimate self-defense is open and has been subject to debate. However, in the absence of an armed attack that has already occurred, resorting to self-defense is legitimate only in cases of a real, looming, and imminent attack. In essence, distinctions between unilateralism and multilateralism, states and non-states, and deterrence, preemption, and preventive war are fundamental. A denial of these distinctions is politically and morally unacceptable.

President Bush's first strike doctrine spells out in detail the case for striking first for the sake of self-defense. According to his *National Security Strategy*:

> For centuries, international law recognized that nations need not suffer an attack before they can lawfully take action to defend themselves against forces that present an imminent danger of attack. Legal scholars and international jurists often conditioned the legitimacy of preemption on the existence of an imminent threat – most often a visible mobilization of armies, navies, and air forces preparing to attack. We must adapt the concept of imminent threat to the capabilities and objectives of today's adversaries. Rogue states and terrorists do not seek to attack us using conventional means. They know such attacks would fail. Instead, they rely on acts of terror and, potentially, the use of weapons of mass destruction-weapons that can be easily concealed, delivered covertly, and used without warning ... To forestall or prevent such hostile acts by our adversaries, the United States will, if necessary, act preemptively.[20]

Condoleezza Rice has elaborated on this by claiming:

> Preemption is not a new concept. There has never been a moral or legal requirement that a country wait to be attacked before it can address existential threats... But this approach must be treated with great caution. The number of cases in which it might be justified will always be small. It does not give a green light to the United States or any other nation to act first without exhausting other means, including diplomacy. Preemptive action does not come at the beginning of a long chain of effort. The threat must be very grave. And the risks of waiting must far outweigh the risks of action.[21]

The Bush administration's version of self-defense and its arguments in favor of a first strike doctrine rest on the larger view that warfare has been transformed by terrorism in general and 9/11 in particular. As Colin Powell argues, "It's a different world.... it's a new kind of threat."[22] And in several important respects, war has changed along the lines the administration suggests, although that transformation is nothing new as terrorism has been an ongoing threat to the US for a number of decades. Prevailing wisdom suggests that non-traditional enemies, namely terrorist groups and rogue states, are prepared to wage modern warfare by concealing their movements, weapons, and intentions by attacking civilians, military personnel, technologies, and infrastructure and shirking their commitments to international law. Exacerbated by the 9/11 terrorist attacks, American policymakers are motivated by the fear of nuclear, chemical, and biological weapons falling into the hands of terrorists and irresponsible rogue states. President Bush contends in his 2002 *National Security Strategy* that Americans face enemies who "reject basic human values and hate the United States and everything for which it stands."[23] Although vulnerability could be reduced, it is impossible to achieve complete immunity.

As the argument goes, America's vulnerability to terrorism and its fear of WMD proliferation has legitimized the Bush Administration's assumption of a more offensive military posture grounded on self-defense. But it is the character of potential threats from states that becomes extremely important in evaluating the legitimacy of Bush's first strike doctrine. Thus, the assertion is that 9/11 demonstrates that the US will continue to be confronted by rogue states that oppose America's goal of preventing the proliferation of WMD in the hands of dangerous leaders, such as Saddam Hussein and Kim Jong Ill, and the potential spread of those weapons to non-state terrorists. Indeed, these twin threats have contributed to a political environment that has allowed Bush to significantly alter America's strategic national security doctrine. According to historian John Lewis Gaddis:

> It took a shock like 9/11 to produce something that was this dramatic ... I have to say that 10 years into the Post-Cold War era, there was very little sign of a comprehensive grand strategy. There were strategies toward particular countries and with regard to particular issues, but very little effort to pull it altogether. 9/11 forced us to get our grand strategic act together. And this is the way it normally happens, it seems to me, in history.[24]

But while 9/11 may have justified America's right to use force as a offensive response against states that sponsored terrorist attacks on the US, such as the Taliban, the Bush Administration makes a questionable and controversial moral jump when it assumes that "rogue states" not directly affiliated with anti-US terrorist activity or the 9/11 attacks desire to harm the US with WMD and pose an imminent or future military threat. Does the president blur the distinction between "rogue states" and terrorists and erase the difference between terrorists and those states in which they reside with the following: "We make no distinction between terrorists and those who knowingly harbor or provide aid to them."[25] Any tentative answer must acknowledge, in the first place, that such distinctions make a difference.

There is also a strong difference between the intentions and capabilities of so-called rogue states. The first strike doctrine sees a major national security threat in the accelerating horizontal "proliferation" of destructive capacities, which it suggests is due to rising technical capacities of states beyond the traditional great powers. Importantly, it makes no distinction between the acquisition of what it terms "the world's most destructive technologies" and the intention to turn those technologies into usable weapons.[26]

The Long Tradition of US Offensive Force and Interventionism

The Bush Administration's assertion of a right to flex its military might against so-called rogue states and terrorists via preemptive force and preventive war is both a political response to the terrorist attacks of 9/11 and consistent with the tradition of US interventionism. But while offensive force is certainly not a new development or concept, its expression in the form of a public national security doctrine and the president's claim of a moral right to preempt or prevent threats is a highly expansive interpretation of that history. Thomas Paine conceived America as "an asylum for mankind" and John Winthrop once spoke of a shining "city on a hill," words which later formed the basis of Manifest Destiny and American exceptionalism.[27]   Indeed, there has been a crusading element to America's existence: namely, to tell the world about the success of its experiment and to extend to others the benefit of its wisdom.

Since the early days of the American Republic, presidents have embodied this nationalist and idealist yearning that has transformed US foreign policy into a moral crusade or visionary quest for spreading US values throughout the world via armed intervention. For example, a 1975 congressional study makes clear the long history of US armed intervention around the globe since 1798. Prior to its entry in World War II, America intervened 163 times in foreign nations with its armed forces, and has averaged one armed intervention per year since the end of that war.[28] While the scope of armed intervention has historically focused on Latin America, the Caribbean, and East Asia, the US has recently used force in Somalia, Liberia, the former Yugoslavia, Afghanistan, and Iraq.

In the very early years of the Republic, the US made it clear that it intended to support peoples who wanted independence, but would only serve as an exemplar in doing so. Americans sought to safeguard their daring new adventure in government by shunning all foreign quarrels and overseas obligations. As the 18th century ended, President George Washington admonished his countrymen to "steer clear of permanent alliances," and Thomas Jefferson attempted to strike a delicate balance between trade and national security by warning "Peace, commerce, and honest friendship with all nations, entangling alliances with none."[29] On 4 July 1821 Secretary of State John Quincy Adams even enshrined America's aversion to imperialism with the following precept:

> Wherever the standard of freedom and independence has been or shall be unfurled, there will America's heart, her benediction, and her prayers be. But she goes not abroad in search of monsters to destroy. She is the well-wisher to the freedom and independence of all. She is champion and vindicator only of her own. She will commend the general cause by the countenance of her voice,   and   the   benignant sympathy of her example. She well knows that by once enlisting under other banners than her own, were they even the banners of foreign independence ... the fundamental maxim of her policy would insensibly change from liberty to force ... She might become the dictatress of the world. She would no longer be the ruler of her own spirits.[30]

Interestingly, the words of America's early leaders did not prevent the US from using offensive military force to expand westward in violation of treaties with Native Americans, to extending northward into Canada in search of more living space, and quelling Barbary pirate attacks on US commercial interests in North Africa. According to Adams's yardstick, only a direct threat to national survival could justify America's entry into foreign wars; that is, non-interventionism would be the benchmark of American foreign policy. But Adams was directing his words toward Europe, in particular Great Britain and France.

Non-interventionism and restraint were certainly not the case within the Western Hemisphere as America believed its moral concerns extended to what it perceived as its own geographic sphere of influence. Just two years after Adams' speech, in 1823, President James Monroe altered America's approach to the world by enunciating his famous Monroe Doctrine to Congress, which Adams ironically drafted. The doctrine combined the ingredients of moralism with American self-interest, a mix that has often perplexed and bemused others, by stating that the US would prevent any attempt by European powers "to extend their systems to any portion of this hemisphere as dangerous to our peace and security." The second part of the doctrine pledged that, in exchange, the US vowed "never to entangle ourselves in the broils of Europe."[31]

For all the considerable virtue attached to such a pronouncement, namely idealism and self-interest, President Monroe never consulted the Latin American countries covered under his declaration, thereby triggering an everlasting resentment and anger in the region. Of course, the United Kingdom gave America enough leeway to utter such a bold decree since it controlled the Atlantic sea lanes which spared the US from having to more rapidly build up its own navy. Although the US enforced the Monroe Doctrine inconsistently, according to whatever interpretation of the national interest suited it at the time, it was enforced over and over again by Monroe's successors. From 1806 until today, the US intervened more than 100 times with its armed forces in Latin America, including brief military forays against coastal areas, armed attacks on pirates, efforts to secure the construction of the Panama Canal, violent overthrows of anti-US governments, forcible takeovers of property for repayments of debts, and arrests of renegades sometimes direct assistance to get rid of dictatorships. There was always a publicly stated moral imperative behind each action. It ranged from forestalling chaos, to saving the lives and property of Americans, to extending democracy abroad. Lurking in the shadows were US economic interests.

The greatest period of US dominance in the region started with President Theodore Roosevelt and ended with President Franklin Roosevelt. American soldiers occupied five countries for decades: Cuba, the Dominican Republic, Panama, Haiti, and Nicaragua. The rationale was to uphold US values in unsettled situations south of the border; President Theodore Roosevelt even formulated a corollary to the Monroe Doctrine, arrogating to the US the right of "preventive enforcement" to seize governments that failed to pay their debts.[32] However, each occupation turned out to be debacles of one sort or another, and the moral arguments soon appeared shabby and thin. Since the American public eventually saw no moral basis for these usurpations, it withdrew its mandate from heaven, leading President Franklin Roosevelt to withdraw the remaining US forces in the region as a gesture from the good neighbor to the north. However, the US never really embraced interdependence until corporate desires drove it to enter the North American Free Trade Agreement (NAFTA) in 1993.

It was President Woodrow Wilson who broke the notion of non-entanglement in European affairs by sending American soldiers into World War I in 1917. Then, at the Versailles Peace Treaty, Wilson took a major step toward an unprecedented global commitment by advancing the concept of the League of Nations, in order to promote the morally broader ideas of freedom and self-determination in America's revolutionary heritage. As he said with a very American sense of certainty: "We have come to redeem the world by giving it liberty and justice."[33] Although Wilson failed to make the political argument in defense of US membership in the League in the US Senate, he made a strong moral case for internationalism, or Wilsonianism. As summed up by Robert Nisbet:

> From Wilson's day to ours the embedded purpose, sometimes articulated in words, more often than not – of American foreign policy, under Democrats and Republicans alike oftentimes, had boiled down to America-on-a-Permanent-Mission – a mission to make the rest of the world a little more like America the Beautiful.[34]

The ruination of World War II changed all of these reservations. America realized that it had to become a permanent participating member of the post-war world order because its very survival was at stake in a new world characterized by atomic weapons. In the ensuing Cold War, the US needed allies, both democratic and undemocratic. President Roosevelt proposed that the US back the United Nations Charter, which was drafted by his own State Department. The UN would be unlike the League of Nations; it was designed to be uniquely configured to America's national interests as well as its idealism. This body struck a balance between America's moral foundations and the growing extent of its global power, namely giving the veto power on the Security Council to, at the time, the five most powerful states and allowing other member nations to debate and vents their views in a General Assembly. The UN would provide the political veil America needed to advance its Cold War interests visa vie its nemesis, the USSR

President Truman rallied the US around the Truman Doctrine's containment and deterrence strategies, the Marshall Plan, and the Bretton Woods global monetary system (which fixed the exchange rates of allied governments on the US dollar), in order to counter the spread of Soviet power and Communism. Such a sweeping appeal touched upon the preoccupations of Americans, who were held together by a fierce sense of Anti-Communism. Besides, the strategy worked for decades. Presidents Eisenhower, Kennedy, and Johnson enforced Truman's foreign policy goals as a way of halting the USSR and protecting US business interests. However, both Johnson and Nixon tilted too far toward national security arguments alone, eventually losing their moral standing in Southeast Asia.

President Carter may have elevated human rights to a serious concern in his foreign policy; however, he applied the policy in such a haphazard and unconvincing way that he could not find moral support at home or even address America's national interests. President Reagan appealed to America's moral soul by calling the USSR an "Evil Empire" and demanding that Gorbachev "tear down that wall," but he stumbled over Iran-Contra, ordered a military invasion of the helpless island of Grenada, rapidly increased military spending resulting in soaring budget deficits and a national debt that would constrain his successors, and openly supported right wing death squads in Central America.

During the Cold War, America's long preoccupation of at times embracing dictatorships in defense of US interests eroded its moral strength. US support for brutal and dictatorial regimes at the height of the Cold War, namely the Shah in Iran, Saddam Hussein in Iraq, Ferdinand Marcos in the Philippines, Manual Noriega in Panama, and General Augusto Pinochet in Chile at the expense of the democratically elected Salvador Allende, demonstrated that it would abandon its moral principles in order to contain the USSR. Clearly, the national security strategy of containing and deterring Soviet Communism was first and foremost among America's foreign policy priorities.

America's refusal to abandon its support of repressive regimes in the Middle East in the Post-Cold War world has resulted in a strong moral contradiction. The growing movement favoring democracy and human rights in the Middle East has not shared the remarkable successes of its counterparts in Eastern Europe, Latin America, Africa and parts of Asia. Today, most Middle Eastern governments remain autocratic, especially those in Saudi Arabia, Pakistan, Syria, and Jordan. In fact, the US has reduced– or maintained at low levels– its economic, military and diplomatic support to Arab countries that have experienced substantial political liberalization in recent years while increasing support for autocratic regimes such as Saudi Arabia, Kuwait, Egypt and Morocco. Jordan, for example, received large-scale US support in the 1970s and 1980s despite widespread repression and authoritarian rule; when it opened up its political system in the early 1990s, the US reduced foreign aid. Aid to Yemen was cut off within months of the newly unified country's first democratic election in 1990. America's recent embrace of the brutal regime of Islam Karimov in Uzbekistan and its relative silence regarding Russian atrocities in Chechnya have paradoxically bolstered Al-Qaida's claims that the US supports the oppression of Muslims and props up repressive anti-Muslim governments.

In other words, the problem with the appealing vision outlined in the Bush Doctrine's ambitious promotion of freedom and democracy is that it is unlikely to be pursued faithfully, given America's traditional support of autocratic regimes. The difficulty is not whether or not America will get tough with adversarial governments; the problem is if America will get tough with repressive governments on its "side" in the war on terrorism. Democratic enlargement seems to fall by the wayside when it came to "friends" of the US. While many endorse the principle of democracy promotion, few have been willing to practice it.

In the absence of East-West tensions, US foreign policy meandered under Post-Cold War Presidents George HW Bush and Bill Clinton. As observed by National Security Adviser Condoleezza Rice:

> The United States has found it exceedingly difficult to define its 'national interest' in the absence of Soviet Union. That we do not know how to think about what follows the US-Soviet confrontation is clear from the continued references to the 'post-Cold War period.' Yet such periods of transition are important, because they offer strategic opportunities. During these fluid times, one can affect the shape of the world to come.[35]

For example, President George Bush Sr. seemingly fought the drug war by eventually ousting the long time American-backed Noriega and restoring democracy but without first seeking the consent of the United Nations Security Council. But then he secured the backing of the UN Security Council for his assault against Iraq in 1991, which instantly gave him moral authority, though this could be interpreted as an attempt at rescuing the hides of oil companies under the guide of protecting a defenseless country. He also had morality on his side when he sent troops to Somalia to prevent against a widespread humanitarian crisis, but his efforts ended in disaster and withdrawal.

This is why President Clinton sidestepped the issue of sending US troops to Rwanda, especially in the wake of the disastrous humanitarian intervention in Somalia initiated under Bush Sr. Although he was able to temporarily build up his moral credentials when he ordered US troops to Haiti in 1994, he had difficulties in sustaining sympathies for China with his economic interests-based policy of engagement. Clearly, the issues of human rights violations and alleged Chinese financial support for his 1996 reelection eroded his moral footing. Even more, with the end of the Cold War, Clinton faced a public, which felt that since the US won the Cold War on the global level, the US should look more inward.

The threat of global governance, blue-helmeted peacekeepers, multilateralism, and international rules and treaties featured prominently in the highly conservative agendas in Congress. Deprived of Anti-Communism as the belief holding disparate forces together, populist conservatives found that attacks on the UN and international organizations resonated with a more economically and culturally insecure America. Rejecting as liberal hogwash the "assertive multilateralism" of Clinton's Secretary of State Madeleine Albright, the Republican Congress appealed to America's culture of individualism, making simultaneous cases against the domestic welfare state and multilateralism in foreign policy. In an unprecedented speech by a US legislator before the UN, then-Senator Jesse Helms, Chair of the Senate Foreign Relations Committee, drew a clear marker:

> If the UN respects the sovereign rights of the American people, and serves them as an effective tool of diplomacy, it will earn and deserve their respect and support. But a UN that seeks to impose its presumed authority on the American people, without their consent, begs for confrontation and, I want to be candid with you, eventual US withdrawal.[36]

Clinton's foreign policy measures were tempered by such popular legislative sentiments. Evidence of this ambivalent multilateralism is plentiful. For example, between 1993 and 1995, US foreign policy toward the war in Bosnia-Herzegovina was driven by the view that the US would only intervene if the fighting expanded beyond Bosnia and Croatia. The war ended only when Clinton unilaterally forced the warring sides to the peace table at Dayton, Ohio in 1995, allowing only a diplomat from the United Kingdom a minor voice representing the European Union (EU). Although the NATO air campaign against Serbian forces in Kosovo eventually ended the fighting, it largely fulfilled US unilateral interests since the bombing was largely carried out by US forces under the public guise of NATO and military operations were given tacit support from Russia in exchange for US economic inducements.[37] Also, over the objections of the EU and Canada, Clinton continued implementing US sanctions against European and Canadian businesses operating in Iran, Libya, and Cuba. Moreover, Clinton's inability in October 1999 to lead the US Senate to supply advice and consent on the Comprehensive Nuclear Test Ban Treaty (CTBT) furthered an image of the US as unwilling to engage with other nations. In addition, Clinton began testing a national missile defense system that would eventually contribute to George W. Bush's decision to withdrawal from the Anti-Ballistic Missile Treaty of 1972.

After 9/11, President George Bush Jr. and his national security team began chipping away at a host of treaties and conventions they believed constrained US power.[38] Leaving aside the concern that as global sheriff the US will address only military threats to its security, the Bush Administration's strong ambivalence toward multilateralism deprived international institutions the necessary powers to respond to nontraditional security issues, such as conflicts over natural resources, public health and infectious diseases, international crime, and environmental degradation. Neoconservative advisers, namely Secretary of Defense Donald Rumsfeld, Deputy Secretary of Defense Paul Wolfowitz, and Vice-President Richard Cheney, hold a view that leaves little or no room for consideration of proposals for new forms of global governance to address non-security issues and non-traditional, yet very real threats. For example, Bush's decision to renounce the Clinton Administration's support for the International Criminal Court (ICC) is reflective of an anti-multilateral streak. Bush's opposition to the Kyoto Protocols on climate change and his desire to undermine efforts to establish international norms on fossil fuels are additional examples of US unilateral trends.

Such details underscore fundamental shifts in the policy direction of the Bush presidency. For the Bush foreign policy team, at stake is the ability of the US to flex its global might. To make the 21st Century a "New American Century," neoconservatives who gained the upper hand in the administration have pushed for a fundamental reordering of US global engagement with offensive military strategies designed to fill the Post-Cold War void with American precepts. For Bush, strategies of realism and liberal internationalism that worked in tandem to promote American global power during the Cold War are outdated in today's world, a world they see one in which the US is no longer constrained by another superpower. With its attendant balance-of-power politics, coalitions and alliances, deterrence, and containment, realism is seen no longer applicable in what Bush and most of his team see as a unipolar world characterized by major power imbalances between the US and the world. Likewise, Wilsonian strategies of enlightened self-interest designed to build economic and political alliances under US global leadership have been deemed, for the most part, unnecessary and out of touch with today's global power structure. So, too, are liberal geopolitical strategies such as the democracy-centered "enlargement" policies and humanitarian interventionism of Bush Sr. and Clinton that stressed a new world order of inclusion and rules.

Whether one describes the current structure of the international system as unipolar, bipolar, or multipolar, it is indisputable that the US possesses significant military, political, economic, and cultural influence in the world. Paradoxically, the attacks of 9/11 and their aftermath have given the US a renewed sense of vulnerability, yet have also affirmed US global dominance. The combination of US vulnerability and American global primacy has reinforced anti-multilateral tendencies in US foreign policy.

However, some may consider the US war against Iraq in 2003 as reflective of morally problematic elements in this trend toward anti-multilateralism. First, the Bush Administration claimed that the US has a moral and political right to use preventive force against any regime it deems as a rogue state seeking WMD. Second, the administration perceives that the goal of US military action should be the overthrow of so-called threatening rogue regimes that support terrorism and pursue such weapons in defiance of international organizations. Third, neoconservatives assert a right on the part of the US to act unilaterally if others are not willing to do so. In the build to the US/UK invasion of Iraq, while Bush did publicly seek some measure of UN and allied support, it is significant that the American case for war was made in the context of a strategic doctrine that placed a priority on maintaining US global supremacy, the power to utilize preemptive and preventive force, on a firm rejection of deterrence and containment, and on a strong dismissal of traditional approaches to non-proliferation.

Critics of what is perceived by some as an assault on multilateralism, whether it be on climate change, international justice, ballistic missile defense, or any other attempt to institute international norms and rules, argue that US interests and national security have been morally undermined by the flexing of offensive military force in Iraq. The thickening web of multilateral regimes and treaties is regarded, as one astute observer of multilateralism noted, as Lilliputian attempts to tie down Gulliver.[39] Even more alarming than the adverse impact on any one international problem addressed by these multilateral efforts under US attack is the possibility that the result may be the disintegration of the entire post-World War II moral and political framework of multilateralism, thrusting global affairs into a Hobbesian world where unrestrained power prevails.[40]

Clearly, there have been strong moralizing elements in the tradition of US intervention that still hold true today. According to Nisbet, "the single most powerful cause of the present size and the worldwide deployment of the military establishment is the moralization of foreign policy and military ventures that has been deeply ingrained, especially in the minds of presidents for a long time."[41] But such words should be tempered by a realism that suggests America has often times placed its political interests above its moral objectives, as evidenced by its past embrace of dictators and its support for repressive regimes. Walter Russell Mead contends, "popular enthusiasm for military intervention can be limited. Revulsion against atrocities does not quickly or universally translate into the political will to put American forces in harms way."[42] We should therefore be mindful of the words of Reinhold Neibuhr who observed, "Moral pretensions and political parochialism are the two weaknesses of the life of a messianic nation."[43]

George W. Bush and Democratic Moralism

The assertion of a first strike strategic national security doctrine and the long history of US interventionism have invariably been couched in terms of a democratic moralism that has been on the rise since Woodrow Wilson in varying forms. President Bush's doctrine taps America's deep moral roots and messianic mission. However, instead of promoting Wilsonian liberal values, the missionaries driving US foreign policy today are more comfortable with stark moral contrasts, linking America's post-9/11 mission to a conflict between good and evil.

Bush's moral simplicity has helped him ease the American transition from the war on terrorist networks to the much broader confrontation with what he calls the "axis of evil" and other so-called "evildoers." The grand moral scale of Bush's approach has been driven by the goal of conquering evil and a dismissal of concerns about the means employed. But Bush has been consistent with the moral irony of US foreign policy. For example, his spoken vision of the world in terms of "good and evil" and "us and them" should be tempered by his administration's continued support for repressive regimes in Pakistan, Saudi Arabia, Israel, and China, and rejection of human rights conditions on US global aid.

Such moral convictions and contradictions are consistent with the idealistic image of America as a "city upon a hill," a perception in contrast to the evil forces it is attempting to eradicate. Barry emphasizes, "Over the past five centuries, American society has continued to believe in its own moral transcendence, but the city on the hill has experienced major urban renewal."[44] At the initiation of the Cold War, the moral values of the city were commonly regarded as Western principles. The collapse of the USSR led many to believe in the perfection of the American ideal. For Barry, "neoconservative 'end of history' and 'clash of civilization' interpretations of history fortified the American conviction that its Judeo-Christian transatlantic culture constituted the epitome of civilization." He goes on to suggest that those who dissent from this ideal, namely Western Europe, are regarded as "moral relativists, political opportunists, and weak-kneed partners afraid to speak evil's name."[45]

So what is really new about Bush? After all, there is a long tradition of American presidents claiming high moral ground and seeking the blessings of the almighty in their pursuit of US foreign policy objectives. Howard Fineman contends "Every president invokes God and asks his blessing. Every president promises, though not always in so many words, to lead according to moral principles rooted in biblical tradition. The English writer GK Chesterton called America 'a nation with the soul of a church,' and every president, at times, is the pastor in the bully pulpit."[46] However, Bush occupies a unique position within this tradition since he possesses a deeply rooted mission. Bush's friend former Secretary of Commerce Donald Evans contends that Bush's sense of mission "gives him [Bush] a desire to serve others and a very clear sense of what is good and what is evil."[47]

9/11 drove the president to believe that God actually chose him to guide America on his personal mission. After the attacks, Bush claimed "I'm here for a reason," prompting one close adviser to state that Bush "really believes he was placed here to do this as part of a divine plan."[48] According to Fineman, "it has taken a war, and the prospect of more, to highlight a central fact- this president and this presidency is the most resolutely 'faith-based' in modern times, an enterprise founded, supported, and guided by trust in the temporal and spiritual power of God."[49] This has led Professor Michael Genovese to pose the question: "did September 11 change Bush, or did it unleash him?"[50]

Bush's strategy against "evildoers" incorporates many of the conventional features of American exceptionalism, interventionism, and manifest destiny. However, the Bush Administration has largely dropped the notion that US global leadership should operate within a framework of rules, norms, and institutions designed to benefit all nations. As a result, the US is increasingly seen as less benign. Under Bush, the salient features of US global engagement are its aggressive anti-multilateralism, renewed militarism and disdain for diplomacy, and strict moral interpretation of right and wrong, good and evil, and us or against us. Underlying these currents is the language of anti-terrorism, which has replaced Anti-Communism as the organizing principle in Post-9/11 American politics.

Thus, the emerging Bush strategy is an agenda of preemption, preventive war, and hegemony distinguished by a moral simplicity that according to Bush justifies America's wars against "evildoers." Bush's warning that you are "either with us or with the terrorists" reflects a one-dimensional approach to foreign policy. The president's morally simplistic worldview also relegates realism to the backburner. For example, in a key foreign policy speech at West Point on 1 June 2002, Bush outlined a supremacist agenda of international security. Not only would the US no longer count on coalitions of great powers to guarantee collective security, it also would prevent the rise of any potential global rival. As for the "the moral clarity" that Bush's supporters say he uses to interpret world politics, we should welcome the words of Bryan Hehir, former head of the Harvard Divinity School:

> The invocation of moral reasoning for contemplated policy decisions is to be welcomed as long as the complexity of moral issues is given adequate attention. Moral reasoning can indeed support military action, at times obligate such action. It also, equally importantly, can restrain or deny legitimacy to the use of force. To invoke the moral factor is to submit to the full range of its discipline.[51]

How would the world respond? Bush suggested two explanations in his West Point speech, both of which most ethicists and political scientists would find plausible. The first is that great powers prefer management of the international system by one world power as long as it's relatively benign. International conflict shifts to trade and other relatively minor quarrels, none worth fighting about. As Bush's NSS puts it: "No people on earth yearn to be oppressed, aspire to servitude, or eagerly await the midnight knock of the secret police."[52]

Another related issue in the Bush strategy is America's long-term objective of removing the causes of terrorism and tyranny. The president is convinced now more than ever that poverty does not cause terrorist activity and a social embrace of tyranny; rather, it was resentment emerging from the absence of representative institutions in their own societies. Hence, as Bush insists, the ultimate goal must be to spread democracy everywhere. The US must carry out the mission initiated by Woodrow Wilson: the world, quite literally, must be made safe for democracy, even those parts of it, like the Middle East, that have so far resisted that tendency. Terrorism – and by implication the authoritarianism that breeds it – must become as obsolete as slavery, piracy, or genocide: "behavior that no respectable government can condone or support and that all must oppose."[53]

Offensive wars against rogue states and terrorists have therefore been legitimized by Bush as a necessary means of protecting America's most sensitive moral and cultural values, namely democracy, freedom, and security. However, as Stanley Hoffman has claimed, the US can produce "an activism that others see as imperialistic: for we expect them to join the consensus, we ignore the boundaries and differences between 'them' and 'us,' we prod them out of conviction that we act for their own good, and we do not take resistance gracefully."[54]

Notes

1. *Declaration of Independence* and the *Constitution of the United States* (New York: Bantam Books, 1998), Edited by Pauline Maier, 22.
2. Bush's quote can be found in Walter Pincus and Dana Millbank, "Kay Cites Evidence Of Iraq Disarming Action Taken in '90s, Ex-Inspector Says," *Washington Post*, (28 January 2004).
3. Rice is quoted in Jay Tolson, "The New American Empire?" *US News and World Report*. (13 January 2003), 39.
4. Rice is quoted in Nicholas Lehmann, "The Next World Order: The Bush Administration May Have a Brand-New Doctrine of Power," (April 2002), 1.
5. George W. Bush, "Statement by the President in Address to the Nation," (11 September 2001),
    http://www.whitehouse.gov/news/releases/2001/09/20010911-16.html
6. Wolfowitz   is   quoted   in   "The   War   Behind   Closed   Doors,"
    http://www.pbs.org/wgbh/pages/frontline/shows/iraq/etc/cron.html

7. George W. Bush, "Address to a Joint Session of Congress and the American People," 20 September 2001, http://www.whitehouse.gov/news/releases/2001/09/20010920-8.html
8. George W. Bush, "State of the Union," (29 January 2002), http://www.whitehouse.gov/news/releases/2002/01/20020129-11.html
9. Ibid.
10. Ibid.
11. George W. Bush, "Graduation Speech at West Point." (1 June 2002), http://www.whitehouse.gov/news/releases/2002/06/20020601-3.html
12. George W. Bush, *The National Security Strategy of the United States of America*, (17September 2002), 12 and 19, http://www.whitehouse.gov/nsc/nss.html.
13. Ibid., 19.
14. Ibid., 33.
15. Betty Glad and Chris J. Dolan, eds., *Striking First: The Preventive War Doctrine and the Reshaping of US Foreign Policy* (New York: Palgrave-Macmillan, 2004).
16. For more, see: Lea Brilmayer, *American Hegemony: Political Morality in a One-Superpower World.* (New Haven: Yale University Press, 1994); Eugene Gholz, Daryl G. Press, and Harvey M. Saplosky, "Come Home America: The Strategy of Restraint in the Face of Temptation," *International Security* 21, 4 (Spring 1997): 5-48; Christopher Herrick and Patricia B. McRae, *Issues in American Foreign Policy.* (New York: Addison Wesley Longman, 2003); Robert Kagan, "The Benevolent Empire," *Foreign Policy* 111 (Summer 1998): 24-35; David M. Malone and Yuen Foong Khong, *Unilateralism & US Foreign Policy.* (Boulder, CO: Lynne Rienner Publishers, Inc., 2003); Joseph S. Nye Jr., *The Paradox of American Power: Why the World's Only Superpower Can't Go it Alone.* (2002: New York: Oxford University Press); Stewart Patrick and Shepard Foreman, *Multilateralism & US Foreign Policy.* (Boulder, CO: Lynne Rienner Publishers, 2003).
17. Richard N. Gardner, "The Comeback of Liberal Internationalism." *Washington Quarterly* 13, 3 (September 1990): 23-29; Robert Jervis, "Realism, Neoliberalism, and Cooperation: Understanding the Debate." *International Security* 24, 1 (Summer 1999): 42-63; Stephen D. Krasner, *Sovereignty: Organized Hypocrisy.* (Princeton, NJ: Princeton University Press, 1999); Andrew Moravcsik, "Taking Preferences Seriously: A liberal Theory of International Politics." *International Organization* (Autumn 1997): 513-553; Robert Tucker, "Alone or With Others," *Foreign Affairs* 78, 6 (November/December 1999): 15-20.
18. Steven Holloway, "US Unilateralism at the UN: Why Great Powers Do Not Make Great Multilateralists." *Global Governance*, 6, 3 (July-September 2000): 361-381; Charles Krauthammer, "The Unipolar Moment" *Foreign Affairs* (1990/1991): 23-32 and "A World Imagined: The Flawed Premises of Liberal Foreign Policy." *The New Republic* (March 15, 1999); William Kristol and Robert Kagan, "Toward a Neo-Reaganite Foreign Policy." *Foreign Affairs* (July/August 1996): 18-32.
19. See Chapter VII, Article 51, *Charter of the United Nations*, http://www.un.org/aboutun/charter/chapter7.htm (accessed February 10, 2004).
20. "The National Security Strategy of the United States of America," 17.
21. Condoleezza Rice, "A Balance of Power that Favors Freedom," Wriston Lecture, Manhattan Institute, October 1 2002: http://www.manhattan-institute.org/html/wl2002.htm (retrieved March 31, 2004).

22. Colin Powell, "Perspectives: Powell Defends a First Strike as Iraq Option," interview, *New York Times*, (8 September 2002), 18.

23. *The National Security Strategy of the United States*, Chapter V, http://www.whitehouse.gov/nsc/nss.html.

24. John Lewis Gaddis, Interview, *PBS: The War Behind Closed Doors*. Public Broadcasting Corporation. 2002.

25. *National Security Strategy*, Chapter III.

26. *National Security Strategy*, 13.

27. See: Thomas Paine, *Common Sense* (New York Penguin Books), Edited by Isaac Kramnick, 1983, 31. Winthrop is quoted in Elizabeth Connelly and Arthur M. Schlesinger Jr., *John Winthrop: Politician and Statesman* (Chelsea House Publishing, 2000).

28. US Congress, House, Committee on Foreign Relations, *Background Information on the Use of US Armed Forces in Foreign Countries, 1975 Revision*, Committee Print (94th Congress, 1st Session, 1975).

29. See: George Washington, "Farewell Address to the People of the United States," *Independent Chronicle*, September 26, 1796. Jefferson's quote is found in Stephan Howard Browne, *Jefferson's Call for Nationhood: The First Inaugural Address* (College Station: Texas A&M University, 2003).

30. John Quincy Adams, "An Address Celebrating the Anniversary of Independence, at the City of Washington on the Fourth of July," 4 July 1821.

31. See: E. Root, "The Real Monroe Doctrine," In *Addresses on International Subjects*, R. Bacon and J. B. Scott, eds. (Cambridge: Cambridge University Press, 1916), 105-123.

32. Richard H. Collin, *Theodore Roosevelt's Caribbean: The Panama Canal, The Monroe Doctrine, and the Latin American Context* (Baton Rouge, Louisiana, 1990); Edmund Morris, *Theodore Rex* (New York: Random House, 2001).

33. Wilson is quoted in Arthur Schlesinger, Jr., "America and Empire," in *The Cycles of American History* (Boston: Houghton Mifflin, 1986), 129.

34. Robert Nisbet, *The Present Age: Progress and Anarchy in Modern America*. (New York: Harper and Row, 1988).

35. Condoleezza Rice, "Promoting the National Interest," *Foreign Affairs* (January-February 2000): 45-62.

36. Helms is quoted in Barbara Crossette, "Helms, in Visit to UN, Offers Harsh Message." *New York Times* (21 January 2000).

37. See Mark Danner, "Marooned in the Cold War: America, the Alliance, and the Quest for a Vanished World," *World Policy Journal* (Fall 1997): 1-23; Nicholas Lemann, "The Next World Order: The Bush Administration May Have a Brand-New Doctrine of Power," *The New Yorker* (1 April 2002); Benjamin Schwartz, "The Vision Thing: Sustaining the Unsustainable," *World Policy Journal* (Winter 1994-1995): 101-121.

38. See: Richard Falk, "The New Bush Doctrine," *The Nation*, (15 July 2002); Stewart Patrick, "Don't Fence Me In: A Restless America Seeks Room to Roam," *World Policy Journal*, Fall 2001; Stewart Patrick, "Multilateralism and Its Discontents: Causes and Consequences of US Ambivalence," in Patrick and Shephard Forman, eds., *Multilateralism and US Foreign Policy* (Boulder, CO: Lynne Rienner Publishers, 2002).

39. Tom Barry, "The US Power Complex: What's New," *World Policy Journal* (November 2002). See also Patrick, "Multilateralism and Its Discontents."

40. Barry, "The US Power Complex."
41. Nisbet, *The Present Age*, 29.
42. Walter Russell Mead, *Special Providence: American Foreign Policy and How is Has Changed the World.* New York: Routledge, 2002, 288.
43. Reinhold Niebuhr and Alan Heimert, *A Nation So Conceived.* (New York: Charles Scribner's Sons, 1963), 150.
44. Barry, "The US Power Complex."
45. Ibid. See also: Robert Kagan, "Power and Weakness," *Policy Review* (June/July 2002).
46. See Howard Fineman, "Bush and God," *Newsweek* (March 10, 2003), 25.
47. All quotes in this paragraph can be found in Howard Fineman, "Bush and God," *Newsweek* (March 10, 2003), 25.
48. The first quote can be found in Bob Woodward, *Bush at War.* New York: Simon & Schuster, 2003, 205. The second quote is in Michael Hirsch, "America's Mission," *Newsweek*, Special Edition, December 2002- February 2003, 10.
49. Fineman, "Bush and God," 25.
50. Michael Genovese, "George W. Bush and Presidential Leadership: The Un-Hidden Hand Presidency of George W. Bush," in Betty Glad and Chris J. Dolan, eds., *Striking First: The Preventive War Doctrine and the Reshaping of US Foreign Policy* (New York: Palgrave-Macmillan, 2004).
51. Quoted in Stanley Hoffmann, "The High and the Mighty," *The American Prospect* vol. 13 no. 24, (13 January 2003).
52. Ibid., 9.
53. George W. Bush, The National Cathedral, "President's Remarks at National Day of Prayer and Remembrance," (14 September 2001), http://www.whitehouse.gov/news/releases/2001/09/20010914-2.html
54. Stanley Hoffman, *Gulliver's Troubles, or the Setting of American Foreign Policy* (New York: McGraw-Hill, 1968), 195.

Chapter 2

Just War and Political Power

Theoretical Framework

Just war theory is useful for explaining the preemptive and preventive use of force. It is realist in its appreciation for the political dynamics of power and diplomacy, but internationalist and pacifist in its moral implications. The use of force, especially offensive force, must be subjected to an ethical analysis of political power and its limitations. President Bush's efforts to raise America's offensive military might in the wake of 9/11 shows that just war theory can still be applied today as his administration has brought into focus self-defense, national sovereignty, justice, protection of social identity, and cultural survival. However, America's specific interest in conducting the war on terrorism against the Al-Qaida terrorist network has been expanded to include targeting and terminating states and a fundamental reshaping of the international order.

Just war theory grudgingly accepts the reality that national sovereignty is a strong force in a chaotic world in which every state is free to judge the ethics and justice of its own interests on whether or not to engage in war and conflict. However, just war theorists believe that the moral force of international law imposes boundaries and limits with regard to how states go to war, conduct war, and terminate hostilities. Debates over the morality of war stem from the Nuremberg and Tokyo war crimes trials and the proliferation of nuclear weapons during the Cold War. Concerns about just war principles have also been raised several times to describe the war in Vietnam, Gulf War I, and Bosnia and Kosovo in the late 1990s. Conceptions of justice are consequential in the politics of war since they impact levels of public support for policies, relations with allies, and positions of power from which policymakers operate.

The political and moral challenge for the US should be to craft a foreign policy that protects Americans from global terrorism while managing the flow of power and acknowledges judicial limits established by international law. Thus, ambitious military crusades transgress legitimate political limits. Bringing a just war perspective to bear on US foreign policy after 9/11 means calling attention to the reality that the war on terrorism cannot be formulated solely in terms of advancing the national interest. Of course, America's national interests are at stake, but those interests must be brought into relationship with global politics and international law and ethics, the multilateral foundations of which were built by the US during the Cold War.

Just war theory was developed over the span of many centuries, from a variety of Catholic theologians, including St. Augustine of Hippo, St. Thomas Aquinas, and Grotius to Jean Bethke Elstain, Douglas Lackey, Paul Ramsey, and Michael Walzer.[1] Even today the most explicit references to just war theory are likely to come from Roman Catholic sources, but implicit references to its arguments may arise from anywhere because of the way in which it has become incorporated into Western thought. The result has been a rich conceptual framework that allows us to examine the primary phases of war: *jus ad bellum* (justification for going to war), *jus in bello* (conduct of justifiable acts in wartime), and *jus post bellum* (justifiable imposition of peace once major combat has ceased). According to Francisco Suarez, the advantage of just war theory is primarily exhaustive, since "periods must be distinguished with respect to every war: its inception; its prosecution, before victory is gained; and the period after victory."[2]

Jus ad bellum

Jus ad bellum requirements revolve around five principal elements: *just cause, right intention, legitimate authority, last resort,* and *likelihood of success.*[3] In order to get an overall sense of just war and to justify the grave consequences of waging offensive warfare, those who are considering the use of preemptive or preventive force need to establish *Just Cause.* However, any state or group will always explain that war is pursued in the name of Just Cause. Nazi Germany provides examples of causes which most people today would regard as unjust, but which the Nazis themselves believed were quite just.

In order to tentatively address such concerns, Just Cause should be understood as "responding to aggression" and "punishing injustice" inflicted upon a government and its citizens. Seen as one of the primary sources of the just war tradition, St. Augustine developed the idea of promoting just cause for war in terms of responding to aggression. St. Thomas Aquinas qualifies St. Augustine's idea by claiming that "A just war is wont to be described as one that avenges wrongs, when a nation or state has to be punished for refusing to make amends for wrongs inflicted by its subjects, or to restore what has been seized unjustly."[4] According to Francisco de Vitoria, a nation has just cause when it attempts to right a violation of its sovereignty.[5] Francisco Suarez argued that just cause is more than responding to an afflicted aggression; it also includes the right of a state or nation to inflict punishment on those responsible for the injustice.[6] Hugo Grotius and Emmerich Vattel would later claim that the prevention of injustice is consistent with the principle of just cause.[7]

Just Cause is often framed as one of the fundamental moral requirements in the just war framework.[8] Some have agreed with Aquinas, de Vitoria, Suarez, Grotius, Vattel, and other thinkers in interpreting Just Cause as a response to aggression.[9] In 1974, the UN General Assembly defined aggression as "the use of armed force by a State against the sovereignty, territorial integrity or political independence of another State."[10] The notion of sovereignty is derived from the right of citizens to construct a society in which governmental authority is derived from their consent and sustained by the concept of justice.[11]

Interpreting Just Cause as a response to aggression makes things easier for the "aggressor-defender" conception. The use of military force can be legitimately consistent with Just Cause if the response to aggression is also framed in terms punishing injustice, although the legitimate authority of a sovereign government does not necessarily guarantee its moral justification.[12] Force may be used to address injustices such as human rights violations, state sponsorship of terrorism, and the use of WMD. A dangerous and repressive government lacks necessary ethical and moral legitimacy and, as a result, its sovereign authority can erode.[13]

Among the widely used reasons states use to establish Just Cause is the assertion of a right to self-defense. The use of military force in response to an ongoing or recent attack is considered the legitimate form of self-defense. Taken in association with the just war principle of legitimate authority and in consideration of the fear of WMD proliferation, offensive warfare cannot be considered a regular instrument of enforcing national security policy. The legitimacy of a preemptive attack is based on evidence that an aggression and an injustice are actually about to happen. It is the yet-to-occur aggression and injustice that places the claim of a right to self-defense in a suspect classification.

How far does "self defense" extend? When conceptual and economic interests are understood to be global and when democracy and human rights are defined more broadly than ever before, the notion of self-defense expands and enlarges. But a broad conception of the self is not necessarily legitimate and neither are the values to be defended completely obvious.[14] Policymakers must therefore grapple with the notion of anticipatory self-defense. According to Michael Walzer, preemptive warfare may be a legitimate form of anticipatory self-defense only if it used to obviate a real and actual threat, in which the potential aggressor is about to inflict an injustice, is in active preparation to engage in violently aggressive behavior, and if the injustice and aggression are imminent and looming. Preventive war involves the use of offensive warfare against non-imminent threats to thwart future aggressive intent and to avert potential injustice.[15]

During the Cold War, America confronted more globally-defined threats, such as the Soviet Union, its Eastern allies, and Communism and the spread of nuclear technology and weaponization.[16] For many, 9/11 reaffirmed the ideas that America's national identity and survival continue to be assaulted by so-called rogue states and terrorists on a global scale. Others agree but temper such beliefs with the argument that Al-Qaida is the specific threat. Bush's *National Security Strategy* is reflective of the former as it only embraces nations that conform to America's broadly defined goals:

> In the 21st Century, only nations that share a commitment to protecting basic human rights and guaranteeing political and economic freedom will be able to unleash the potential of their people and assure their future prosperity. People everywhere want to be able to speak freely; choose who will govern them; worship as they please; educate their children – male and female; own property; and enjoy the benefits of their labor. These values of freedom are right and true for every person, in every society and the duty of protecting these values against their enemies is the common calling of freedom-loving people across the globe and across the ages.[17]

International law does not disallow states to exercise the right of anticipatory or preemptive self-defense in terms of Just Cause. A literal interpretation of Article 51 of the UN Charter suggests that self-defense is only lawful after an attack occurs. This is absurd if it means that a state must let itself be harmed, perhaps fatally, before it can respond with force. In *Nicaragua v. the United States* (1986), the International Court of Justice did not dismiss the possibility of some limited form of anticipatory self-defense out of hand. The decision held, "no view on ... the lawfulness of a response to the imminent threat of an armed attack."[18] However, there exists no general acceptance of a preventive self-defense doctrine within the UN beyond possibly 'interceptive' self-defense; for example, an action of sufficient magnitude that clearly has a hostile intent can be 'defended' against before the aggressor's forces execute the attack. In the absence of an imminent threat, the right of self-defense in support of preventive war does not hold.

At what point does self-defense become indistinguishable from aggression? As Richard Betts has argued, "When security is defined in terms broader than protecting the near-term integrity of national sovereignty and borders, the distinction between offense and defense blurs hopelessly... Security can be as insatiable an appetite as acquisitiveness – there may never be enough buffers."[19] The projection of the self-conception of the US onto the world by American leaders could lead to interventions in a number of countries at the expense of being looked upon by the world community as an aggressor nation with imperial designs. Thus, any self-defense conception must be narrowly confined to immediate risks to life and health within borders or to the life and health of citizens abroad.

Based on these suggestions, the exercise of legitimate offensive force in terms of "responding to aggression" and "punishing injustice" could only occur if several necessary conditions were met. First, self-defense cannot be invoked to protect imperial interests or to promote hegemony. Second, in which threats must be assessed in terms of immediacy and strong evidence must be identified that an attack is imminent, inevitable, and likely in the instant future. This demands indisputable and incontrovertible evidence demonstrating that a potential aggressor has both the real and actual capability and intention to do immediate harm. Third, preemption should succeed in reducing the threat. If preemption is likely to fail, it should not be undertaken. Fourth, military force is necessary, however, only after all legitimate policy options have been exhausted in due time.

Just Cause acknowledges that self defense and sovereignty are powerful forces in a world in which every state is free to judge the ethics and justice of its own interests. However, "punishing injustice" and "responding to aggression" set moral parameters regarding how and for what reasons states go to war. These conceptions are consequential in initiating war since they impact levels of public support for war policies, relations with allies, and positions of power in the international system. Therefore, the challenge is to craft a case for just cause that protects citizens from terrorism, acknowledges the flow of power, and recognizes moral and political limits established by international law. Ambitious military crusades transgress legitimate political and moral limits of just cause. While US interests are at stake, they must be brought into a relationship with Just Cause.

Right Intention involves the means by which the cause will be achieved, which of course must be moral, ethical, fair, and just. We should be mindful of the tendency to confuse just cause with right intention because both seem to speak about goals or aims.[20] However, whereas the former is concerned with the basic principles for which one is fighting, the latter has more to do with the immediate goals and the means by which they are to be achieved. Put simply, just cause may be pursued with unjust intentions and the intentions themselves may have very little to do a just cause. A government could launch an offensive war for the just cause of "expanding democracy," but the immediate intentions of that war may be to eliminate persons who express doubts about democracy. The mere fact that a country is waving the bloody shirt of liberty does not mean that it intends to achieve those goals through fair and reasonable means.

The subjective nature of Right Intention is highly problematic, since its realization is not implied in a nation's case for legitimate cause. Keeping this in mind, in the past, offensive wars have been waged with the general intentions to strike first to head off another power (preemptive war) or to prevent a potential aggression sometime in the future (preventive war). A moral interpretation of the specific intentions associated with preemptive and preventive wars should deal with two questions regarding the partiality of right intentions. First, what specific issues are the right ones? A state's general intention to defend itself from an attack is consistent with Right Intention. Second, there exists a very tenuous relationship between the conduct of offensive warfare and right intentions, since offensive wars can appear as naked aggression. For example, while it is difficult to dispute the idea that the Iraqi military had a rightful intention to wage defensive warfare against invading militaries in 2003 for some, others believed such resistance was wrong, believing that the US-UK desires to topple Saddam and replace him with a democratic government represented morally superior intentions.

Christian political thought laid the foundation for Right Intention. St. Augustine, who believed Christians should not wholly dismissed the necessity of military force, put forth the notion that any just war should be waged with the intention of attaining peace.[21] He also warned against the influence of personal intentions of leaders who had responsibility for waging warfare and advanced a conception of the state as a force for promoting peace.[22] In "Contra Faustum," he argued that "the real evils of the war are love for violence, revengeful cruelty, fierce and implacable enmity, wild resistance, and lust for power, and such like."[23] In the *City of God*, St. Augustine even went so far as to suggest "He then who prefers what is right to what is wrong, and what is well organized to what is perverted, sees that peace of unjust men is not worthy to be called peace in comparison with peace of the just."[24] However, while St. Augustine supplies us with a rich foundation to understand the importance of right intentions in waging war, his development of the principle helped pave the way for justifying the promotion of religious wars and other crusading missions.[25] Similarly, the Islamic tradition, which emerged a few centuries following St. Augustine, is also based related concerns. The idea of jihad holds that while all selfish motivations, namely greed, glory, and lust, are unjust, the only right intention is the service of Islam.[26]

Right intention has also come to imply that states possess the right to wage military force in defense of others. According to just war analysis, the term "others" does not have to constitute another state; that is, the term could also include a collection of individuals whose fundamental rights are or will be threatened by states or non-state entities. This involves humanitarian interventions, which involves states using offensive force in order to protect innocent victims of violent repression and to prevent human catastrophe. According to George Kent, humanitarian intervention includes "assistance provided to people within a nation by outsiders without the consent of the national government."[27] Paul Christopher narrows this definition to cases where intervening states utilize "armed forces in a coercive role to cause some effect in the internal affairs of another state, and withdraws its armed force once the humanitarian objective has been met."[28] However, humanitarian intervention is a contested practice as international actors hold conflicting ideological and arbitrary interpretations of its application as a rightful intention.

Humanitarian intervention can therefore be perceived as coercive action against a state that does not consent to the intervention.[29] Such intervention involves one essential component: imminence; that is, humanitarian intervention is justified when far reaching human rights violations occur within a country whose government is unable or unwilling to protect its citizens at the very moment the mass killing occurs. The problem here is that the level of imminence is not clearly apparent. When it is decided to intervene in a state to alleviate human suffering, the intervening forces must violate the territorial integrity and sovereignty of another state. The state that has been subjected to outside intervention has a legitimate case that it is the victim of foreign aggression and that it has just cause to defend itself. How can we know who has the more rightful case?

In order to provide a tentative answer to this dilemma, we can point to the United Nations Charter. While sovereignty is a prevailing concept in the Charter, the concept of human rights is widely embraced as a fundamental moral reality. Such a viewpoint is grounded in the tradition of the social contract, in which state sovereignty is derived from individuals who consented to the formation of the state. A state has violated the social contract when it has violated the human rights of its citizens. However, the international community is justified in using military force only when the level of human suffering reaches the point of imminence, not months or year after the mass suffering and devastation has subsided.[30]

According to *Legitimate Authority*, a war cannot be just if it has not been justified by recognized authorities. This may seem to make more sense in a medieval setting where one feudal lord might try to wage war against another without seeking the authorization of the king, but it still has relevance today.[31] The main problem with this principle lies in identifying who or what is the "justified authority." On a very basic level, Legitimate Authority involves the role of a state's military preparedness for both offensive and defensive purposes. However, one state's preparedness can be perceived by both states and non-state entities as a threat and mutual threat perceptions may lead to military buildups and aggressive intentions, resulting in what realists would describe as a "security dilemma."

In order to prevent military actions from violently spiraling out of control, most states have entered into multilateral organizations, such as the United Nations, and international institutions, like the Non-Proliferation Treaty (NPT), that are empowered to enforce restraint.[32] In essence, the power of a national state to determine and define its own domestic sovereignty has evolved alongside the promotion and maintenance of international order and peace.[33] Although the idea of Legitimate Authority refers to domestic state institutions as justifiable sources of military force, a state's national interests or national security concerns are not the sole legitimating forces for waging offensive force. A state's power to wage warfare in any form should therefore be derived from its global commitments as an entity in the global system and be consistent with the rule of international law.[34] Of course, the post-Westphalia international system, which is organized around the idea of non-intervention in the internal sovereignty of other state, has been repeatedly sullied by the exercise of both defensive and offensive military force.

Therefore, the principle of Legitimate Authority involves legal parameters concerned with state sovereignty, self-defense, and multilateralism. Since World War II, the US has acknowledged the United Nations Security Council as a multilateral organization designed to constrain the use of military force by sovereign states and has acknowledged the importance of international laws governing military restraint. These checks are reinforced by the Charter of the United Nations. Article 2, Chapter I of the Charter calls on all member states to "settle their international disputes by peaceful means in such a manner that international peace and security, and justice, are not endangered."[35] It also obligates member states to refrain from threatening other members with military force: "All Members shall refrain in their international relations from the threat or use of force against the territorial integrity or political independence of any state, or in any other manner inconsistent with the Purposes of the United Nations."[36] Article 51 of the United Nations Charter represents the most significant and meaningful elaboration on this premise by preserving for member states the right of self-defense: "Nothing in the present Charter shall impair the inherent right of individual or collective self-defense an armed attack occurs against a Member of the United Nations, until the Security Council has taken measures necessary to maintain international peace and security."[37]

With these issues in mind, is it possible for the US via the Bush Doctrine to circumvent the primary international organization, the United Nations Security Council, and still be in conformance with Legitimate Authority? On a domestic level, the legislative powers of the US Congress and executive powers of the president are grounded on a sovereign public and to some extent are constrained by the US Constitution.[38] On an global level, America's formal membership in the United Nations and its endorsement of the Charter of the United Nations, which has been acknowledged and endorsed by other UN member-states, has not answered the question of who or what is really and actually capable of using offensive force as a legitimate authority in situations beyond those involving in response to an attack that has already taken place.[39] However, the UN Security Council is world's only forum for legitimizing the use of preemptive and preventive force, pacifying conflicts in general, safeguarding against unilateral and arbitrary military actions, and for protecting international law.

The principle of *Last Resort* is the idea that war should never be the first option in resolving disputes.[40] Although it may at times be a necessary option, it should only be chosen when all non-military options have been exhausted. While it is more difficult to criticize a state for engaging in war after these options have been exhausted, this is a condition that is difficult to judge as having been fulfilled. It is always possible to try one more round of negotiations or impose one more sanction in order to avert war. Because of this, war may never truly be a "final option" and other options may simply not be reasonable. Moreover, how do we decide when it is no longer reasonable to try to negotiate more?

In essence, Last Resort involves a state grappling with fears of deadly threats and the degree of urgency with which it acts to wage offensive warfare to head off additional violence or potential attacks. However, decisiveness and urgency can sometimes produce hasty and rash choices. Thus, we should seek to differentiate between credible threats, means, and capabilities from simple aims, fears, and ambiguities.[41] A state's ability to make these distinctions will largely determine whether or not it exhausted all available non-military options before deciding to wage offensive military force as a last resort.

To understand these complexities, a threshold of credible fear is needed. Such a threshold perceives that simple fears of future attacks are not enough to claim a right to exercise offensive force before other choices are considered. Hostile intent coupled with a capacity to do immediate harm on the part of the aggressor is a justifiable and credible threshold of fear for any government to exercise preemptive or preventive war. With respect to the use of offensive military force after 9/11, the threshold of credible fear encourages us to consider two questions: 1) Have aggressors harmed us in the recent past and do they wish to harm us again in the near future?; 2) Are these adversaries moving their forces into position to do significant and ominous harm and could peace be attained and danger averted if force is used?[42] While it might be tempting to assume that secrecy on the part of a potential adversary is a sure sign of aggressive intentions, it may simply be a desire to prepare a deterrent force that might itself be the target of aggression.

The distinction between credible and simple fear is absolutely consequential.[43] During the Cold War, credible fears of nuclear warfare deterred the world's major powers from risking conventional wars between them, not to mention the use of nuclear weapons because of the danger of an uncontrollable nuclear exchange. Nuclear annihilation was allayed when it was realized that containment and deterrence were the only morally and politically acceptable strategies to employ against the Soviet Union and the East.[44] The entire school of Cold War-era realist thought and nuclear preclusion allowed the US to embrace containment and deterrence as workable foreign policy strategies against Soviet expansionism and proliferation.[45] With the Bush Doctrine, the reverse seems true: the fear of WMD proliferation actually appears as a legitimate case for exercising both offensive military force against the states accused of producing them and terrorists who are thought to be seeking them.

If fear was justified during the Cold War on the grounds of morality, rationality, and strategy, when and how will we know today if the threats of terrorism and WMD have been significantly reduced or eliminated? The moral and political nature of fear may be that once a state has suffered a surprise attack, its government and people are justified in responding with force and vigilance. Indeed they may, out of simple fear or paranoia, be aware of threats to the point of hypervigilance—seeing small threats as large, and squashing all challengers and rivals no matter how minor they may in fact be with brutality.[46]

According to Neta Crawford, credible fear should be lowered in the context of the contemporary war on terrorism and WMD counter-proliferation. However, the consequences of lowering the threshold may increase instability and elevate the prospect of prematurely exercising offensive force.[47]   But as Richard Betts cautions, if fear really justifies assault, then offensive military force could be limitless since, according to the Bush administration's own arguments, we cannot always know with certainty what the other side has, where it might be located, or when it might be used.[48] If one attacks on the basis of a simple fear, or a suspicion that a potential adversary may someday have the intention and capacity to harm you, then Last Resort has not been met.[49]

For our purposes, a fine balance must be struck. On the one hand, the threshold of evidence and warning cannot be too low, where simple apprehension that a potential adversary might be out there somewhere and may be acquiring the means to attack the US could trigger the exercise of offensive force.[50]   Non-military options must be exhausted prior to making the decision to wage preemptive or preventive warfare, otherwise last resort is not met. Did the US allow enough time for the UN weapons inspection process to effectively work prior to making the decision to attack Iraq and overthrow Saddam Hussein? Were the no-fly zones working to degrade Iraq's alleged WMD capacities? Were economic sanctions useful in containing the ability of Saddam to fund terrorist organizations?

On the whole, Last Resort identifies a fine line between the legitimate exercise of offensive force and aggression driven by paranoia. The US must be prepared to accept vulnerability and a minimum level of casualties and uncertainty and should avoid the tendency to exaggerate the threat, which almost always heightens fear.[51] On the other hand, the threshold of evidence and warning for justified fear cannot be so high that those who might be about to do harm cannot be stopped or the damage they inflict be mitigated. What is required is a maximization of an understanding of the capabilities and intentions of potential adversaries and a rational prioritization of all available options before offensive force is used against credible, real, and imminent threats.

While of *Likelihood of Success* has not been as conceptually developed as several of the other just war requirements, it remains an essential element that cannot remain unaddressed. Hugo Grotius identified the principle as a force that states had to contend with when making the decision to go to war or in response to an ongoing attack.[52]   While some scholars prefer to consider the principle in conjunction with other principles, it will be treated in this book as significant component of our just war analysis. While the principle carries more than one label (likelihood, probability, reasonable, or hope of success), the problem lies with the term "success." For many, success equals victory and the lack of victory means failure. In almost any type of war, success can mean almost anything, such as halting an advancing military, obliterating an opposing army, capturing territory, counting deaths and casualties, eliminating terrorist networks or cells, locating illegal or banned weapons, overthrowing a dangerous and threatening government, or severing a state's relationship with terrorists.[53] Another drawback is in the tendency of states to redefine victory as events in the war unfold.

The Bush Administration's strategic doctrine of justifying first strikes raises several questions. Does the president mean that success in wars that directly or indirectly emanate from the 9/11 attacks is to be determined by the actual elimination of terror-related forces? Will the war on terrorism be conducted on a permanent basis? How will it be known when the US achieves victory and how will the American people know when they are finally safe? Moreover, how many terrorists need to be killed or captured and what specific governments should be overturned? The difficulty we have in grasping the ethical and political meaning is quite immense. Defining victory in any war against non-state terrorists and states pursuing WMD is morally ambiguous at best. When it comes to wars against terrorists, even those conducted militarily on the offensive, it might be more just and realistic to define counter-terrorism in terms of success and failure, rather than in terms of war. Unlike a conventional military campaign, a war on terrorism really has no enemy capital to capture, standing army to defeat, or industrial base to destroy. Even a terrorist organization that is divided and demoralized still has the capability to kill innocent civilians.

Any response to aggression that intends to seek out and kill terrorists contradicts Bush's very description of war because, in the end, the object of war is not just victory, but peace. Therefore, the likelihood of American success in offensive military campaigns is directly connected with the successful establishment of a peaceful outcome. Peace entails some reconciliation with one's adversary, whether in victory or defeat, and an inclusive reconstitution of political community. The 20th Century's struggles that pitted liberalism and capitalism against fascism and totalitarianism strained this conception; however, in the end, for Germany, Japan, and Italy and later the USSR, Americans came to appreciate the distinction between the objects of war and the people who survived. A US-led "crusade" against "evildoers" that leaves no enemy behind with which to build a later peace obliterates this distinction and is a questionable element in the Bush Administration's efforts to increase the likelihood of success. A scorched earth campaign is less likely to achieve America's aim to prevail against terrorism and seems more likely to plant the new seeds of extremism throughout the world.

There is no question that a successful counter-terrorism policy is difficult to measure. Unlike a conventional military campaign, capturing or destroying enemy capitals and industrial bases will most likely not lead to the discovery, capture, and defeat of every terrorist. Even a divided and demoralized terrorist organization operating within the boundaries of one state still has the capability to lash out and kill many innocents.

Clearly, success against terrorism is quite difficult to attain and measure. The struggle against terrorists have therefore led the US to pay specific attention to the behavior of so-called rogue states and to promote of a policy of regime change, which calls for the elimination of dangerous governments and the establishment of democratic societies in order to promote success. The Bush Administration defines rogue states as those governments that seek to build and development WMD programs and sponsor terrorist activities. The Bush Administration has pointed to the fact that democracy is no longer just a Western value but a universal one, having spread to Latin America, Asia, and Africa. Success could be driven by a strategy that concentrates on overthrowing repressive regimes and hopes such efforts have a ripple effect. For example, an American invasion of Iraq could result in the overthrow of Saddam Hussein and thereby serve as a deterrent against other dictatorships.

Jus in bello

Once war is underway, a main criterion is *Proportionality*, which requires that, when engaged in warfare, actions be relative to objectives. Included here are the use of methods that are not evil in themselves, such as the use of torture, rape, ethic genocide, and WMD. Any military action will necessarily be destructive on some level, but we must ask what we expect to gain from that action and whether the resulting good outweighs whatever evil came from the destruction.[54] It's easy to come up with extreme situations in which this criterion would apply. Quickly killing fighters in order to capture an extremely important city with no further loss of life would be just, while using a nuclear bomb in order to wipe out a minor observation post would be unjust. Outside of such extremes, however, the situation is murkier and it can be difficult to determine just how proportional an action really is.

A cursory analysis of proportionality might conclude that the principle is nothing more than simple formula that calls on a state to maximize benefits and minimize costs. The proportional utilization of offensive military force demands more as we should focus on the destructive impact of war in proportion to the goals sought.[55] Every destructive action has to assess against the minimization of destructiveness. As eloquently stated by John Rawls, "The means employed must not destroy the possibility of peace or encourage a contempt for human life that puts the safety of ourselves and of mankind in jeopardy."[56] The disproportional and unnecessary use of violence to prevail on the battlefield, that is utilizing immoral means to achieve a self-described moral end, make the eventual case for establishing a real and actual peace quite difficult indeed.

Proportionality is a principle of distinction that prohibits any attack expected to cause a loss of civilian life (or injury) or civilian property damage that is "excessive in relation to the concrete and direct military advantage anticipated."[57] Terrorist attacks against civilians are simply not consistent with proportionality.

However, proportionality also applies when civilians or civilian objects are not the intended target. This test is difficult to measure since it requires comparing dissimilar moral values. How can we assess whether or not suffering was justifiably inflicted against a military target in order to maximize the military objective? How can we know that the weapons used were excessive?

Therefore, the inherent "value" of an object depends on many varied factors; that is, the circumstances of the conflict, culture, historical and experiential base. In an attack that may be expected to cause significant loss of life to military objects, what does "expected" mean? How does one calculate the likelihood of damage and injury to military targets? What about harm that does not amount to physical damage or suffering? Consider the increasing importance the US and its allies are placing on targets guided by high technology guidance systems. Given the new capability to cause enormous levels of both physical and non-physical "suffering," does proportionality govern this reality?

The Bush Administration's view of future war poses a number of possible challenges to the principle of proportionality. Consider the transformation of battlefields into spaces where combat is virtual and non-linear. No longer will non-combatants be separated from the battle area by limitations in the range of weaponry.[58] Even today, attacks can be launched from continents away with pinpoint accuracy. The inevitably of targeting errors and technical flaws in weapon systems will place non-combatants and civilian objects in jeopardy.

Another key requirement is *Non Combatant Immunity*, or discriminating between combatants and noncombatants. Put simply, killing and injuring combatants is commensurate with just war while deliberately targeting non-combatants is not.[59] Generally speaking, this seems like a noble principle. Unfortunately, non-combatant casualties and damage to civilian properties are inevitable. Therefore the main question is how much warring parties avoid attacking non-combatants. The problem is distinguishing between combatants and noncombatants, since enemy combatants and terrorists hide and operate in the shadows and can easily blend in with civilian populations.

International laws of armed conflict provide clear provisions concerning the proper treatment of both non-combatants and combatants. For example, Article 51 of the Geneva Conventions holds that military force that does not or cannot discriminate between combatants and non-combatant civilians is illegal and immoral.[60] The most serious violations are considered war crimes, including deliberately targeting non-combatants, torture and inhuman treatment, humiliation, hostage-taking, using civilians as human shields, unlawful deportation and confinement, and depriving a person of a right to a fair trial.[61]

While the role of non-combatants in any war is certainly a complicated and controversial one, non-combatant casualties are always a constant factor, because the reality is that non-combatant casualties will happen.[62] Since Non-combatant Immunity recognizes this, military forces must significantly minimize non-combatant deaths and injuries and damage to civilian objects. Moreover, the use of nuclear weapons, especially against high value target regions in or near highly populated areas, cannot be considered consistent with the Principle of Non-

Combatant Immunity.[63] The same holds for military or political efforts designed to terrorize civilian populations are absolutely prohibited.

As the development and extensive utilization of advanced and sophisticated weaponry has quickened, adherence to non-combatant immunity has become more difficult to maintain.[64] According to Michael Walzer, combatants must therefore assume additional risk to themselves in order to ensure non-combatant immunity.[65] This is quite contradictory since advanced technologies are intended to minimize non-combatant casualties. But in the conduct of military operations, constant care must be taken to spare the non-combatant civilian population and civilian objects from the effects of hostilities.[66] Parties to a conflict are therefore required to take precautionary measures with a view to avoiding and minimizing incidental loss of civilian life, injury to civilians, and damage to civilian objects.

Observance of non-combatant immunity demands that considerable attention and responsibility be placed on military forces recognizing and appreciating who is and who is not a combatant. In other words, legal status is important under laws of armed conflict. Of course, non-combatants are granted broad protections under international law; in contrast, while combatants are somewhat protected, they are far more constrained in their actions. The objective, again, is to minimize the destructiveness of warfare and to concentrate its effects on legitimate combatants.

Non-combatant status is also impacted by the level of support a person has supplied to the war effort. According to Jeffrie Murphy, civilians that possess weapons, deliver war-related materials, knowingly harboring soldiers, actively taking part in terrorist activities, or working at munitions sites fall into the chain of agency.[67] Civilians in the chain of agency are considered combatants and because they are inseparable from the fighting. However, civilians who perform purely non-military functions are generally considered non-combatants.

Who then is a combatant? Article IV of the Geneva Convention (Protocol 3) specifies that lawful combatants fall into the following categories: "(a) that of being commanded by a person responsible for his subordinates; (b) that of having a fixed distinctive sign recognizable at a distance; (c) that of carrying arms openly; [and] (d) that of conducting their operations in accordance with the laws and customs of war.[68] In the case *Ex parte Quirin* (1945), the US Supreme Court defined a lawful combatant as an individual authorized by a governmental authority or international laws of armed conflict to engage in hostilities. A lawful combatant may be a member of a regular armed force or an irregular or guerilla force can be tried and convicted for crimes against humanity.[69]

In contrast, an unlawful combatant is considered a person who takes part in hostilities without being authorized to do so.[70] This includes civilians who play a role in the hostilities as well as violent parties to a conflict that do not comply with Article IV. The US Supreme Court perceives unlawful combatants as those who fail to conform to internationally accepted rules of war and therefore do not qualify for POW status.[71] Unlawful combatants violate laws of armed conflict and are justifiable targets.[72] Not surprisingly, most individuals captured and detained by US military forces have been given unlawful enemy combatant status. This designation has allowed the US to hold captured enemy combatants indefinitely and to deny them certain habeas corpus rights that lawful combatants and prisoners of war traditionally receive. It is important to stress that international constraints and laws governing armed conflict are formally recognized by the United States Constitution, which guarantees due process protections for "persons" and not just for citizens.

Jus post bello

Francisco Suarez has argued there is a third element in the just war framework, which requires that just peace be established following a legitimate case for war and a justifiably conducted war.[73] Once hostilities have ceased, those most grievously harmed have a natural right to some reasonable expectation that a just society acknowledge the fact that atrocious crimes have been perpetrated on them, and fairly judge and exact punishment from the perpetrators. The purpose of a legitimately established just peace is to promote reconciliation between warring parties and to promote a lasting peace in the wake of major hostilities.

For any war to be consistent with justice, it must be waged in a manner that encourages eventual peace. War is not absolute, and the criteria for when a just peace should emerge and considered morally acceptable is at the heart of Immanuel Kant's theory of international just and peace.[74] On the whole, *jus post bellum* requires that warring parties recognize that the goal of war should be the moral attainment of a state of peace. According to Masek, "a warring nation must avoid acting according to principles that would destroy the possibility of a lasting peace."[75] If a state of peace is not attained, the case for just war is not possible.

There are several necessary conditions for concluding war in order to bring about a just peace: *Just cause for termination, right intention, discrimination,* and *likelihood of a successful peace.*[76] For Brian Orend, *Just Cause for Termination* involves: "a reasonable vindication of those rights whose violation grounded the resort to war in the first place."[77] Unjust gains from aggression have been eliminated, victims' rights reinstated, a formal apology issued to civilians, renouncing the gains of its aggression and a submission to the reasonable principles of punishment, including compensation, war crimes trials, and perhaps rehabilitation. *Just Cause for Termination* addresses the issue of the appropriate punitive measures imposed on aggressive nations, measures that must be consistent with the goal of ensuring an enduring state of peace, not merely the attaining of a temporary cessation of hostile actions in an encompassing atmosphere of war.

The idea of *Right Intention* seeks to answer the question: how far may the victors go in establishing peace? Does it simply halt major hostilities or should it punish the vanquished for their actions? What are justifiable goals in waging war? According to Walzer, "The theory of ends in war is shaped by the same rights that justify the fighting in the first place most importantly, by the right of nations, even of enemy nations, to continue national existence and, except in extreme circumstances, to the political prerogatives of nationality."[78] Moreover, imposing perpetual rule over a defeated nation and promoting economic motivations are not justifiable peaceful ends. On the whole, *jus post bellum* considerations prevent against the total destruction and domination of the enemy. Walzer also warns against rushing so quickly toward a cessation of major hostilities in order to head off "unjust" establishment of peace is established.[79] A just peace, the proper goal of war, is one that lays the foundation for harmonious relations between belligerents, rather than preserving the conditions that give rise to conflicts.

Right Intention also excludes motives such as revenge. The wounded must be treated in a humane fashion, lawful enemy combatants cannot be humiliated, tortured, or executed, and revenge-taking will not provide the required stabilizing influence of jus post bellum. In addition, publicly placing blame on those most clearly responsible for atrocities and exacting fair retribution is the purpose of holding war crimes tribunals against those responsible for committing crimes against humanity.

Discrimination demands there are strong differentiations between non-combatants and military and political leaders. As was the case with the *jus in bello* requirement of Non-Combatant Immunity, legitimate non-combatants simply cannot be targeted. If they are, the prospects for the legitimate establishment of a just peace simply wither away. Relaxing restrictions on the treatment of civilians who conceal their identities as combatants but claim civilian immunity is not consistent with discrimination.[80] Moreover, although insurgents and terrorists may argue that their tactics are the only means of countering a clearly identifiable military force, their claims necessarily erode.

In terms of a *likelihood of successful peace*, unjust aggression has to be defeated and the pre-war status quo be restored. It could be argued that in a defensive war against aggression, the leaders who launched the aggression should be brought to justice. Beyond this, it is more important to obtain reparations for victims and to impose some constraints on the future war making capacity of the aggressor. The US adhered to this route in the first Gulf war. Regime change was rejected by the US recognition of Iraqi sovereignty. Sovereignty can be deprived of in cases of repeated aggression or in the aftermath of a humanitarian intervention to stop mass murder. In such cases, the murderous regime is justly overthrown. What happens after that? The occupying authority power has to maintain law and order and engage in a peaceful reconstruction of that which was destroyed during major combat.

The likelihood of a lasting peace also necessitates the establishment of local legitimacy. The new government has to be non-aggressive and non-murderous, obviously, but it also has to command sufficient support among its own people so that it isn't dependent on the coercive power of the occupying army. Democracy is the strongest form of local legitimacy, but not the only one. It was what the allies aimed at in Germany and Japan after WWII, which were both occupied and governed militarily for an extended period. If something like that is necessary for a democratic transformation, however, then you have to worry about the legitimacy of the occupation before you can even begin to worry about the legitimacy of a successor regime. In the case of Iraq, the need for legitimacy is the strongest argument for international participation to resurrect an independent national state.

It should be noted that *jus post bellum* is a highly difficult concept to apply to what appears as a permanent war on terrorism against terrorist groups such as Al-Qaida. Just War theory certainly has some difficulties. It relies upon ambiguous criteria which, when questioned, prevent anyone from readily applying them and concluding that a war definitely is or is not just. This does not, however, mean that the criteria are meaningless. Instead, it demonstrates that ethical questions are never clear-cut and that there will always be gray areas where well intentioned people will not necessarily agree. The criteria are helpful in that they provide a sense of where wars can "go wrong," assuming that they aren't inherently wrong to begin with. Although they may not define absolute boundaries, at the very least they do describe what nations must strive towards or what they must move away from in order for their actions to be judged reasonable and justified.

Some have suggested that just war theory is obsolete. To make such a contention would be to hold that politics and power are obsolete. To evaluate America's first strike doctrine and foreign policy in the absence of just war principles would be to deny the tradition its capacity to shed light on the irreducible moral component of exercising offensive force. What we must do is retrieve and develop the just war tradition to take account of the new challenges and realities of the 21st Century. 9/11 demonstrates how urgent this task is.

Realist Conceptions of War and Morality

One cannot understand the moral consequences of a first strike-oriented foreign policy in the absence of a greater understanding and appreciation for the role and fluctuation of power in the international system. Foreign policy in general is nothing more than a statement of power and influence expressed in terms of values, ethics, interests, and ambitions. Realism, the most useful theoretical paradigm in explaining power relationships, presents us with a rich and deep understanding of the moral elements and implications resulting from the exercise of power.[81]

In a world based on self-help and self-interest, a central tenet of realism involves governments arming themselves in response to a security dilemma.[82] Stefano Guzzini contends that the security dilemma arises when "one actor's quest for security through power accumulation ... exacerbates the feelings of insecurity of another actor, who in turn will respond by accumulating power."[83] In such a world of mutual distrust, one state cannot be certain that another state or non-state is arming for its own defense and not for an offensive capacity. Thus, the security dilemma holds that states will seek to build up their own defenses. According to Robert Jervis, a vicious circle or spiral of security develops, with fear and misperception exacerbating the situation.[84] Security dilemmas are thus not wholly driven by anarchy or nature.[85] Rather they are constructed because social identities and interests are constituted by changing collective meanings.

While many hold that realism has excluded moral and ethical components of power, a sharper analysis reveals a somewhat different picture. Realism does not make the very broad assertion that justice, ethics, and morals have no place in explaining war and conflict. Probably the most important contributions of realism in the 20th Century have been made by so-called traditionalists, in particular Edward Hallett Carr and Hans Morgenthau. Not only did they formulate a theory of power as such, their insights are deep and relevant to examining the ethical dimensions of the war on terrorism. It is a mistake to believe that Carr was dismissive of the notion of change in the international system and was not wedded to the belief that the state was the final evolutionary form of global politics. Carr predicted that the nation-states would pass through a tumultuous period of integration and disintegration in their search for 'optimal size. He envisaged other political units which were not necessarily territorially based, such as religious, ideological, or ethnically-based groups.[86]

Morgenthau paid significant attention to human nature's conception of power. His first principle of political realism claims "politics, like society in general, is governed by objective laws that have their roots in human nature."[87] In Morgenthau's view, realism posits that global instability and inequalities in power are "the result of forces inherent in human nature." According to this approach, "to improve the world one must work with those forces, not against them."[88] Yes, Morgenthau's state-centric theory is clearly set, but it is not pre-destined and unchangeable. The political, cultural, ethical, and strategic environments will largely determine the forms of power a state chooses to exercise, just as the fluctuation of power in personal human relationships change over time. Therefore, we should not be committed to a rejection of the view that realism cannot explain how power and morality are inextricably linked. Morgenthau also anticipated that the forces of globalization would render the nation-state no longer valid: "the sovereign nation-state is in the process of becoming obsolete."[89] He stresses that a final task that a theory of international relations can and must perform is to prepare the ground for a new international order radically different from that which preceded it.

Variants of neo-realism proposed by Kenneth Waltz, Christopher Layne, and John Mearshimer were developed intellectual extensions of the theoretical tradition.[90] Neorealists emphasized the overall distribution of power among states and were skeptical of the degree with which international institutions and multilateral organizations could manage conflict. The anarchic international system is treated as a separate domain, in which a state's capabilities determine its power and behavior and ethics have no independent explanatory power. According to Peter J. Katzenstein, Peter Gourevitch, and Snyder and Diesing, states can utilize culture, ethics, and domestic political structures in a highly strategic fashion to advance their own self-interests.[91]

It would be misleading to assert that neo-realist perspectives do not acknowledge the importance of norms, rules, and values. Gilpin has developed a compelling argument about war and change, in which he does not neglect sociological insights as necessary for understanding the context of power.[92] He contends, "Specific interests or objectives that individuals pursue and the appropriateness of the means they employ are dependent on prevailing social norms and material environment ... In short, economic and sociological approaches must be integrated to explain political change"[93] Waltz was concerned with morality and culture when he argued that anarchic structures tend to produce "like units," allowing for what he calls 'socialization' and 'imitation' processes.[94] Similarly, Stephen Krasner suggested that domestic social factors could change state interests and has even acknowledged that the influence of norms and ideas become "embedded in institutions, often for haphazard reasons, which then constrain the options available to policy makers."[95] If domestic social and cultural forces matter, then realism is not necessarily about power; economic and social forces may shape the dimensions of power.[96]

However, the relatively minimalist treatment of culture and social phenomena increasingly resulted in a presupposition that neo-realism paid scant attention to the explicit relationship between morality and power. It was the suspicion that the international system transformed itself culturally faster than would have been predictable from changes in military and economic capabilities that triggered the interest in social identities.[97] Reconstruction of the theory was vital in order to save realism from becoming obsolete. The realization of this has triggered a shift in realist thinking and gave way to the emergence of a 'constructivist' interpretation of realism.

In recent years, Francis Beer and Robert Harriman have formulated a "post-realist" interpretation of power and the security dilemma, in which state-level actors are not the only important characters in international relations.[98] International organizations, domestic political processes, public opinion, and individuals influence global events. In other words, the sources of power do not necessarily flow from war, but from complex international interactions arising from social, economic, and political factors that explain the complexity of war and conflict. Foreign policy does not have to be determined by broad national interests defined in terms of benefits and costs and means and ends. Decision-makers are therefore shaped by a relative mixture of their desire for power, their interpretations of history and its lessons, unique perceptions that shape their views of policy situations and their political decisions, and a concern for legal, ethical, and moral rules.[99]

The relationship between morality, ethics, and power leaves room for a greater nexus between just war theory and realism. The just war framework is an important framework that supplies a contemporary understanding of warfare by providing an ethical perspective to structure and limit the use of military force. The argument presented here illustrates how political actors use notions of just war to supplement realism in foreign policymaking. Policymakers also tend to accentuate or diminish different elements of just war theory in support of or opposition to the use of military force. A primary reason for why the US military fights with greater attention to non-combatant immunity is that policymakers have learned that killing non-combatant civilians makes it difficult to achieve political goals; there are concrete reasons for waging a just war. Modern technology heightens the ability of America to engage in just war. Even so, the rules of engagement will often require soldiers on the ground to accept greater risks than they might otherwise do in order to reduce the risks they impose on civilians.

In sum, there exist significant elements of realism that do not deny the validity of the moral dimensions and ethical consequences of war and conflict. Morals and ethics shape a state's expression of its foreign policy. Just war theory is not only a framework for understanding warfare; it is a theoretical tradition that helps shape power, conflict, and cooperation.

Notes

1. See: St. Augustine of Hippo, *City of God*, David Knowles, Ed. (New York: Penguin Classics, 1972); St. Thomas Aquinas, *Summa Theologica*, Part III (New York: Ave Maria Press, 1997); Hugo Grotius, *The Rights of War and Peace*, book 2, chapter 1-2, section 1, translated by AC Campbell (Washington, DC: M. Walter Dunne, 1901); Michael Walzer, *Just and Unjust Wars: A Moral Argument with Historical Illustrations.* 2d ed. (New York Basic Books, 1992); Paul Ramsey, *The Just War: Force and Political Responsibility* (New York: Scribner's, 1968); Jean Bethke Elstain, *Just War Theory* (New York: New York University Press, 1991); Douglas Lackey, *The Ethics of War and Peace* (New York: Prentice-Hall, 1988).
2. Suarez is quoted in Davida E. Kellogg, "Jus Post Bellum," *Parameters* (Autumn 2002): 87-99.
3. James Turner Johnson, *Can Modern War Be Just?* (New Haven: Yale University Press, 1993); James Turner Johnson, *Morality and Contemporary Warfare* (New Haven: Yale University Press, 1999; James Turner Johnson, *Just War Tradition and the Restraint of War* (Princeton: Princeton University Press, 1981).
4. Thomas Aquinas, *Summa Theologiae* HaHae, q. 40, Tr. *Fathers of the English Dominican Province* (Chicago: William Benton, 1952).
5. J. Bathelemey, *The Founding Fathers of International Law* (Paris: V. Giard & E. Briere, 1904).
6. Ibid.
7. Emmerich de Vattel, *The Law of Nations or the Principles of Natural Law*, book 3, Chapter 3, §26 (Paris: Guillaumin, 1863), 19, 363.
8. Alex Moseley, "Just War Theory," in *The Internet Encyclopedia of Philosophy*: http://www.utm.edu/research/iep/j/justwar.htm
9. Leslie C. Green, *The Contemporary Law of Armed Conflict.* (Manchester, Canada: Manchester University Press, 1993).
10. United Nations General Assembly, Resolution 3314, "Definition of Aggression": http://jurist.law.pitt.edu/3314.htm
11. Walzer, *Just and Unjust Wars*, 54.
12. Johnson, *Just War Tradition and the Restraint of War,* 328.
13. David Luban, "Just War and Human Rights" *Philosophy and Public Affairs*, Vol. 9, No. 2. (Winter 1980): 160-181.
14. See Neta Crawford, "The Slippery Slope Toward Preventive War," *Carnegie Council on Ethics and International Affairs,* (2 March 2003), http://www.cceia.org/viewMedia.php/prmTemplateID/8/prmID/868
15. Walzer, *Just and Unjust Wars*.

16. For thorough and compelling accounts of American foreign policy during the Cold War (1945 to 1989), see: Stephen E. Ambrose, *Rise to Globalism*. (Middlesex, England: Penguin Books, 1997); Steven W. Hook and John Spanier, *American Foreign Policy Since World War II*. (Washington DC: Congressional Quarterly Press, 2000); and Mead, *Special Providence*. Several studies are concerned with the use preemption in response to nuclear proliferation during the Cold War. See: Marc Trachtenberg, *History and Strategy* (Princeton: Princeton University Press, 1991), 103-18, 132-46; C. L. Sulzberger, *An Age of Mediocrity: Memoirs and Diaries, 1963-1972* (New York: Macmillan, 1973), 463; Robert S. Litwak, "The New Calculus of Pre-emption," *Survival* 44 (Winter 2002-03), pp. 61-62; Robert M. Lawrence and William R. Van Cleave, "Assertive Disarmament," *National Review*, (10 September 1968), 898-905; Richard K. Betts, "Nuclear Proliferation After Osirak," *Arms Control Today* 11 (September 1981), 1-7; William Burr and Jeffrey T. Richelson, "Whether to 'Strangle the Baby in the Cradle': The United States and the Chinese Nuclear Program, 1960-64," *International Security* 25 (Winter 2000/01), 54-99.

17. George W. Bush, "The National Security Strategy of the United States of America," (17 September 2002), 12, http://www.whitehouse.gov/nsc/nss.html.

18. ICJ Reports 1986, Military and Paramilitary Activities in and against Nicaragua (Nicaragua v. United States of America), Merits, Judgment, 14.

19. Richard K. Betts, *Surprise Attack: Lessons for Defense Planning* (Washington, DC: Brookings Institution, 1982), 14–43.

20. Christopher, *The Ethics of War and Peace*, 40; Hehir, "Intervention: From Theories to Cases," 5-6; Walzer, *Just and Unjust Wars*; Robert Holmes, *On War and Morality* Princeton, NJ: Princeton University Pres, 1989), 196; US Catholic Bishops, "Pastoral Letter: The Challenge of Peace: God's Promise and Our Response," in Jean Bethke Elstain, ed., *Just War Theory* (New York: New York University Press, 1992).

21. St. Augustine, *The City of God*, book 19, chapter 12 in Marcus Dods, *Great Books of the Western World* vol. 16 (Chicago: Encyclopedia Britannica, 1990).

22. St. Augustine, "Contra Faustum," in Marcus Dods, *The Works of Aurelius Augustine*, vol. 6, *Writings in Connection with the Manichean Heresy*, book 22, chapter 74 (Edinburgh: T. and T. Clark, 1872).

23. Ibid., Chapter 74.

24. St. Augustine, *City of God*, book 19, chapter 12, 587.

25. Paul Christopher, *The Ethics of War and Peace: An Introduction to Ethics and Moral Issues*, Second Ed. (Upper Saddle River, NJ: Prentice-Hall, 1999), 40.

26. John Kelsay, *Islam and War* (Louisville: Westminster-John Knox Press, 1993).

27. George Kent, "Humanitarian Intervention," in Donald A. Wells, *An Encyclopedia of War and Ethics* (Westport, CT: Greenwood Press, 1996), 214. For further development of humanitarian interventionism, see: David Fisher, "The Ethics of Intervention," *Survival* 36, 1 (Spring 1994): 51 and J. Bryan Heir, "Intervention: From Theories to Cases," *Ethics and International Affairs* 9 (1995): 5-6.

28. Christopher, *The Ethics of War and Peace*, 193.

29. See: Robert Jennings and Arthur Watts, Eds., *Oppenheim's International Law*, Vol. 1, Ninth ed (London: Harlow Essex, 1992).

30. Robert Phillips and Duane Cady, *Humanitarian Intervention: Just War Versus Pacifism* (Lanham, MD: Rowman & Littlefield, 1996), 28.

31. A.J. Coates, *The Ethics of War* (Manchester, England: Manchester University Press, 1997); Stephen D. Krasner, *Sovereignty: Organized Hypocrisy* (Princeton, NJ: Princeton University Press, 1999); Heather Wilson, *International Law and the Use of Force by National Liberation Movements* (Oxford: Clarendon Press, 1988).

32. See Michael Howard, George J. Andreopoulos, and Mark R. Shulman, *The Laws of War: Constraints on Warfare in the Western World* (New Haven, Yale University Press. 1994).

33. Krasner, *Sovereignty*.

34. Coates, *The Ethics of War*.

35. Chapter I, Article 2, *Charter of the United Nations*, http://www.un.org/aboutun/charter/chapter1.htm

36. Ibid.

37. See Chapter VII, Article 51, *Charter of the United Nations*, http://www.un.org/aboutun/charter/chapter7.htm

38. The Constitution divides war powers between the Congress and the President. This division was intended by the framers to ensure that wars would not be entered into easily: it takes two keys, not one, to start the engine of war. The Constitution's division of powers leaves the President with some exclusive powers as Commander-in-Chief (such as decisions on the field of battle), Congress with certain other exclusive powers (such as the ability to declare war and appropriate dollars to support the war effort), and a sort of "twilight zone" of concurrent powers. In the zone of concurrent powers, the Congress might effectively limit presidential power, but in the absence of express congressional limitations the President is free to act. Although on paper it might appear that the powers of Congress with respect to war are more dominant, the reality is that Presidential power has been more important--in part due to the modern need for quick responses to foreign threats and in part due to the many-headed nature of Congress. In the wake of the Vietnam War, a relatively rare effort by Congress to limit the President's power in the area of overseas military actions came in the War Powers Act of 1973, which required the President to report on troop commitments into hostile situations within 48 hours and required withdrawl of troops within 60 to 90 days unless the deployment were authorized by Congress. For more see: Constitution of the United States (New York: Applewood Books, 1995), Article I and Article II; Louis Fisher, Presidential War Power (Lawrence, KS: University Press of Kansas, 2004).

39. On 1 January 1942, 26 Allied nations signed the Declaration of the United Nations endorsing the Atlantic Charter, which committed themselves to defeat the Axis powers and to not to make a separate peace. Representatives of 50 nations met in San Francisco April-June 1945 to complete the Charter of the United Nations. In addition to the General Assembly of all member states and a Security Council of 5 permanent and 6 non-permanent members, the Charter provided for an 18-member Economic and Social Council, an International Court of Justice, a Trusteeship Council to oversee colonial territories, and a Secretariat under a Secretary General. The goal was to create an international organization to prevent future wars. By a 89 to 2 vote, the US Senate supplied advice and consent to the US membership in the UN Charter on 28 July 1945. The United Nations came into existence on 24 October 1945, after 29 nations had ratified the Charter. For more see: Townsend Hooper and Douglas Brinkley, *FDR and the Creation of the UN* (New Haven: Yale University Press, 2000).

40. Richard J. Regan, *Just War: Principles and Cases* (Washington DC: Catholic University of America Press, 1996); Bruno Coppieters, *Federalism and Conflict in the*

Caucuses London: Royal Institute for International Affairs, 2001); Jonathan Glover, *Humanity: A Moral History of the Twentieth Century* (London: Pimlico, 2001), 224; D.A. Baldwin, "The Sanctions Debate and the Logic of Choice," in *International Security* 24, no. 3 (Winter 1999/2000), 87-92.

41. Neta C. Crawford, "Just War Theory and the US Counterterror War," *Perspectives on Politics* (March 2003).

42. These concepts have been developed by Immanuel Kant. For more, see: Immanuel Kant, "To Perpetual Peace: A Philosophical Sketch," in Immanuel Kant, *Perpetual Peace and Other Essays on Politics, History and Morals* (Hackett Publishing Co., 1983), 107–143:110.

43. Walzer, *Just and Unjust Wars*.

44. Geoffrey Goodwin, *Ethics and Nuclear Deterrence* (New York: St. Martins Press, 1982); Walzer, *Just and Unjust Wars*.

45. Realism, of course, is not a monolithic theoretical tradition and its broad use here should not be construed as to suggest that its variants or schools have been overlooked. The specific incarnations of realism include neo-realism, traditional realism, classical realism, and constructivist realism. For an overview see, Scott Burchill, "Introduction," in Scott Burchill, ed., *Theories of International Relations*, (London: Macmillan Press, 1996), 1. For more see: Edward Hallett Carr, *Nationalism and After* (London: Macmillan, 1945); Hans J. Morgenthau, *Politics Among Nations: The Struggle for Power and Peace.* (New York: Knopf, 1985); Hans J. Morgenthau, "The Intellectual and Political Functions of Theory," in Der Derian, (1995); Kenneth Waltz, *Theory of International Politics* (Reading, Mass.: Addison-Wesley, 1979; John J. Mearshimer, "The False Promise of International Institutions," *International Security* 19, no. 3 (Winter 1994/1995): 5-49; Christopher Layne, "The Unipolar Illusion: Why Great Powers Will Rise," *International Security* 17, no.2, (Spring 1993): 5-51; Peter J. Katzenstein, *Between Power and Plenty: Foreign Economic Policies of Advanced Industrial Countries* (Madison: University of Wisconsin Press, 1978; Peter J. Katzenstein, *The Culture of National Security: Norms and Identity in World Politics* (New York: Columbia University Press, 1996); Glenn H. Snyder and Paul Diesing, *Conflict Among Nations: Bargaining, Decision-making and System Structure in International Crises* (Princeton: Princeton University Press, 1977); Robert Gilpin, *War and Change in World Politics* (Cambridge: Cambridge University Press, 1981); Robert Gilpin, "The Richness of the Tradition of Political Realism," Robert Keohane, ed., *Neorealism and its Critiques.* New York: Columbia University Press, 1986.

46. Chris Brown, *International Relations Theory: New Normative Approaches* (New York: Columbia University Press, 1992).

47. Neta Crawford, "The Slippery Slope to Preventive War," *Ethics and International Affairs* March 2, 2003.

48. Betts, *Surprise Attack,* 142 and 143.

49. Neta C. Crawford, "Just War Theory and the US Counterterror War," *Perspectives on Politics* (March 2003).

50. Crawford, "Just War Theory and the US Counterterror War."; Richard K. Betts, "The Soft Underbelly of American Primacy: Tactical Advantages of Terror," *Political Science Quarterly,* vol. 17, no. 1 (Spring 2002), 19–36.

51. Michael Doyle, *Ways of War and Peace: Realism, Liberalism, and Socialism.* (New York: WW Norton, 1997).

52. Hugo Grotius, *The Rights of War and Peace*, book 2, chapter 24, sections 4-8 (Washington DC: M. Walter Dunn, 1901, 280-284).
53. Coates, *The Ethics of War*.
54. John Rawls, *A Theory of Justice* (Cambridge, MA: Belknap Press, 1971); Sheldon H. Harris, *Factories of Death* (London: Routledge, 1995); Michael Ignatieff, *Virtual War* (London: Chatto and Windus, 2000); Christopher, *The Ethics of War and Peace*; Walzer, *Just and Unjust Wars*.
55. Coates, *The Ethics of War*.
56. Rawls, *A Theory of Justice*.
57. United Nations Office of the High Commissioner for Human Rights, "Protocol Additional to Geneva Conventions of 12 August 1949, and Relating to the Protection of Victims of Non-International Armed Conflicts (Protocol II): Geneva, 8 June 1977," Provision 5.
58. Michael Ignatieff, *Virtual War* (London: Chatto and Windus, 2000).
59. Walzer, *Just and Unjust Wars*; Coates, *The Ethics of War*; Jeffrie Murphy, "The Killing of the Innocent," in *War, Morality, and the Military Profession*, 2nd Ed., ed. Malham M. Wakin (Boulder, CO: Westview Press, 1986), 346; Michael Ignatieff, "Annals of Diplomacy: Balkan Physics," *New Yorker* May 10, 1999); Ramsey, *The Just War*; Steven P. Lee, *Morality, Prudence, and Nuclear Weapons* (Cambridge University Press, 1993); David Fisher, "Priorities in Just Deterrence," in *Just Deterrence: Morality and Deterrence into the Twentieth Century*, ed. Malcolm McCall and Oliver Ramsbotham (London: Brassy's, 1900).
60. United Nations Office of the High Commissioner for Human Rights (UNHCR), "Protocol Additional to Geneva Conventions of 12 August 1949, and Relating to the Protection of Victims of Non-International Armed Conflicts (Protocol 1): Geneva, 8 June 1977," Article 51: http://www.unhchr.ch/html/menu3/b/93.htm
61. Coates, *The Ethics of War*.
62. Jeffrie Murphy, "The Killing of the Innocent," in *War, Morality, and the Military Profession*, Second Ed., ed. Malham M. Makin (Boulder, Co: Westview Press, 1986.
63. Lee, *Morality, Prudence, and Nuclear Weapons*; Ramsey, *The Just War*.
64. Michael Ignatieff, "Annals of Diplomacy: Balkan Physics," *New Yorkers* (10 May 1999).
65. Michael Walzer, *Just and Unjust Wars* (New York: Basic Books, 1977).
66. Johnson, "Threats, Values, and Defense: Does the Defense of Values by Force Remain a Moral Responsibility?"
67. Murphy, "The Killing of the Innocent."
68. UNHCR, "Geneva Convention relative to the Treatment of Prisoners of War Adopted on 12 August 1949 by the Diplomatic Conference for the Establishment of International Conventions for the Protection of Victims of War, held in Geneva from 21 April to 12 August, 1949," Article 4: http://193.194.138.190/html/menu3/b/91.htm
69. See *Ex parte Quirin,* 317 US 1 (1945).
70. George Aldrich, "The Taliban, Al Qaeda, and the Determination of Illegal Combatants," *American Journal of International Law*, Vol. 96 (2002): 892.
71. *Ex parte Quirin*.
72. I. Detter, *The Law of War* (Cambridge: Cambridge University Press, 2000).
73. Francisco Suarez, "The Three Theological Virtues," Disputation XIII, in: *Selections From Three Works*, ed. G. L. Williams, A. Brown, and J. Waldon, *Classics of*

International Law, Vol. 2, ed. James Brown Scott (Oxford, Eng.: Clarenden Press, 1944), 836.

74. Immanuel Kant, *Groundwork of the Metaphysics of Morals*, Translated and edited by Mary Gregor (Cambridge University Press: Cambridge, 1998).
75. Lawrence Masek, "All's Not Fair in War: How Kant's Just War Theory Refutes War Realism." *Public Affairs Quarterly*, Vol. 16, no. 2 (April 2002).
76. Brian Orend, *War and International Conflict: A Kantian Perspective* (Toronto: Wilfrid Laurier University Press, 2001).
77. Ibid.
78. Walzer, *Just and Unjust Wars,* 123.
79. Ibid.
80. Davida Kellogg, "On the Importance of Having an Honorable Enemy—Moral Asymmetry in Modern Warfare and the End of the Just War Tradition," Can Nations Handle National and International Crises Ethically?—The 4th Canadian Conference on Ethical Leadership, Royal Military College, Kingston, Ontario, 7-9 November 2001.
81. It is important that we do not consider Realism as a monolithic theoretical tradition. Heterogeneity is a strength because there are few benefits to be gained from theoretical purity. Thus, I use the term Realism very broadly, unless otherwise specified as, for example incarnations in neo-realism, traditional realism, classical realism, and constructivist realism. For an overview see, Scott Burchill, "Introduction," in Scott Burchill, ed., *Theories of International Relations*, (London: Macmillan Press, 1996), 1.
82. John H. Herz, ""Idealist Internationalism and the Security Dilemma," *World Politics* 2, no. 2 (January 1950): 157-180.
83. Stefano Guzzini, *Realism in International Relations and International Political Economy: The Continuing Story of a Death Foretold*, Routledge (New York 1998):35.
84. Robert Jervis, *Perception and Misperception in International Politics*, Princeton University Press (Princeton 1976).
85. Alexander Wendt, "Anarchy is What States Make of It: The Social Construction of Power Politics," *International Organization* 46, no.2 (Spring 1992): 391-425.
86. Edward Hallett Carr, *The Twenty Years' Crisis 1919-1939* (London: Macmillan, 1951).
87. Edward Hallett Carr, *Nationalism and After* (London: Macmillan, 1945).
88. Hans J. Morgenthau, *Politics Among Nations: The Struggle for Power and Peace,* 6th ed., McGraw-Hill (New York 1985), 3.
89. Morgenthau, "The Intellectual and Political Functions of Theory," in Der Derian, (1995), 50.
90. Kenneth Waltz, *Theory of International Politics* (Reading, Mass.: Addison-Wesley, 1979; John J. Mearshimer, "The False Promise of International Institutions," *International Security* 19, no. 3 (Winter 1994/1995): 5-49; Christopher Layne, "The Unipolar Illusion: Why Great Powers Will Rise," *International Security* 17, no.2, (Spring 1993): 5-51.
91. Peter J. Katzenstein, *Between Power and Plenty: Foreign Economic Policies of Advanced Industrial Countries* (Madison, Wis: University of Wisconsin Press, 1978; Peter J. Katzenstein, "Introduction," in Katzenstein, ed., *The Culture of National Security: Norms and Identity in World Politics* (New York: Columbia University Press, 1996), 17; Peter Gourevitch, "The Second Image Reversed: The International Sources of Domestic Politics," *International Organization* 32, (1978): 881-913; Glenn H.

Snyder and Paul Diesing, *Conflict Among Nations: Bargaining, Decision-making and System Structure in International Crises* (Princeton: Princeton University Press, 1977).

92. Robert Gilpin, *War and Change in World Politics* (Cambridge: Cambridge University Press, 1981); Robert Gilpin, "The Richness of the Tradition of Political Realism," Robert Keohane, ed., *Neorealism and its Critiques.* New York: Columbia University Press, 1986.

93. Gilpin, *War and Change in World Politics*, xii-xiii.

94. Waltz, *Theory of International Politics*, 74-77.

95. Krasner's quote is from: Stephen Krasner, "The Accomplishments of International Political Economy," in *International Relations Theory*, ed., Paul R. Viotti and Mark V. Kauppi (Boston: Allyn and Bacon, 1999), 193-194. See also: Stephen D. Krasner, "Regimes and the Limits of Realism: Regimes as Autonomous Variables," in Krasner, ed., *International Regimes*, (Ithaca: Cornell University Press, 1983), 362-364.

96. Of course there is no dominant argument or paradigm influence of the international system on domestic social and cultural patterns. However, the research and theory of Peter Katzenstein, Ronald Rogowski, and Jeffery Frieden demonstrate that such patterns are not only important, but consequential to the formation of a state's national interests and foreign policy. See: Peter J. Katzenstein, *Small States in the World Economy* (Ithaca: Cornell University Press, 1985); Ronald Rogowski, *Commerce and Coalitions* (Princeton: Princeton University Press, 1989); Jeffery Frieden, "'Invested Interests': The Politics of National Economic Policies in a World of Global Finance," *International Organization* 45 (1991): 425-451.

97. Yosef Lapid and Friedrich Kratochwil, "Revisiting the 'National': Toward an Identity Agenda in Neo-Realism?" in Lapid and Kratochwil, eds., *The Return of Culture and Identity in International Relations Theory*, (Boulder, CO: Lynne Rienner, 1996): 124.

98. Francis A. Beer and Robert Harriman, *Post-Realism: The Rhetorical Turn in International Relations (Rhetoric and Public Affairs Series)*. East Lansing: Michigan State University Press, 1996.

99. Ibid.

Chapter 3

Just Cause

Framing Just Cause

Just cause is both concerned with responding to aggressions and punishing injustices that have been conducted and preventing aggression and injustice that could actually occur. While this provides some clarity, such an interpretation is still quite vague. Although the basic elements suggest that the ethical components of just cause are the presence of aggression and injustice, what defines aggression and what constitutes injustice? In the absence of a violent attack, when a state senses an aggression, it must put forth evidence to the world that demonstrates the aggression is about to happen. Moreover, when a state claims to be the victim of an injustice, it has to indicate that a threat has already or is about to wrong it.

Self-defense is a key element in the application of President Bush's first strike doctrine. According to its elements, it makes little moral sense to suggest that the US must wait until a North Korea, Iraq, or Iran actually launches a ballistic missile or supplies weapons related technologies or logistical support to terrorists before it can legitimately do something about it. In fact, the 2002 *National Security Strategy* perceives that in the hands of certain states, the mere possession of WMD is an aggression itself. Therefore, the Bush Administration's interpretation of self-defense is an expansive one grounded on anticipated aggression and injustice.

The principle of just cause is probably the most essential component in just war theory, since it defines the moral goals and ethical reasons that lead nations into war. Throughout the 1990s, US civilian and military personnel were targeted several times within the US and abroad by Al-Qaida terrorists. Among these were terror attacks in Somalia, the World Trade Center in 1993, Oklahoma City in 1995, the Khobar Towers in Saudi Arabia, American embassies in East Africa in 1998, and the USS Cole in Yemen in 2000. However, the devastating terrorist attacks of 11 September 2001 on the United States were unlike any other attack in recent memory. Did the use of offensive force against Afghanistan and Iraq in the wake of the 9/11 attacks meet the necessary requirements of just cause? To understand this, just cause is interpreted here as "punishing injustice" and "responding to aggression."

Punishing Injustice

In the days following the attacks, the Bush Administration began making the claim that the injustice inflicted on the US on 11 September 2001 justified an aggressive military response against bin Laden, the Al-Qaida leadership, and the Taliban in Afghanistan in terms of necessary and just cause. On 7 October 2001, President ordered US forces to implement Operation Enduring Freedom, which combined powerful air attacks with the insertion of special forces and intelligence agents on the ground. The goals were to eliminate Al-Qaida's terrorist bases and to degrade and then terminate the Taliban's hold on power, which the US believe would thwart future terrorist attacks against the US. Therefore, the US would combine a defensive use of force to topple the Taliban and disperse the Al-Qaida leader with offensive military force in order to wage an ongoing presence to obviate future and additional attacks against America at home and abroad. In a speech delivered to the nation on 7 October, the president assured that all personnel in the US military that: "Your mission is defined. The objectives are clear. Your goal is *just*."[1]

The American blow against the injustice of 9/11 would be intended not only to destroy terrorist bases in Afghanistan but also to demonstrate to other nations that there is a heavy cost to be paid for those who shelter enemies of the US. A principal element in the US military strategy was aiding the Northern Alliance, a beleaguered rebel alliance that at the time of the 9/11 attacks claimed just a sliver of Afghanistan's territory. The alliance was further weakened by the assassination of its leader, Ahmed Shah Massoud, who died in an Al-Qaida suicide bomb attack just two days before 9/11.

Combating terrorism in such a context meets the requirements of just cause. The deliberate murder of innocent civilians for any reason can never be justified and cannot be interpreted other than as a moral affront to those involved and to civil society as a whole. On a national level, to correct the injustice, the US made the legitimate claim that the fear caused by the 9/11 attacks and the potential for additional attacks imposed a heavy toll on the regular functioning and operation of regular life in the United States. On the global level, the US argued that its vulnerability proves that other states are equally as vulnerable and that steps should be taken by all governments to thwart future attacks.

In order to punish the 9/11 terrorists, it became reasonable for the Bush Administration to correct the injustice through the prevention of future injustices via a forward-looking approach that combined both defensive responses and offensive measures to obviate future threats. However, in order for the Bush Administration's cause to be just, correcting the injustice demanded knowledge of the enemy terrorists and their state sponsors. In this case, the "enemy" is not an organized military with territorial location pursuing the understood aims of a sovereign government. Rather, the "enemy" is a network of terrorists or non-state actors driven by unknown motivations and hiding from both detection and accountability with a leadership protected by a reclusive rogue regime. In his speech to a joint session of Congress on 20 September 2001, Bush carefully explained:

Who attacked our country? The evidence we have gathered all points to a collection of loosely affiliated terrorist organizations known as al Qaida ... Al-Qaida is to terror what the mafia is to crime. But its goal is not making money; its goal is remaking the world – and imposing its radical beliefs on people everywhere ... There are thousands of these terrorists in more than 60 countries. They are recruited from their own nations and neighborhoods and brought to camps in places like Afghanistan, where they are trained in the tactics of terror. They are sent back to their homes or sent to hide in countries around the world to plot evil and destruction.[2]

He also singled out the Taliban for supplying money and arms to Al-Qaida in order for it to execute the 9/11 attacks: "It is not only repressing its own people, it is threatening people everywhere by sponsoring and sheltering and supplying terrorists. By aiding and abetting murder, the Taliban regime is committing murder."[3]

Before any military response could be conducted by the US against Al-Qaida and the Taliban, the Bush Administration had to present some evidence that 9/11 was actually carried out by bin Laden's elusive network with the support of the Afghani government. The US supplied irrefutable evidence that the 9/11 hijackers were indeed Al-Qaida operatives to all members of NATO. This included evidence that the plot was hatched in Afghanistan, polished in Germany and funded through Al-Qaida cells in the United Arab Emirates. Coordinated largely by 9/11 ringleader Mohammed Atta, the evidence suggests that the hijackers handled all the plot's details themselves, which included financing for flight training in Florida, identification for renting cars and apartments, computer programs, and maps. Immediately prior to the attacks, bin Laden's operatives even spoke of engaging in "very big attacks on America."[4] The evidence was then confirmed by Pakistani intelligence services, which acknowledged that the US possessed "sufficient grounds for indictment."[5] The later seizure by the US and Northern Alliance of key targets in Afghanistan and eventual capture of Al-Qaida operation leaders Abu Zubaydah and Khalid Sheikh Mohammed confirm that the nineteen 9/11 hijackers were indeed Al-Qaida operatives. There is also evidence of bin Laden's public threats against the US. In a pronouncement issued in 1996 his stated goals were to drive the Americans out of Saudi Arabia. But in his second pronouncement, issued in 1998, he declared that it was the duty of all Muslims to kill US citizens and their allies.[6]

But could the US establish a greater nexus between the Taliban, bin Laden and Al-Qaida? Following the expulsion of bin Laden from the Sudan in May 1996 by President Omar Hassan Ahmed Bashir, the Taliban, which by mid-1996 had assumed control over most of Afghanistan, had offered bin Laden and Al-Qaida safe harbor. There is evidence to suggest that bin Laden financed much of the Taliban's effort to consolidate its hold on Kabul. In exchange, the Taliban supplied bin Laden with logistical support to build, maintain, and secure terrorist training camps and planning sites in Afghanistan's rugged mountainous terrain. When the US demanded that that the Taliban hand over bin Laden and the Al-Qaida leadership in September, Afghani Foreign Minister Wakil Ahmed Muttawakil openly refused, claiming that bin Laden "was a friend in time of need, and that it would be very much cowardly to leave him at this stage in his life."[7]

This evidence of collaboration between the Taliban and the Al-Qaida leader made Afghanistan a legitimate target for the US to respond to the injustice of 9/11.

The US also made similar claims of injustice against the government of Saddam Hussein in Iraq. The American argument was centered on its view that Iraq was in was in violation UN Security Council Resolutions 687 and 1441, which demanded that Iraq submit to full cooperation with United Nations inspectors ensuring that its weapons of mass destruction, delivery systems, and facilities for manufacturing such weapons are destroyed. Conflicts over access for UN inspectors to alleged Iraqi weapons of mass destruction have always been the primary issue of debate between the Iraqi government and the United Nations. For the US, these conflicts was proof that Iraq has not submitted to full compliance with 687 and 1441 and that it retains the right to use force against Saddam as insurance.

Although Resolutions 687 and 1441 were highly detailed, no military enforcement mechanisms were specified. Nor did the Security Council specify any military enforcement mechanisms in subsequent resolutions. As is normally the case when it is determined that governments violate all or part of UN resolutions, any decision about the enforcement of its resolutions is a matter for the UN Security Council as a whole. Individual members of the Council are not authorized to interpret the coherence of international law enforcement provisions. The most explicit warning to Iraq regarding its noncompliance came in UN Security Council Resolution 1154, which stated that: "the Council was determined to ensure immediate and full compliance by Iraq without conditions or restrictions with its obligations under resolution 687 ... and that ... any violation [of its obligations] would have the severest consequences for Iraq."[8] Although this resolution warned Iraq of the "severest consequences" if it continued its refusal to comply, the Security Council declared that it alone had the authority to "ensure implementation of this resolution and peace and security in the area."[9]

Ever since the end of the first Gulf War, both the Clinton and the Bush Administrations saw no reason why the US needed to compromise its foreign policy objectives of ensuring full compliance. After almost eleven years of enforcing UN mandated no-fly zones over northern and southern Iraq, which were designed to protect the Kurds and the Shiites from Iraqi air attacks, and witnessing UN weapons inspectors being allowed in or expelled from potential examining WMD sites, the US began a public campaign for what it called "regime change" in Iraq. In 1998, President Clinton even signed the Iraq Liberation Act, which quickened the pace towards a post-Saddam and democratic Iraq that would acknowledge its international commitments to disarmament. While inspections took place during the 1990s, increasing tension between the inspection teams and Iraq between 1996 and 1998 eventually lead to the cessation of inspections by late 1998. In response, in December 1998, President Clinton ordered Operation Desert Fox, a four day joint US-UK bombing campaign. It was not until November 2002 that UN inspectors resumed their duties in Iraq following the passage of UN Security Council Resolution 1441.

After the 9/11 attacks, the Bush Administration believed that the current, unprecedented level of US power in the world would be sufficient to invade Iraq, bring stability to the country, and then form a new government that would have the support of the Iraqi people, while at the same time cooperating with US interests. The most enthusiastic supporters of this plan were a group known as the "vulcans," a coalition of neo-conservative Reaganite policymakers and thinkers firmly entrenched in the Department of Defense, the Vice-President's office, and those in private interest groups.[10] Among the most important are Secretary of Defense Donald Rumsfeld, Deputy Defense Secretary Paul Wolfowitz, Vice-President Dick Cheney and his chief of staff Lewis (Scooter) Libby, *Weekly Standard* Editor and co-founder of the "Project for a New American Century" William Kristol, head of the Iraqi National Congress (INC) Ahmad Chalabi, and former Reagan Assistant Secretary of Defense and Defense Policy Board Chair Richard Perle. The vulcans question the validity of containment and deterrence, promote an aggressive assertion of hegemony, are critical of US membership in multilateral organizations, and are active proponents of using offensive force against states.

Most of the vulcans identify with President Reagan's Evil Empire speech of 1983 in envisaging a world defined by dichotomous notions of good and evil. The vulcans argue that in the absence of the USSR, US power should be used to change the world, to promote so-called democratic ideals, and have an evangelical interpretation of international politics that sees American power as a moralizing force. In addition, they perceive multilateral cooperation as beneficial if it is consistent with American interests. According to Perle:

> Multilateralism is fine in principle. What is not fine is having our interests adversely affected by the inability to gain a sufficient degree of multilateral support. And what is not fine is subsuming US interests, particularly where security is concerned, in some larger notion that, if the only option in unilateral, we should be paralyzed ... So, multilateralism is preferable, if we can get a consensus. But if the only way you can get a consensus is by abandoning your most fundamental interests, then it is not helpful.[11]

The vulcans targeted Presidents Bush Sr. and Clinton for failing to take advantage of the demise of the USSR in order to promote US interests and assert global US supremacy. In January 1998, the PNAC even issued an open "Letter to President Clinton on Iraq," in which they warned the White House that "the policy of 'containment' of Saddam has been steadily eroding over the past several months," and that a new strategy "should aim, above all, at the removal of Saddam's regime from power."[12] For vulcans, America's use of overwhelming force against Iraq, even conducted via a unilateral approach would be a necessary springboard to demonstrate the preeminence of US power.

America's argument was grounded in the idea that the failure of the UN and other international organizations to force Iraqi compliance with UN Security Council resolutions calling for the dismantling of its alleged WMD arsenal threatened its national security and therefore represented an injustice according to international law. The Bush Administration further claimed that Saddam's failure to comply threatened the lives of innocent citizens everywhere and, so the argument goes, when innocent lives are threatened, governments are justified in using force to counter threats, protect citizens, and therefore punish the injustice.[13] However, as Richard Betts has cautioned, "When security is defined in terms broader than protecting the near-term integrity of national sovereignty and borders, the distinction between offense and defense blurs hopelessly ... Security can be as insatiable an appetite as acquisitiveness – there may never be enough buffers."[14]

Responding to Aggression

In order to build its case for military force against targets in Afghanistan as an appropriate response to the aggression of 9/11, the Bush Administration chose to characterize the 9/11 attacks as "acts of war." While Bush's immediate statements on had cast the terrorist attacks as "criminal acts" and that the terrorists would inevitably be "punished" and "justice" would be served, on the very next day, the president and his advisers began emphasizing the language of war. President Bush, Secretary of State Colin Powell, and other administration officials were now explicitly calling the attacks "acts of war" and declared that the US "at war" with a network of terrorists and their state sponsors responsible for the attacks.[15]

The Bush Administration's immediate shift toward interpreting the attacks as acts of war, rather than international crimes, carries several implications. In doing so, the administration reserved for itself judgments over the legitimacy of the cause for using military force. More importantly, the administration could now heighten America's grievances beyond 9/11 to include offensive military force within the realm of "responding to aggression." The matter was no longer simply about finding the specific perpetrators and holding them accountable. According to Secretary of State Colin Powell, the US intends to build "a strong coalition to go after these perpetrators, but more broadly, to go after terrorism wherever we find it in the world."[16]

It was clear that the US was preparing powerful military strikes if the Taliban, as expected, refused to hand over Osama bin Laden and shut down his terrorist network. Thus, when President Bush and his top aides talked about military action to end Afghanistan's support for terrorism, they were focusing the military response on the Taliban in order to undermine their control over the country, which in turn would decapitate the Al-Qaida leadership. While early war plans were still being considered, the Bush Administration insisted that responding to the aggression of 9/11 meant that no option would be excluded.

President Bush himself perceived and clearly communicated his belief that the 9/11 attacks initiated a war that required America to assume "new" defensive and offensive capabilities in order to respond to the terrorists' aggressions prevent additional terror attacks. On 20 September, in a speech before a joint a session of Congress, he argued: "Our response involves far more than instant retaliation and isolated strikes. Americans should not expect one battle, but a lengthy campaign… It may include dramatic strikes, visible on TV, and covert operations, secret even in success."[17]

The president also made attempts to frame this war not a clash of civilizations; rather, it would be a moral struggle between "us and the terrorists," or the humane and civilized world versus militants who are willing to shed the blood of civilians but unwilling to acknowledge their identities or motivations. Secretary Powell seemingly acknowledges the administration's metaphoric and political, rather than literal, use of the term "war": "[we are] speaking about war as a way of focusing the energy of America and the energy of the international community; it is a long-term campaign, which is why we are characterizing it as a war – if not in the technically legal sense of war."[18]

There are several problems with the Bush Administration's strategy in conducting its war on terrorism. The most evident characteristic is that this war was initially thought to be non-territorial. Since the Al-Qaida terrorist network spans a multitude of nations on every continent, individuals prepared to commit terrorist attacks are at the global level. However, the problem with the Bush counter-terrorism response is that not only does his strategic doctrine target the network, it also seeks to overthrow "rogue states" that have harbored, supported, or abetted them. Such an approach puts the US war on terrorism on morally and politically questionable grounds because its desire to target states represent attempts to maintain some semblance of territoriality in a non-territorial war. The Bush Administration therefore leaves open the possibility of targeting states that did not sponsor the 9/11 attacks and conjures up the question of whether or not the US even has the resources to target every state in which Al-Qaida operates. Most important, Bush's focus on state sponsors is belied by the growing evidence that the principal state within which Al-Qaida terrorists planned and trained for the 9/11 was indeed the United States.

Another problem with the Bush argument is that the war on terrorism will also be in large measure non-military. Battles will not only be waged in fields and mountains, but also within the financial systems of the global economy and in the hearts and minds of the world's people. Powell acknowledged this dimension in observing that this war "may be military action, but it can also be economic action, political action, diplomatic action and financial actions."[19] These assessments are highly inconsistent with the principle of just cause, since Bush is defining all options in open-ended and limitless terms of war and redefining traditional notions of waging war.

However, a complete effort to fight terrorism means more than just conducting a morally ambiguous and politically risky war on terrorism. Any global campaign against terrorism involves examining the reasons why and how economic forces give rise to the type of passionate and violent anti-US hostility carried out by Al-Qaida. Depressed economic conditions and poverty and the failure of repressive Arab governments to address such concerns have combined with deep anti-US sentiment in many Islamic countries to form a potential breeding ground of terrorism and political violence. For example, rising social inequality illustrates that most Arabs have not benefited from the vast oil wealth generated over decades by many of the Middle Eastern states. According to a 2002 UN Development Program report on human development, twenty per cent of Arabs lives on less than $2 per day with many living on or below the $1 per day income benchmark for "dire poverty." Also, unemployment throughout the Middle East (except Israel) is also among the highest in the developing world and stands at about fifteen per cent. This equates to a total number of unemployed at 20 million people. Moreover, an additional 6 million Arabs annual enter the labor market. Most disturbing are staggering rates of illiteracy. About 65 million adult Arabs are illiterate, two-thirds of them women. The overall adult literacy rate in the region is twenty per cent compared to a global average of seventy-nine per cent. In terms of combined school enrolment in basic education, the average rate in the Middle East of sixty percent is lower than the global average of sixty-four per cent. While the link between social and economic conditions and terrorism is certainly debatable, the nexus must be more fully understood. Although terrorists may not be the poorest people, the nations they tend to come from are likely at the bottom of the world's economic hierarchy.[20]

The Bush Administration's response to the aggression on 9/11 only addresses the "democratic deficit" in many areas of the Muslim world and has overlooked important economic and social factors. In his 20 September speech, the president focused strictly on the absence of democracy in countries that breed terrorism:

> why do they hate us? They hate what we see right here in this chamber – a democratically-elected government. Their leaders are self-appointed. They hate our freedoms – our freedom of religion, our freedom of speech, our freedom to vote and assemble and disagree with each other."[21]

But one wonders if the Bush Administration fully grasps the scope and terms of this hatred and why it is so pervasive in the Muslim world. The terrorist attacks on 9/11 assaulted the world quite literally and conceptually by destroying and/or damaging symbols of military power and wealth with suicidal and civilian means, resulting in the death or injury of thousands of military personnel and innocent citizens from a number of different countries. Quite contrary to Bush's emphasis that Al-Qaida attacked America's "democratically elected government" and "our freedoms," the global signs of US national security policy and US foreign economic policy were struck. If democracy and freedom were actually under assault on 9/11, then why did Al-Qaida strike at the United States and not against other democratic societies, in particular Western Europe or Japan? America was assaulted and terrorized on 11 September 2001 because of the foreign policies, economic interests, and political power it projects onto the world. Moreover, the hatred that Bush speaks of cannot strictly be met by political resolve and military power. Until America assumes a generosity of spirit and a moral commitment to addressing the same global problems that directly contribute to terrorism and anti-Americanism, it will have an uphill battle to fight in the war on terrorism.

The primary basis for America's argument against Iraq was that its national security was being threatened by Saddam's alleged maintenance of a clandestine program to accumulate a WMD program since the end of the Gulf War of 1991 and was a state sponsor of terrorist organizations, including Al-Qaida. The most accusatory statements were directed at Iraq from President Bush himself. Bush cautioned that "Saddam Hussein aids and protects terrorists, including members of Al Qaida," and went on to accuse Iraq of possessing "25,000 liters of anthrax, 38,000 liters of botulinum, 500 tons of sarin, mustard, and VX agent, 30,000 munitions capable of delivering chemical agents," building "mobile biological weapons labs," and pursuing "five different methods of enriching uranium for a bomb."[22] In referring to Iraq's alleged nuclear capability, Bush even claimed that Saddam was "six months away from developing a weapon."[23] Bush expanded on his accusation by claiming that Iraq had intentions to someday use its alleged WMD arsenal: "Facing clear evidence of peril, we cannot wait for the final proof – the smoking gun – that could come in the form of a mushroom cloud ... We have every reason to assume the worst, and we have an urgent duty to prevent the worst from occurring.[24]

Vice-President Dick Cheney made even more forceful accusations that Saddam's alleged WMD programs were not only real, they were certain and that UN could not be an effective guarantee of enforcing compliance with international law. On 26 August 2002, Cheney claimed, "there is no doubt that Saddam Hussein now has weapons of mass destruction... A return of inspectors would provide no assurance whatsoever of his compliance with UN resolutions. On the contrary, there is a great danger that it would provide false comfort that Saddam was somehow 'back in his box'".[25] Secretary of Defense Rumsfeld even claimed that Saddam's WMD should be obvious to all nations: "Any country on the face of the earth with an active intelligence program knows Iraq has weapons of mass destruction."[26] The Bush Administration, however, has not publicly provided any substantive evidence that Iraq possesses WMD, having only admitted that it possessed extensive intelligence that this was the case.[27]

Based on these assertions, the Bush Administration suggested that Saddam's government and its alleged illegal unconventional arsenal were inseparable; one could not be eliminated without the other. Hence President Bush's longstanding commitment to "regime change," which is simply the corollary of the Iraqi regime's incapacity to part with its WMD and which in any case has been explicit US policy since former President Clinton signed the 1998 Iraq Liberation Act. Iraq's relentless pursuit of WMD capability has long been the regime's topmost priority, a vital matter of prestige and protection against external and internal enemies alike.

Also, in attempting to make its case, the Bush Administration did not distinguish between weapons intentions from capabilities. In failing to do so, the US framed its accusations strictly in terms of undisputed facts and unavoidable conclusions. First, it claimed that since 1991 Iraq has continued to possess and develop banned weapons, notwithstanding the presence or absence of UN weapons inspectors. Such American beliefs flew in the face of UN weapons inspectors who claimed Iraqi WMD programs were being eliminated by UNSCOM. Second, the Bush Administration was justifying a potential offensive war against Iraq based on a presumption that the containment of tyrants and terrorists in general are antiquated foreign policy strategies and will especially not work against the threat posed by Saddam. The argument is that all previous international efforts, ranging from unsuccessful inspections and collapsing economic sanctions to the limited use of military force, have failed to disarm Iraq. Third, deterrence is unlikely to remain effective, since the Bush Administration is driven by the perception that Saddam's frequent expulsion of UN weapons inspectors must prove that he possesses WMD and, due to this perception, is therefore a "grave and gathering danger" to American interests.[28] Above all, it was thought that Saddam's reckless history of aggression and fully matches the menace of the means at his disposal. While Iraq's potential for developing WMD should not be totally discounted, Saddam's refusal to allow UN inspectors to return and his lack of full cooperation prior to their departure do not necessarily mean he is hiding something.

America's accusations were thought to be confirmed by intelligence assessments by the United Kingdom. On 24 September 2002 the UK released a dossier entitled "Iraq's Weapons of Mass Destruction," an official report of Prime Minister Tony Blair's Labor government. The report also concluded that Iraq possessed chemical and biological agents and a small number of limited range missiles that could deliver chemical and biological and potentially nuclear warheads to neighboring countries. In terms of the Iraq's motivations in developing its inventory of WMD, Blair: "Intelligence reports make clear that [Saddam Hussein] sees the building up of his WMD capability, and the belief overseas that he would use these weapons, as vital to his strategic interests, and in particular his goal of regional domination ... What I believe the assessed intelligence has established beyond doubt is that Saddam has continued to produce chemical and biological weapons, that he continues in his efforts to develop nuclear weapons, and that he has been able to extend the range of his ballistic missile programme.... the threat posed to international peace and security, when WMD are in the hands of a brutal and aggressive regime like Saddam's, is real."[29]

The question of whether Iraq did in fact possess WMD or even the capability to rapidly develop them became clear as the US has failed to turn up any evidence. Dr. David Kay, who directed the Iraq Survey Group and the US weapons hunt, reported no discoveries of finished weapons or banned delivery systems, chemical or biological agents, or ready-to-start uranium production lines. The group, in a series of interviews, admitted that throughout 2003 and early 2004 the prospects of finding WMD were scant.[30] Frustrated, Kay states, "We have found no actual W.M.D... I just don't know. We're looking for them."[31] What was found was a weapons arsenal far less capable than US analysts judged before the war. According to Kay's deputy, Major John Sutter, "there is no single large missile that we found or chemicals."[32]

Despite American and British justifications of possible ongoing Iraqi efforts to procure WMD, not one has been able to put forward evidence that the Iraqis were actually doing so, though they have certainly done so in the past. The dilemma facing the international community was that its process of disarming Iraq was accused of being ineffective by the US. But the reality was that in the aftermath of the 1991 Gulf War and the subsequent inspections regimen, virtually all Iraq's stockpile of chemical and biological weapons, missile delivery systems, and capability of producing such weapons were destroyed. Inspectors with the United Nations Special Commission (UNSCOM) were withdrawn from Iraq in late 1998 before their job was complete, however, under orders by President Clinton prior to a heavy four day US bombing campaign in Operation Desert Fox. The Iraqi government did not allow them to return until November 2002. Prior to that time, UNSCOM reportedly oversaw the destruction of 38,000 chemical weapons, 480,000 liters of live chemical weapons agents, 48 missiles, six missile launchers, 30 missile warheads modified to carry chemical or biological agents, and hundreds of pieces of related equipment with the capability to produce chemical weapons.[33]

The International Atomic Energy Agency confirmed UN reports of Iraqi disarmament by declaring that it no longer possessed a nuclear program. In late 1997, UNSCOM Director Richard Butler reported that UNSCOM had made "significant progress" in tracking Iraq's chemical weapons program and that 817 of the 819 Soviet-supplied long-range missiles had been accounted for. Several dozen Iraqi-made missiles remained unaccounted for, but were considered outmoded and unable to be launched. Though Iraqi officials would periodically interfere with inspections, in its last three years of operation, UNSCOM was unable to detect any evidence that Iraq had been further concealing prohibited weapons. The development of biological weapons, by contrast, is much easier to conceal, due to the small amount of space needed for their manufacture. Early UNSCOM inspections revealed evidence of the production of large amounts of biological agents, including anthrax, and charged that Iraq had vastly understated the amount of biological warfare agents it had manufactured.[34]

In response, UNSCOM set up sophisticated monitoring devices to detect chemical or biological weapons, though these devices were dismantled in reaction to the 1998 US bombing campaign. Frightening scenarios regarding mass fatalities from a small amount of anthrax assume that the Iraqis have developed the highly sophisticated means of distributing these them by missile or aircraft. However, there are serious questions as to whether the alleged biological agents could be dispersed successfully in a manner that could harm troops or a civilian population, given the rather complicated technology required. For example, a vial of biological weapons on the tip of a missile would almost certainly either be destroyed on impact or dispersed harmlessly. To become lethal, highly concentrated amounts of anthrax spores must be inhaled and then left untreated by antibiotics until the infection is too far advanced.

What the US and the UK failed to see was that Saddam demonstrated that he cared first and foremost about his own survival and protecting his power, not risking his position by threatening the US. He presumably recognized that any effort to use weapons of mass destruction would inevitably lead to his own destruction. This is why he did not use them during the Gulf War. A US invasion, which would be designed to topple Saddam, this logic of self-preservation might no longer be operative. Although it was thought that a US invasion would dramatically increase the likelihood of his ordering the use of WMD, this did not occur. Saddam's leadership style has always been to protection his direct control of his government; his distrust of subordinates is one of the factors ensuring his survival. It is extremely unlikely that he would go to the risk and expense of developing WMD only to pass them on to terrorists. If he does have such weapons at his disposal, they would be for him and nobody else.[35]

Most observers believed that while Iraq constituted a regional threat in 1990, when it invaded Kuwait, it did not meet the definition of a threat between 2001 and 2002. Scott Ritter, former head of the UN inspections process and a former US Marine officer, contended that ninety to ninety-five per cent of Iraq's weapons of mass destruction were confirmed destroyed and that there is no evidence that Iraq retained any of its weapons or capacity for producing them.[36] On 27 January 2003, International Atomic Energy Agency (IAEA) Director Mohammed El Baradei reported there was no evidence that demonstrated a banned clandestine nuclear weapons program in Iraq.[37] Even Secretary Colin Powell stated on 24 February 2001, that "He (Saddam Hussein) has not developed any significant capability with respect to weapons of mass destruction. He is unable to project conventional power against his neighbors."[38]

The inability of the US to uncover WMD in Iraq following the March 2003 invasion leads us to tentatively assert that the pre-war policy of imposing sanctions and enforcing no-fly zones may have actually worked and confirms prewar evidence demonstrating some measure of Iraqi disarmament. David Kay admitted, "The Iraqi's engaged in quite a bit of destruction and dispersal before the war."[39] Referring to Kay's investigation, Barton Gellman elaborates, "Leading figures in Iraqi science and industry, supported by observations on the ground, described factories and institutes that were thoroughly beaten down by 12 years of conflict, arms embargo and strangling economic sanctions. The remnants of Iraq's biological, chemical and missile infrastructures were riven by internal strife, bled by schemes for personal gain and handicapped by deceit up and down lines of command."[40]

These assertions have recently been confirmed by official American and British policymakers. Secretary Rumsfeld admitted that the weapons may not have even existed. "We don't know what happened... It is also possible that [Saddam's government] decided they would destroy them prior to a conflict."[41] The Central Intelligence Agency (CIA) disclosed that pre-war intelligence was highly flawed and inaccurate.[42] On 31 May 2003 that UK Foreign Secretary Jack Straw expressed doubts that Iraqi WMD ever existed. According to Dan Plesch and Richard Norton-Taylor, "The [British] foreign secretary [Jack Straw] reportedly expressed concern that claims being made by Mr. Blair and President Bush could not be proved. The problem was the lack of corroborative evidence to back up the claims" and according to Straw, "Much of the intelligence were assumptions and assessments not supported by hard facts or other sources."[43] Not only did the US and UK fail to produce any evidence that Iraq was in possession of illegal WMD, it failed to effectively refute reports from international sources suggesting that Iraq was in compliance with UN inspectors.

Prior to the first Gulf War, when Saddam was actually at his strongest militarily, the development and use of such weapons required significant investment and external support. Quite ironically, much of this actually came from the West. This included providing biological weapons to Iraq for use in its war against Iran in the 1980s. According to US Senator Robert Byrd (D-WV), between 1985 and 1988, the nonprofit American Type Culture Collection ordered and the Reagan Administration approved 11 shipments of bio-related technologies to Iraq that, including anthrax, botulinum toxin and gangrene.[44] Then, between 1 October 1984 and 23 October 1993, the US Centers for Disease Control and Prevention in Atlanta supplied Iraqi scientists with nearly two dozen viral and bacterial samples, including the plague, West Nile, and dengue fever. This was confirmed by a letter written in 1995 by then-CDC director David Satcher in response to a congressional inquiry.[45]

The argument that Saddam used chemical weapons against the Kurds and Iranian soldiers at Hallabja occurred during the time that Iraq was a military ally of the US. In fact, the Reagan administration provided Iraq with critical battle planning assistance and strategic intelligence against Iran in the Iran-Iraq war in the 1980s. This also included "the furnishing of chemical and biological materials by the United States to Iraq which markedly enhanced Iraq's CBW [Chemical and Biological Weapons] capability."[46] Furthermore, as Dilip Hiro contends, "if concerns about chemical weapon usage were real, why was there no concern, or even condemnation at the time it actually happened, when it was a well-known incident?"[47] Moreover, President Reagan had dispatched Special Middle East envoy and Bush Secretary of Defense Donald Rumsfeld to meet with Saddam in 1983 and again in 1984 to extend military aid and commodity credits to Iraq.[48] At the time, the US Senate unanimously issued sweeping sanctions in response to Saddam's use of chemical weapons that would have denied Iraq access to most US technology; however, the measure was terminated by President Reagan.[49]

Months after the war has ended, the hunt for the weapons still has not revealed anything that could establish just cause of the American invasion and occupation of Iraq, or even come close to matching the fearful scenario portrayed by the Bush Administration. Iraqi WMD and their immediate availability and danger, was absolutely central to America's case for war in Iraq in March 2003. Undercutting the White House's ever changing and evolving public rationale for the war on Iraq, former chief US weapons inspector David Kay now states:

> I don't think they existed ... I don't think there was a large-scale production program in the 90s ... I think we have found probably 85 per cent of what we're going to find ... I think the best evidence is that they did not resume large-scale production and that's what we're really talking about.[50]

Clearly, Saddam's regime in 2002 and 2003 a weak shadow of the semi-fearsome military force it had been at the time of the first Gulf War; that it had no significant chemical, biological or nuclear weapons programs or stockpiles still in place; and that the UN inspections and the US-UK bombing campaign in the 1990s had been much more effective than their critics had believed at destroying the remnants of these programs, which simply eroded into dust. So, the question is why did the US place so much attention on making such strong WMD allegations, which turned out to be false? As Paul Wolfowitz stated almost two months after the war ended, the administration chose to emphasize the allegations simply because "it was the one reason everyone could agree on."[51]

At the same time it was claiming a political and moral right to exercise offensive military force to eliminate the WMD threat, the Bush administration also suggested that the Iraqi government was connected to Al-Qaida and the 9/11 attacks on the US. President Bush has argued, in referencing Saddam Hussein and Osama bin Laden, that the two are "equally as bad, equally as evil and equally as destructive" and that "you can't distinguish between Al Qaida and Saddam when you talk about the war on terror."[52] On 5 February 2003, Secretary Powell argued before the UN Security Council that Iraq was harboring an Al-Qaida terrorist cell led by Abu Musab al-Zarqawi. Powell also said that senior Iraqi and Al Qaida leaders had met at least eight times since the early 1990s.[53] Ansar al-Islam, an Islamist militia group, was also suspected of ties to Al-Qaida, and was based in a lawless part of northeast Iraq, though it was not known to have cooperated with Saddam. Further evidence put forth by the US that Iraq was linked to Al-Qaida came in the form of White House leaks to the media about alleged evidence of a meeting in Prague between an Iraqi intelligence officer and one of the hijackers of the doomed airplanes that crashed into the World Trade Center.[54]

One audio recording, allegedly by bin Laden, in February 2003, was used as circumstantial evidence in demonstrating a very general nexus between Al-Qaida and Saddam's government. The recording called on Muslims to rise up, and was supportive of Iraqi people in the event of war, but also said that the people of Iraq should rise up to overthrow Saddam.[55] Yet, Secretary Colin Powell focused on this in establishing a nexus between Al Qaida and Iraq during his public presentation before the UN on 5 February even though it was highly unlikely that this was the case because bin Laden supported the killing of Saddam. Besides, at the time, over 150,000 US soldiers were already in place for an invasion of Iraq. It could be argued that bin Laden was really responding to the US military buildup in the event of an invasion and that his audio recording was not evidence that Al-Qaida enjoyed an actual presence in Iraq with Saddam's state sponsorship that could be effectively linked with the 9/11 attacks.

Subsequent investigations by the FBI, CIA, and Czech intelligence have uncovered no supporting materials proving that any such meeting took place. None of the hijackers were Iraqi, no major figure in Al Qaida is Iraqi, and no funds to Al Qaida have been traced to Iraq. On the whole, aside from making general and open-ended claims that senior Al-Qaida leaders had received cooperation from Saddam's government, the US never provided specific information or even evidence of Iraqi state sponsorship of Al-Qaida terrorist activity or on the acquisition of WMD from Iraqi sources.

Moreover, the independent commission investigating the government's handling of the 9/11 terror attacks reported there is "no credible evidence" that

Saddam's government cooperated with Osama bin Laden and the Al-Qaida network on conducting attacks against the United States, including those on 11 September 2001.[56] The commission states "there have been reports that contacts between Iraq and al-Qaida also occurred after bin Laden had returned to Afghanistan [in 1996], but they do not appear to have resulted in a collaborative relationship... Two senior bin Laden associates have adamantly denied that any ties existed between al Qaida and Iraq. We have no credible evidence that Iraq and al Qaida cooperated on attacks against the United States."[57] The findings contradict the position taken by both Bush and Cheney that Iraq and Al-Qaida had a cooperative relationship.

Iraq's past terrorist links have primarily been limited to such secular groups as Abu Nidal, a now-largely defunct Palestinian faction opposed to Yasser Arafat's Palestine Liberation Organization (PLO). At the height of Iraq's support of Abu Nidal in the early 1980s, Washington dropped Iraq from its list of countries that sponsored terrorism so the US could bolster Iraq's war against Iran. Baghdad was reinstated to the list only after the Iraqi invasion of Kuwait in 1990, even though American policymakers were unable to cite any increased Iraqi ties to terrorist groups. Abu Nidal himself was apparently murdered by the Iraqis in his Baghdad apartment, perhaps as an effort to deny the Bush administration an excuse to attack. A recent CIA report indicates that the Iraqis have actually been consciously avoiding any actions against the United States or its facilities abroad, presumably to deny Washington any excuse to engage in further military strikes against their country. The most clear example American counter-terrorism policymakers could cite of such Iraqi-backed terrorism was the 1993 plot by Iraqi agents to assassinate former President George Bush. In response, President Bill Clinton ordered the bombing of Baghdad, hitting an Iraqi intelligence headquarters as well as a nearby civilian neighborhood.

Although Secretary of Defense Donald Rumsfeld insisted that Saddam was backing international terrorism, he was unable to present any evidence that he did so against the US on 9/11. In fact, the State Department's annual *Patterns of Global Terrorism* does not list any serious act of international terrorism by Iraq between 2000 and 2003.[58] However, it is known that Saddam had assisted radical Islamists in Iraqi Kurdistan to undermine pro-American Kurdish groups. Iraq has indeed sponsored terrorism against Israel and the Kurds and has sought to eliminate Iraqi opponents abroad. However, Saddam has remained true to the unwritten rules of state sponsorship of terror: never get involved with a group that cannot be controlled and never give a WMD to terrorists who might use it to undermine his power.

In the end, the US never provided substantive evidence that Iraq was involved in Al-Qaida activities other than making open-ended accusations or producing WMD technologies. No specific claims were made that Iraq had plans to attack or assist an attack on any other state with the weapons Bush accused Saddam of being in unlawful possession of. Just cause does not permit a state to take offensive military force against another in the absence of evidence or beyond the threshold of credible fear.

Notes

1. George W. Bush, "Presidential Address to the Nation," (7 October 2001), http://www.whitehouse.gov/news/releases/2001/10/20011007-8.html
2. George W. Bush " Address to a Joint Session of Congress and the American People," (20 September 2001), http://www.whitehouse.gov/news/releases/2001/09/20010920-8.html
3. Ibid.
4. Editorial, "The New Enemy," *Economist* (15 September 2001), 15.
5. John Cloud, "The Manhunt Goes Global," *Time* (15 October 2001), 50.
6. Lisa Breyer, "Roots of Rage," *Time* (1 October 2001), 52-54.
7. Muttawakil is quoted in Hannah Bloch, "Land of Endless Tears," *Time* (24 September 2001), 61.
8. United National Security Council Resolution 1154, (2 March 1998), http://www.un.org/Depts/unscom/Keyresolutions/sres98-1154.htm
9. Ibid.
10. Used primarily as a way of identifying their policy interests of unilateralism, idealism, and global preeminence with the Roman god who forged fire with iron, the source of the term "vulcans" can be traced to Paul Wolfowitz, Donald Rumsfeld, and Richard Perle in comparison with other Bush advisers. Prior to the publication of *Striking First*, there has been a paucity of research concerned with the relationship between Bush and the vulcans. One excellent study is: Ivo Daadler and James Lindsay, *America Unbound: The Bush Revolution in Foreign Policy* (Washington DC: Brookings Institution Press, 2003), chapter 2. Also, a nice documentary that describes the general roles of the vulcans was produced by the Public Broadcasting Service on the special *Frontline*. See: "The War Behind Closed Doors," http://www.pbs.org/wgbh/pages/frontline/shows/iraq/interviews/perle.html
11. Richard Perle, "The War Behind Closed Doors," http://www.pbs.org/wgbh/pages/frontline/shows/iraq/interviews/perle.html
12. Project for the New American Century, "Letter to President Clinton on Iraq," January 26, 1998, http://www.newamericancentury.org/iraqclintonletter.htm.
13. See Neta Crawford, "The Slippery Slope Toward Preventive War," *Carnegie Council on Ethics and International Affairs*, (2 March 2003), http://www.cceia.org/viewMedia.php/prmTemplateID/8/prmID/868
14. Richard K. Betts, *Surprise Attack: Lessons for Defense Planning* (Washington, DC: Brookings Institution, 1982), 14-43.
15. Bush is quoted in Dana Milbank, "Bush Calls Attacks 'Acts of War,'" *Washington Post* (12 September 2001), 1.
16. Powell is quoted in Jane Perlez, "Powell Says It Clearly: No Middle Ground On Terrorism," *New York Times* (13 September 2001), 1.
17. Ibid.
18. Colin Powell, "Powell Very Pleased with Coalition-Building Results', (13 September 2001), usinfo.state.gov/topical/pol/terror/01091366.htm
19. Ibid.
20. United Nations Development Programme, *Human Development Report 2002: Deepening Democracy in a Fragmented World* (New York: Oxford University Press, 2002). See the online report at: http://hdr.undp.org/reports/global/2002/en/pdf/complete.pdf

21. Bush "Address to a Joint Session of Congress and the American People," http://www.whitehouse.gov/news/releases/2001/09/20010920-8.html

22. George W. Bush, "State of the Union," (28 January 2003), http://www.whitehouse.gov/news/releases/2003/01/20030128-19.html

23. Bush is quoted in Dana Milbank, "For Bush, Facts are Malleable," *Washington Post* (22 October 2002), 1.

24. Bush's quote can be found in Walter Pincus and Dana Millbank, "Kay Cites Evidence Of Iraq Disarming Action Taken in '90s, Ex-Inspector Says," *Washington Post* (28 January 2004).

25. Richard Cheney, "Vice President Speaks at VFW 103rd National Convention," (26 August 2002), http://www.whitehouse.gov/news/releases/2002/08/20020826.html

26. Quoted in John F. Cullihan, "Preempt Iraq," *National Review* (16 December 2002), 5.

27. Ibid.

28. See President Bush's speech before the General Assembly of the United Nations: George W. Bush, "President's Remarks at the United Nations General Assembly," (12 September 2001), http://www.whitehouse.gov/news/releases/2002/09/20020912-1.html

29. Blair is quoted in: "Full Text of Tony Blair's Forward to the Dossier on Iraq," *The Guardian* (24 September 2002), 1.

30. Barton Gellman provides an excellent and thorough examination of the inability of US forces to uncover WMD in post-Hussein Iraq. See: Barton Gellman, "Iraq's Arsenal was Only on Paper," *Washington Post*, (7 January 2004), A1. First reports on US inspections can be found in Douglas Jehl and Judith Miller, "Draft Report Said to Cite No Success in Iraq Arms Hunt," *New York Times*, (25 September 2003), 1.

31. David Kay, "Chasing Saddam's Weapons," http://www.pbs.org/wgbh/pages/frontline/shows/wmd/interviews/kay.html

32. John Sutter, "Chasing Saddam's Weapons," http://www.pbs.org/wgbh/pages/frontline/shows/wmd/interviews/kay.html

33. For more, see UNSCOM, "Report to the Security Council," (25 January 1999), http://www.fas.org/news/un/iraq/s/990125/index.html

34. Ibid.; Stephen Zunes, "The Case Against War," *The Nation* (12 September 2002), 23.

35. There are several sources on the leadership style, beliefs, and political personality of Saddam Hussein as leader of Iraq. Betty Glad, "Figuring Out Saddam Hussein," in Marcia Lynn Whicker, James P. Pfiffner and Raymond A. Moore, eds., *The Presidency and the Persian Gulf War*, (Westport, Connecticut: Praeger, 1993) 65-83; Said K. Aburish, *Saddam Hussein: The Politics of Revenge*, (New York, New York: Bloomsbury Publishing, 2000); Efraim Karsh and Inari Rautsi, *Saddam Hussein: A Political Biography*, (New York, New York: The Free Press, 1991).

36. See the special interview published in *The Guardian* on 19 September 2002 between Scott Ritter and journalist Williams Rivers Pitt: http://www.guardian.co.uk/Iraq/Story/0,2763,794771,00.html

37. See Mohamed El Baradei, International Atomic Energy Agency, (27 January 2003), "The Status of Nuclear Inspections in Iraq" including a February 14th update at: http://www.iaea.org/NewsCenter/Statements/2003/ebsp2003n005.shtml

38. Colin Powell, US Secretary of State, "Press Remarks with Foreign Minister of Egypt Amre Moussa," (24 February 2001): http://www.state.gov/secretary/rm/2001/933.htm

39. Kay, "Chasing Saddam's Weapons."

40. Gellman, "Iraq's Arsenal was Only on Paper," A1.

41. Rumsfeld is quoted in "Rumsfeld: Iraq May Have Destroyed Weapons," *USA Today* (28 May 2003), 22.

42. Scott Shepherd, "Saddam Not Part of 9/11 Attacks," *Atlanta Journal-Constitution,* (18 September 2003), 1B; Robert Schlesinger, "C.I.A. Takes Blame for Iraq Charge," *Boston Globe* (12 July 2003), A1.

43. Dan Plesch and Richard Norton-Taylor, "Straw, Powell, Had Serious Doubts Over Their Iraqi Weapons Claims," *The Guardian* (31 May 2003), 1.

44. Paul J. Nyden, "Will the US Reap What it has Sown?," *West Virginia Gazette* (27 September 2002), 1.

45. To view a copy of the letter, please see: Dean Foust and John Carey, "A US Gift to Iraq: Deadly Viruses," *Business Week* (20 September 2002), 34.

46. Patrick Tyler, "Officers Say US Aided Iraq Despite Use of Gas," *New York Times* (18 August 2002), 1.

47. Dilip Hiro, "When US Turned a Blind Eye to Poison Gas," *The Observer* (1 September 2002), 1.

48. Jeremy Scahill, "The Saddam in Rumsfeld's Closet," *CommonDreams.org* (2 August 2002), 1,http://www.commondreams.org/views02/0802-01.htm. For more background information on Rumsfeld's meetings with Hussein and the extension of American support to Iraq, see: Dana Priest, "Rumsfeld Visited Iraq in 1984 to Reassure Iraqis," *Washington Post* (19 December 2003), A42.

49. Ibid.

50. Kay is quoted in Tabassum Zakaria, "US Weapons Hunter Quits," *Boston Globe* (24 January 2004), 1.

51. "War in Iraq: How the Die was Cast Before Transatlantic Diplomacy Failed," *Financial Times,* (27 May 2003), 1.

52. George W. Bush, "President Bush, Colombia President Uribe Discuss Terrorism," (25 September 2002), http://www.whitehouse.gov/news/releases/2002/09/20020925-1.html

53. Colin Powell, "Remarks to the United Nations Security Council," (5 February 2003), http://www.state.gov/secretary/rm/2003/17300.htm

54. Tony Karon, "How Close Were Iraq and Al-Qaida?" *Time* (30 July 2003), 11.

55. David L. Greene, "Bin Laden Tape Exhorts Iraqis," *Baltimore Sun* (12 February 2003), 1.

56. The National Commission on Terrorist Attacks Upon the United States, *The 9/11 Report.* (New York: St. Martins Press, 2004).

57. Quoted in Dan Eggen, "9/11 Panel Finds No Collaboration Between Iraq, Al Qaida," *Washington Post,* June 16, 2004, A01. See the full report: The National Commission on Terrorist Attacks Upon the United States, *The 9/11 Report.*

58. See the annual reports at: http://www.state.gov/s/ct/rls/pgtrpt/

Chapter 4

Right Intentions

The Partiality of Intentions

The importance of seeking to project rightful intentions in waging offensive warfare is absolutely essential in meeting our requirements for building a case for just war. Any state can attack another with just cause, but go to war with the partial or biased intention of occupying territory and exploiting resources. This, however, illustrates the main problem with the principle of right intentions as one's good or bad intentions cannot be adequately or objectively assessed. In order to judge whether or not America's efforts to wage offensive warfare after 9/11 are right and good, one potential tactic would be to analyze US intentions after offensive military force has been applied. However, policymakers with influence over US foreign policy do not openly reveal their specific intentions to the public.

How can we test the principle of right intentions for our assessment here? According to Bruno Coppieters and Boris Kashnikov, a state's intention to wage war should be directed at promoting just cause.[1] While a state may have multiple intentions in waging offensive war, the intention to act in accordance with the principles of just cause should supersede other legitimate intentions. The goal, however, is not to realize moral ideals or promote the ethical purity or perfection of just cause; the diversity of intentions should be acknowledged and respected as long as territory is not occupied and resources not exploited.

Of course, it is impossible to presume that all policymakers and citizens will consent to some pure just cause objective and that no other intentions exist. But our interpretation here allows for a measured degree of flexibility in promoting rightful intentions, since it holds that as long as just cause predominates, other remaining goals can contribute to the case for right intentions. The methods used by the US must be moral and ethical and its goals have to be just in order for rightful intentions to exist.

Searching for Higher Ground

Since the 9/11 attacks, the US has had to struggle to establish Rightful Intentions in waging offensive warfare. In Afghanistan, in the direct aftermath of the attacks and with the devastation still firmly etched in the minds of Americans, President Bush took the appropriate steps toward building an international coalition against Al-Qaida and gathering support for the use of force in Afghanistan in response to 9/11 and to prevent future attacks. American officials not only contacted traditional allies such as Great Britain, but also international organizations, multilateral institutions, and other Muslim and non-Muslim nations for their support. The support of the world was a prerequisite not only for attacking Al-Qaida and the Taliban, but for maintaining an ongoing American-led anti-terrorist presence in the region.

Bush's coalition building efforts proved to be very successful. Virtually all nations extended some measure of support to the US in building a vast global anti-terrorist coalition to combat Al-Qaida and the Taliban. On 12 September, the United Nations Security Council unanimously denounced the attacks as a grave threat to peace and security and the North Atlantic Treaty Organization referred to Article 5 of its Washington Treaty by claiming that the attacks on the US were an attack on all NATO member states. Although very critical of past US military deployments, China and Russia pledged their support in exchange for a pledge from the US to hunt down terrorist in their own nations. This was especially important to Russia, which had been waging anti-terror campaign against Chechen Muslims since 1995. Muslim governments, especially Saudi Arabia, Egypt, and Jordan shied away from making public commitments to the US, claiming that any military action be under the sole authority of the UN Security Council.

President Bush even successfully obtained the support of the Taliban's natural ally, Pakistan. In fact, Pakistani President Pervez Musharrev pledged his unwavering support to the US in exchange for the lifting of economic sanctions on Pakistan, which were imposed after Pakistan successfully tested a nuclear weapon in 1998 in response to India's detonation of a nuclear device. Musharrev's support was quite surprising given that most of the Taliban's leaders, including Mullah Mohammed Omar, were educated in refugee camps and mosques throughout western Pakistan. The Pakistani intelligence services worked very closely with the Taliban in the Afghani civil war of the early to mid 1990s. In fact, following the Taliban's assumption of power in Afghanistan, only Pakistan, Arabia, and the United Arab Emirates officially recognized the Taliban.

Once the military response was set to occur and with a far-reaching anti-terror coalition in place, the US had to make sure that its prime focus was on conducting military action in Afghanistan. The US campaign would be comprised of punishing air assaults, the deployment of special operations forces in association with clandestine intelligence officers, and the eventual introduction of regular ground forces. It was also intended for US Special Forces and intelligence officers to coordinate attacks with the Northern Alliance. Important here is that there was a tacit recognition that to go further by carrying out a Soviet-style occupation with thousands of troops would place the US at odds with much of the Islamic world and is fraught with danger. However, short of that, Bush was prepared for a more forceful plan than launching cruise missile strikes, similar to those ordered by President Clinton in 1998.

Administration officials indicated that military action against Afghanistan need not be an urgent matter without the element of surprise. Indeed, the Pentagon would need time to position its forces in order to carry out major attacks in Afghanistan, far from American bases. But administration officials were aware that politically it will be easier to take action while world outrage over the terrorist attacks against the World Trade Center and the Pentagon was still fresh in the minds of the American public. The military action planned for Afghanistan would be part of a broader diplomatic as well as military policy of holding nations accountable that provide aid and comfort to terrorists.

Capturing or even killing bin Laden was priority one. In past missions, the US military tried to capture the Somali warlord Muhammad Farah Aidid. And it failed numerous times before the invasion of Iraq and eventual capture of Saddam Hussein in December 2003 to break his hold on power despite numerous missile attacks including some devised to kill the Iraqi leader. The first Bush administration was successful in apprehending Manuel Noriega in Panama largely because the US had many logistical advantages, including the use of its own bases and airfields inside Panama. But bin Laden has been elusive and based himself in a rugged region, remote from American bases and forces. Vice President Dick Cheney even declared that the US was not even sure that if bin Laden was is still in Afghanistan. Faced with a difficult task of tracking him down, the Bush Administration has responded by enlarging the problem. The theory is that while the Al-Qaida terrorists may be hard to find, the Taliban was not.

Although many of the same issues were apparent, US intentions seemed quite different when examining the case for offensive war against Iraq. A key element has been a moral argument that it sought to "liberate" the Iraqi people from Saddam's ruthless dictatorship. Implicit in the "liberation" intention has been the conviction that Iraq can and must be assisted to build a democratic form of government. However, we cannot forget that the case for against Iraq was grounded on the American argument that it possessed WMD in violation of UN Security Council resolutions and was a state supporter of Al-Qaida. In the words of Elliott Abrams, Bush's National Security Council director of Near East Affairs, "a by-product of the war is the liberation of the Iraqi people."[2]

It is debatable as to whether or not the US confronts a potentially more perilous and complicated situation in Iraq. However, what is known is that In its most far reaching expression, the US believes a democratic transformation of Iraq will shake Middle Eastern autocracies to their foundations and finally extend the global wave of democratization to a region that has long resisted it. Realistically, only recognition of the obstacles and dangers, cooperation with international organizations, and a sober reflection on the lessons of post-conflict reconstruction could make a democratic transformation possible. It will require a prolonged and internationalized engagement with Iraq, costing billions of dollars and thousands of lives over a number of years.

After over 35 years of Saddam's repression, Iraqis are now torn between several conflicting positions: a gratitude for their liberation from tyranny, nationalist resentment over their occupation by a foreign power, hesitancy to recognize a new Iraqi government independent of the US, an urgent need for economic assistance and political stability, and a profound resentment at years of international sanctions and economic ruin. Relief has transformed into anxiety, hope into distrust, and expectation into bitterness at all the suffering and destruction caused by war and isolation. Iraqis are also intensely divided along the obvious cleavage lines of Sunni Kurds, Arab Sunnis, Shiites, and other small minorities along a bewildering and shifting series of political, historical, economic, and family cleavages.

In the near term, only a massive military presence will be able to establish order and hold the country together. In early 2003, former US Army chief of staff, General Eric Shinseki, estimated this would require roughly 200,000 soldiers, nearly as large an occupying force as the one that fought to overthrow Saddam. It was not a good sign when the Bush administration appeared to chastise him for this honest appraisal before the war. Order cannot be restored and democracy and freedom promoted on the cheap. It was hoped that this peace-implementation force could be much broader in composition in order to suppress the domestic insurgencies and terrorist infiltrations that have frequently taken place since President Bush declare an end to major combat in May 2003.

Defense of Others

Does the intention to alleviate human suffering meet the necessary requirements for rightful and moral intentions? The notion of defending victims of repression, atrocities, and crimes against humanity via humanitarian interventions has been considered rightful intention for resorting to war.[3] Humanitarian intervention that occurs without the consent of a relevant government can be justified only in the face of ongoing or imminent genocide or comparable mass slaughter.[4] Encouraging military action to meet lesser abuses may mean a lack of capacity to intervene when atrocities are most severe. The invasion of Iraq, in the absence of formal approval from the UN damages the international legal order which itself is important to protect rights. Therefore, humanitarian intervention should be reserved for situations involving imminent mass killing. Also, because of the substantial risks inherent in the use of military force, humanitarian intervention should be exceptional and reserved for dire circumstances. Military action must be the last reasonable option to halt or prevent slaughter and should not be used for humanitarian purposes if effective alternatives are available. Moreover, the intervention must be guided primarily by a real humanitarian purpose and the prime reason for military action. Furthermore, every effort should be made to ensure that the means used to intervene themselves are consistent with international law and significant multilateral authority.

In Afghanistan, there were clear humanitarian objectives in bringing an end to the bloody civil war, which had engulfed the nation since the Soviet Union withdrew its occupation forces in 1989. The Taliban, under the direction of Mullah Muhammad Omar, enforced public order by instituting a very strict interpretation of the Sharia or Islamic law. Public executions and floggings became regular events at soccer stadiums and "frivolous activities" were outlawed. Men were required to wear beards and were beaten if they did not. The Taliban also engaged in a concerted effort eliminate all "non-Islamic" influence within their realm of control. Most Western technologies, namely television, music, and the Internet were banned for civilian use. Also, in 2001, the Taliban's Radio Shariat and Bakhtar news agency issued edicts requiring Afghan Hindus to wear distinctive clothing and carry personal identification cards made by the Kabul-based Council of the Ulema. Then in March 2001, the Taliban's Ministry of Information destroyed the ancient and revered Afghan Bamiyan Buddha statues, which at the time were the tallest Buddha statues in the world, claiming that the images were "offensive to Islam." The Taliban's moves against Afghan Hindus were designed to hasten their exodus from Afghanistan.

Humanitarian aid workers and fellow Muslims also fell victim to Taliban atrocities. Police from the Ministry for the Prevention of Vice and Promotion of Virtue made it a regular practice to raid several internationally funded and staffed hospitals in Kabul, beating staff members and forcing the hospitals to at times suspend operations because male and female staff allegedly mixed in dining areas and operating wards. It was also reported that police executed several Afghani relief workers for assisting with international aid personnel. The Taliban's policy of murdering civilians was also widespread. In January 2001, the predominantly-Sunni Taliban massacred hundreds of civilian Hazaras, a Shiite Muslim ethnic group in the central highlands of the country. The Taliban then blocked the delivery of international humanitarian aid to large parts of the Hazarajat region. In 1998, Taliban forces executed between 2,000 and 5,000 civilians in Mazar-i-Sharif, the majority of them ethnic Hazaras, Uzbeks, and Tajiks and raped hundreds of women and young girls. Those who were spared were forced to become Sunni Muslims.

Most shocking was the Taliban's treatment of women. When the Taliban assumed control over Kabul in 1996, they immediately forbade girls to go to school and barred women from working outside the home. They even prohibited women from leaving their homes without a male relative; those who defied the edicts risked being beaten and executed by the police. The restrictions were devastating for thousands of Afghan war widows, who had been reduced to selling their possessions or begging to feed their families. The Taliban even significantly reduced women's access to health care by decreeing that women could only be treated by the handful of women doctors in Kabul. In addition to these abuses were other constraints, such as chopping off fingers if women were caught wearing nail polish. According to the Taliban, this was to safeguard and protect women.

The US effort to alleviate these grave humanitarian issues in Afghanistan was based on a strategy which held that any use of American military force would be tempered by the notion that America's struggles were against bin Laden, the Al-Qaida leadership and its terrorist camps, and the Taliban as a state sponsor, not Islam or the Afghani people. In his 20 September speech, Bush declared, "The terrorists practice a fringe form of Islamic extremism that has been rejected by Muslim scholars and the vast majority of Muslim clerics, a fringe movement that perverts the peaceful teachings of Islam... The terrorists are traitors to their own faith, trying, in effect, to hijack Islam itself. The enemy of America is not our many Muslim friends; it is not our many Arab friends. Our enemy is a radical network of terrorists, and every government that supports them."[5] The president reiterated his comments to the people of Afghanistan on 7 October, the day on which Operation Enduring Freedom commenced: "The United States of America is a friend to the Afghan people, and we are the friends of almost a billion worldwide who practice the Islamic faith. The United States of America is an enemy of those who aid terrorists and of the barbaric criminals who profane a great religion by committing murder in its name."[6] In order to make sure that it was following these pledges, the US began a humanitarian campaign of air dropping thousands of ready-made meals and medicine to civilians.[7]

But the US was fighting an uphill battle by claiming that its struggle was not against Islam and the people, since popular antipathy toward America even in the immediate aftermath of the 9/11 in the Muslim world was and continues to be particularly intense. Much-touted US efforts at public diplomacy have made little progress. In predominantly Muslim countries surveyed by the Pew Global Attitudes Project, anger toward the US was very high even in the months following the 9/11 attacks and strong anti-US sentiment has remained pervasive since the attacks. Interestingly, bin Laden, is viewed favorably by sixty-five per cent in Pakistan, fifty-five per cent in Jordan, and forty-five per cent in Morocco. Even in Turkey, where bin Laden is highly unpopular, as many as thirty-one per cent say that suicide attacks against Americans and other Westerners are justifiable. Majorities in all four Muslim nations surveyed doubt the sincerity of the war on terrorism. Most Muslims perceive US actions as reflective of a greater intention to control oil and to dominate the world.[8]

Ironically, US efforts to fight terrorism have resulted in the fostering rather than diminution of anti-Americanism in the Muslim world. The US embrace of repressive governments during the Cold War, especially the Royal family in Saudi Arabia, the Shah of Iran and his allowance by the Carter Administration to seek medical treatment in the US, and Saddam as a bulwark against the Ayatollah Khomeini in Iran, has contributed to a history of US anti-Islam policies. Moreover, America's recent embrace of the brutal regime of Islam Karimov in Uzbekistan and its relative silence regarding Russian atrocities in Chechnya have paradoxically bolstered Al Qaida's claims that the US supports the oppression of Muslims and props up repressive anti-Muslim governments.

However, it is America's continued support for Israel that has strengthened its anti-Muslim perception throughout the Islamic world. An April 2002 Zogby International poll conducted in several predominately-Muslim countries reported that more than ninety per cent of respondents disapproved of US policy toward the Palestinians.[9] While many Arabs also dislike America for other reasons, its perceived arrogance and supposed hostility to Islam, as well as its support for repressive Arab regimes, Palestinian issues have struck a particularly raw nerve since the outbreak of the second intifada in September 2000. Moreover, *Al-Jazeera* now broadcasts images of dead and wounded Palestinians into homes and coffeehouses across the Muslim Middle East and Central Asia.

While Israel has peace treaties with two of its neighbors, Egypt and Jordan, the Jewish state remains a regional outcast whose close ties to America and possession of nuclear weapons are among its most important strategic deterrents. Before, ever since President Truman recognized Israel in May 1948, the two countries have had what many term a "special relationship" shaped by American admiration for Israeli democracy, Cold War power politics, US distaste for Arab aggression and terrorism, long-standing congressional support for Israel, US guilt over turning away Jewish refugees fleeing Nazi Germany, the clout of the pro-Israel lobby in the US Congress, and Christian interest in the holy land. Moreover, Israel is a primary recipient of foreign aid, receiving $2.1 billion in military financing and $600 million in economic aid a year.[10]

Bin Laden's proclamations reflect these perceptions. The US is deemed by him as an aggressor against Islam due to the presence of US troops in Saudi Arabia since the end of the Gulf War. In addition, the "protracted blockade" against Iraq is viewed as an assault on the Iraqi people. In other words, the United States has become the embodiment of the *dar al-harb*, or engagement in aggression against Islam. Bin Laden of course lacks the religiously mandated authority to wage such war or to issue fatwas, as they do not bear the mantle of succession to the Prophet Muhammad. This is why the struggle against the US is depicted by Al-Qaida as a defensive war.

With respect to Iraq, from the outset, the public campaign to oust Saddam was grounded on the accusation that he possessed WMD in violation of international law and deserved to be overthrown because of his alliances with terrorists groups, namely Al-Qaida. Moreover, the US claimed that illicit Iraqi WMD programs were a threat to US national security because of Saddam's perceived linkage with terrorist activities. In the days and months leading up the US invasion, the case for war was not primarily grounded in terms of humanitarianism. But given America's inability to locate alleged illicit Iraqi WMD programs and its failure to uncover evidence of an Al-Qaida presence in the country, the Bush Administration's argument for war has evolved toward a humanitarian rationale centered squarely on Saddam's human rights abuses. While other reasons are still regularly mentioned, the humanitarian intention, along with the democratic intention, has gained prominence.

The question is not whether Saddam was a ruthless leader; rather, the real question should be concerned with the actual conditions present in Iraq under Saddam at the same time humanitarian intervention was being considered. These conditions should emphasize levels of mass abuse and repression in terms of imminence. In other words, human suffering has to represent an imminent threat. In other words, a humanitarian intervention has to occur at the same time as the mass human catastrophe is occurring, not years later in retrospect. Now that the war's proponents are relying so heavily on a humanitarian argument given the absence of WMD and an Iraqi-Al-Qaida nexus, the need to assess this claim has grown in importance.

Was genocide or comparable mass slaughter underway or imminent in Hussein's Iraq between 2001 and 2003? Brutal as Saddam's reign had been, the scope of the Iraqi government's killing in this period was not of the exceptional and dire magnitude that would justify humanitarian intervention. This does not discount the reality that after years of Sunni dominated, Bath Party rule, the Iraqi government murdered roughly 200,000 to 300,000 Iraqi civilians, mostly Shiites and Kurds. However, at the time America was building its public case for war, Saddam's murderous reign had subsided. However, there were times in the past when the killing was so intense that humanitarian intervention would have been justified; for example, during the 1988 Anfal genocide, in which the Iraqi government slaughtered some 100,000 Kurds. Human Rights Watch even advocated military intervention in 1991 after George HW Bush encouraged domestic insurrection and then failed to aid the Kurds and Shiites. But on the eve of the American invasion in 2003, the Iraqi government was not engaged in the type of killing near this magnitude, or had been since 1991.[11]

The present "better late than never" argument for humanitarian intervention does not represent a rightful intention. The argument put forth by President Bush and proponents of the US invasion and occupation now argue that if Saddam committed mass atrocities in the past, his overthrow now prevents his resumption of atrocities. This argument is groundless. Recall that Bush grounded his original case for war on the grounds that Saddam was accumulating WMD for the purpose of threatening the Middle East and the US. Moreover, the administration stressed the potential for those weapons falling into the hands of terrorists. America's failure to locate evidence suggesting illegal Iraqi WMD intentions or capabilities has resulted in a redefinition of the original justification for the war, which has evolved into one based on a humanitarian rationale out for political expediency. This re-definition falls far short of meeting rightful intentions for offensive war.

Moreover, the humanitarian argument in Iraq cannot be justified if other equally or more needy places are ignored. Of course, Iraqi repression was severe, but the case might be made that repression elsewhere was worse. For example, an estimated three million or more have lost their lives to violence, disease, and exposure in recent years during the conflict in the eastern Democratic Republic of Congo, yet intervention was late and, compared to Iraq, modest. Also, the various civil wars in the Sudan between Christians and the Islamic military government and among various disparate black and Arab Muslim groups has resulted in the deaths of hundreds of thousands of persons and produced no American-led humanitarian intervention. The most devastating case was in 1994 in Rwanda when the Clinton Administration sat idly by and witnessed mass genocide of the Tutsi population by Hutu militants, which ultimately resulted in the slaughter of roughly 1 million people over the span of four months. Israel has been a sore point for many, as they have nuclear weapons and are accused by human rights groups and others of countless abuses of human rights violations and military occupations of Palestinian areas. Turkey has for years had a harsh crackdown on Kurds and North Korea regularly imprisons, tortures, and executes thousands. If Saddam's repression warrants military intervention, it would be callous to disregard the plight of the Iraqi victims simply because victims in other countries were neglected. However, moral necessity requires political consistency.

What about the role of the US in support of Iraq towards the end of the Cold War? Following the hostage crisis in Teheran and the overthrow of the Shah, the

US threw its support behind Saddam throughout the 1980s in the hope of preventing the spread of the Shiite Iranian revolution. When Saddam ordered chemical attacks against Iranian troops in the 1980s, he did so based on strategic intelligence reports of Iranian troop movements supplied by the Reagan Administration supplied.[12] After the Anfal genocide against Iraqi Kurds in 1988, both the Reagan and first Bush administrations gave Baghdad billions of dollars in agricultural credits and import loan guarantees.[13] The Iraqi government's ruthless suppression of the 1991 uprising by Iraqi Shiites and the Kurds after the Gulf War ceasefire was facilitated by the first Bush Administration's concession to Saddam that Iraq could use its helicopter gunships in violation of its no-fly zone commitments. What makes this case even more morally questionable is that President George HW Bush had encouraged the uprising in the first place.[14] America's support for Saddam in the 1980s against Iran and in the 1991 uprising reinforced an image that it was more important for the US to defeat Iran or check Iranian influence inside Iraq than to discourage or prevent large-scale slaughter and a humanitarian catastrophe. This perception has deeply resonated among Iraqi Shiites.

We should also take into consideration the reality that the humanitarian crisis in Iraq has been caused, to a great extent, by fourteen years of sanctions that devastated Iraqi civilians as much as it limited the means with which Saddam Hussein could fund WMD programs and terrorist activities.[15] On 6 August 1990, the Security Council responded to Iraq's invasion of Kuwait by adopting Resolution 661, which prohibited all imports and exports except "supplies intended strictly for medical purposes, and, in humanitarian circumstances, foodstuffs."[16] However, since Iraq's currency income was highly dependent on exports, the proceeds of which were frozen by international banks, it was simply unable to import any humanitarian goods. In addition, by March 1991, UN military forces destroyed or disabled Iraq's civilian infrastructure, including electric power stations, irrigation facilities, and water and treatment sewage plants. The sanctions were justified in order to force Iraq into complying with new conditions imposed by cease-fire agreements and UN Security Council resolutions banning WMD.

Despite an impending human catastrophe, the Security Council failed to alleviate the negative impact of the sanctions until August 1991, after UN missions showed civilian suffering. In Resolutions 706 and 712, the Security Council proposed an oil-for-food program aimed at allowing Iraq to sell $1.6 billion of oil every six months.[17] The amount allowed to purchase food and medicine for the civilian population was roughly $1.8 billion, far below the UN-estimated $22 billion needed to repair damage to the civilian infrastructure. The Security Council did not revisit the issue until April 1995, when it passed an altered oil-for-food measure with the passage of Resolution 986.[18] In May 1996, Saddam and the UN agreed to a deal permitting the sale of $1 billion in oil revenue over a renewable 90-day period in order to pay for food and medicine. Thirty per cent of the profits would pay for war reparations, 15 per cent toward humanitarian supplies for 3 million Kurds, five to ten per cent for UN operations, and five to ten per cent for maintenance of the oil pipelines, leaving about $1.6 billion for Iraq's remaining population of 18 million, less than $7.50 per person every month. [19]

The so-called oil-for-food deal never effectively addressed the widespread hunger and disease in Iraq. There has been an alarming reappearance of malnutrition and the UN estimated a five-fold increase in child mortality due to hunger, disease and unsanitary conditions.[20] Sanctions resulted in shortages in medical supplies, namely syringes, IV sets, blood bags, oxygen, anesthesia, and linens. The UN Children's Fund (UNICEF) reported increases in diabetes, cancer and kidney disease, and preventable infections, such as diarrhea, pneumonia, whooping cough and typhoid.[21] It could be argued that because sanctions more closely resemble a state of war than of peace, UN-imposed sanctions should be governed by more permissive laws of war, rather that the strict civilian immunities of human rights.

The Security Council, the US, and the UK shoulder a large measure of responsibility for these violations of human rights and humanitarian law by maintaining sanctions without taking effective measures to minimize harm to the population. The Council has refused to entertain less drastic measures only after UN and independent reports publicly revealed the extent of civilian cease-fire resolutions that would result in the lifting of sanctions. It defies logic, however, for the Security Council to hold the welfare of a nation hostage to the good behavior of a dictator. And while it is troubling that a repressive regime, through sheer indifference to its own population, can exert leverage over UN policy, it is even more disturbing that the international community has acquiesced to a policy that effectively constitutes illegal collective punishment.

The invasion of Iraq failed to meet the test for a humanitarian intervention and therefore cannot be used by the Bush Administration to suit is rightful intentions for war. Most important, the killing in Iraq at the time was not of the exceptional nature that would justify such intervention. In addition, intervention was not the last reasonable option to stop Iraqi atrocities. Intervention was not motivated primarily by humanitarian concerns. It was not conducted in a way that maximized compliance with international humanitarian law. It was not approved by a legitimate multilateral authority or by the Security Council. And while at the time it was launched it was reasonable to believe that the Iraqi people would be better off, it was not designed or carried out with the needs of Iraqis foremost in mind.

Democracy and Freedom

Immediately after the 9/11 attacks, the American view was that to prevent authority from breaking down in Kabul in a post-Taliban government and to eliminate Afghanistan as an attractive haven for terrorists, the US must promote a strong sense of stability within the country and in the entire region of Central Asia. To do so, the US favored establishing enduring state political and economic structures that would be acceptable by the various ethnic groups in Afghanistan. Stability and security within Afghanistan and between its neighbors and the building of viable political and economic institutions is a prerequisite for the state's future viability in the world community.

Such a task would be fraught with significant challenges. The most challenge dealt with the question of how much political power should be consolidated in a new post-Taliban central government in Kabul. For the Bush Administration, the building of central authority would be done via the creation of a national army that could target Al-Qaida and Taliban holdouts with US military support. Complicating matters was the long standing tradition of power in the hands of local warlords and religious councils scattered throughout the various Afghani provinces and villages. Thus, it was believed that any new stable political system or structure of a national army would be based on some form of power-sharing between a national government and strong local and provincial leaders.

For Afghanistan to begin the process towards building stable relations with the West, the Bush Administration believed certain social and economic reforms had to be undertaken to end Taliban repression and eliminate Al-Qaida. One goal was to promote gender considerations into a post-Taliban governmental structure. Another emphasized the long-term importance of creating strong political parties in promoting discipline within institutions and reducing the importance of individual leaders, bridging ethnic differences, and encouraging political participation in the country. The need to guarantee the security of the voting public before and during elections was also an urgent need, and a primary duty of the new national army. One way of promoting a sense of national unity and stability was to schedule national elections before regional elections to facilitate the development of a broader national electorate, rather than cause regional or ethnically divided polities.

If promoting stability appeared tough, then building Afghanistan's economy, promoting foreign trade, and constructing infrastructural links connecting it with others seemed virtually impossible. Any peace and long-term economic viability in Afghanistan would have to be built on the restoration of productive agriculture. According to the UN Food and Agriculture Organization (FAO), "The shortest path to national stability will be for the rural population to return to their fields and produce the nation's food." Roughly eighty-five per cent of Afghanistan's population is dependent on agriculture and the Bush Administration made $39 million available to improve access to food in rural and urban areas by increasing food production and generating income by providing basic inputs such as seeds and fertilizer.[22]

Development programs would also focus on the rehabilitation of irrigation, reforestation, seed multiplication, the promotion of high-value crops to reduce poppy production, veterinary services and integrated pest management. This made the need to improve the status of women in Afghanistan as they are traditionally responsible for food availability, family income, nutrition, health care and education in Afghanistan. However, twenty years of civil war left an estimated half a million households without a male provider.

The US believed that if these measures were implemented, Afghani farmers would ultimately abandon opium production through the development of alternative crops, credit, and foreign markets. But the fight against poppy production could only be won if the US made an attempt to improve the household and community welfare especially in the rural areas. Since poppy production accounted for roughly half of Afghanistan's economy in 2001, that eradication would have to come at the expense of farmers' livelihoods. Besides, Afghanistan is the world's largest producer of opium, accounting for roughly 70 per cent of the world's total supply.[23] While the post-Taliban government of US-backed President Hamid Karzai did issue a decree in January 2002 forbidding poppy cultivation and trading and began an ambitious eradication campaign, it was resisted by his government's weak authority over the provinces and delays in international assistance for alternative crops and farmer support.

While somewhat of a different case, the goal of promoting stability in Iraq appeared more immediate. The social, economic, and political conditions for establishing democracy in Iraq are far from favorable. Unlike Germany, Japan, and Italy in the wake of WW II, Iraq has no prior experience with multiparty government (with the important exception of the post-1991 experiment with democracy in the autonomous Kurdish areas in the north). In particular contrast to post–World War II Europe, Iraq sits in a region that is hostile to democracy and in a cultural zone that lacks a lasting democratic tradition (and, apart from Lebanon and Turkey, has never had one).

This does not mean that Iraq does not have democratic potential. To be sure, Iraq does have impressive human capital: scientists, engineers, businesspeople, artists, and intellectuals, many of the best of whom stand ready to return from exile. But the obstacles are quite high. In 2003, illiteracy was estimated at more than sixty per cent, with seventy-seven per cent of women unable to read while joblessness and economic displacement are pervasive and services in shambles.[24] The economy depends almost entirely on foreign-exchange earnings from oil. Oil may generate the wealth to rebuild the country, but in developing countries, it also generates the pervasive corruption that undermines democracy and stability.

The challenges in building an Iraqi democracy are formidable and morally questionable. One key reason is that American legitimacy in the Middle East in general is fragile as are US intentions in witnessing the emergence of an Iraqi democracy. But in the face of an American invasion and occupation, jubilation and gratitude will most likely be met with impatience, confusion, anger, grieving, and even nationalist loathing since Iraqi suspicion is rife of American hegemonic intentions. This raises a greater dilemma. A democracy built on strong institutions takes decades to effectively build and evolve. However, the US will not have much time to convey its rightful intentions; that is, to frame the post-war context in a way that clearly underscores ownership of the democracy by the Iraqi people. This will be a delicate task because, initially, there will be no legitimate representatives of the Iraqi people to hand authority over to; if the US simply designates a few Iraqis to govern in the name of a sovereign democratic Iraq, they would be probably be rejected as an American client regime.

The Slippery Slope

American intentions can also be viewed from an economic standpoint, especially since American offensive force has been applied to the oil-rich regions of Central Asia and the Middle East. The collapse of the Cold War and the disintegration of the USSR created a vacuum in Central Asia and a US presence in Afghanistan could provide it with strategic access to the Caspian Sea region, in particular to its large proven and unproven reserves of oil and gas. Driven by the sense of injustice caused by the 9/11 terror attacks, an overthrow of the Taliban and the establishment of an American "client regime" allows the US to create a new political framework within which it will exert its influence over the region. In Iraq, for years, the US has intended to secure and stabilize the flow of oil to and from the Middle East with a friendly government in Baghdad. For decades, oil has been a major US concern about Iraq in internal and unpublicized documents.[25] Moreover, the desire to manage Iraqi oil is linked with America's promotion of the dollar, which in turn, is supported by the greater American view that all OPEC global oil sales transactions continue to be conducted in US dollars.

On the whole, unimpeded access to affordable energy is a paramount geo-strategic interest of the US at the core of American national security policy as oil fuels America's economy. For example, in 2000, Americans consumed a total of 19.7 million barrels of petroleum (crude oil and petroleum products) per day, or about one-quarter of total world oil production. Roughly 50 per cent of that total oil consumption is imported. This demand for oil is expected to grow to 26.7 million barrels of petroleum per day by 2020 with about 60 per cent imported.[26]

As domestic sources of oil supplies erode, the nation's increasing reliance on imported oil makes the US vulnerable to oil supply disruptions and threatens America's economic and energy security. American transportation relies heavily on oil, accounting for two-thirds of US petroleum use in 2000 and consumption is expected to continue through 2020. Throughout this forecast period, the level of gasoline consumption should remain steady at about forty-five per cent of all the petroleum used in the US, as gasoline consumption increases from 8.5 to 11.8 million barrels per day. In addition, more than fifty per cent of the fuel used by the transportation sector is imported, far more than any other part of the US economy.[27] To keep up with this dependence, the US steadily increased its dependence on foreign oil. In 1993, total imports as a share of petroleum products broke fifty per cent for the first time. In 2004, imports of 11.5 million barrels per day comprise fifty eight per cent of petroleum products.[28]

At the same time, US oil production has been steadily declining since 1970. Although US petroleum production is expected to remain virtually unchanged (9.03 million barrels per day in 2000 to 9.95 million barrels per day in 2020) over the next two decades, oil consumption is expected to rise from 19.7 million barrels per day in 2000 to 26.7 million barrels per day in 2020, a thirty-five per cent increase.[29] This combination will make it impossible for the US to improve its energy security by using more domestic petroleum, even if it were to tap every oil deposit. That would delay the inevitable and the US would still have to reduce its use of petroleum products and turn to alternative fuel sources.

While there is no question that the US is dependent on foreign oil, the level of oil dependence does not give a full indication of how vulnerable the US is to a supply disruption. Today, there are four major sources that supply roughly one-third of the US oil supply: Canada, Mexico, Venezuela, and the Persian Gulf region (Bahrain, Iran, Iraq, Kuwait, Qatar, Saudi Arabia and the United Arab Emirates). Trade agreements with Canada and Mexico, and the proximity of these sources should make their supplies less vulnerable to disruptions. In 2000, the Persian Gulf supplied twelve per cent of US oil consumption; by 2020 it will supply almost sixteen per cent.[30] This region will continue to increase its influence in world oil markets as supplies in other regions are exhausted.

The US first experienced oil supply disruptions from the Persian Gulf region in the 1970s, when two sudden and sharp oil price hikes rocked the American economy. Although America's ability to offset major oil supply disruptions has improved somewhat since the 1970s, several factors are contributing to America's vulnerability. Oil production facilities are primarily concentrated in the Persian Gulf region and the region's share of worldwide petroleum exports is expected to grow. A supply disruption from the Gulf would impact oil prices worldwide.

The global extent of American power is grounded largely in terms of it military influence and logistical ability to persuade transport routes for fossil fuels and other strategic material supplies demanded by other industrial states. For example, the US is the world's leading power and its military spending is greater than all of the next 13 countries ranked beneath it.

Table 1 Global Military Expenditures, 2004

Country	Billions (US dollars)
United States	399.1
Russia	65.0
China	47.0
Japan	42.6
United Kingdom	38.4
France	29.5
Germany	24.9
Saudi Arabia	21.3
India	15.6
South Korea	14.1
Israel	10.6
Iran	4.8
North Korea	2.1
Iraq	1.4

Source: Center for Defense Information, Fiscal Year 2004 (most recent year available). See: http://www.cdi.org/issues/usmi/

While oil reserves on US territory are increasingly scarce, there is a growing tension to search for more foreign sources of oil. In the short term, most oil imports over the next several decades will come from the Organization of Petroleum Exporting Countries (OPEC), which is dominated by nations from the Arab Middle East. Saudi Arabia leads with 25 per cent of the world's proven reserves, followed by Iraq with 11 per cent, Kuwait, the United Arab Emirates and Iran each with 9 per cent, and Venezuela at 7 per cent. While the small number of proven oil reserves in the Caspian region cannot solve expected shortfalls in US oil consumption, a long term presence in Central Asia could decrease American energy dependence on OPEC and the Middle East.

The US presence has allowed it access to oil flows throughout Central Asia. Since Central Asian oil is "non-OPEC oil," energy supplies are less likely to be affected by the price and supply policies applied by the oil-exporting cartel. Flows of large volumes of oil extracted from the Caspian Sea area through non-OPEC lands could erode the power of OPEC, as well as its ability to maintain high oil prices and to use oil as political leverage. An American foothold in Afghanistan could begin the formal process of challenging OPEC's power over international energy exchanges. The goal is therefore to reduce dependency on any particular region, namely the Arab Middle East, and reduce the possibility that a political upheaval in one country/region will significantly affect oil supplies and possibly bring about a global economic crisis. According to a US oil expert, "The addition of Caspian oil could weaken the OPEC monopoly, providing greater leverage over the pricing policies of Saudi Arabia and other OPEC countries, ultimately contributing to lower world oil prices."[31]

Therefore, the struggle to influence Caspian Sea energy becomes a driving force in US foreign policy toward Central Asia in general and Afghanistan in particular because oil remains the lifeblood of the American and world economies. The maintenance of America's global superpower status demands that it control and influence oil and gas production at every stage: discovery, pumping, refining, transporting, and marketing. The American Petroleum Institute, voice of the major US oil companies, has referred to the Caspian region as "the area of greatest resource potential outside of the Middle East."[32] Vice-President Dick Cheney, speaking of the Caspian Sea basin in 1998 when he was head of the US oil corporation Halliburton, stated "I cannot think of a time when we have had a region emerge as suddenly to become as strategically significant as the Caspian."[33]

America's desire to influence Central Asian oil via Afghanistan should not be a surprise. According to George Monbiot, US-based Unocal Corporation, which is headquartered in El Segundo, California, had been negotiating with the Taliban since 1995 to build "oil and gas pipelines from Turkmenistan, through Afghanistan and into Pakistani ports on the Arabian sea."[34] Ahmed Rashid claimed that the US and Pakistan actually helped install the Taliban in hopes of bringing stability to Afghanistan, with the greater hope of securing a pipeline project under the supervision of Unocal. However, Unocal reneged on the project following America's missile strikes on Afghanistan conducted in response to the 1998 terrorist attacks on US embassies in Kenya and Tanzania.[35] The 9/11 terrorist attacks provided the Bush administration a legitimate reason to invade Afghanistan and topple the Taliban, which supplied safe harbor to Al-Qaida. Following the Northern Alliance's capture of Kabul in November 2001, the US quickly engineered the rise to power of two former Unocal employees: Hamid Karzai, the new interim president of Afghanistan, and Zalmay Khalizad, the Bush administration's Afghanistan envoy.[36]

For reasons both of world strategy and control over energy resources, the US is therefore determined to secure for itself a dominant geo-strategic role in Central Asia. At a minimum, an immediate task of US power has been to ensure that no competing state or coalition gains the ability to diminish its influence. This includes checking Russia's monopoly over oil and gas transport routes in the region, promoting US energy security through diversified supplies, constructing multiple pipelines that traverse US-controlled Afghanistan, and denying other potential powers, namely China, leverage over Central Asian oil and natural gas resources.

The stakes in Iraq may be greater because it possesses the world's second largest proven oil reserves, estimated at 115 billion barrels or 11 per cent of the world total and its gas fields are extensive. Moreover, it also estimated that Iraq holds at least 110 trillion cubic feet of natural gas.[37] Oil companies will most likely gain production rights over these rich fields of Iraqi oil, worth hundreds of billions of dollars. Exxon Mobil, Royal Dutch-Shell, British Petroleum-Amoco, Chevron-Texaco, and TotalFinaElf currently dominate the world oil industry. American and British corporations have long held a three-quarter share in Iraq's oil production, but they lost their position with the 1972 nationalization of the Iraq Petroleum Company. The nationalization, following ten years of increasingly rancorous relations between the companies and the government, rocked the international oil industry, as Iraq sought to gain greater control of its oil resources. After nationalization, Iraq turned to France and Russia for funds.[38]

During the 1990s, Russia's Lukoil, China National Petroleum Corporation and France's TotalFinaElf held contract talks with Saddam's government over plans to develop Iraqi fields as soon as sanctions are lifted. Lukoil reached an agreement in 1997 to develop Iraq's West Qurna field, while China National signed an agreement for the North Rumailah field in the same year (China's oil import needs from the Persian Gulf will grow from 0.5 million barrels per day in 1997 to 5.5 million barrels per day in 2020, making China one of the region's most important customers). France's Total at the same time held talks for future development of the Majnun field.[39]

American and British corporations have been very concerned that their rivals might gain a major long-term advantage in the global oil business. "Iraq possesses huge reserves of oil and gas – reserves I'd love Chevron to have access to," enthused Chevron CEO Kenneth T. Derr in a 1998 speech at the Commonwealth Club of San Francisco, in which he pronounced his strong support for sanctions.[40] Sanctions have kept America's and Britain's rivals in check, a clear advantage. A post-Saddam government would provide them with an advantage over their competitors with a post-Saddam government.

The US quest for energy security and its link with a post-Saddam Iraq has been noted via a 1997 report from the James A. Baker Institute of Public Policy at Rice University, which claimed that the US would be threatened over the next decade by significant oil shortages. In particular the report addressed "The Threat of Iraq and Iran" to the stable flow of oil from the Middle East. It concluded that Saddam remained a threat to Middle Eastern security and still had the military capability to exercise force beyond Iraq's borders.[41]

The Bush Administration reiterated this theme by endorsing a second report, this time issued by the Council of Foreign Relations (CFR), concluding that "The United States remains a prisoner of its energy dilemma. Iraq remains a de-stabilizing influence to ... the flow of oil to international markets from the Middle East. Saddam has also demonstrated a willingness to use his own export program to manipulate oil markets. Therefore the US should conduct an immediate policy review toward Iraq including military, energy, economic and political/ diplomatic assessments."[42] When Vice President Cheney's Energy Task Force issued its own national energy strategy, it declared in that "The [Persian] Gulf will be a primary focus of US international energy policy."[43] Following the recommendations of Cheney's Task Force, the Bush Administration even hoped to increase foreign investment in under-developed Iraq oilfields. On 16 January 2003, just two months before the US invasion, *Wall Street Journal* reported that the White House, State Department, and Department of Defense had been meeting informally with executives from Halliburton, Schlumberger, ExxonMobil, ChevronTexaco and ConocoPhillips to plan the postwar expansion of oil production from Iraq.[44]

Prior to the US invasion in March 2003, Saddam extended offers of oil exploration to France, China, Russia, Brazil, Italy, and Malaysia in exchange for the lifting of economic sanctions. The possibility of the US overthrowing Saddam would disrupt these plans. According to Faisal Qaragholi of the Iraqi National Congress (INC), a post-Saddam government "will examine all the contracts that Saddam has made, and we will cancel all those that are not in the interest of the Iraqi people and will reopen bidding on them."[45] Ahmad Chalabi, leader of the Iraqi National Congress, a once-US favorite as heir to the Iraqi leadership, was quoted as saying: "American companies will have a big shot at Iraqi oil."[46]

Moreover, revelations by former Secretary of the Treasury Paul O'Neill inform us that the Bush Administration started planning for an invasion of Iraq immediately after the presidential inauguration. According to O'Neill, Iraq was "Topic A" at the very first meeting of the Bush National Security Council, just ten days after the inauguration. "It was about finding a way to do it. That was the tone of the President, saying 'Go find me a way to do this.'"[47] Immediately after the presidential transition, Cheney's National Energy Policy Development Group studied the challenge posed by French, Russian and other companies. One of the documents made public after a long court case, is a map of Iraq showing its major oil fields and a two-page list of "Foreign Suitors for Iraqi Oilfield Contracts." The list showed more than 40 companies from 30 countries with projects agreed or under discussion, but not a single US or UK deal.[48] The list included agreements or discussions with companies from Germany, India, Italy, Canada, Indonesia, Japan and other nations, along with the well-known French, Russian and Chinese deals. The report, released in May 2003, warned of US oil shortfalls that might "undermine our economy, our standard of living, our national security."[49]

As war talk increased in the US and at the UN, oil issues came into the open. The influential Heritage Foundation published "The Future of a Post-Saddam Iraq" in September 2002 which called for the privatization of the Iraqi National Oil Corporation (INOC) and warned that competitor companies would lose their Saddam-era contracts. The companies, the Bush Administration and the Iraqi opposition held many meetings over post-war oil. The *Washington Post* even reported that companies were "maneuvering for a stake" in postwar Iraq and that the war could cause major "reshuffling" of world petroleum markets. Former CIA Director James Woolsey told the *Post* that the US would use access to post-war oil as a bargaining chip to win French and Russian support.[50]

The US is not just interested in strictly extracting oil from Iraq or preventing rivals from gaining a foothold; a concern may be with exerting financial influence with oil-producing countries over the long term. The US current budget deficit has soared to an unprecedented $503 billion in 2002, almost five per cent of GDP, an indication that the US economy is growing increasingly more dependent on an inflow of foreign assets.[51] The rapidly growing budget deficit is largely the result of increased US military spending and reduced government revenue due to tax cuts. The deficit adds to the instability of the dollar, making foreign dollar-holders nervous about the future strength of the currency and the future value of dollar-denominated US assets. Moreover, the US trade deficit, its net exports and imports, has grown considerably in the last decade. In 2002, the US trade imbalance in goods and services and income payments was at 418,038 million dollars.[52] At stake here is the US goal of preserving the dollar against competing currencies, namely the euro.

The economic component to American military intervention in Afghanistan and Iraq is a significant matter because it has the potential of reducing the moral significance of US offensive military measures against terrorism and WMD. This is disappointing to many since it is examined in the wake of 9/11, which was planned by Al-Qaida and the Taliban from within the borders of Afghanistan. It is, however, problematic to view the US intervention in Afghanistan strictly in terms of securing oil. Although the key motivation is to prevent future terrorist attacks against the US, the evidence presented here suggests that the need for oil is no doubt an essential component in American foreign policy toward Central Asia and has been legitimized and facilitated by the injustice imposed on the US by 9/11.

Notes

1.   See: Bruno Coppieters and Boris Kashnikov, "Right Intentions," in Bruno Coppieters and Nick Fotion, *Moral Constraints on War: Principles and Cases* (Lanham, MD: Lexington Books, 2002), chapter 4.

2.   Abrams is quoted in: Michael Flach, "Administration Officials Defense Operation Iraqi

Freedom," *Catholic Herald*, (10 April 2003).

3. Michael Walzer, *Just and Unjust Wars: A Moral Argument With Historical Illustrations* (New York: Basic Books, 1977); James Turner Johnson, *Morality and Contemporary Warfare* (New Haven: Yale University Press, 1999).
4. Walzer, *Just and Unjust Wars*.
5. George W. Bush, "Address to a Joint Session of Congress and the American People," (20 September 2001), http://www.whitehouse.gov/news/releases/2001/09/20010920-8.html
6. George W. Bush, The White House, "Presidential Address to the Nation," (7 October 2001), http://www.whitehouse.gov/news/releases/2001/10/20011007-8.html
7. "Pop Tarts in the Dust," *Economist*, (20 October 2001), 18.
8. The Pew Research Center for the People and the Press, Pew Global Attitudes Project, "A Year After Iraq War," (16 March 2004), http://people-press.org/reports/display.php3?ReportID=206
9. The Zogby poll is cited in Ann McFeatters, "Zogny Poll: Most Arabs Think US Biased Against Palestinians," *Pittsburg Post-Gazette*, (13 April 2002), 1.
10. Warren Bass, *Support Any Friend: Kennedy's Middle East Policy and the Making of the US-Israeli Alliance* (Oxford: Oxford University Press, 2004); Avner Cohen, *Israel and the Bomb* (New York: Columbia University Press, 2004); Peter Grose, *Israel in the Mind of America* (New York: Knopf, 1983).
11. Human Rights Watch, *Iraq's Crime of Genocide: The Anfal Campaign Against the Kurds* (New Haven: Yale University Press, 1995).
12. Just Hilterman, "America Didn't Seem to Mind Poison Gas," *International Herald Tribune*, (17 January 2003); David Leigh and John Hooper, "Britain's Dirty Secret, *The Guardian*, (6 March 2003), Patrick Tyler, "Officers Say US Aided Iraq in War Despite Use of Gas," *New York Times*, (18 August 2002), 1.
13. Michael Dobbs, "US Had Key Role in Iraq Buildup," *Washington Post*, (30 December 2002), 1; Dana Priest, "Rumsfeld Visited Baghdad in 1984 to Reassure Iraqis," *New York Times*, (19 December 2003), 1.
14. Peter W. Galbraith, "The Ghosts of 1991," *Washington Post*, (12 April 2003), 1.
15. David Cortright, "A Hard Look at Iraq Sanctions," *The Nation*, (3 December 2001); Walter Russell Mead, "Deadlier Than War," *Washington Post*, March 12, 2003; John Mueller and Karl Mueller, "Sanctions of Mass Destruction," *Foreign Affairs* 78 no. 3 (May/June 1999), 43-53.
16. See United Nations Security Council Resolution 661 at: http://ods-dds-ny.un.org/doc/RESOLUTION/GEN/NR0/575/11/IMG/NR057511.pdf?OpenElement
17. See United Nations Security Council Resolution 706 and Resolution 712 at: http://ods-ddsny.un.org/doc/RESOLUTION/GEN/NR0/596/42/IMG/NR059642.pdf?OpenElement and http://ods-dds ny.un.org/doc/RESOLUTION/GEN/NR0/596/48/IMG/NR059648.pdf?OpenElement
18. See United Nations Security Council Resolution 986 at: http://ods-dds-ny.un.org/doc/UNDOC/GEN/N95/109/88/PDF/N9510988.pdf?OpenElement
19. Food and Agriculture Organization of the United Nations, *Technical Cooperation Programme: Evaluation of Food and Nutrition Situation in Iraq* (New York: United Nations, September, 1995).
20. Ibid.
21. United Nations Children's Fund (UNICEF), *Proposal for Water and Environmental Sanitation Project* (New York: United Nations, August 1994), 1.

22. See: http://www.fao.org/world/afghanistan/index_en.htm. The source for these numbers and the quote in this paragraph can be found in Food and Agriculture Organization of the United Nations, "Peace and Stability in Afghanistan Depend on Productive Agriculture- Appeal for US $39 million Launched," (21 January 2002),http://www.fao.org/WAICENT/OIS/PRESS_NE/english/2002/2180-en.html

23. See United Nations Information Service, "United Nations Calls for Greater Assistance in Afghanistan to Fight Poppy Cultivation," (22 October 2002), 1.

24. US Department of State, Office of Women's Issues, "U.S. Policy on Iraqi Women's Political, Economic, and Social Participation," (7 August 2003).

25. Michael Renner, "The New Oil Order," *Foreign Policy in Focus* (14 February 2003), 1.

26. Energy Information Administration, "Annual Energy Outlook 2004 with Projections to 2025, Market Trends – Energy Demand," http://www.eia.doe.gov/oiaf/aeo/demand.html#trans

27. Energy Information Administration, "Annual Energy Outlook 2004 with Projections to 2025.Market Trends - Oil and Natural Gas," http://www.eia.doe.gov/oiaf/aeo/gas.html

28. Ibid, http://www.eia.doe.gov/oiaf/aeo/gas.html#aopoi.

29. Energy Information Administration, "Annual Energy Outlook 2004 with Projections to 2025, Market Trends – Energy Demand," http://www.eia.doe.gov/oiaf/aeo/demand.html#trans

30. See Table A21 "International Petroleum Supply and Disposition Summary," http://www.eia.doe.gov/oiaf/aeo/pdf/appa.pdf

31. Shaffer, Brenda. "Caspian Oil Fields Rise In Significance With Gulf Volatility." *Investor's Business Daily* General News (8 November 2001).

32. Cheney is quoted in Marjorie Cohn, "Cheney's Black Gold: Oil Interests May Drive US Foreign Policy," *Chicago Tribune* (10 August 2000), 1.

33. Ibid.

34. George Monbiot, "America's Pipe Dream," *The Guardian* (23 October 2001), 1.

35. Ahmed Rashid, *Taliban: Militant Islam, Oil and Fundamentalism in Central Asia* (New Haven: Yale University Press).

36. Sayed Salahuddin, "Afghan Power Brokers," *Christian Science Monitor* (10 June 2002), 1.

37. Energy Information Administration, "Iraq Country Analysis Brief," March 2004: http://www.eia.doe.gov/emeu/cabs/iraq.html

38. Joe Stork, *Middle East Oil and the Energy Crisis* (New York: Monthly Review Press, 1975), 188-194.

39. Energy Information Administration, "Annual Energy Outlook 2004 with Projections to 2025 Market Trends - Oil and Natural Gas," http://www.eia.doe.gov/oiaf/aeo/gas.html

40. www.chevrontexaco.com/news/archive/chevron_speech/1998/98-11-05.asp

41. Baker Institute Study 3, "The Political, Economic, Social, Cultural, and Religious Trends in the Middle East and the Gulf and Their Impact on Energy Supply, Security, and Pricing View," http://www.rice.edu/projects/baker/Pubs/studies/bipp_study_3/index.html#top

42. Edward Morse, Task Force Report, Council on Foreign Relations, *Strategic Energy Policy: Challenges for the 21st Century Independent Task Force Report* (Washington DC: Council of Foreign Relations, 2001).

43. Quote can be found in: Howard Witt and Bob Kemper, "US Claim to Iraq Oil is No Sure Bet," *Chicago Tribune* (20 November 2002), 1.

44. Nick Paton Walsh, Julian Borger, Terry Macalister, and Ewen MacAskill, "US begins secret talks to secure Iraq's oilfields; Fears that wells will be torched if regime falls," *The Guardian* (23 January 2003), 1.
45. Robert Collier, "Oil Firms Wait as Iraq Crisis Unfolds," *San Francisco Chronicle* (29 September 2002), 1.
46. Ibid.
47. Ron Suskind, *The Price of Loyalty: George W. Bush, the White House and the Education of Paul O'Neill* (New York, Simon & Schuster, 2004) 174-75.
48. Ibid; Dan Morgan and David B. Ottaway, "In Iraqi War Scenario, Oil is Key Issue as U.S. Drillers Eye Huge Petroleum Pool," *Washington Post*, (15 September 2002), 1.
49. The Cheney documents were made public in response to a law suit by the conservative organization Judicial Watch. The administration challenged Judicial Watch in court, but eventually lost. The "Foreign Suitors" list includes Shell, but lists no contract results with the company. Exxon, Chevron and BP are not on the list at all. Two small UK firms, Branch Energy and Pacific Resources are also to be found on the list.
50. Morgan and Ottaway, "In Iraqi War Scenario, Oil is Key Issue as U.S. Drillers Eye Huge Petroleum Pool," 1.
51. US Department of Commerce, Bureau of Economic Analysis, 2002.
52. Ibid.

Chapter 5

Legitimate Authority

Self-Defense and International Commitments

The American case for legitimate authority rests on the presumption that contemporary threats are similar to those traditionally presented by states. There is some merit to this argument. As international law relating to the recourse to force developed over the centuries, culminating in the formation of the UN Charter in the wake of WW II, the main purpose of the law was to address conventional threats posed by states. When the charter was adopted in 1945, its framers sought to prevent the types of conflict that had precipitated World War I circumstances in which regular armies engaged in clear, overt acts of aggression against other states. As a consequence, Article 2, Section 4 of the UN Charter prohibits the threat and use of force and Article 51 acknowledges a state's inherent right of self-defense if an armed attack occurs. Even if UN Charter provisions are understood in light of customary international rules present before 1945, then the Charter's focus is still on states using traditional force in a conventional fashion.

The Bush Administration has contended that, because of the contemporary threats posed by terrorism and WMD, these requirements may not always make sense as it may be too late to endorse any form of offensive military action. While offensive military force is not a new development, what makes the Bush Doctrine different is that it relaxes the international legal requirements of immediacy and necessity. The 2002 *National Security Strategy* claims "[w]e must adapt the concept of imminent threat to the capabilities and objectives of today's adversaries... [t]he greater the threat, the greater is the risk of inaction—and the more compelling the case for taking anticipatory action to defend ourselves, even if uncertainty remains as to the time and place of the enemy's attack."[1]

What should be the international legal standard for preventing terrorist attacks and obviating WMD threats? If there is a group such as Al-Qaida that has been attacking the US, the US could simply engage in standard self-defense against the ongoing violence. What about states or groups that have yet to commit violent attacks, although they seem likely to act at some point in the future? Short of an imminent attack, when would a state lawfully be able to preempt that group? Although it is a reality that contemporary international law dealing with offensive force in terms of self-defense does not adequately address the problem of WMD and terrorism, no clear legal standard exists to determine when offensive force would be permissible in such cases.

Legitimate Self-Defense

The Bush Administration's argument that the right of self-defense in Article 51 supplied relevant authority to use force in response to the 9/11 attacks and to wage offensive warfare against the Taliban and the Al-Qaida leadership in Afghanistan needs to be reexamined in terms of its legal significance. In particular, the US legal position should be assessed according to the principle of *jus cogens*, or the obligation not to use force, which is enshrined in Article 2, Section 4 of the UN Charter:

> All Members shall refrain in their international relations from the threat or use of force against the territorial integrity or political independence of any state, or in any other manner inconsistent with the Purposes of the United Nations.[2]

Thus, according to Article 2, Section 4, UN member states are obligated not use military force in any capacity against other members and must adhere to its general prohibition against the unilateral use of force conducted independent of UN authorization. Furthermore, in *Nicaragua v. United* States, the International Court of Justice (ICJ) acknowledged a general exclusion on the use of force as it currently exists in the UN Charter.[3] Given this prohibition, it is also relevant that we consider the exceptions to Article 2, Section 4. More specifically, whether or not: US actions against the Taliban and Al-Qaida are justified in terms of a right of self-defense; the role of the Security Council was formally required in light of the evidence presented; and whether or not the consistency of the use of force to prevent future terrorist attacks with customary international law requirements was met under international legal parameters.[4]

Article 51 of the UN Charter holds that nothing "shall impair the inherent right of individual or collective self defense if an armed attack occurs against a member of the United Nations."[5] Article 51 also gives a state the right to repel an attack that has already occurred or is ongoing as a temporary measure until the UN Security Council can take steps necessary for international peace and security. While a strict viewpoint holds that it is difficult to perceive how Article 51 is applicable to the 9/11 attacks, a loose perspective contends that even if Article 51 is not satisfied, the use of force may still be justified.

For the self-defense provision in Article 51 to be relevant in the case of the US invasion of Afghanistan in October 2001, it is necessary that there be an "armed attack" within the meaning of the UN Charter. The definition of an "armed attack" is broad, as it is conveyed in *Nicaragua v. United States* (1986) where the International Court of Justice held that the concept covers "the sending by or on behalf of a state of armed bands, groups, irregulars or mercenaries" and a state's "substantial involvement therein."[6] Do the 9/11 attacks on the US by Al-Qaida with the sponsorship of the Taliban meet the requirements for an "armed attack?" While the 9/11 terrorist attacks appear to be clearly within the definition of "armed attack" committed by "armed bands," it is difficult to see how action by Al-Qaida is connected to the state of Afghanistan. The ICJ rejected the notion that mere assistance to rebels or terrorists was an "armed attack."[7] Given these realities, there is room to argue that the US was not a victim of 'armed attack' within the meaning of Article 51 and the US use of force is contrary to Article 2, Section 4.

However, the terms of Article 51 acknowledge the right of self-defense if an armed attack has occurred or is occurring. In *Nicaragua,* while the ICJ rejected the argument that assistance represented an "armed attack," it did hold that the use of force in individual or collective self-defense is legitimated in light of grave acts, which do constitute an "armed attack."[8] Furthermore, the UN General Assembly has elaborated on *Nicaragua* to define aggression as "the sending by or on behalf of a State of armed bands, groups, irregulars, or mercenaries, which carry out acts of armed force against another State of such gravity as to amount to '… an actual armed attack conducted by regular forces."[9]

Now that Article 51 has been addressed it is appropriate to move on to the role of the Security Council. In considering the role of the Security Council, it is a requirement that any measures taken in self-defense 'shall be immediately reported to the Security Council' and then the Security Council will take 'measures necessary to maintain international peace and security'. There is no doubt the US did report its action and in response the Security Council passed two resolutions condemning the 9/11 attacks and announced a number of measures to fight terrorism.[10]

However, on 12 September 2001, the Security Council passed Resolution 1368, which recognized the inherent right of individual or collective self-defense in accordance with the UN Charter, but the operative part of the resolution described the attacks as "terrorist attacks," not "armed attacks." The resolution did condemn the attacks as a threat to international peace and stability and called on all member states to "work together urgently to bring to justice the perpetrators, organizers, and sponsors of these terrorist attacks."[11] 1368 contained no explicit approval of the use of military force. For example, the resolution can be see in contrast to Resolution 678, adopted in 1990 after Iraq's invasion of Kuwait, which authorized all member-states cooperating with Kuwait to use "all necessary means" to force Iraq to comply with UN Security Council resolutions to withdraw from Kuwait and restore peace.[12]

Resolution 1368 refers to the right of self-defense that exists under the terms of the UN Charter. Thus, the Security Council did not take a position on whether the Charter's conditions for the use of force to thwart additional attacks in self-defense had been satisfied in the case then under consideration, in contrast to UN Security Council Resolution 661 (1990), which also made reference to the right of self-defense but at the same time linked this right to "the armed attack by Iraq against Kuwait."[13] It should be noted that neither the right of self-defense nor the design of Resolution 1368 referred to in statements made in the Security Council in connection with the resolution's adoption, although the president would later state that the US would not distinguish between terrorists and those who sponsor them.[14]

Finally, it could be argued that the use of force is a far-reaching intrusion into state sovereignty and thus ought to require clear legal authority. Given these arguments, it must be clear that, legally speaking, Resolution 1368 does not in itself approve America's use of force against Afghanistan. It remains to be seen if the resolution represents political acceptance of the idea that the right of self-defense may be appropriate in some cases of terrorism. It is puzzling why the Security Council did not express its opinion on the right of self-defense via a simple reference to Article 51 of the UN Charter.

Interestingly, the Security Council did issue Resolution 1373 under Chapter VII of the UN Charter, which specified that all member states had the individual and collective responsibility to avoid supporting and financing terrorist activities and promote an open exchange on information to prevent additional attacks. In contrast to 1368, the adoption of 1373 under Chapter VII demanded that member-states are bound by international law to prevent the financing of terrorism. Like 1368, Resolution 1373 provides no explicit acknowledgement of a right of the US to attack another state in response to 9/11 or to conduct offensive military operations to prevent future terrorist activity.[15] And since no debate took place in the Security Council in connection with the adoption of Resolution 1373, there is no guidance for purposes of interpretation.

The Security Council also went on to pass Resolution 1377 and Resolution 1378. 1377 was largely a declaration on the need to follow previously adopted resolutions and the need for implementing measures against terrorism. Like 1368 and 1373, 1377 failed to authorize the use of force.[16] Resolution 1378 affirmed the Security Council's "international efforts to root out terrorism."[17] However, since the resolution was adopted after the US engaged in military operations against Afghanistan, the use of force should be seen as a key element of the international efforts referred to in the resolution. Furthermore, it could be argued that "to root out" could be construed to mean "expose" or to "bring to justice" accused terrorists. "To root out terrorism" does not imply the use of military force to prevent additional attacks and in response to attacks that already occurred, since it is possible that these goals might be attained without resorting to military action.

Most important, supporting international efforts is not the same as authorizing them. Since 1378 was not adopted under Chapter VII and because authorization of force ought to have a reasonably clear legal basis, the resolution should not be considered as providing such legitimate authority. Politically, Resolution 1378 supplies less ambiguous support for the use of the force against Al-Qaida; however, it is significant that the resolution neither precisely states which international efforts should be engaged nor authorizes the use of military force by member states as a response or as preemptive and preventive measures for potential attacks.

Each resolution does have legal significance and the right of self-defense has not been constrained. The resolutions' coupling of terrorism and self-defense may be a relevant point of interpretation in evaluating the right of states to response to terrorist attacks. However, the resolutions do not state that governments have the moral right to engage offensive military operations against states with the goal of obviating additional terrorist acts beyond or independent of the legitimate parameters set by the UN Security Council. It can be reasonably concluded that neither Resolution 1368 or 1373 formally authorized the use of offensive military force to preempt or prevent future attacks.

Do these resolutions apply to America's use of offensive military force to prevent future attacks from Afghanistan? Although Article 51 supplies a UN member state with the right of self-defense to use force in response to an armed attack, it is unclear as to whether or not the Charter legitimates the use of preemptive or preventive force to thwart future aggression that appear looming and imminent. For clarity, we can point to relevant legal boundaries established by customary international law, which predates the UN Charter, but is acknowledged as legitimate. Self-defense as a politically legitimating factor on the road to war has a long history, dating to Hugo Grotius in 1625.[18] Historically, the legitimate claim of self-defense included the right to preemptive use of force. This "inherent moral right" was not absolute, however. In 1842, US Secretary of State Daniel Webster helped to clarify self-defense in the 1837 *Caroline* case with England; that is, the conditions under which America could exercise the right to preempt an attack with military force in self-defense. Preemptive force had moral limitations and could only be justified when "the necessity of that self-defense is instant, overwhelming, and leaving no choice of means and no moment for deliberation [the act of self-defense must also involve] nothing unreasonable or excessive."[19]

In other words, in order for force to be legitimate in terms of self-defense under international law, there must be a demonstrated need that it be immediate and necessary.[20] In terms of immediacy, "on-the-spot" and measured responses to a terrorist armed attack are permissible. Although politically difficult, this view appears to suggest that US action should have been immediate for it to be legitimate under the international law established in *Caroline*. However, a reasonable delayed response is equally as acceptable, since there is a critical need to gather evidence demonstrating that the accused actually carried out the attacks.[21] Necessity of self-defense was realized when American efforts to convince the Taliban to peacefully hand Osama bin Laden over to the US failed, thereby indicating to the world community that future attacks coordinate from Afghanistan were not only possible, but imminent.

Thus, according to international law in the case of the use of offensive force against ongoing threats from within Afghanistan, the US possesses a moral and political right of self-defense to obviate additional imminent attacks, given that the 9/11 attacks suggested the possibility of future violence from the Taliban and Al-Qaida. It should be stressed here that this interpretation of self-defense *only applies to Afghanistan*. Any expansion of this interpretation to include other national security concerns beyond Afghanistan would not meet the requirements of legitimate authority. In other words, a view that claims the right to use force without an actual attack or an imminent threat of one would be discredited and illegitimate. A doctrine grounded on the notion of a general appeal to "preventive self-defense" would require the consent and authorization of the UN Security Council, which was created, in large measure by the United States, as a collective security apparatus to forestall such unilateral action.

There is room for disagreement about the precise interpretation of Article 51 and customary and modern international law. However, in the case of America's use of offensive military force to prevent attacks against Afghanistan, the US argument in terms of a right of self-defense is strong. Although UN resolutions failed to explicitly supply an authorization to use force, Article 51 supplies legitimate authority to wage war in response to the 9/11 attacks and to prevent future attacks. As it has been demonstrated in Chapter 3, the US put forth credible evidence suggesting that the Taliban supplied support and safe haven to Al-Qaida that allowed terrorists to carry out the 9/11 attacks and other potential acts of aggression. Article 51 further allows a state to use offensive force to destroy a government that has conspired with terrorist organizations.

Taking the Law into its Own Hands?

In a press conference held on 6 March 2003, President Bush was asked whether the United States would be seen as defiant of the United Nations if it launched a war against Iraq without explicit authorization from the Security Council. In response, Bush answered, "As we head into the 21st century, when it comes to our security, we really don't need anybody's permission."[22] It's hard to see this remark as anything other than a repudiation of the framework of international law governing the use of force, as set in the United Nations Charter. The Bush Administration pointed to UN Security Council Resolution 1441 and its emphasis on imposing "serious consequences" should Iraq fail to fully comply with UN weapons inspectors. In other words, the US argued that a war against Iraq was already authorized by existing UN Security Council resolutions and that another resolution was simply not necessary.

How convincing was President Bush's argument? In the US, there has been comparatively little public discussion about the existing UN resolutions, and how far they authorize an attack against Iraq under present circumstances. In the UK, by contrast, the legality of the prospective war was an urgent political question. On 9 March 2003, Prime Minister Tony Blair's cabinet secretary of state for international development, Clare Short, warned that she would resign if he took the country into war without a further UN resolution: "I will not uphold a breach of international law."[23]

Two key variables should be noted at this time. First, the decision by the US and the UK not to seek the passage of an additional UN Security Council resolution explicitly authorizing the use of offensive military force against Iraq was made in the face of anticipated French, German, and Russian obstructionism. In particular, France and Russia made it known that they would veto any new US or UK sponsored resolution authorizing force against Iraq.[24] Second, the American and British case against Iraq was based on a lack of significant hard evidence demonstrating that Iraq was in actual possession of chemical, biological, or nuclear weapons. Thus, the US and UK had to confront the reality that the case for an invasion was at best questionable.

The US should be justifiably worried about states that possess WMD. But simple accusations or the mere possession of such weapons does not amount to an armed attack and therefore does not meet the acknowledged requirements of legitimate self-defense. To be sure, Iraq has been prohibited by the Security Council from any development of nuclear weapons following its defeat in the Persian Gulf War of 1991. This prohibition is embodied in the suspension of the UN military campaign against the Iraqi occupation of Kuwait.

Those arguing in favor of broader right of preventive self-defense to encompass a legitimate US case for war against Iraq based their contentions on the word "inherent" in Article 51. The argument is that Article 51, by pledging not to "impair the inherent right of self-defense," left intact and unchanged the law of customary self-defense predating the adoption of the UN Charter. The "inherent right" argument is very weak, given its emphasis on customary international law, which evolved well before the adoption of the UN Charter. At the time of the *Caroline* case, the use of force was generally lawful as an instrument of national policy. The UN Charter was adopted for the very purpose of creating a far wider prohibition on force than existed under treaty or custom in 1945, let alone 1842. Even if earlier custom allowed preemptive self-defense, arguing that it persisted after 1945 for UN members requires privileging the word "inherent" over the plain terms of Article 2, Section 4 and the words "armed attack" in Article 51. The drafters specifically designed the Security Council to meet threats to the peace, preserving the right of a state to act unilaterally only in cases of an actual armed attack or to preempt an impending attack based on clear evidence. In cases lacking objective evidence of an armed attack, the Charter requires multilateral decision-making. Permitting such an expansive interpretation of self-defense at the sole discretion of a single state is fundamentally at odds with the Charter's design. It is an exception that would overthrow the prohibition on the use of force in Article 2, Section 4 and thus the very purposes of the UN. The International Court of Justice in *Nicaragua* rejected the right to use force in the absence of an armed attack, as have most governments.

Thus, in cases where there is an absence of an actual armed attack or an absence of actual evidence that an armed attack is imminent and about to occur, any utilization of preventive or preemptive action must be conducted through the UN and be authorized by the Security Council. Prior to the March 2003 invasion, no state appealed to the Security Council, because they were not convinced that Iraq was threatening them. Based on the evidence that the Bush Administration has made public, there does not appear to be anything close to sufficient legal grounds for the US to convince the Security Council to approve the use of military force against Iraq in America's self-defense. This may explain why the Bush Administration refused to go before the United Nations on this matter in support of an additional resolution specifically authorizing war. In the absence of such authorization, any military action against Iraq would be illegal and might be viewed as an act of aggression.

The position assumed by the US in making the claim that it possesses legitimate authority is quite problematic because it is based on a political and moral right of unilateral enforcement of UN Security Council resolutions and the exercise of preventive self defense. There is no firm moral or political basis in international law for the American case for war. Iraq has not been shown to have carried out "an armed attack" on the United States. No evidence has been offered that assigns any responsibility to Iraq for the attacks on the United States made on 9/11 or any other attacks. Iraq has not been shown to be a credible threat to the US. Allegations of illegal Iraqi WMD possession do not constitute an "armed attack" on anyone; nor do they justify unilateral US military action. If such weapons are a threat to its neighbors or anyone else, including the US, this is a matter for UN action, not unilateral American military action. While the US also accused Iraq of establishing links with Al-Qaida, this does not constitute an "armed attack" on anyone. If such links constitute a serious threat, this too is a matter for UN action, not for unilateral American action. A US attack against Iraq, absent evidence of an Iraqi armed attack against the US, would violate international law and be contrary to America's international commitments.

The specific debate over legitimate authority therefore pitted international legal restraints against America's perception and interpretation of its own right of self-defense. United Nations Security Council Resolution 687, which was formally agreed to by Saddam Hussein on 6 April 1991, required Iraq to dismantle its WMD programs and submit to verification inspections by United Nations (UN) agencies.[25] However, the US claimed between 1991 and 2003 that Iraq had not fulfilled these obligations and was therefore in or violation of international law. It also made the greater argument that the inability of the UN to enforce its own resolutions represented an injustice that was in dire need of correction, since any accumulation of WMD by Iraq was a threat to regional stability in the Middle East. Moreover, it was argued that the likelihood of those alleged weapons falling into the hands of terrorist organizations like Al-Qaida represented a threat to America's national security interests in the wake of the 9/11 terrorist attacks.

On 8 November 2002, the UN Security Council unanimously passed Resolution 1441, which was to "afford Iraq ... a final opportunity to comply with its disarmament obligations ... and to set up an enhanced inspection regime with the aim of bringing to full and verified completion the disarmament process established by resolution 687 and subsequent resolutions of the Council.[26] Resolution 1441 provided UN inspection teams with an unprecedented mandate for unconditional access to all of Iraq, including Saddam's presidential palaces. It also demanded that Iraq declare a full list of its WMD programs, including any chemical, biological and nuclear facilities that are claimed not to be related to weapons purposes. The resolution stated, "any false statements or omissions in the declarations submitted by Iraq pursuant to this resolution and failure by Iraq at any time to comply with, and cooperate fully in the implementation of, this resolution shall constitute a further material breach of Iraq's obligations and will be reported to the Council for assessment."[27] Should Iraq hamper the mission of UN inspectors or fail to comply with its disarmament obligations, the UN Security Council would "convene immediately... to consider the situation and the need for full compliance with all of the relevant Council resolutions in order to secure international peace and security... [and]... recalls, in that context, that the Council has repeatedly warned Iraq that it will face serious consequences as a result of its continued violations of its obligations."[28] Important to stress here is that 1441 did not authorize the use of military force against Iraq if it was determined to be in material breach.

Resolution 1441 was carefully drafted to suggest that authorization to use force should rest on a simple determination of fact; that is, whether Iraq was complying completely with its disarmament obligations. The implication is that, once it is clear that Iraq has not taken its "final chance," "serious consequences" are likely to follow. In this context, the phrase "serious consequences" is clearly intended to suggest the possibility of the use of force. But despite this, there is nothing in the resolution that gives any UN member state, aside from the Security Council itself, the right to decide when the final chance has been exhausted as well as to define the meaning of "serious consequences."

The US made it clear that unilateral military action was a viable option in the absence of any UN resolution formally authorizing the use of military force to implement UN resolutions. Following the UN Security Council's unanimous vote in favor of 1441, US Ambassador to the UN John Negroponte contended that if the Security Council failed to act decisively in the event of further Iraqi violations that the US would not be constrained by the UN from acting to "defend itself against the threat posed by Iraq or to enforce relevant United Nations resolutions and protect world peace and security."[29] Thus, the US claimed that it retained the right to use military force in self-defense and unilaterally enforce UN resolutions, a position inconsistent with the UN Charter.

Under international law, the use of force against states is strictly limited. Again, Article 2, Section 4 of the UN Charter is clear in calling on all member states to avoid using military force and is considered an unconditional and authoritative norm in international law. This is especially the case in the absence of an actual armed attack or clear evidence demonstrating that an attack is imminent. In other words, there is no 'wiggle room' for a member state to claim that its use of military force was consistent with the spirit or provisions of international law. Any alteration of the law via preventive or preemptive self-defense and the unilateral enforcement of Security Council resolutions must be approved by UN member states.

Hence, the international legal avenues on which a state can wage offensive military force are: 1) when a state has suffered an actual armed attack or when it is confronted with an actual imminent attack, thereby allowing the state to legitimately appeal to a right of self-defense consistent with Article 51 (as specified at the beginning of this chapter); and 2) in cases when the right of self-defense as spelled out in Article 51 does not apply, the use of offensive military force must be conducted via a UN Security Council resolution consistent with Articles 39 and 42. Article 39 gives the Security Council the power to "determine the existence of any threat to the peace, breach of the peace, or act of aggression and shall ... decide what measures shall be taken... to maintain or restore international peace and security."[30] Article 42 adds, "Should the Security Council consider that measures ... be inadequate or have proved to be inadequate, it may take such action by air, sea, or land forces as may be necessary to maintain or restore international peace and security. Such action may include demonstrations, blockade, and other operations by air, sea, or land forces of Members of the United Nations."[31] For example, Article 42 was used to authorize the UN military response via Resolution 678 against Iraq in the Gulf War of 1990–91: "The Security Council, acting under Chapter VII of the Charter ... authorizes member states cooperating with Kuwait ... unless Iraq fully implements all resolutions ... to use all necessary means to implement and uphold ... all relevant resolutions and restore international peace and security to the area."[32]

The focus on Article 42 and Resolution 678 is in need of further elaboration. First, the authorization must not only be adhered to by Iraq, but also by the United States and indeed all UN member-states. Second, it provides them with broad authority to what is considered necessary, including the use of military force, to secure implementation of the resolutions requiring Iraq's withdrawal from Kuwait. When the UN Security Council adopted Resolution 687 in April 1991, the UN maintained Iraq's obligation to agree unconditionally to the destruction of WMD and to accept inspections for verification purposes.

According to articles 39 and 42, in the absence of Article 51 and legitimate self-defense, no member state has the right to enforce any resolution against Iraq with offensive military force unless the Security Council determines there has been a breach of its resolution, decides that all non-military means of enforcement have been exhausted, or explicitly authorizes military force. This is what the Security Council did in November 1990 with Resolution 678 in response to Iraq's occupation of Kuwait in violation of Security Council resolutions passed that August. If the US could unilaterally claim the right to invade Iraq due to that country's violation of Security Council resolutions, other Security Council members could logically also claim the right to invade other member states that are in violation of UN Security Council resolutions. The US insistence on the right to attack unilaterally could seriously undermine the principle of collective security and in doing so would open the door to international anarchy. On the whole, articles 39, 42, and 51 are clear as to when military force is allowed.

Thus, Resolution 1441 did not authorize the use of force for three main reasons. First, resolutions adopted by the security council in the past, including Resolution 678 passed in 1990 after the Iraqi invasion of Kuwait, show that the language used to authorize force is bold and consistent. Member states are "authorized" to "use all necessary means" or "take all necessary measures" in pursuit of a specified goal. These words are absent from Resolution 1441. Second, as a matter of principle international law precludes UN member states from relying on any implied authorization to use force. Third, the use of force without "clear collective authorization" would be in conflict with the fundamental principles of the UN Charter. This is also true of earlier resolutions. Resolution 687 did not authorize the use of force to enforce the 1991 ceasefire agreement. The UN Secretary General, Kofi Annan, made it clear: "If the US and others were to go outside the security council and take unilateral action they would not be in conformity with the [UN] charter."[33]

The mere passage of Resolution 1441 does not alter the situation. America claimed that 1441 implied the authorization of military force. Some could argue that diplomatic and political reality may preclude the Council from publicly authorizing actions that its members privately desire or at least would accept. The American insistence on enforcing Resolutions 687 and 1441 was grounded on the idea that member states who were unwilling to enforce it were threatening US national security. The general political pressure to find implied authorization in Security Council acquiescence or ambivalence rests on construing the purpose of the UN to maintain international peace and security as requiring forceful action to remove threats to the peace. President Bush believes so-called rogue states that flout UN resolutions or otherwise threaten US national security ought to be penalized. Thus, in the absence of effective UN sanctions, world order requires that individual states or regional organizations provide an effective remedy.

Moreover, Resolution 687 was a creature of its own as it was designed to address a particular situation at a particular time, and it authorized the states acting in coalition with Kuwait to take specified action. The ceasefire declared by Resolution 687 was conditional on Iraq fulfilling the conditions required of it at the immediate time. However, a close reading of the text of the resolution makes clear that the ceasefire will come into effect if Iraq simply accepts the terms of the resolution. Resolution 687 goes on to state that it is then up to the Security Council to "take such further steps as may be required for the implementation of the current resolution."[34] This signaled that the Security Council regarded the matter of Iraq "as being back under its control as far as the use of force is concerned."[35] No individual state or group of states acting outside the clear authorization of the Council retained the right to use force, even to punish Iraq for breaches of the resolution or to compel its compliance.

Put simply, the UN Charter demands that offensive force must be explicitly authorized by the Security Council. The absence of such approval is in direct contradiction to the expressed purposes of the Charter and the promotion of a stable world via collective security. But while the original maintenance of collective security remains an important goal of the UN Charter, another key purpose was promoting an international system that strongly favors resolution of disputes by peaceful means. The presumption of peaceful means requires that all forms of ambiguity be interpreted before warfare is initiated. Put simply, Security Council authorizations of force must be clear and unambiguous. Article 42 reflects the presumption of peaceful means by specifying that the Council may decide to authorize the use of force only after determining that all other measures have been exhausted.

Security Council authorization to use force is often inferred from the Council's condemnation of a nation's action as a threat to the peace. But making that inference is unwarranted; it contradicts the Charter's requirement that the Security Council must determine both that a threat to the peace exists and that peaceful means cannot resolve the situation. In many cases, as in the US confrontation with Iraq over its expulsion of UN weapons inspectors in 1998 or even in the Kosovo crises of 1998 and 1999, the Council may declare a threat to the peace without expressing a need for military action. Thus, the requirement of explicit Security Council approval of uses of force reflects the substantive value that force not be used too hastily to resolve international disputes. Resolution 1441 did not do this, nor did it provide an explicit authorization to use force against Iraq in 2003.

A world order that would allow nations to use force unilaterally under the guise of creative or disputed interpretations of vague language in Security Council resolutions or by the Council's failure to act undermines the UN Charter. A related argument sometimes made is that the 1991 Gulf War ceasefire agreement referred to in Resolution 687 was dependent on Iraq's carrying out of its disarmament obligations. Iraq has failed to carry these out fully and Resolution 678 authorized the use of force against Iraq. However, Resolution 687 says the Security Council is empowered to take steps "as may be required for the implementation of the present resolution."[36] It does not state or imply that UN members themselves may do so in a unilateral fashion. Also, the primary thrust of 678 relates more to Iraq's failure to withdraw from Kuwait rather than to Iraq's possession of WMD. Since international law does not allow the US, or any other country, to take offensive military action against Iraq for the purpose of enforcing any of the disarmament resolutions passed by the UN, it is clear that just cause has not been met.

In the end, by declining to support a UN Security Council resolution explicitly authorizing force, the UN disagreed with the US assessment of the Iraqi threat and the method of dealing with it. The Security Council's refusal was an indication that the US simply failed to characterize military action as an urgent necessity under the *Caroline* formula of self-defense established in 1837. Recall that the formula holds that the use of armed force and the violation of another state's territory could be justified only if: 1) an armed attack is launched; 2) if an armed attack is imminent and there is an urgent necessity for preemptive action against that attack; 3) there is no practical alternative to military action; 4) and if the action taken is limited to what is necessary to stop or prevent the infringement.

It appears there was no basis of authority in international law for the US or any other state using military force to 'implement or enforce' any current Security Council resolution on Iraq based on its claim of a right of self-defense. Because no evidence indicating an Al-Qaida presence was found and in the absence of sufficient evidence that Iraq was in illegal possession of WMD, the case for establishing legitimate authority was not been made for legally employed offensive force under preemptive self-defense. However, obtaining international agreement to possibly expanding the legal boundaries of self-defense would likely be difficult if states believe this is merely an attempt to unilaterally override the UN Security Council. If the threat to international peace and security posed by Iraq via its refusal to give up its alleged WMD was really a "grave and gathering danger," as claimed by President Bush, then the record of the UN Security Council suggests that it would supply its authorization for the use of force to promote America's claim that it legitimately possesses a right of self-defense and a right to unilaterally enforce Security Council resolutions on its own with offensive force against Iraq.

On the whole, the US-led invasion of Iraq violated the basic rules of the UN Charter requiring countries to exhaust all peaceful means of maintaining global security before taking military action, and permitting the use of force in self-defense only in response to actual or imminent attack. The UN Security Council's refusal to approve a specific resolution authorizing the use of military force against Iraq revealed that the weapons inspection process initiated by Security Council Resolution 1441 should have been permitted to continue before military action could be authorized. By withdrawing the resolution and issuing an ultimatum to Saddam to leave the country or face attack, the US grounded its case for offensive war solely on its own sovereign right to self-defense and its intention to enforce Resolution 687 and Resolution 1441. As a result, the US failed to live up to its international commitment of adherence to the UN Charter, thereby weakening its adherence to the principle of legitimate authority.

The US war against Iraq on the allegations that existed at the time should be regarded as in violation of international law and the UN Charter and should not stand as legal precedent for an expansive interpretation of self-defense. It provides an occasion to reaffirm the fundamentally sound idea embodied in international law that force can only legally be used under conditions of palpable defensive necessity. The invasion of the Iraq stands more as an indication of American unilateralism within the context of regime-changing military interventions. If this pattern were to be established it would have produced what might be called a geopolitical norm; that is, use of power in a predictable pattern to achieve specified goals. The main feature of such a norm would be a repudiation of the authority of international law and the UN Charter by state practice that violates a consensus that joins the views of the majority of states and world public opinion.

Consequences for International Law

The exercise of armed military action in self-defense is legal only when it is conducted against actual armed attacks and when threats are imminent. In the absence of necessity and imminence, offensive military force must be authorized by the UN Security Council. In Afghanistan, the reality is that the US possessed a legal right of self-defense to wage offensive warfare to prevent likely or potential armed attacks because it was the victim of terror attacks on 9/11 and because the threat of future aggression from the Taliban and Al-Qaida was imminent. The US also had the right to attack the Taliban and Al-Qaida in Afghanistan before the 9/11 attacks, if it possessed evidence demonstrating that the terror attacks were imminent and actually about to occur. In other words, *the US did not have to wait to be attacked.*

However, the US invasion of Iraq has done grave damage both to the ethical norms of restraint and to international legal constraints adhered to by the US itself. The use of offensive force against Iraq to eliminate its alleged WMD was largely the result of an American strategy of preventive war or preventive self-defense that is incompatible with the just war principle of legitimate authority and unlawful with respect to international legal constraints. Moreover, offensive force was conducted entirely without legal justification and, more importantly, waged in the absence of an imminent threat. When a state is threatened by another, but is not the victim of an armed attack, self-defense simply does not hold. To exercise offensive force in the absence of an armed attack, a state must seek clear and formal UN authorization to wage war consistent with articles 39 and 42. No UN resolution authorized war against Iraq to enforce its disarmament obligations or to topple Saddam.

The US played a leading role in the adoption of the UN Charter, and since that time, it has been careful to make only those legal arguments relative to the use of force that it could accept in the hands of others. The Bush Administration began the war on terrorism after 9/11, invoking Article 51, going to the Security Council and even to other governments, building a consensus around the view that what it was doing was not only lawful, but legitimate and righteous. It has supported other states' right to do the same. The invasion of Iraq is in stark contrast. As stated in his 2002 West Point speech, Bush indicated that "not only will the United States impose preemptive, unilateral military force when and where it chooses, but the nation will also punish those who engage in terror and aggression and will work to impose a universal moral clarity between good and evil."[37]

This is a mischaracterization of the law, and no other justification has been suggested. Implied authority has been invoked by the United States in the case of its invasion of Iraq; however, there is no reason to believe that the resolutions authorized an invasion in the first place. Rather, if an official argument is given at all for an invasion of Iraq, it is likely to be one of preventive war, not preemptive force. The Bush Administration has established a dangerous and illegitimate precedent by taking the position that it alone has a special legal status, in which it has rights not available to others.

The invasion of Iraq does establish one precedent that the US itself has opposed since 1945: anticipatory self-defense. Any state that believes another regime poses a possible future threat, regardless of the evidence, could cite the US invasion of Iraq. Anticipatory self-defense not only undercuts the restraint on when states may use force, it also eliminates the restraints on how and why states use force, and is therefore illegitimate.

Notes

1. George W. Bush, *The National Security Strategy of the United States of America*, (17 September 2002), 12 and 19: http://www.whitehouse.gov/nsc/nss.html.
2. Chapter I, Article 2, *Charter of the United Nations*, http://www.un.org/aboutun/charter/chapter1.htm

3. See: *Nicaragua v USA* (1986) International Criminal Court, (27 June 1986),
    http://www.icj-cij.org/icjwww/icases/inus/inusframe.htm.   In this case, Nicaragua
    brought an action against the United States in the International Court of Justice for
    mining sovereign waters and orchestrating the military activities of the contras. Rather
    than contest the allegations against it, the US withdrew its support of the court and
    refused to appear at the proceedings. Conversely, when the US brought an action
    against Iran for the American hostage crisis, Iran followed suit by rejecting the
    jurisdiction of the court.
4. Martin Dixon, *Textbook on International Law* (London: Blackstone Press, 2000); John
    Bassett Moore, *A Digest of International Law*, Vol. II (1906), 412.
5. Chapter VII, Article 51, *Charter of the United Nations*,
    http://www.un.org/aboutun/charter/chapter7.htm
6. *Nicaragua v. United States* (1986):
    http://www.icj-cij.org/icjwww/icases/inus/inusframe.htm. It should be noted that the
    United States does not officially recognize the jurisdiction of the ICJ. For an excellent
    reference on legal ramifications concerning "armed attacks," see: Thomas Franck,
    Recourse to Force: State Action   Against Threats and Armed   Attacks (Cambridge,
    UK: Cambridge University Press, 2003.
7. Ibid.
8. *Nicaragua v. United States* (1986): http://www.icj-
    cij.org/icjwww/icases/inus/inusframe.htm
9. Ibid.
10. David W. Greig, 'Self-defence and the Security Council: What Does Art. 51 Require?,'
    40 *International and Comparative Law Quarterly* (1991): 366.
11. See United Nations Security Council Resolution 1368 at: http://ods-dds-
    ny.un.org/doc/UNDOC/GEN/N01/533/82/PDF/N0153382.pdf?OpenElement
12. See United Nations Security Council Resolution 678 at: http://ods-dds-
    ny.un.org/doc/RESOLUTION/GEN/NR0/575/28/IMG/NR057528.pdf?OpenElement
13. See United Nations Security Council Resolution 660 at: http://ods-dds-
    ny.un.org/doc/RESOLUTION/GEN/NR0/575/10/IMG/NR057510.pdf?OpenElement
14. George W. Bush, "Statement by the President in Address to the Nation," September 11,
    2001, http://www.whitehouse.gov/news/releases/2001/09/20010911-16.html
15. See United Nations Security Council Resolution 1373 at: http://ods-dds-
    ny.un.org/doc/UNDOC/GEN/N01/557/43/PDF/N0155743.pdf?OpenElement
16. See: United Nations Security Council Resolution 1377 at: http://ods-dds-
    ny.un.org/doc/UNDOC/GEN/N01/633/01/PDF/N0163301.pdf?OpenElement
17. See: United Nations Security Council Resolution 1378 at: http://ods-dds
    ny.un.org/doc/UNDOC/GEN/N01/638/57/PDF/N0163857.pdf?OpenElement
18. Hugo Grotius, *The Rights of War and Peace*, book 2, chapter 1-2, section 1, translated
    by AC Campbell (Washington, DC: M. Walter Dunne, 1901), 1625.
19. Daniel Webster, in a letter to Lord Ashburton, August 6, 1842, set out in John Bassett
    Moore, *A digest of International Law*, Vol. II (1906), 412 (quoted by Ackerman, op.
    cit., 2).
20. Anthony Arend and Robert C. Beck, International Law and the Use of Force: Beyond
    the UN Charter Paradigm (London: Routledge, 1994).
21. Thomas Franck, *Recourse to Force: State Action Against Threats and Armed Attacks*
    (Cambridge, UK: Cambridge University Press, 2003); David Rodin, War and Self-
    Defense (Oxford, UK: Oxford University Press), 2003.

22. George W. Bush, "President George W. Bush Discusses Iraq in National Press Conference," (6 March 2003),
    http://www.whitehouse.gov/news/releases/2003/03/20030306-8.html
23. Short's quote can be found in Andrew Rawnsley, "I will not Uphold a Breach of Law or Undermine the UN," *The Guardian* (10 March 2003), 1.
24. Edith M. Lederer, "Britain May Introduce New Resolution Authorizing Force Against Iraq: France and Russia Balk," *Boston Globe*, (7 February 2003).
25. See United Nations Security Council Resolution 687 at: http://ods-dds-ny.un.org/doc/RESOLUTION/GEN/NR0/596/23/IMG/NR059623.pdf?OpenElement
26. See United Nations Security Council Resolution 1441 at: http://ods-dds-ny.un.org/doc/UNDOC/GEN/N02/682/26/PDF/N0268226.pdf?OpenElement
27. Ibid.
28. Ibid.
29. John Negropante, "US Wants Peaceful Disarmament of Iraq, Says Negroponte," (8 November 2002), United States Department of State, Office of International Information Programs. See: http://usinfo.state.gov/topical/pol/terror/02110807.htm
30. Chapter VII, Article 39, *Charter of the United Nations*,
    http://www.un.org/aboutun/charter/chapter7.htm
31. Ibid.
32. See United Nations Security Council Resolution 678 at: http://ods-dds-ny.un.org/doc/RESOLUTION/GEN/NR0/575/28/IMG/NR057528.pdf?OpenElement
33. Anan is quoted in Karen DeYoung and Peter Slevin, "Full US Control Planned for Iraq," *Washington Post* (21 February 2003), 1.
34. See United Nations Security Council Resolution 687 at: http://ods-dds-ny.un.org/doc/RESOLUTION/GEN/NR0/596/23/IMG/NR059623.pdf?OpenElement
35. Ibid.
36. Ibid.
37. US, President, George W. Bush, "Graduation Speech at West Point." (1 June 2002).

Chapter 6

Last Resort

Fear Factor

Among the most important factors associated with President Bush's first strike doctrine is the potential danger that it places the use of offensive military force at the forefront of US national security policy based on a general fear of potential threats and attacks. The doctrine's primary assumption has been illustrated by President Bush who has stated: "time is not on our side, I will not wait on events while dangers gather. I will not stand by as peril draws closer and closer."[1] In a speech at West Point in June 2002, the president reiterated, "If we wait for threats to materialize, we will have waited too long."[2] But is it really the case that the US is facing such imminent threats to its survival? Has the Bush Administration made a coherent attempt to distinguish between the intentions and capabilities of supposed threats? Could not Bush's strategy of taking military actions based on such ambiguous and possibly exaggerated assessments and allegations lead the US to spend its blood and treasure in wasteful ways?

The Bush Doctrine's emphasis on the specific threats (real and perceived) of terrorism and weapons of mass destruction proliferation complicates the available options and compels further development of last resort. For what does it mean to say that all non-military options have been tried when confronted with lethal terrorists, which recognize no other form of power except the use of violence and that is largely immune (unlike a conventional state) from international legal, diplomatic, or economic pressures? The charge that US military action in Afghanistan after 9/11 was morally dubious because all other possible means of redress had not been tried and found wanting could be a misreading of terrorist intentions. With respect to the counter-proliferation of WMD, the "last" in last resort can mean "only," in circumstances where there is reason to believe that non-military actions are unavailable because the threat is credible, imminent, and actual. The United Nation's tradition of utilizing weapons inspections compels member states to allow for sufficient time for the inspections to run its course. Otherwise, the decision to wage preemptive or preventive war could be a hasty one, and therefore be inconsistent with the just war requirement of last resort.

The Bush Administration is justified in emphasizing America's s vulnerability to terrorist attacks and the immediate threat of WMD proliferation. The administration has also argued that it cannot wait for a smoking gun if it comes in the form of a "mushroom cloud." And, yes, there may be little or no evidence in advance of a terrorist attack using nuclear, chemical, or biological weapons. Yet, under this view, the requirement for evidence is reduced to a fear that the other has, or might someday acquire, the means for an assault. President Bush seems to have set the bar for offensive force very low with his *National Security Strategy* since it fails to ask how much and what kind of evidence is necessary to justify preemption and preventive war and downplays the importance of distinguishing credible fears from simple fears.

Military Force as Credible Choice

It has been evident from the 9/11 attacks that the magnitude of the devastation and suffering along with their exposure of American vulnerability meant an urgent recourse to war on the part of the US. The abrupt and catastrophic nature of the attacks made the use of force inescapable as there were no credible alternatives to an all-out American invasion of Afghanistan. Politically, the US could not utilize limited retaliatory missile strikes, issue economic sanctions, depend on law enforcement, or use diplomacy reinforced by sanctions. In other words, past responses would not be sufficient to reduce the threat or prevent additional attacks. Indeed, the Bush Administration had benefited from the fact that Osama bin Laden and his Al-Qaida leadership operated from terrorist bases in Afghanistan under the protection of Taliban rule since 1996. Moreover, Afghanistan had very little contact with the outside world, except for diplomatic ties with Pakistan and Saudi Arabia. The Taliban had also been refused the right to represent Afghanistan in the UN. For the most part, Afghanistan was already being treated as a pariah state that engaged in severe human rights abuses and crimes against humanity.

This background added to America's case against the Taliban and Al-Qaida in Afghanistan as legitimate enemies responsible for planning and carrying out the 9/11 attacks. In his speech to a joint session of Congress and the American people on 20 September 2001, President Bush articulated a series of non-negotiable demands known as "punish and coerce" to the Taliban regime focusing almost exclusively on Al-Qaida:

1. the immediate transfer of Osama bin Laden and the Al-Qaida leadership to the US and the termination of their presence from Afghanistan;
2. release all foreign citizens imprisoned within the country; third, protect all journalists, international humanitarian workers and religious personnel, and foreign diplomats;
3. close down every terrorist training camp;
4. and provide the US with access to all terrorist training facilities and funding sources.

For President Bush, these demands were not subject to debate and if the Taliban failed to comply with each, it would share in the fate of Al-Qaida. When the Taliban via a meeting of Muslim clerics convened in Kabul by leader Mullah Mohammed Omar requested evidence of bin Laden's involvement in the 9/11 attacks, their request was immediately dismissed. In response, on 7 October 2001, President Bush and Prime Minister Tony Blair launched the invasion of Afghanistan in retaliation for the 9/11 attacks and to prevent additional violence.

How can all of this be examined from the perspective of the just war principle of Last Resort? Based on the struggle on the part of the US for urgent military action against Al-Qaida in Afghanistan, we could safely presume that America's initial restraint in the days and weeks following the attacks was not influenced by the view that military force should be put off until non-military alternatives were completely exhausted. America's restraint, while conveying a sense of measured and thoughtful resoluteness, was driven by the practical reality that any use of military force against the Taliban and Al-Qaida demanded enough time to prepare for the invasion. Furthermore, it took several weeks to persuade Pakistani President Musharrev to switch allegiance and embrace the use of military force against an Afghani government that Pakistan was sustaining with financial and military means. It also required enough time to build an international coalition strong enough to topple the Taliban to establish closer ties with the Northern Alliance, which at the time of the 9/11 attacks controlled only five to ten per cent of Afghanistan. Besides, given the non-negotiable demands and the very tight relationship between Taliban and Al-Qaida leaders, the chances of these demands being considered were virtually non-existent. Any potential war had to produce the total collapse of the Taliban regime and a degradation of the Al-Qaida presence in Afghanistan. It was, however, generally believed that most members of the Al-Qaida leadership might elude capture.

It is possible to appraise the recourse to war by relying on a flexible interpretation of last resort given the far reaching impact of the 9/11 attacks. In Chapter 5, we assessed the restraining influence of international law and the United Nations as relevant forces and the importance of identifying and adhering to limits is of great significance. These factors are important in acknowledging the destructiveness of war as a means to resolve conflict and to stress the importance of not setting a precedent of rushing into an unnecessary war. In its response, the US had been innovative in devising a quick and devastating response.

The refusal to negotiate with the Taliban over the demands issued by President Bush and its rebuff by the Taliban created the impression that the US was not genuinely interested in a peaceful resolution or pursuing non-military alternatives. However, there were good reasons not to rely on a diplomatic approach, given the unlikelihood that Al-Qaida could be seriously weakened without destroying the Taliban's hold on power in Afghanistan. Interestingly, that case was never made in public, and as a result, an impression was created throughout the Muslim world of an American rush to war. An International Gallup Association poll conducted in 37 countries shortly after the 9/11 attacks found large majorities in most countries favoring a legal response over a military one given the image of America in the Middle East and Central Asia; only in Israel, India, and the United States did majorities favor quick military action.[3] The consideration of potential significant civilian casualties and concerns about the polarizing effects of a sustained bombing campaign were of particular concern. The retributive aspect of such a campaign also raised international legal issues. For Muslim and Arab governments especially, action against an Islamic state was much more disconcerting than an attempt to neutralize Al-Qaida. Again, in the specific setting of urgency, with credible dangers of further attacks, the necessity for war in the context of Afghanistan seemed at the time compelling, and in retrospect, has been validated both by the political changes in Afghanistan, and even more so by present indications of the weakening of Al-Qaida.

In general, can non-military options effectively address the problem of terrorism? Would cutting off terrorists' funds, enhancing intelligence and prosecutions, strengthening international law, and building goodwill toward the US really work? A network such as Al-Qaida or any other non-state terrorist group possesses no recognized or functioning economy that could be damaged or isolated from the international community. Also, while Al-Qaida certainly has coherent anti-US political goals, it is not likely that its leadership could be convinced to consider non-violent policy-oriented means in its struggles. The utilization of non-military options in associated with military force against Al-Qaida should be interpreted as crucial elements in an overall anti-terrorism effort.

In framing the potential usefulness of non-military options, the reality of the political and economic situation in Afghanistan was more complex than it seemed. While the use of economic sanctions is a likely alternative to war, were they a practical policy alternative to the use of force against the Taliban? As opposed to the Al-Qaida terrorist network, Afghanistan has an economy, although a very poor and impoverished one with almost non-existent economic institutions aside from its extensive production of illicit opium. Moreover, the Taliban had engaged in a far-reaching campaign to eradicate opium poppy production since it seized power in 1996. Therefore, it was unlikely that it would crumble in the face of economic sanctions. Besides, sanctions are more effective in the long run and a delayed US response could result in Taliban and Al-Qaida leaders eluding capture.

While it appeared that the American public would consent to non-military options, given the horrific 9/11 attacks, most believed that a failure to take military action in response to the attacks would increase the chances of terrorist attacks in the future. A poll conducted in October 2001 revealed that over eighty per cent of Americans favored "using American military force against terrorist groups that were behind the September 11 attacks."[4] However, eighty-six per cent favored other non-military measures, including "building goodwill toward the US by providing food and medical assistance to people in poor countries" and seventy-nine per cent supported "building goodwill toward the US by helping poor countries develop their economies."[5] Support for these measures was higher than for using "military force against groups in other countries that have committed international terrorist acts, but were NOT behind the September 11 attacks," which was favored by seventy-seven per cent.[6] Seventy-four per cent favored "putting greater pressure on both Israel and the Palestinians to reduce their level of conflict" and sixty-three per cent supported "making a major effort to be seen as even-handed in the Israeli-Palestinian conflict."[7] Provided that many believed that US military action in Afghanistan was justified in terms of legitimate self-defense, the increased readiness to embrace military solutions is not surprising.

However, removing the Taliban led to the greater question of what political force would replace them? And what would be the effect on political stability in

Afghanistan and the entire region of Central Asia? Finally, there was the practical issue of getting the job done: No one doubted that removing the regime would require a commitment of ground troops. In the weeks leading up to the war, the Bush Administration exhibited an artful ambiguity about the goals and nature of the prospective military operation in Afghanistan. Even had the Taliban leadership been ready to rid themselves of bin Laden and his top associates, several elements of the US ultimatum made their compliance unlikely. By some accounts there were as many as 3,000 Al-Qaida fighters in Afghanistan, the majority of them involved in the Taliban's war against the Northern Alliance. Acceding to American demands could mean defeat in the civil war.

To address these complex and dynamic issues, the US plan hastily came together in the days after the 9/11 attacks. Initially the goal of regime replacement did not necessarily imply unleashing the Northern Alliance or completely uprooting the Taliban in the south. Instead, the US aimed to pressure and weaken the Taliban through a combination of air attacks, special operations, and limited support to the Northern Alliance war effort. President Bush also hoped to induce a split in the Taliban by eliminating the most intransigent elements most closely connected to bin Laden, including Mullah Mohammed Omar, defense minister Obeidullah Khan, and justice minister Mullah Nooruddin Turabi.[8] The belief was that a weakened Taliban could blend more effectively with other Pashtun forces being assembled by the US and Pakistan. The final step would be the creation of a unity government incorporating the Northern Alliance.

This hurried plan contrasted with the experience of preparing for operations Desert Storm and Allied Force. In those cases, months of diplomatic work and economic sanctions preceded the onset of military action; these earlier operations also benefited from simpler strategic circumstances and stronger pre-war alliance arrangements. Out of speed and haste, key elements of the initial plan proved to be impracticable. The decision to launch such an ambitious campaign immediately after the 9/11 attacks put an impossible set of tasks before the US State Department. Not only did it have to assemble a multi-national political framework in weeks rather than months, it had to do so under conditions of a war whose objectives and direction were unclear.

It could be asserted from the perspective of last resort that a course of action based strictly on maximizing non-military alternatives was not considered an actuality. Since military action was not possible until early October 2001, the Bush Administration was just going through the motions. Does this mean that the US failed to meet the test of last resort? No. President Bush effectively put forth a series of legitimate demands before the US Congress and American people, which was broadcast throughout the world. The Taliban certainly received the message as it called for a council of Muslim clerics to consider America's demands and forge a response. The consequences of not utilizing military force were not only politically devastating for President Bush in the US, but would result in a waste of an opportunity to eliminate a dangerous government with a history of harboring among the most violent and threatening terrorists in the world.

Hypervigilance

Any assessment of last resort against Iraq should address the following general questions: does the Bush Doctrine deny unfriendly yet unthreatening states the ability to create peaceful ambiguity that they are in possession of WMD or sponsoring terrorism?; is the use of preemptive force or preventive war to eliminate such fear and ambiguity based on credible or simple fears?; and does the strategy hastily eliminate non-military options too quickly and is it dangerous? Recall that the key issues involved in a possible invasion of Iraq were enforcing Iraqi disarmament of potentially deadly and threatening WMD and ending its support for international terrorist organizations, including Al-Qaida. The US case for war was grounded in its argument that sanctions, no-fly zones, and UN weapons inspections could not effectively guarantee Iraqi compliance or terminate its relationships with terrorists. According to the Bush Administration, the resulting ambiguity and fear left the US with no choice but to invade Iraq in 2003.

In arriving at its decision for war, the Bush Administration made a game-theoretic calculation that the Cold War era strategy of deterrence and containment no longer apply to the post-9/11 world. Saddam Hussein's Iraq provided the best case for testing the validity of the Bush Doctrine's emphasis on eradicating the fear and ambiguity of alleged Iraqi WMD possession and state sponsored terrorism. In the absence of its application, the doctrine of striking first is meaningless. For the US, these twin threats have caused a passionate need for urgent action against a regime that may or may not have held caches of nuclear, biological and chemical weapons in violation of UN resolutions. America's fear of banned Iraqi WMD appeared strong because that was what Saddam wanted the US and the world to believe; the evidence was Saddam's use of chemical weapons against the Kurds and Iranians in the 1980s. However, in rejecting the weapons inspections, sanctions, and the no-fly zones as ineffectual and embracing offensive military force in 2003, did the Bush Administration fall for an elaborate deception and, in response, hastily erase non-military options in favor of offensive military force?

Weapons Inspections

Since the termination of the first Gulf War, Iraq engaged in a foreign policy of uncertainty regarding the true nature of its weapons programs after Saddam agreed to dismantle them via UN weapons inspections established in Resolution 687. Between 1991 and 2002, instead of committing to full compliance, Saddam chose to accept sanctions and no-fly zones over inspections. Although no one in the international community knew exactly what it was actually trying to do, Iraq took no public actions to reduce the level of fear and ambiguity surrounding its WMD programs. Saddam's cat-and-mouse game with weapons inspectors was both his goal and his strength in the international arena.

WMD fear and ambiguity further guaranteed that the US would distrust the UN as much as it feared Saddam. America's misgivings about the UN actually reinforced Saddam's power as it coincided with intensifying anti-Americanism inside Iraq and around the Muslim world and rising international worries of US global power. Moreover, the environment of suspicion guaranteed that only a massive military invasion would be the only way for the US to eliminate the ambiguity, distrust, and fear.

The ability of the UN inspectors to carry out their mission generated even greater fear about Iraq's willingness to comply whether or not Saddam possessed WMD capability. Moreover, Secretary of State Colin Powell's dramatic yet false presentation before the UN Security Council in February 2003 was overshadowed by the reality that America's evidence in support of offensive warfare to enforce Iraqi disarmament was not credible, but inconclusive and driven by simple fear and distrust. The Bush Administration, in interpreting Iraq's refusal to remove the fear and ambiguity caused by its disrespect for UN resolutions as overtly hostile acts, has sent an unambiguous signal that it will seek military solutions that eliminate such indistinctness. However, the strategy may not inherently make the world a safer place because the desire to eliminate fear and ambiguity places considerable attention and significance on the alternative of offensive military force before non-military alternatives.

One way to stop the potential of Iraq developing WMD would be by strongly supporting the rigorous inspection process approved by the Security Council in Resolutions 687 and 1441. If such weapons were found, the UN inspections team would have to dismantle them. With 1441, Iraq agreed to allow the inspectors unfettered access, yet the Bush Administration declared its intention to invade anyway by placing a massive military force in Kuwait as the inspections were underway.

Despite episodes of Iraqi non-cooperation with and harassment of weapons inspectors during the 1990s, UN inspections were successful in discovering and decommissioning the vast majority of Iraq's offensive military capability. Iraq certainly developed and deployed WMD in the 1980s, but the Gulf War and UN sanctions and inspections reversed and retarded its capabilities. Even before the passage of Resolution 1441, the International Atomic Energy Agency (IAEA) declared that Iraq no longer has a nuclear program.[9] The greatest success of the UN disarmament mission was in the nuclear realm. IAEA inspectors found an alarmingly extensive nuclear weapons program when they entered Iraq in 1991, and they set out to destroy all known facilities related to the nuclear program and to account for Iraq's entire inventory of nuclear fuel. In 1997, the IAEA and UNSCOM (United Nations Special Commission in Iraq) concluded that there were no "indications that any weapon-useable nuclear material remain[ed] in Iraq" or "evidence in Iraq of prohibited materials, equipment or activities."[10] After four months of resumed inspections in 2002-2003, IAEA Director-General Mohamed El Baradei confirmed that, according to all evidence, Iraq had no nuclear weapons and no program to redevelop them. He reported to the UN Security Council in March 2003 that inspectors had found "no indication of resumed nuclear activities ... nor any indication of nuclear-related prohibited activities at any inspected sites." The IAEA's report noted, "During the past four years, at the majority of Iraqi sites, industrial capacity has deteriorated substantially."[11]

From 1991 to 1998, UNSCOM identified and dismantled almost an estimated ninety to ninety-five per cent of WMD.[12]   At one time, Iraq may have pursued biological agents, but no evidence was found that it was in the advanced stages of complex missile delivery systems necessary to make these potential bioweapons a credible threat.[13]   In conjunction with the IAEA, it conducted hundreds of inspection missions at weapons sites and documentation centers, systematically uncovering and eliminating Iraq's nuclear weapons program and most of its chemical, biological, and ballistic missile systems. After four months of additional inspections from November 2002 until March 2003 – which included 237 missions to 148 sites – the UN Monitoring, Verification, and Inspection Commission (UNMOVIC) confirmed the depleted state of Iraq's WMD capabilities.

In the US, these accomplishments were muted. Both the Clinton and Bush administrations interpreted each weapons report as confirmation of Saddam's non-compliance rather than as a measure of its success. There was a lingering belief that behind each new discovery lay more banned weapons. After 9/11, the achievements of UN disarmament were ignored, and Saddam's defiance was taken as confirmation that deadly stockpiles existed, when in fact they were eliminated. Despite these suspicions, the process of disarmament was successful. As former chief UN weapons inspector Hans Blix, director of UNMOVIC has claimed, "the UN and the world had succeeded in disarming Iraq without knowing it."[14]

Even more problematic, especially in the immediate aftermath of the 9/11 attacks, America lacked credible evidence linking Iraq to Al-Qaida. Despite active support of Abu Nidal and other secular terrorist groups in the 1980s, Iraqi support for international terrorism has since declined markedly; the last act of anti-American terrorism the US government tied to Iraq was in 1993. In 2001, the State Department's annual study, *Patterns of Global Terrorism*, did not list any acts of international terrorism linked directly to Iraq.[15]   Indirect support has been limited to some financial aid to families of Palestinians- including relatives of suicide bombers – killed in their struggle against Israel, a practice common in other Arab states as well.

International opposition to an invasion was significantly high, especially given that the weapons inspections were successful. When the inspections conducted by Hans Blix and UNMOVIC were suspended in March 2003, it appeared as if the US and its allies prematurely made the decision to wage war to ensure full weapons compliance and to sever Iraq's ties to international terrorists, namely Al-Qaida. By contrast, the 1991 Gulf War was widely viewed as an act of collective security in response to aggression by Iraq against Kuwait, and it had the support of several important Arab and European allies. In 2002 and 2003, US allies emphasized their opposition to a unilaterally declared war. Arab governments in the region have repeatedly stated that they did not view Iraq as a threat and feared serious political ramifications in the event of a US invasion. NATO, in its mid-November 2002 summit, refused an American request to pass a resolution endorsing military action and instead reiterated its support for the UN. Only the British government expressed support for US military action against Iraq, although Prime Minister

Tony Blair was appeared restrained by public opinion from active participation in a war lacking UN authorization.

In light of the opposition, the US could have broadened the international containment of Iraq. To carry out such a proposal, the president had to allow for the continuation of the UN weapons inspections process. The policy has time and again proven more durable than critics expected and has accomplished much with fewer risks and potential costs than entailed by military action. In addition to bolstering international support for the coalition by making tradeoffs in other foreign policy areas, steps that could be taken to reinforce the policy's key points of shoring up UN weapons inspections by including more non-Anglo-American professional UNSCOM staff members; keeping tight restrictions on Iraqi imports and closing the loopholes for oil exports via Iranian waters, Turkey, and Jordan, thus ensuring that Saddam does not benefit from easing sanctions; extending the no-fly and no-drive zones if Saddam takes provocative military measures; and developing and announcing a credible policy on when and how force will be used.

Besides, before the 2003 invasion, a majority of Americans favored trying to achieve Iraqi disarmament through a lengthy process of UN inspections before resorting to war, rather than trying to achieve regime change. A strong majority favored the UN setting a deadline for Iraqi compliance and authorizing the use of military force if it does not comply. If Iraq allows in inspectors but interferes with their work, a majority favored using military force through the UN and after the inspectors completed their mission; however, a very strong majority thinks that it is unlikely that Saddam will allow the UN to perform the necessary inspections. In September 2002, only thirty per cent chose the argument that "The US should invade Iraq to remove Saddam, whether he cooperates with UN inspectors or not, because the UN inspectors might not find all his weapons." A very strong sixty-eight per cent chose instead the argument that "If Iraq allows the UN to conduct unrestricted inspections, the US should agree to not invade Iraq to remove Saddam as long as Iraq continues to cooperate, because we should only go to war as a last resort."[16] Other polls have also found a readiness to refrain from military action as long as Iraq is cooperating with inspections, and a readiness to wait longer to see if this will happen. Another September 2002 poll found that "If Iraq agrees to let United Nations weapons inspectors back into the country," seventy-seven per cent felt the US should "hold off on attacking Iraq." Asked whether the US should "take military action against Iraq fairly soon, or…wait and give the United Nations more time to get weapons inspectors back into Iraq," fifty-seven per cent preferred to give the UN more time. Only thirty-six per cent preferred taking action soon.[17]

Such viewpoints reflect a readiness to wait for efforts at UN inspections to work themselves out, even if it took several years for the inspections to be completed. If it does prove possible to disarm Iraq, a majority is ready to abandon the goal of regime change through military force. When asked, "Which concerns you more: that the Bush administration might move too quickly to take military action against Iraq, or the Bush Administration might not move quickly enough?" fifty-two per cent said that they were concerned that it would move too quickly, while forty per cent were concerned that it would not move quickly enough.[18]

Another poll similarly confirmed the American people's skepticism, after being asked "Suppose it does prove possible to disarm Iraq of any weapons of mass destruction it may have, should the US still invade Iraq in an attempt to overthrow Saddam's government, or should it not?" 56 per cent said the US should not invade while forty-three per cent said that it still should.[19] However, if Iraq allows in UN inspectors and does not fully cooperate with them, eighty-one per cent support using military force, but only with formal UN authorization for war.[20]

A deterrence strategy would largely limit itself to preventing Iraqi use of force, without the level of emphasis on restricting Iraqi military capabilities. Also, accepting that Saddam is likely to remain in power and that UN sanctions can be sustained only at a high political price, the US could avoid using offensive force by de-emphasize Iraq as a foreign policy issue. Should Iraq use military force or support terror attacks against the US and its allies, the Bush Administration could retain the option of responding with swift and intense offensive military force. The US military presence in Kuwait would be largely over the horizon, with periodic exercises signaling the US commitment and ability to deter Iraqi aggression. Rather than emphasize a special arms control regime for Iraq, US diplomacy would deal with the Iraqi problem in the context of a global counter-proliferation strategy. US military planners would not lose sleep over any Iraqi plan to waste money rebuilding its conventional military capabilities.

No Fly Zones

Further questioning the need for an invasion, Iraq's military capabilities had been severely weakened by the enforcement of US-UK no fly zones between April 1991 and March 2003. Sustaining the zones, however, was a costly exercise; the price tag for the southern zone in September 2000 was $1.4 billion, up from $850 million for both the northern and southern zones in 1999. The total cost of enforcing both zones since the end of the first Gulf War in 1991 was $7 billion.[21] But the rhetoric surrounding both the southern and northern zones still reiterates the formulas used to justify them since 1991. These formulas held that the no-fly zones protect civilian populations – Kurds in the north and the Shiites in the south – and that they are part of an international policy of "containing Iraq" and protecting its neighbors from attack. But the actual history of these zones displayed a considerable gap between publicly declared intentions on the road to what appeared as an eventual choice for offensive war.

The original no-fly zone was first declared in the northern region by President George HW Bush in early April 1991 to protect coalition aircraft during the airdrops of aid to Kurdish refugees on the Turkish border and then to protect coalition ground troops advancing into northern Iraq as part of Operation Provide Comfort. Britain, France and the US asserted that the zone was consistent with the terms of UN Security Council Resolution 688, which called on Iraq to cease its repression of civilian populations.[22] However no explicit endorsement in the form of a Security Council resolution was obtained for either Operation Provide Comfort or the zones. When UN ground troops were withdrawn in mid-1991, the no-fly zone was left in place to protect the Kurds and the international humanitarian workers based in the north. After the Iraqi government decided, in October 1991, to withdraw its ground troops from three northern provinces, the region came under Kurdish control but had no formalized status. It was part of Iraq but not under government control. The no-fly zone and the presence of international humanitarian staff may have deterred the Iraqi regime from trying to retake the northern region with military force.

In August 1992, remaining members of the Gulf War coalition announced the establishment of the southern no-fly zone south of the 32nd parallel just north of Najaf. The immediate trigger for action was the UN Human Rights Special Rapporteur's report on the increasing Iraqi military pressure on the Shiite population.[23] However, the Rapporteur had envisaged some form of monitoring on the ground, rather than a no-fly zone. The announcement of the zone avoided the necessity for ground action of any kind, while it allowed the US to appear tough after one of the many disputes over weapons inspections that had occurred in July 1992. UN Resolution 688 was invoked to justify the intervention. Gradually, the US began to justify the southern no-fly zone more as a means of reassuring its allies that Iraqi planes would be kept far away from their airspace by destroying them one-by-one.

The result, however, was an Iraqi military incursion into Erbil in September 1996, the first major movement of Iraqi troops into the Kurdish-controlled zone since 1991. Opposition members fled or were killed and all UN humanitarian aid personnel left the country. Instead of challenging the short-lived Iraqi incursion, or attacking the advancing Iraqi troops, the US chose to attack targets in the south and unilaterally extend the southern no-fly zone to the 33rd parallel. It was the collapse of UNSCOM's role at the end of 1998 that led the Clinton Administration to adopt "aggressive enforcement" of the no-fly zones as part of its so-called "enhanced containment" of Iraq. Soon after Operation Desert Fox in December 1998, President Clinton quietly sanctioned changes in the rules of engagement for US aircraft operating in the no-fly zones. This allowed US pilots to strike at any part of the Iraqi air defense system, not just those that directly target their aircraft.

Interestingly, no UN resolution or other international authority legitimized the zones, which were the scene of intensifying air-to-ground fights between US and British warplanes and an obsolete Iraqi defense system. Yet the zones became more controversial because UN Security Council Resolution 1441 restarted the UN weapons inspections process. The legal justification for the zones was based on a shaky interpretation of several past UN resolutions, especially 678 and 688. Resolution 678 invoked Chapter 7 of the UN Charter, which authorized member states to use military force, thus legitimizing the war to expel Iraq from Kuwait. Resolution 688, passed after Saddam violently suppressed internal revolts by Kurds in northern Iraq and Shiite insurgents in the south, condemned the Iraqi repression, but did not authorize the no-fly zones. Through the imposition of the zones, the US and UK were enforcing 688 and creating an aerial umbrella over Kurdish and Shiite in the absence of UN legitimization. That legal theory awkwardly combines 678's authorization of force with 688's condemnation of

Iraq's internal actions, even though 688 specifically does not cite Chapter 7 of the UN Charter. In any case, neither 678 nor 688 make any reference to the zones, nor do any other UN resolution; in reality, both the northern and southern zones were unilateral creations by the US, UK, and France. For more than a decade, the US and UK have played a lethal cat-and-mouse game over Iraq.

However, by early 2003, the combined force of the air patrols and new UN weapons inspections resulted in a degradation of the Iraqi military forces to barely one-third of their pre-Gulf War strength. Iraq's navy was virtually nonexistent, and its air force was a fraction of what it was before the war. Military spending by Iraq has been estimated at barely one-tenth of its level in the 1980s, and the country is presumed to have no more functioning missiles. None of Iraq's immediate neighbors have expressed any concern about a possible Iraqi invasion in the foreseeable future. Bush seemed unable to explain why Iraq was considered such a threat that it was necessary to invade the country and replace its leader.

Sanctions

Sanctions issued by the UN Security Council are particularly useful in adhering to the principle of last resort because they demonstrate international disapproval of a particular state and, if effective, could actually remove the need for warfare. This does not mean there are moral and ethical drawbacks with economic sanctions. As argued in Chapter 4, the major drawback is that sanctions have a fateful impact on the civilian population and could be resulting in humanitarian catastrophe.

Following the passage of Resolution 1441, the previously unacknowledged success of UN weapons monitoring and disarmament became clear. However, few have gone a step further to identify the primary reason for this success: the UN-enforced sanctions regime. Dismissed by those predisposed to the war option as the only method to ensure compliance and by those who stressed the humanitarian tolls, sanctions have had few defenders. The evidence now shows, however, that sanctions forced Baghdad to comply with the inspections and disarmament process and prevented Iraqi rearmament by blocking critical imports. And although many critics of sanctions have asserted that the system was beginning to break down, the "smart" sanctions reform of 2001 and 2002 in fact laid the foundation for a technically feasible and politically sustainable long-term embargo that furthered US strategic and political goals.

The story of the nearly thirteen years of UN sanctions on Iraq is extensive. On 6 August 1990, four days after Iraq's invasion of Kuwait, the UN Security Council passed Resolution 661, imposing comprehensive sanctions on Iraq and establishing a committee to monitor them. For the first six years, comprehensive sanctions cut Iraq off from all world trade and shut down its oil exports, devastating its economy and society. Coupled with the damage caused by Gulf War bombing and the enforcement of the southern and northern no-fly zones, sanctions helped spur a severe humanitarian crisis that resulted in hundreds of thousands of preventable deaths, increased levels of anti-Americanism through the Muslim world, and produced enhanced support for Saddam among the Iraqi populace.

Sanctions were met with considerable skepticism from the start when they failed, only after five months, to force Iraq's withdrawal from Kuwait. Nor did they persuade Iraq to comply with the full range of demands in the ceasefire agreement after the Gulf War. Yet the US viewed sanctions as a punitive instrument and refused to consider even a partial lifting of sanctions in exchange for partial Iraqi compliance. The American position was contradicted by UN Security Council Resolution 687, which stated that sanctions should be lifted once Iraq lived up to UN disarmament obligations and consented to inspections. Meanwhile, Saddam exploited the humanitarian crisis in Iraq and anti-American sentiment to win international support for the lifting of sanctions.

But despite such political failings and the humanitarian cost, sanctions forced Iraq to make significant concessions on disarmament. In October 1991, as Iraq's resistance to disarmament became evident, the Security Council approved Resolution 715 mandating continuous IAEA monitoring to prevent Iraqi rearmament.[24] Although Saddam resisted, he eventually yielded in November 1993, which resulted in the installation of monitoring equipment at weapons facilities in 1994 and routine UNSCOM inspections. The pressure of UN sanctions was responsible for this concession. However, Iraqi officials told UN officials they wanted concrete assurances that sanctions would be lifted before Iraq would agree to full disarmament so it could reenter the international community.

Once the ongoing monitoring system was in place, sanctions continued to help force Iraq to disarm. There were numerous disputes between UN officials and the Iraqi government, ranging from the confrontation between Dr. David Kay and Iraqi weapons officials in 1991 to the conflicts in late 1998 that prompted UNSCOM to withdraw and President Clinton to order Operation Desert Fox. At several points, UNSCOM had to cajole Iraqi leaders to end their obstructionism, using sanctions and dangling the prospect that they might some day be lifted, to assure compliance. In 1995, for instance, the UNSCOM threatened to prolong sanctions in order to get Iraqi officials to disclose past efforts to produce VX nerve gas. Without further revelations, they warned, the chances of Iraq's getting the sanctions lifted would be much reduced. In 1997, as Iraqi harassment of inspectors increased, UNSCOM again used the threat of continuing sanctions to overcome resistance. In the face of Iraqi obstruction, the Security Council passed Resolution 1115 in June 1997, which prevented any action to lift sanctions and threatened unspecified measures until compliance was attained.[25]

In addition to driving the disarmament process, sanctions undermined Iraqi military capabilities and prevented rearmament by keeping a significant portion of Iraq's oil wealth out of Saddam's hands. Contrary to President Bush's assertion that Iraq was a "grave and gathering danger," the Iraqi military and weapons programs had, in fact, steadily eroded under the weight of sanctions. Estimates of the total amount of oil revenue denied to Iraq totaled roughly $250 billion. For the first six years of sanctions, Iraq sold no oil except to Jordan. After the oil-for-food program began, oil sales generated, according to UN figures, $64.2 billion in revenue. Sanctions also blocked foreign investment and oil development, which could have increased Iraq's oil output to as much as seven million barrels a day by the late 1990s (in comparison to roughly three million barrels a day in July 1990).[26]

No sanctions regime can be one hundred per cent effective. In the case of the oil-for-food program, smuggling and black marketeering became common practice. George A. Lopez and David Cortright claim Saddam did everything to evade sanctions, mounting elaborate oil-smuggling and kickback schemes to siphon dollars from the UN oil-for-food program. Lopez and Cortright refer to a report conducted by the General Accounting Office (GAO) that put Iraq's illicit earnings at $1.5 billion to $2.5 billion a year. An updated GAO report estimated that illegal Iraqi revenues from 1997 through 2002 amounted to $10.1 billion, about fifteen per cent of total oil-for-food revenues during that period.[27]

Still, sanctions worked remarkably well as only a fraction of total oil revenue generate from the oil-for-food program ever reached the Iraqi government. The funds that Saddam illegally obtained were grossly insufficient to finance a large-scale military development programs or WMD programs. Saddam's government had no other major source of income, due in large measure to the devastating economic and financial impact of the sanctions. Most revenues from smuggling and kickbacks went toward paying the salaries of Iraq's Republican Guard and to maintaining Saddam's presidential palaces. As a result, almost no money was available for the development of nuclear, chemical, or biological weapons systems, however much Saddam might have wished to rebuild his arsenal. A regime that had previously spent lavishly on its war machine was denied the means to rebuild its war-ravaged military.

Indeed, US government figures show a drop in Iraqi military spending and arms imports after 1990. Iraqi defense expenditures plummeted from over $15 billion in 1989 to less than $1.4 billion a year through the 1990s.[28] The cumulative decline in arms imports from 1991 to 1998 was more than $47 billion, a deficit that Iraq's illicit schemes could not address.[29] According to the Center for Strategic and International Studies, the Iraqi army found itself with "decaying, obsolete, or obsolescent major weapons."[30]

Sanctions also prevented the import of specific items that could be used for the development of long-range ballistic missiles and nuclear, chemical, and biological weapons. The US especially, but other major powers as well, made a major investment in sanctions enforcement; the Security Council remained united in its resolve to deny Iraq the means to rebuild its weapons programs; and the dragnet was highly effective in denying Iraq the means to redevelop WMD. In response, the US, UK, France, Spain, and others mounted a massive effort to block shipments of prohibited weapons to Iraq. The State Department scrutinized oil-for-food contracts to screen for possible weapons imports.[31] The US Navy established the Maritime Interception Force, a multinational operation that over a ten-year period searched more than 12,000 vessels in the northern Persian Gulf. Such measures led to a series of high-profile successes. Based on CIA intelligence analysis, on 10 November 1995 UNSCOM and the Jordanian government intercepted a shipment of 240 Russian missile-guidance gyroscopes and accelerometers bound for Iraq. The next month, after dredging a section of the

Tigris River in Baghdad, a team of scuba divers directed by UNSCOM discovered more than 200 additional missile instruments and components. These parts included Russian-made gas pressure regulators, accelerometers, GIMBAL position indicators, and gyroscopes and derived from dismantled Russian submarine-launched ballistic missiles (SS-N-18s) designed to deliver nuclear warheads to targets more than 4,000 miles away.[32] A combination of watchful external intelligence and inspectors on the ground prevented the guidance systems from ever being used.

Similarly, the specialized aluminum tubes that were a source of controversy in the prewar debate never reached Iraq. Regardless of whether they were to be used for uranium enrichment, as the administration claimed, or for conventional rockets, as UN experts reported, the tubes were intercepted before arriving, according to a UK September 2002 dossier.[33] The dossier documented foiled Iraqi attempts to purchase vacuum tubes, a magnet production line, a large filament-winding machine, fluorine gas, and other items that could have nuclear weapons-related applications. As long as sanctions remained effective, the report found, "Iraq would not be able to produce a nuclear weapon." It also noted that "sanctions and the earlier work of the inspectors had caused significant problems for Iraqi missile development," by preventing Iraq from buying potential ingredients of rocket fuel such as magnesium powder and ammonium chloride.[34]

Ironically, rather than bolstering the case for sanctions, the interdiction of prohibited items was often seen as a sign of their failure. Those skeptical of sanctions focused on Iraq's attempts to smuggle material in the first place, not on their having been thwarted. Inflated assumptions mistook Iraq's intentions for real capabilities, even in the face of evidence showing how deteriorated the latter were.[35] In reality, sanctions had left the Iraqi war machine in utter ruin.

The amalgamation of sanctions and inspections eroded Iraq's weapons programs and constrained its military capabilities. The renewed UN resolve demonstrated by the Security Council's approval of a "smart" sanctions package in May 2002 showed that the system could continue to contain and deter Saddam. Unfortunately, only when American and British military forces invaded in March 2003 did these successes become clear: the Iraqi military that confronted them had, in the previous twelve years, been decimated by the strategy of containment that the Bush Administration had called a failure in order to justify war in the first place. In the end, the Bush Administration's intense level of urgency in discerning the fear and ambiguity associated with Iraq's alleged possession of WMD and its supposed support for terrorism and Al-Qaida determined to a great extent the resort to war. Those who feared that Iraq could easily rebuild its WMD stockpiles if restrictions were relaxed, that it could supply weapons to Al-Qaida, that it could regain regional influence and military might if sanctions were eased and the no-fly zones removed, and that it is eager to pursue regional domination and revenge, were more predisposed to a more offensive military strategy. Those who believed Saddam was politically isolated at home and may be overthrown preferred a combination of inspections, no-fly zones, and sanctions on the grounds that the containment strategy was sustainable while Saddam was in power.

Striking First Only as Last Resort

From the perspective of Last Resort, the 2002 *National Security Strategy* puts forth the view that "Given the goals of rogue states and terrorists, the United States can no longer solely rely on a reactive posture as we have in the past... The inability to deter a potential attacker, the immediacy of today's threats and the magnitude of potential harm that could be caused by our adversaries' choice of weapons do not permit that option. We cannot let our enemies strike first."[36] In Afghanistan, striking against the Taliban and the Al-Qaida leadership was common sense. Immediately following the 9/11 attacks and based on a credible set of fears that it might come under attack again soon, the US simply could not be expected to wait to exhaust all of its non-military options before attacking the Taliban and Al-Qaida on their home turf. Moreover, any non-military measure, namely sanctions and diplomatic isolation, would not produce an outcome suitable to meet President Bush's legitimate list of demands. As a result, the Taliban shared in Al-Qaida's fate in Afghanistan. Once the Taliban was overthrown by the weight of American and British military power, a massive strike that began on 7 October 2001 has now evolved into an ongoing offensive military campaign that demands a permanent military presence in Afghanistan.

The choice to engage in offensive warfare against Iraq as a measure to ensure the elimination of WMD and to sever its ties with Al-Qaida is another matter. Not only did the military action violate the UN Charter as demonstrated in Chapter 5 and set a dangerous international precedent, it was a war the Bush Administration did not have to wage because it was based on the simple fear that the UN Security Council failed to ensure Iraqi WMD compliance. In terms of last resort amid an ambiguous environment, President Bush's choice to invade, militarily occupy, and maintain an ongoing presence reversed over sixty years of American strategic doctrine and thinking and was based on simple fear. Consistent with his doctrine of US global preeminence and right to wage offensive warfare, the choice to launch to war to eliminate alleged Iraqi WMD and dissolve its so-called ties with Al-Qaida was essentially made on the grounds that the new enemies America confronts in the post-9/11 world are dissimilar to then risk-averse Soviet Union. What the Bush Doctrine ignores is history, because at the very same time George Kennan and the Truman Administration were framing strategies of deterrence and containment, the Soviet ruler had long been Joseph Stalin, a leader not known for his risk-aversion. There is no reason or argument that suggests rogue states seeking WMD cannot be contained or deterred with non-military means along the same lines the sustained American strategic doctrine during the Cold War.

The form of deterrence and containment that Bush now claims is archaic has proven to be successful in reducing the potential for disaster. This is important, given that the pre-war combination of inspections, containment, sanctions no-fly zones was actually working. Even Kay admits, "The Iraqi's engaged in quite a bit of destruction and dispersal before the war."[37] Referring to Kay's investigation, Barton Gellman elaborates, "Leading figures in Iraqi science and industry, supported by observations on the ground, described factories and institutes that were thoroughly beaten down by 12 years of conflict, arms embargo and strangling economic sanctions. The remnants of Iraq's biological, chemical and missile infrastructures were riven by internal strife, bled by schemes for personal gain and handicapped by deceit up and down lines of command."[38] The CIA also disclosed that intelligence the president used to claim that Saddam was seeking uranium to build nuclear weapons was false.[39]

And of course, we now know, via Dr. David Kay, who directed the Iraq Survey Group and the US weapons hunt, there have been no discoveries of finished weapons or banned delivery systems, chemical or biological agents, or ready-to-start uranium production lines. The group, in a series of interviews, admitted that throughout 2003 and early 2004 the prospects of finding WMD were scant.[40] Frustrated, Kay states, "We have found no actual WMD... I just don't know. We're looking for them."[41] What was found was a weapons arsenal far less capable than US analysts judged before the war. According to Kay's deputy, Major John Sutter, "there is no single large missile that we found or chemicals."[42]

Moreover, there was no credible evidence to suggest that Iraq had any relationship with Al-Qaida. The independent commission investigating the government's handling of the 9/11 terror attacks even reported there is "no credible evidence" that Iraq cooperated with Al-Qaida on conducting attacks against the US, including 9/11. The commission stated "there have been reports that contacts between Iraq and al-Qaida also occurred after bin Laden had returned to Afghanistan [in 1996], but they do not appear to have resulted in a collaborative relationship... Two senior bin Laden associates have adamantly denied that any ties existed between Al-Qaida and Iraq. We have no credible evidence that Iraq and Al-Qaida cooperated on attacks against the United States."[43] The findings contradict a series of public statements by both President Bush and Vice-President Cheney that Iraq and Al-Qaida had a cooperative relationship.

Notes

1. George W. Bush, "State of the Union," (29 January 2002), http://www.whitehouse.gov/news/releases/2002/01/20020129-11.html
2. George W. Bush, "Graduation Speech at West Point." (1 June 2002), http://www.whitehouse.gov/news/releases/2002/06/20020601-3.html
3. International Gallup Association, Poll on International Terrorism in the United States, September 2001): http://www.gallup-international.com
4. *Program on International Policy Attitudes* (PIPA), "do you favor or oppose using American military force against terrorist groups that were behind the September 11 attacks?" 1-4 November 2001.
5. *Program on International Policy Attitudes* (PIPA), "What about building goodwill toward the US by helping poor countries develop their economies?" 1-4 November 2001.

6. *Program on International Policy Attitudes* (PIPA), "What about using American military force against groups in other countries that have committed international terrorist acts, but were NOT behind the September 11 attacks?" 1-4 November 2001.

7. *Program on International Policy Attitudes* (PIPA), "What about putting greater pressure on both Israel and the Palestinians to reduce their level of conflict?" 1-4 November 2001.

8. Pamela Constable, "US Hopes To Attract Moderates In Taliban; Powell Sees Them In 'New Afghanistan'," *Washington Post*, (17 October 2001, 24; Doyle Mcmanus and John Daniszewski, "US Seeks Signs of Split in Taliban," *Los Angeles Times*, (3 October 2001, 1.

9. See the full text of Mohamed El Baradei's 27 January 2003 report "The Status of Nuclear Inspections in Iraq" including a February 14th update at: http://www.iaea.org/NewsCenter/Statements/2003/ebsp2003n005.shtml

10. "The Implementation of United Nations Security Council Resolutions Relation to Iraq, Report by the Director-General" (United Nations: August 1998). Another interesting and related source is Gary B. Dillion, "The IAEA Iraq Action Team Record: Activities and Findings," In *Iraq: A New Approach*, Carnegie Endowment for International Peace, (Washington, D.C.: Carnegie Endowment for International Peace, September 2002).

11. This quote and the one found in the sentence prior to it can be found in Mohammed El Baradei, International Atomic Energy Agency, (7 March 2003), "The Status of Nuclear Inspections in Iraq: An Update,"
http://www.un.org/News/dh/iraq/elbaradei-7mar03.pdf

12. William Rivers Pitt, *The Guardian*, "Special Interview with Scott Ritter," 19 September 2002, http://www.guardian.co.uk/Iraq/Story/0,2763,794771,00.html; For more, see UNSCOM, (25 January 1999), "Report to the Security Council.": http://www.fas.org/news/un/iraq/s/990125/index.html

13. Barton Gellman, "Iraq's Arsenal was Only on Paper," *Washington Post*, (7 January 2004), A1; Douglas Jehl and Judith Miller, "Draft Report Said to Cite No Success in Iraq Arms Hunt," *New York Times*, (25 September 2003), 1; Rumsfeld is quoted in "Rumsfeld: Iraq May Have Destroyed Weapons," *USA Today* (28 May 2003), 22.

14. Hans Blix, *Disarming Iraq* (New York: Pantheon Books, 2004).

15. See the 2001 report at: http://www.state.gov/s/ct/rls/pgtrpt/2001/

16. Program on International Policy Attitudes (PIPA), "Americans on an invasion of Iraq to remove Saddam Hussein," 25 September-1 October 2002, 1.

17. *ABC News*, "If Iraq agrees to let UN Weapons inspections back into the country, do you think the United States should hold odd on attacking Iraq, or not?," (13 September 2002), 1.

18. *CBS News/New York Times*, "What concerns you more: that the Bush Administration is (might move too quickly) to take military action against Iraq, or the Bush Administration (might not move quickly enough)?," (26 September 2002), 1.

19. *Program on International Policy Attitudes* (PIPA), "Should the US still invade?," (26-30 September 2002) 1.

20. *ABC News*, "If Iraq agrees to admit the weapons inspectors, but then interferes or does not cooperate with them, in that case would you favor or oppose having US forces take military action against Iraq?," (14 September 2002), 1.

21. House Budget Committee Report, "The Cost of War and Reconstruction in Iraq: An Update," (30 September 2003),
http://www.house.gov/budget_democrats/analyses/iraq_cost_update.pdf;
Sarah Graham-Brown, "No-Fly Zones Rhetoric and Real Intentions," *Middle East Report Online*, (20 February 2001), http://www.merip.org/mero/mero022001.html

22. See United Nations Security Council Resolution 688 at: http://ods-dds-ny.un.org/doc/RESOLUTION/GEN/NR0/596/24/IMG/NR059624.pdf?OpenElement

23. United Nations General Assembly Report A/RES/46/134 can be read at: http://www.un.org/documents/ga/res/46/a46r134.htm

24. See United Nations Security Council Resolution 715 at: http://ods-dds-ny.un.org/doc/RESOLUTION/GEN/NR0/596/51/IMG/NR059651.pdf?OpenElement

25. See United Nations Security Council Resolution 1115 at: http://ods-dds-ny.un.org/doc/UNDOC/GEN/N97/168/32/PDF/N9716832.pdf?OpenElement

26. See the website for the United Nations Office of the Iraq Program at: http://www.un.org/Depts/oip/; Bob Davis and Hugh Hope, "Once an Economic Dynamo, Iraq is Now Financial Riddle," *Wall Street Journal*, (9 April 2003), 1.

27. George A. Lopez and David Cortright, "Containing Iraq: Sanctions Worked," *Foreign Affairs*, July/August 2004. To view the GAO report, entitled "UN Confronts Significant Challenges in Implementing Sanctions Against Iraq," please go to the website: http://www.gao.gov/new.items/d02625.pdf. For additional information on lost Iraqi revenues resulting from the sanctions, see: Bob Davis and Hugh Hope, "Once an Economic Dynamo, Iraq is Now Financial Riddle," *Wall Street Journal*, (9 April 2003, 1.

28. Ibid., 12.

29. Ibid.

30. Anthony H. Cordesman, "If We Fight Iraq: Iraq and the Military Balance," *Center for Strategic and International Studies*, (28 June 2002), http://www.csis.org/burke/mb/fightiraq_mb.pdf

31. US Department of State, "Saddam Hussein's Iraq," September 1999.

32. Vladimir Orlov & William C. Potter, "Mystery of the Sunken Gyros," *Bulletin of the Atomic Scientists*, November/December 1998, Vol. 54, No. 6: 1. The bulletin can be read at: http://cns.miis.edu/research/iraq/gyro/

33. Michael White and Brian Whitaker, "UK War Dossier a Sham, Say Experts," *The Guardian*, (7 February 2003), 1.

34. Prime Minister Tony Blair, "Iraq's Weapons of Mass Destruction - The assessment of the British Government," (24 September 2002),
http://www.number10.gov.uk/output/Page271.asp

35. Walter Russell Mead, "Deadlier Than War," *Washington Post*, (12 March 2003); Rachel Bronson, "No Containing Iraq," *Newsday*, (13 March 2003); John Mueller and Karl Mueller, "Sanctions of Mass Destruction," *Foreign Affairs* 78 no. 3 (May/June 1999), 43-53; David Cortright, "A Hard Look at Iraq Sanctions," *The Nation*, (3 December 2001); US Department of State report, "Saddam Hussein's Iraq," September 1999, www.usia.gov/regional/nea/nea.htm

36. George W. Bush, *The National Security Strategy of the United States*, (17 September 2002), http://www.whitehouse.gov/nsc/nss.html.

37. David Kay, "Chasing Saddam's Weapons,"
http://www.pbs.org/wgbh/pages/frontline/shows/wmd/interviews/kay.html

38. Gellman, "Iraq's Arsenal was Only on Paper," A1.
39. Scott Shepherd, "Saddam Not Part of 9/11 Attacks," *Atlanta Journal-Constitution,* (18 September 2003), 1B; Robert Schlesinger, "C.I.A. Takes Blame for Iraq Charge," *Boston Globe* (12 July 2003), A1.
40. Barton Gellman provides an excellent and thorough examination of the inability of US forces to uncover W.M.D. in post-Hussein Iraq. See: Gellman, "Iraq's Arsenal was Only on Paper," A1. First reports can be found in Jehl and Miller, "Draft Report Said to Cite No Success in Iraq Arms Hunt," 1.
41. Kay, "Chasing Saddam's Weapons."
42. John Sutter, "Chasing Saddam's Weapons," http://www.pbs.org/wgbh/pages/frontline/shows/wmd/interviews/kay.html
43. Dan Eggen, "9/11 Panel Finds No Collaboration Between Iraq, Al Qaeda," *Washington Post*, (16 June 2004), A1.

Chapter 7

Likelihood of Success

"Peace and Freedom Will Prevail"

In attempting to make the case that the US would prevail, President Bush repeatedly referred to America's use of offensive military force since the 11 September 2001 terrorist attacks as a legitimate strategy in its broader war against terrorists and rogue states. But what represents victory? On this, Bush was clear:

> Our war on terror begins with Al-Qaida, but it does not end there. It will not end until every terrorist group of global reach has been found, stopped and defeated.[1]

The president also contended:

> We will not waver; we will not tire; we will not falter; and we will not fail. Peace and freedom will prevail.[2]

If the United States wanted to wage a successful campaign against terrorists, it had to recognize that suppressing terrorism would take years of cooperation with other countries in areas such as intelligence sharing, police work, managing financial flows and monetary transactions, and regulating immigration. In the wake of the 11 September 2001 attacks, the US helped to create the UN Counter-Terrorism Committee to coordinate international law enforcement efforts, and to deny financing and safe haven for Al-Qaida and other terrorist networks. Many have cooperated with the US on these efforts because it is in their national security interests to do so. However, it remains to be seen if the invasion of Iraq and the practice of offensive military force to promote regime change against rogue states unraveled international cooperation on security issues or undermined America's broader global war against terrorism

America's Frustration with Terrorism

For years, policymakers and the public have morally and politically struggled to set effective policies that would be successful enough to prevail against terrorism and the capabilities of terrorist groups. America's general frustration with terrorism is largely centered on the notion that terrorists employ non-conventional tactics that fall beyond traditional rules of engagement. The frustration is driven largely by the civilian devastation associated with particular terrorist attacks, the fact that most people regard terrorism as an unethical method of exercising influence and dissent, and by the reality that terrorist organizations are not legitimately recognized states in the traditional sense.

The Likelihood of Success Against Al-Qaida

The likelihood of success against terrorism would be quite difficult to attain. America's frustration is due in large part to America's moral and political struggle to understand and deal with the Al-Qaida terrorist network. In order to be successful against Al-Qaida, America has to understand its origins and how it operates. The origins of Al-Qaida (the "base") can be found in the Afghan uprising against the 1979 Soviet invasion and eventual occupation.[3] Thousands of Muslims and other volunteers from around the world flocked to Afghanistan as *mujahideen*, a group of warriors fighting to defend fellow Muslims against the atheist and Communist USSR. Osama bin Laden became the primary financier for the mujahideen, which forced the Soviets to withdraw from Afghanistan by 1989. In that same year, bin Laden returned from Afghanistan to his Saudi Arabia where he founded an organization to aid veterans of the Afghan war, many of whom went on to fight against the Serbs in Bosnia, the Americans in Somalia, and the Russians in Chechnya. After Saddam Hussein invade Kuwait in 1990, bin Laden lashed out at the Saudi royal family for allowing US troops to be stationed in Saudi Arabia and was immediately expelled for inciting anti-government activities.

After his expulsion from Saudi Arabia, bin Laden established preliminary headquarters for Al-Qaida in Khartoum, Sudan under the protection of its military government. The first actions of Al-Qaida against American interests were attacks on US forces in Somalia. A string of terrorist attacks followed, including the 1993 bombing of the World Trade Center, the 1996 bombing of the Khobar Towers in Dhahran, the 1998 US Embassy bombings in Nairobi and Dar Esalam, the 2000 bombing of the USS Cole in Aden, and the 9/11 attacks. Under pressure from Saudi Arabia and the US, Sudan eventually expelled bin Laden, who moved his operations to Afghanistan where he was able to set up terrorist camps. During this time, Al-Qaida forged alliances with other radical groups (see Figure 7.1).

Figure 7.1 Known Al-Qaida Affiliates

> Egyptian Islamic Jihad;
> Jemaah Islamiyah (Southeast Asia);
> the Salafist Group for Preaching and Combat (Algeria);
> GIA, or Armed Islamic Group (Algeria);
> Al-Ittihad al-Islamiyah (Somalia);
> The Islamic Movement of Uzbekistan;
> Pakistan Scholars Society;
> Partisans Movement (Kashmir);
> Hizb-ut-Tahrir (Central Asia);
> the Al-Jama Al-Islamiyya;
> the Abu Sayyaf group (Philippines);
> and the Hizb ut-Ta hrir organization worldwide.

Al-Qaida is a confederation of these and other smaller groups, which are united by their dedication to attacking Western targets as well as Islamic regimes with Western sympathies. The Al-Qaida leadership oversees a loosely connected and decentralized network of local cells that operate with their blessing and financial support in roughly 38 countries. Each cell operates independently of the leadership and its members do not know the identity of other cells. If one group is arrested they will not be able to betray others.

While on the surface it appears that Al-Qaida and Osama bin Laden are synonymous, bin Laden does not run the network single-handedly. Ayman al-Zawahiri is bin Laden's probable successor and an Egyptian physician who joined the Islamist movement in the late 1970s. He served three years in prison on charges connected to the assassination of Anwar Sadat. After his release he went to Afghanistan, where he met bin Laden and became his personal physician and advisor. Al-Zawahiri is suspected of helping organize the 1997 massacre of 67 foreign tourists in the Egyptian town of Luxor and was indicted in connection with the bombing of US embassies in Tanzania and Kenya. Other key members of Al-Qaida include Mustafa Hamza, Rifie Ahmed Taha, and Mohammed Islambouli, the brother of Khaled Islambouli, Sadat's assassin. Sheikh Omar Abdel Rahman, who is currently serving a life sentence in connection with the 1993 World Trade Center bombing, is revered as a spiritual leader. Mohammed Atef, who was believed to have been killed on 14 November 2001 in a US air strike during operations in Afghanistan, was responsible for Al-Qaida recruitment and training. Atef was suspected of having planned the 1998 US embassy bombings. Following his death, Atef's position within the terror network was replaced by an unknown Al-Qaida operative.

Unlike a distinct terrorist organization in the conventional sense, Al-Qaida has been able to evolve as a massive social movement that seeks to inspire and coordinate with other groups. Although Al-Qaida may have only a few thousand members, it seems to have many more supporters and sympathizers, some of whom may be inspired to terrorist deeds by bin Laden's famous public pronouncements. If Al-Qaida takes losses beyond recuperatation, there is a much broader Islamist movement hostile to the US and sympathetic to Al-Qaida's goals.

Difficulties in Measuring Success

To measure levels of success, the US has appeared to have embraced a so-called "body count" approach in order to provide a concrete measure of success and failure. Such an approach is not only deeply flawed, it is not new in the annals of American thinking. A body count can be misleading because the size of the terrorist cadre is often unknown, and many of those killed or captured are low-level operative and fighters who can easily be replaced by an array of willing recruits. More importantly, it fails to reflect the impact on the adversary's morale, recruitment, fundraising, and residual ability to conduct sophisticated attacks.

Besides focusing on a body count in an offensive war against Al-Qaida terrorists means overlooking the failure of using the same approach prior to the

9/11 attacks. It also misses several frightening characteristics of Al-Qaida, including its tremendous ability to regenerate itself and regain its losses. In *Through Our Enemies' Eyes*, the anonymous author contends that in the years before 9/11, police and security forces worldwide disrupted Al-Qaida cells and arrested many members. In mid-1996, Al-Qaida's senior commander, Abu Ubaydah al-Banshiri, drowned in Lake Victoria. Al-Qaida also lost Ali Muhammad, a leading terrorist trainer, when he was arrested in September 1998. Another huge blow came the next month when German authorities arrested Mamdouh Mahmud Salim, a key logistician. Sidi al-Madani al-Tayyib, Al-Qaida's chief financial officer, was captured by Saudi Interior Ministry police in 1997, along with 300 other bin Laden supporters. As with the arrests and disruptions today, these efforts probably saved thousands of lives; however, they did not stop the growth of the movement, nor did they disrupt plans for carrying out the 9/11 attacks.[4]

Al-Qaida is particularly successful in regenerating lost cells. For example, in August 1997 the home of an Al-Qaida lieutenant, Wadih el-Hage, was raided in Sudan, and he fled the country ironically to Florida. Although this would be a permanent setback for many organizations, a year later the plans he was working on in Sudan led to the destruction of America's Embassy in Kenya in August 1998. Moreover, after several of his Al-Qaida comrades were arrested by the Federal Bureau of Investigation (FBI) in Kenya, his el-Hage's cell launched a series of attacks in Kenya in November 2002 on a hotel frequented by Israelis. The Kenya experience suggests that cells thought to be destroyed are likely to reappear.

Al-Qaida's success is due in large measure to the fact that it is not a coherent organization but a global anti-US, anti-Western insurgency that has distinct, social, cultural, relgious, economic, political and military roots. It cannot be eliminated with a high-profile arrests, deaths, or the overthrow of governments. It requires a painstaking and lengthy struggle to dismantle not only the leadership, but also the broader global network and a massive social, political and economic effort on the part of the US to demonstrate goodwill to the Muslim world and an appreciation of the real causes that lead to terrorist activiity. It also demands a re-examination of US foreign policy issues, namely energy dependence, arms sales, and the Israeli-Palestinian conflict. For the US, success would have to be defined on both a substantive and a conceptual level.

Al-Qaida's worldwide stature as a symbol of resistance may have also allowed it to globalize what were in essence local conflicts. Before 9/11, Al-Qaida constantly strove to turn local movements into ones that shared its global anti-US agenda. On the whole, Islamists appear increasingly anti-American and shutting down terrorist camps in Afghanistan and elsewhere could turn local groups not previously affiliated with Al-Qaida against the US. Although several terrorist organizations, namely Hamas and Hezbollah, are certainly anti-US, they have not as of yet focused on targeting Americans. Given that these groups have recruiting and fundraising networks in Europe and elsewhere, a shift in targeting by these organizations could prove very deadly.

Complicating matters, serious data collection problems have put a more comprehensive and sophisticated approach to measuring success nearly beyond reach. It is difficult to measure precisely the morale or skill of conventional military forces, let alone those of shadowy terrorist organizations. Most of Al-Qaida's money comes from private sources; some of the donors do not know that they are supporting terrorism, believing their contributions support legitimate charities. Even recruitment is difficult to measure. There is no easy way to determine the size of Al-Qaida, the number and scale of its affiliates and proxies; or who its donors, active supporters and potential sympathizers are. Governments often do not know, sometimes deliberately conceal, or may at times exaggerate the Al-Qaida presence operating in their countries.

Then there was the question of whether or not an effort to disperse Al-Qaida, espeically its leadership bases in Afghanistan, would have a real impact and enhance America's likelihood of success? In the information age, Al-Qaida can use computers and cell phones to plan and organize attacks from anywhere in the world. Moreover, Afghanistan's difficult terrain allows Al-Qaida to operate from a highly elusive base. Prior to the American invasion, Afghanistan was a haven for training and recruitment as well as for planning. Al-Qaida and its supporters sent thousands of radicals to Afghanistan, allowing the group to choose the most skilled and dedicated to help with operations and to align itself with significant elements of Afghani culture. The prospect of eliminating Afghanistan as a haven for terrorism and overthrowing other state sponsors might be impossible.[5]

A US invasion of Iraq could increase hostility against America. As a result, the probability of American success in the war on terrorism could be significantly damaged with such an endeavor. According to former counter-terrorism adviser for Presdients Clinton and Bush Richard Clarke:

> The war as seen on television in Islamic countries has dangerously increased the level of frustration, anger, and hatred directed at the United States. It has given radical Islamic terrorists another target, US personnel in Iraq. The seeds of future terrorism have been sown.[6]

America's likelihood of success and of making positive inroads into the Islamic world America would be exceptionally difficult in the face of a US invasion and occupation of Iraq, especially given the long history of US support for brutal ditatorships in the Middle East and Central Asia. If the war against Al-Qaida is about denying terror networks safe harbors and sanctuaries cannot be allowed another sanctuary, would the US actually create another sanctuary in Iraq in the event of an American invasion?

From Terrorists to Rogue States

It was clear from the outset of any offensive military campaign that the struggle to define success in the war on terrorism and the use of body counts to measure levels of success would be unrealistic methods. These difficulties led the Bush

Administration to target so-called rogue states and assert a right to use offensive military force to promote regime change in such state. The primary advantage of regime change is that rogue states represent more clearly identifiable targets than terrorist networks that are more amorphous and obscure targets that present difficulties in measuring success. According to Bush, the focus would be on states as sponsors of terrorism:

> We will starve terrorists of funding, turn them one against another, drive them from place to place, until there is no refuge or no rest. And we will pursue nations that provide aid or safe haven to terrorism. Every nation, in every region, now has a decision to make. Either you are with us, or you are with the terrorists. From this day forward, any nation that continues to harbor or support terrorism will be regarded by the United States as a hostile regime.[7]

Bush's statement appeared to be influenced by Deputy Defense Secretary Paul Wolfowitz, who just three days after the 9/11 attacks, put forth the idea that states would be the primary target in the war on terrorism:

> the president's words are pretty good so let me say these people try to hide but they won't be able to hide forever, they think their harbors are safe but they won't be safe forever, I think one has to say it is not just simply a matter of capturing people and holding them accountable, but removing the sanctuaries, removing the support systems, ending states who sponsor terrorism. And that is why it has to be a broad and sustained campaign.[8]

However, the Bush Administration was not exactly united in such a strategy of defining success in terms of regime change. The same afternoon Wolfowitz made the above statement, Powell retaliated:

> We're after ending terrorism. If there are states and regimes, nations that support terrorism, we hope to persuade them that it is in their interest to stop doing that. I think ending terrorism is where I would leave it, and let Mr. Wolfowitz speak for himself.[9]

On the whole, a rogue state opposes American interests specifically and US global leadership more broadly. Its use as a policy description first emerged when President Reagan termed Libyan dictator Muammar Qaddafi an outlaw.[10] However, in the wake of President Bush's designation of Iran, Iraq, and North Korea as constituting an "axis of evil," the concept of a "rogue state" has been popularized as a response to the changing nature of threats facing the United States and an attempt by the US simplify complex threats that emerged following the collapse of the Soviet Union.[11] Rogue states have also been defined as governments that challenge the emergence of democratic systems since the end of the Cold War and the prevailing international order.[12] In addition to Iran, Iraq, and North Korea, since the end of the Cold War, the term "rogue" has been frequently used by American policymakers to explain the behavior of Cuba, Afghanistan, and Libya.

Rogues are renegade states America believes have engaged in four misbehaviors: 1) seeking and proliferating WMD; 2) supporting terrorism; 3) oppressing their own citizens; and 4) expressing utter disdain for the United States. Other countries that may be associated with one or more of the offensive behaviors, but not all of them, seem to escape the label of rogue, such as Syria, Serbia, China, and Sudan. However, since the accepted norms of behavior have been and continue to be renegotiated, attempts to define rogue states in reference to them invite conceptual confusion and produce a constantly changing roster of rogues.[13] But does toppling a regime really elevate the likelihood of American success in the war against terrorism and WMD proliferation?

Operation Enduring Freedom

When it was launched, Operation Enduring Freedom was implemented under the guise of being a "new war," which gave its architects considerable leeway.[14] However, in the wake of the 9/11 attacks, the impulse to war overwhelmed the attention to how success would be attained and the broader repercussions. Once it came time to carry out the invasion of Afghanistan, the measure of success in Afghanistan came to focus too narrowly on military performance and battlefield achievements. Useful analysis of the war in Afghanistan must begin by revoking the war's treatment as a new style of war itself. War attains meaning only in the context of the strategic international relations and global and regional conditions it influences. These effects are measured in terms of the fate of not only armies, states, and alliances, but people too.

What was the US going to accomplish with Operation Enduring Freedom? Success would be driven by quantitative measures, namely the capture and/or death of thousands of Taliban and Al-Qaida fighters. A disproportionate number of prisoners held by the Northern Alliance militias were foreign fighters, especially Uzbek and Pakistani.[15] An undisclosed number of training camps and facilities affiliated with Al-Qaida would also have to be destroyed, if the US was to demonstrate success in its broader war against terrorism. This proved very difficult on a qualitative level. Yes, thousands of terrorists and terror-related elements would have to be eliminated. If the Bush Administration hoped to be realistically and actually successful, the Taliban itself would have to be driven from its governing power in Afghanistan, reduced as a political force, and both the Taliban and Al-Qaida must be discredited as an ideological and cultural movement in Central Asia. In doing so, however, the US had to presume that Taliban members would likely resume a role in the Afghan polity some as provincial insurgents and leaders of other formations in post-Taliban Afghanistan. In the case of Operation Enduring Freedom, success could not be framed in a complete and absolute fashion.

Although the Al-Qaida and Taliban operations infrastructure in Afghanistan would have to be destroyed, it was difficult to assess the long term costs and benefits of its elimination. The acting assistant director of the FBI's counter-terrorism division, JT Caruso, estimated that Operation Enduring Freedom would only reduce the potential for future deadly attacks by 30 per cent. Furthermore, in the event of a US capture of Osama bin Laden, the decentralized structure of Al-Qaida would result in only a temporary pause in Al-Qaida operations.[16] One might have hoped that Enduring Freedom would have had a greater impact on Al-Qaida's global capabilities given the extensive use of American bombs and missiles, the killing of thousands of enemy fighters, and the capture of thousands more.

Remember that the Taliban regime bore a conditional relationship to Al-Qaida's activities outside Central Asia. In fact, most of the terrorist-related facilities and foreign troops under the control of the Taliban and Al-Qaida in Afghanistan were related to the ongoing civil war against the Northern Alliance. Most of Al-Qaida's capabilities to conduct far reaching terrorist acts resided outside of Afghanistan and fell beyond the scope of Operation Enduring Freedom, calling America's use of force in the country into question in terms of its overall success. The importance of Afghanistan to the extra-regional goals and activities of Al-Qaida was not that it provided a sanctuary and training site for terrorists; rather, Afghanistan served the organization's global activities principally as a recruiting ground for terrorists. The capacity of Al-Qaida to repair its lost capabilities for global terrorism rests on the fact that terrorist attacks similar to 9/11 do not depend on the maintenance of training facilities. Moreover, large terrorist organizations have proved themselves able to operate for very long periods without state sanctuaries and other state-supported safe havens, as long as local sympathetic communities exist. Thus, any successful military action against Al-Qaida had to be broad in scope and to a great extent permanent in nature. Moreover, Al-Qaida may be able to recoup its lost capacity by adopting a more thoroughly clandestine and "state-less" approach to its operations.

The US also held broadly defined objectives that could adversely impact the likelihood of success with the deployment of American military force in Afghanistan. In addition to prevailing against the Taliban and Al-Qaida, the Bush Administration hoped that Operation Enduring Freedom would be successful in: first, deterring rogue states from supporting terrorist attacks against the US on a global level; second, countering any impression that 9/11 attacks would cause the US to avoid using military force and engaging in military operations outside Afghanistan; and third, promoting US national security interests in the immediate region of central and south Asia. Among America's deterrence goals, the US perceived that the destruction of the Taliban as a political and governing body in Afghanistan would encourage other rogue states to avoid sponsoring terrorist attacks against US targets. In terms of success, the problem with the approach was that it most likely would not deter so-called weak rogue states such as Sudan. In addition, strong rogue states that were thought to be in actual possession of WMD programs, such as Libya, Syria, and Iran, might already be deterred from extending state support to Al-Qaida. Furthermore, a long term and broadly defined deterrent-effect would not directly work against a highly decentralized and transnational terrorist network like Al-Qaida, which does not seem dependent on state support for their anti-US operations.

The most significant drawback with the deterrence strategy was that the appealing vision of Operation Enduring Freedom would to a great degree not send a message to allies of the US that are repressive governments, which have terrorist elements within their countries and/or in possession of WMD. This includes Saudi Arabia, Egypt, Uzbekistan, Kuwait, Indonesia, and Pakistan. In the war on terrorism, the administration has clearly sought to align itself with such unsavory governments that for some reason escape the rogue state designation simply because they are politically, economically, and militarily aligned with the US.

The speed and intensity of the US response to the 9/11 attacks certainly undercut any expectation that the attack might lead to a reduction in utilizing military force beyond Afghanistan. Under Bush, the US sought to establish a clear differentiation between pre and post-9/11 policies. Following 9/11, the Bush Administration believed the ferocity of the military response with Operation Enduring Freedom would convey to the world a new message to the world. If America was going to be successful in its war on terrorism, it was fully prepared to reduce its emphasis on multilateralism and to reconsider its participation in arms control agreements and international legal mechanisms. President Bush also believed that US victory in the Cold War allowed America to vigorously exercise the unique prerogatives that promote and secure America's status as the world's sole military superpower. Both see America's unmatched capacity to act wherever it might choose worldwide as a pivotal asset in the effort to maintain US global leadership.

The Bush Administration's approach actually harkens back to Paul Wolfowitz in the first Bush Administration. In his 1992 Defense Planning Guidance draft, Wolfowitz claimed that if the US could not persuade multilateral organizations to cooperate, then it "will go with whoever we can convince and at the same time we'll try to keep the coalitions behind us," but "act alone in defense of our interests" if need be.[17] These ideas framed US global military activism in terms of defending and extending the "strategic depth" afforded the United States as a consequence of Soviet collapse. His belief was that presidents Bush Sr. and Clinton failed to take advantage of the demise of the USSR in order to promote US interests and assert American preeminence. Along with former Secretary of Defense Dick Cheney, Wolfowitz, perceived that the world was brewing with potential conflict and that democracy was not on the rise, but to the contrary, being threatened by rogue states. With Operation Enduring Freedom, the use of force had to be so powerful and overwhelming so other rogue states could witness the demonstration of US power. The principal modus for accomplishing this goal is not an expansion of the community of democratic nations, as the Clinton policy would have it, but an increase in the reach and effectiveness of America's offensive military power. It is not a policy that seeks to make new friends so much as it seeks new ways to eliminate particular rogue states enemies with either multilateral or unilateral power.[18]

Furthermore, the likelihood of success with Operation Enduring Freedom was widely based on the formal objectives advanced in the 2001 *Quadrennial Defense Review* (QDR), which was released on 30 September 2001.[19] Among other objectives, the QDR claimed that the key to success in the post-9/11 world lies primarily in reassuring America allies of its good intentions, challenging America's military competitors, and defeating adversaries who threaten the US and its allies. Based on the Reagan Administration's idea of rolling back Soviet Communism, it places war objectives at the head of US national security interests. Beyond seeking decisive victory, the US was aiming for the defeat of adversaries against potential challengers. The QDR makes several ambitious claims, including "if deterrence fails, decisively any adversary" and occupy "foreign territory until US strategic objectives are met."[20]

The success of Operation Enduring Freedom was, in part, premised on promoting the US position in Pakistan. The original goal was to strengthen American influence in Pakistan and, most importantly, ensure Musharrev's dependence on US support. This, in turn, could reduce nuclear tensions between Pakistan and India and alleviate any humanitarian crisis associated with the expected rush of refugees into Pakistan following the American invasion of Afghanistan. However, Pakistan's increased dependence on the US is a double-edged sword that cuts both ways, since maintaining Musharrev against internal opponents, in particular against remnants of the Pakistani-support Taliban, would not be easy. Guaranteeing an expanded US presence in Central Asia demanded significant American financial investment, long-term political and military commitments, and a risk of destabilizing the country given that much of Northwestern Pakistan exhibits far-reaching anti-US sentiment.

Most important, no one could effectively forecast how the impact of a potential collapse of the Taliban on Afghan society along purely ethnic and tribal lines. The Taliban are an influential organization in Afghanistan with deep-seated and far-reaching roots. The Taliban is one of several mujahideen groups that formed during the Afghan war against the Soviet invasion and occupation of Afghanistan between 1979 and 1989. After the withdrawal of Soviet forces, the Soviet-backed government gave way to the mujahideen. In 1992, Kabul was captured and an alliance of mujahideen set up a new government with Burhanuddin Rabbani as interim president. However, the various factions were unable to cooperate and a civil war ensued.

At the same time, groups of Taliban or "religious students" were loosely organized on a regional basis during the Soviet occupation and civil war. Although they represented a potentially huge force, they didn't emerge as a united entity until the Taliban of Kandahar were chosen by Pakistan to protect a convoy trying to open a trade route from Pakistan to Central Asia. They proved an able force, fighting off rival mujahideen and other warlords and went on to assume total control of the cities of Kandahar and Kabul by late 1996 under leader Mullah Mohammed Omar.

The Taliban's initial popularity with the Afghan people surprised the country's other warring factions. Many Afghans, weary of conflict and anarchy, were relieved to see corrupt and often brutal warlords replaced by the devout Taliban, who had some success in eliminating corruption, restoring peace, and allowing commerce to resume. Although the Taliban managed to reunite most of

Afghanistan, they were unable to end the civil war. Nor did they improve the conditions in cities, where access to food, clean water, and employment actually declined during their rule. A continuing drought and a very harsh winter (2000–2001) brought famine and increased the flow of refugees to Pakistan.

In the context of Afghan history, the rise of the Taliban, though not their extremism, is unsurprising. Afghanistan is a devoutly Muslim nation with a population dominated by Sunni Muslims (other Afghan Muslims are Sufis or Shiites). Most of the Taliban's current leaders were educated in Pakistan, in refugee camps where they had fled with millions of other Afghans after the Soviet invasion. Pakistan's Jami'at-e 'Ulema-e Islam political party provided welfare services, education, and military training for refugees in many of these camps. While the Taliban presented themselves as a reform movement, they have been criticized by Islamic scholars as being poorly educated in Islamic law and history.

Afghanistan's civil war continued until the American bombing campaign of late 2001. However, prior to US intervention in response to the 9/11 attacks, the Taliban's opposition was the Northern Alliance, which at the time held the Northeast corner of the country (about ten per cent of Afghanistan). The Northern Alliance comprised numerous anti-Taliban factions and was nominally led by exiled president Burhanuddin Rabbani. While the Taliban is made up mostly Sunni Muslim Pashtuns, the Northern Alliance includes Tajiks, Hazara, Uzbeks, Turkmen, the largely Shiite Hazara, and some other smaller ethnic groups. In early September, the de factor leader of the Northern Alliance, Ahmad Shah Massoud, died from wounds suffered in a suicide bombing, allegedly carried out by Al-Qaida.

The Taliban regime faced international scrutiny and condemnation for its policies. Only Saudi Arabia, Pakistan, and the United Arab Emirates recognized the Taliban as Afghanistan's legitimate government. After the 9/11 terrorist attacks, Saudi Arabia and the UAE cut diplomatic ties with the Taliban. The UN imposed sanctions on the Taliban, primarily in response to the Taliban's hospitality toward Al-Qaida. The relationship between the Taliban and bin Laden is close, even familial; bin Laden supposedly fought with the mujahideen, has financed the Taliban, and has reportedly married off one of his daughters to Mullah Muhammad Omar. The United Nations Security Council even passed two resolutions, 1267 (1999) and 1333 (2000), demanding that the Taliban cease their support for bin Laden and turn him over for trial.

For the US, Northern Alliance victory meant that the position of Tajik and Uzbek minorities would advance at the expense of the Pashtun majority, most of which comprised the ethnicity of the ruling Taliban. This would likely produce a bipolar division between Pashtuns and non-Pashtuns. The ethnic reframing of the Afghan struggle altered the political implications of US military operations in the country, which had focused almost exclusively on Pashtun areas. Third, the increased salience of ethnic, tribal, and sect lines of division also increased the centrifugal pressures on the international coalition supporting the operation. Notably, a US/Northern Alliance victory could also substantially increase Russian influence in Afghanistan, contrary to US interests and to the dismay of both

Pakistan and Iran. Indian interests (tied to the Tajik militias) also advanced substantially. These developments increased the prospects for intensified regional contention over Afghanistan. The likelihood of success looked more as if military expediency would come to dominate US strategic goals. The Bush Administration first sowed the seeds of this problem when it decided to pursue war objectives without giving enough time or attention to preparation.

Given these overwhelming obstacles to success against Al-Qaida and the Taliban, the US pressed ahead with Enduring Freedom. The US would have to engage in a serious air campaign to disintegrate its enemies. Among the most significant initial targets were air defense installations, command and control facilities, and other political targets. Since a massive US ground assault was not likely for the given the urgent time frame, air power would have to be so devastating as to provide the Northern Alliance and coalition Special Forces with more of a fighting chance against the Taliban.[21] But the US thought the Northern Alliance was unlikely to produce the desired political outcome of establishing stability in the country and consenting to a US military presence.[22]

Although the US possessed military and technological superiority, if military victory was to come in quick fashion, rejoice would have to be tempered with uncertainty for long-term success. On the whole, the likelihood of success with Operation Enduring Freedom was mixed at best. Clearly, in Afghanistan, it was the Taliban that was to suffer the brunt of US military power. Most of the assets and troops under Al-Qaida's control in Afghanistan had to do with the Afghan civil war. The terror network's capacity for conducting global attacks resided largely outside of Afghanistan and fell beyond the scope of Operation Enduring Freedom.

Also in doubt was the broader deterrent-effect. Whereas it was thought that some rogue states would likely become more careful about consorting with or tolerating terrorist organizations, this deterrent effect may not extend to the fragile quasi-states in whose territory organizations like Al-Qaida prefer to nest. Terrorists themselves are notoriously difficult to deter, especially those employing suicidal tactics. These are more likely to be inflamed than tamed by operations like Enduring Freedom and future deployments of US military forces in Muslim nations. Even more, Al-Qaida is not especially dependent on state support for its global activities. None of the terrorist capabilities demonstrated on 9/11, for instance, required a large base infrastructure. Indeed, the Al-Qaida cells that carried out the 9/11 attacks were less dependent on leadership bases in Afghanistan than they were those in the US and Germany.

Operation Iraqi Freedom

The question was not if American forces would prevail militarily against Iraqi forces. But unlike the Gulf War, the US was heading into a conflict with little international legitimacy and motivated by allegations that Iraq was in illegal possession of WMD and providing safe harbor to Al-Qaida. The Muslim world was already simmering because of the US presence in Afghanistan and rising tensions between Israel and the Palestinians. These factors weighed heavily on America's likelihood of success. If US forces could quickly topple or eliminate the Iraqi leadership without inflicting mass suffering or setting off a Middle East cataclysm, the aftermath would be more manageable. Should a violent insurgency take hold in the occupation phase and illicit WMD and an Al-Qaida presence not uncovered, success would be short-lived.

The Bush Administration appeared confident that the US military would succeed on the battlefield and that much of the Iraqi population would aid coalition forces. On 6 February 2003, Vice-President Cheney contended, "the read we get on the people of Iraq is there is no question they would like to get rid of Saddam Hussein and they will welcome as liberators when we come to do that."[23] These words were largely a reflection of Ahmad Chalabi and his Iraqi National Congress, which was closely allied with Deputy Secretary Paul Wolfowitz, his deputy Douglas Feith, and Vice-President Cheney's chief of staff Louis Scooter Libby.[24]

Disarmament

Locating and disarming Iraq of its alleged WMD programs was the original justification for war against Saddam. Therefore, American success in Iraq would have to be assessed against America's case for just cause, which was centered on its ability to disarm Iraq of its WMD programs the US and UK thought Iraq was in actual and real possession. Based on prewar intelligence assessments, the US believed Iraq contained suspected WMD-related sites before the war, and US commanders had expected to find chemical and biological warheads early in the war.[25] However, the likelihood that an American invasion of Iraq would succeed in eliminating its WMD programs or deter other states from producing them may have been ill-conceived, since much of the international community largely believed that pre-war inspections, sanctions, and no-fly zones were successful enough. President Bush remained insistent that Iraq possessed WMD and that the purpose of an invasion would be disarmament because Saddam could have "a nuclear weapon in less than a year."[26] CIA Director George Tenet even suggested that the WMD case against Iraq was a "slam dunk."[27]

Absent compelling evidence of Iraqi possession of illicit and banned WMD in violation of UN Security Council resolutions, the likely costs and risks of a commitment of American military forces to a regime-change campaign in Iraq could outweigh the benefits. Even more, if an American invasion should fail to uncover WMD capabilities and programs or an Al-Qaida-Saddam nexus, the likelihood of a successful American effort in Iraq would not only be significantly lessened, the very claim of success would be baseless and without merit in the first place. Furthermore, a US campaign to overthrow Saddam would entail a large-scale military operation that America would have to assume most of the burden. A largely US campaign could increase the risk of additional terrorist attacks against American or allied targets around the world and even destabilize the Middle East.

Ground Forces

Despite the claims of many regime-change proponents, policymakers could have been under no illusion that Saddam would be overthrown by US air power alone. Given improvements in US air capabilities since the first Gulf War including guided bombs and unmanned aerial vehicles, they would certainly not be enough to topple Saddam. Even laser-guided bombs are generally not accurate enough to destroy armor, and Saddam would be sure to position much of his forces in cities, schoolyards, and hospitals, complicating US targeting options. The use of laser-guided bombs against stationary Iraqi tanks in the Kuwaiti desert in 1991 would be more difficult to replicate in the complex terrain and urban areas in central Iraq.

Iraqi opposition forces were also deeply divided and have a history of infighting, which would require a strong ground force presence. Kurdish, Shiite, and Sunni opposition forces have perhaps one-tenth the strength of Iraqi armed forces. They are outnumbered more than two to one by the dedicated fighters: the Special Republican Guard, the Republican Guard, and the irregular Fedayeen Saddam (Saddam's 'Men of Sacrifice') militia. If convinced that Saddam's regime was on its way out, it was thought that much of the regular Iraqi army would probably stop fighting. Counting on the Iraqi army to quit in the absence of a credible American threat on the ground, however, would be a huge gamble. Thousands could again be slaughtered, Saddam could still hold onto power, and the international coalition against terrorism could be dismayed and fractured by what it would correctly view as not only unilateralist but feckless American leadership. Moreover, the Fedayeen was a fearsome force of Sunni Baathists that could blend in with the civilian population and utilize guerrilla tactics.[28]

For these reasons, a large-scale ground force would have to be credible and large enough to be successful in the invasion, occupation, and subsequent phases of the war. But, what was the appropriate number of troops that would be needed? The actual size of the coalition force (roughly 150,000 troops) was roughly one third the size of the force that ejected Iraqi forces from Kuwait in 1991. The appropriate size of the force and the number of troops was the subject of a major bureaucratic conflict between the civilian leadership and senior military commanders in the US Department of Defense.[29] General Tommy Franks requested more troops than Secretary Rumsfeld was willing to approve.[30] Franks eventually consented to the smaller force because he was given assurances by Rumsfeld that Turkey would allow the US to invade Iraq through its country.[31] After the Turkish parliament rejected the US request, the size of the invasion force was seriously questioned by senior military commanders. Success on the battlefield was defined quite differently among US military leaders.

A Mostly American Burden

Any military invasion of Iraq would have to be undertaken without the UN. Nations in the immediate region worried that a US invasion would produce a refugee crisis and that an American occupation could leave Iraq destabilized in the

Kurdish north and Shiite southeast. If America failed, the global coalition against terrorism could easily weaken, and the US might enjoy less intelligence, law enforcement, and financial cooperation. However, the material benefits that would accrue to countries like Turkey, China, Russia, Jordan, and France if a post-Saddam Iraq could be stabilized would give at least those countries incentive to avoid public condemnations of US military action. It was also believed that Arab states would be relieved, since sanctions would be lifted on a post-Saddam Iraq.

Contrary to prewar assumptions that Iraq's oil revenue would greatly offset American costs, 12 years of sanctions left Iraq incapable of making any significant reimbursement to the US for an occupation or military presence. The cost of preparation, aid to non-combatant allies and the invasion itself amounted to $45 billion.[32] An estimated five-year occupation would cost the US a total of $300 billion and budgetary costs of roughly $9 billion a month.[33] More important, the US must meet an estimated $5 billion in initial humanitarian aid and pay out $8 billion in Iraqi government salaries, as well as about $7 billion for repairs to public utilities and to restore vital services over the next two years.[34]

In many ways, the symbolism of international participation has been a vital component for American success in Iraq. Assembling and maintaining the image of a "coalition of the willing" were absolutely central. However, the actual size of coalition forces was indeed a source of controversy for the Bush Administration ever since the buildup of offensive combat forces in Kuwait began in early 2002 (See Table 1). At the initiation of Operation Iraqi Freedom, of the 34 nations contributing actual combat troops a total of 154,363 troops to the invasion, American troops numbered 130,000 or roughly 84 per cent of total coalition combat troop strength. The second largest combat in the invasion was represented by the UK, with 9,000 troops or roughly 6 per cent. The remaining 32 nations in the coalition contributed only a total of 15,360 troops, or roughly 10 per cent of force strength.[35] The invasion phase would not only be US-led, it would have a distinctive American face and burden. And while the US stressed the number of countries that have sent troops, it has avoided discussions of the small size of the military contingents.[36] Moreover, any dwindling of the coalition following the invasion would further complicate the difficult job of sustaining the force, which is critical to US success in building and securing a post-Saddam Iraq.

The nations included in America's pre-invasion coalition of the willing require an additional ethical and political assessment. The Czech Republic did not allow its troops to leave Kuwait and participate in the invasion, unless chemical weapons were used. Eritrea and Ethiopia are two countries that recently waged a bitter war in the late 1990s, resulting in nearly 100,000 deaths and a tenuous peace. The State Department warns Americans not to visit Honduras, El Salvador, Georgia, Kazakhstan, Philippines, Azerbaijan, and Macedonia. While Japan was a coalition member, Prime Minister Junichiro Koizumi admitted he was "anguished" by his decision to support the US.[37]

Table 1 Combat Troop Contingents in Iraq, March-April 2003

Country	Troops	% of Force Strength
USA	130,000	84.0
UK	9,000	6.0
Italy	3,000	2.0
Poland	2,460	1.6
Ukraine	1,600	1.0
Spain	1,300	0.8
Netherlands	1,100	0.7
Australia	800	0.5
Romania	700	0.4
Bulgaria	480	0.3
Thailand	440	0.3
Denmark	420	0.3
Honduras	368	0.3
El Salvador	361	0.3
Dominican Republic	302	0.2
Hungary	300	0.2
Japan	240	0.1
Norway	179	0.1
Mongolia	160	0.1
Azerbaijan	150	0.1
Portugal	128	0.09
Latvia	120	0.09
Lithuania	118	0.09
Slovakia	102	0.08
Czech Republic	80	0.06
Philippines	80	0.06
Albania	70	0.05
Georgia	70	0.05
New Zealand	61	0.04
Moldova	50	0.03
Macedonia	37	0.02
Estonia	31	0.01
Canada	31	0.01
Kazakhstan	25	0.01
Total Ground Force Strength	154,363	100.00

Sources: Sarah Anderson, Phyllis Bennis, and John Cavanaugh, "A Coalition of the Willing or a Coalition of the Coerced?" (Washington DC: Institute for Policy Studies, February 26, 2003); Eric Leaver and Sara Johnson, "A Coalition of Weakness," (Washington DC: Foreign Policy in Focus, April 2003).

What Do We Do After Toppling Saddam?

To avoid the risk of a potential prolonged conflict among insurgent Shiite, and Sunni groups during a military occupation, the US would need a stable post-Saddam government. Such an effort could require a multi-year military presence by a force of American troops large enough to secure Iraq's borders, patrol the cities, and conduct raids into possible insurgent areas. Residual terrorist attacks would have to be expected, as well as a surge in Arab and Muslim resentment.

Although these realities were certainly conceivable before the war, there was a culture war in the Department of Defense over how many troops would be needed to be successful during the occupation. For Army Chief of Staff General Eric Shinseki and Secretary of the Army Thomas White, a smaller force would make it difficult to successfully stabilize Iraq, eliminate potential insurgents, to secure Iraq's borders, and to provide humanitarian relief. To carry such post-invasion missions, they favored an armed force of roughly 400,000 troops, which was far more than the 75,000 US troops Rumsfeld was willing to provide.[38]

Three weeks before the invasion, the conflict erupted in public when Shinseki claimed the US needed at least "several hundred thousand troops" in the post invasion phase of the war.[39] Rumsfeld rebutted Shinseki, "The idea that it would take several hundred thousand US forces I think is far from the mark."[40] Wolfowitz added, "Some of the higher end predictions we have been hearing recently, such as the notion that it will take several hundred thousand US troops to provide stability in post-Saddam Iraq are wildly off the mark. First, it is hard to conceive that it would take more forces to provide stability in post-Saddam Iraq than it would take to conduct the war itself and to secure the surrender of Saddam's security forces in his army. Hard to imagine."[41] Secretary White would later claim "there is a certain amount of arrogance to both of them in this regard. Neither man I would say is burdened by a great deal of self-doubt. Their view is that they would be absolutely right... Our view is that they were terribly wrong..."[42] Defining success in a post-Saddam government was certainly different for many.

In particular, an American occupation and post-invasion military presence would have to be well-planned in advance. An optimistic partnership between Americans and Iraqis would have to be built from the start. However, any successful occupation should transform the occupied more than the occupier. The US occupation should address the potential side effects associated with the use of destructive military force, such as blackouts, lengthy gas lines, rampant unemployment, and an uncertain future. Schools would have to be rebuilt, children immunized, police forces resurrected, looted government buildings repaired and cleaned, tight controls imposed on Iraqi exiles to prevent corruption, oil pipelines and factories restored, and the Iraqi currency altered. In other words, a US occupational authority should build public confidence in order to win over the populace and to demonstrate that it not only has good intentions, but the will to succeed in constructing a post-Saddam Iraq.

Beyond these bread and butter concerns, the US had to realize that the war would not end with the overthrow or potential capture or death of Saddam. It would also entail confronting disparate resistance forces among them the largely Shitte Mahadi militia led by Moqtada Sadr, a firebrand Shiite Muslim cleric whose father was killed by government agents and remnants of Saddam's own Sunni-dominated Baath Party. But most important, a successful US occupation would have to be conducted in deference to Shiite leader, Grand Ayatollah Ali Sistani, a cleric far more established than Sadr. With tens of millions of loyal followers, Sistani is seen as the most influential leader of Iraq's Shiite majority.

Success = Cooperation

Assessing the likelihood of success is a complex and difficult task. Militarily, given the superiority and determination of American-led forces, it seems fair to conclude that the US would be successful in overthrowing the Taliban regime and toppling Saddam and defeating his forces during major combat. Revealing a considerable level of confidence in Afghanistan, the American public favored going to war even if that meant thousands of casualties for the nation's armed forces. According to a *New York Times* poll, twenty-eight per cent expected fewer than 1,000 American casualties, twenty-eight per cent between 1,000 to 5,000 casualties, and twenty-seven per cent predicted the casualties would be even higher.[43] In Iraq, sixty-four per cent favored the use of military force against Iraq in September 2002 with nearly half (forty-eight per cent) expressing a willingness to accept significant American casualties.[44] The willingness of Americans to accept significant US casualties underscored the public's determination.

However, many of the challenges the US confronted, and still faces in the world today, cannot be resolved with battlefield victories alone. The American military campaign in Afghanistan has not resulted in a degradation of the terror network as a transnational force. Even more damaging to the US case was that although it has been successful in capturing or killing a significant portion of the Al-Qaida leadership with its military efforts in Afghanistan and Central Asia, recent evidence suggests that the terror network has re-generated itself and absorbed the losses.[45] The resilience of Al-Qaida demonstrates that overthrowing the Taliban made little impact on reducing the power of the terror network. Thus, many of the military successes initially attained with America's global anti-terror efforts, in particular with Operation Enduring Freedom and subsequent missions, have been reversed. Counting the number of killed or captured Al-Qaida terrorists is simply not an accurate measure of success.

A successful strategy is one that emphasizes multilateral cooperation and strengthening international institutions to meet these challenges and spreads costs in a more even fashion. As the world's preeminent power, the US has to promote multilateral action and global cooperation on an array of matters, with military concerns being a few among many.[46] Cooperative strategies are the keys to enhancing the likelihood of success for the US against terrorists and so-called rogue states. Given the difficulties of prevailing against a decentralized and far-reaching global terror network like Al-Qaida, there is no question that the use of offensive military force in Afghanistan will not deliver to the US the success it is hoping to attain. Keeping score by counting and publicizing dead or captured terrorists does not make a dent into a global terror network that easily replaces lost members with new recruits and that is more of a social movement than a conventional organization. Coercive military power will remain important in a world of nation-states guarding their sovereignty, but multilateral cooperative power on a transnational level is essential for success against Al-Qaida.

Looking back at the American invasion of Iraq in particular, the Bush Administration tied America's likelihood of success to WMD disarmament and severing ties with Al-Qaida terrorists. However, we know today that the US has failed to locate or discover compelling evidence of banned Iraqi WMD in violation of UN Security Council resolutions. Thus, the costs and risks of the commitment of American military forces to the regime changing campaign against Saddam far outweigh the benefits of the pre-invasion UN-led strategy that combined the use of sanctions with weapons inspections and no-fly zones. The likelihood of a successful American effort in Iraq was significantly diminished and the very claim of success is baseless and without merit in the first place.

The war against Iraq could encourage others to accelerate weapons development in order to defensively deter against potential conventional and unconventional attacks.[47] This runs counter to America's vision of success, which is based on disarming rogue states. Following the American invasions of Afghanistan and Iraq, North Korea has accumulated enough weapons-grade material and built the required weapons delivery systems to deploy two to five nuclear missiles capable of striking targets in East Asia and potentially the Western US. At the same time, Iran has assembled the required components to move forward with an advanced nuclear program. Both rogue states have been allowed to produce self-sufficient WMD programs, due in large measure to the failure to halt the black market network of nuclear materials run by Abdul Qadeer Khan, former director of Pakistan's nuclear weapons program, a supposed US ally in the war on terrorism. The one alleged bright spot was the agreement by Libya's Qadafi to halt WMD production and compensate the families of victims in the bombing of a Pan Am flight in 1989 in exchange for the lifting of sanctions and reintegration into the global economy.[48] Measuring the likelihood of success with military victories is incomplete and inaccurate.

Notes

1.   George W. Bush, "Address to a Joint Session of Congress and the American People," (20 September 2001), http://www.whitehouse.gov/news/releases/2001/09/20010920-8.html
2.   George W. Bush, "Presidential Address to the Nation," (7 October 2001), http://www.whitehouse.gov/news/releases/2001/10/20011007-8.html

3. Al-Qaida is also known as Qa'idat al-Jihad, the Islamic Army for the Liberation of the Holy Places, the World Islamic Front for Jihad Against Jews and Crusaders, the Islamic Salvation Foundation, Osama bin Laden Network.
4. Anonymous, *Through Our Enemies Eyes* (New York: Brassey's Press, 2002).
5. James Risen, "Taliban Chiefs Prove Elusive, Americans Say," *New York Times*, (20 December 2001), 1; Jelinek, "U.S. Keeps Lists for Afghan War," *AP Online*, (30 November 2001).
6. Clark is quoted in Daniel Byman, "Scoring the War on Terrorism," *The National Interest*, Summer 2003, 3.
7. Bush, "Address to a Joint Session of Congress and the American People," http://www.whitehouse.gov/news/releases/2001/09/20010920-8.html
8. Wolfowitz is quoted in "The War Behind Closed Doors," http://www.pbs.org/wgbh/pages/frontline/shows/iraq/etc/cron.html
9. Powell is quoted on the same website, http://www.pbs.org/wgbh/pages/frontline/shows/iraq/etc/cron.html
10. President Ronald Reagan, *Public Papers of the President*, vol. I, "Presidential News Conference," (7 May1986), 563.
11. Michael Klare, *Rogue States and Nuclear Outlaws: America's Search for a New Foreign Policy* (New York: Hill and Wang, 1995).
12. Anthony Lake, "Confronting Backlash States," *Foreign Affairs*, Mar/Apr 1994, 45-55.
13. Francis M. Deng, et al. *Sovereignty as Responsibility: Conflict Management in Africa* (Washington, DC: Brookings Institution Press, 1996).
14. Michael R. Gordon, "A New Kind of War Plan," *New York Times*, (7 October 2001), 1; Michael R. Gordon, "A New War and its Scale," *New York Times*, (17 September 2001), 1; Judy Keen, "Bush Rethinks Principles for 'Different Kind of War'," *USA Today*, (16 October 2001), 13; Don Melvin, "A New Kind of War: Enemy, Victory Hard to Define; Americans Face Long, Expensive Effort," *Atlanta Journal and Constitution*, (18 September 2001), 6; Robert Salladay, "New Kind of Enemy, New Kind of Response; Civilization Confronts Warriors Who Have No Limits," *San Francisco Chronicle*, (30 September 2001), 9.
15. Dexter Filkins, "Foreigners Allied With Taliban Cling to a Surrounded Stronghold," *New York Times*, (18 November 2001), 1. Alex Perry, "Mass Slaughter of the Taliban's Foreign Jihadists," *Time*, (26 November 2001), 60.
16. Walter Pincus, "Al Qaeda to survive bin Laden, Panel told," *Washington Post*, (19 December 2001).
17. Barton Gellman, "The War Behind Closed Doors," http://www.pbs.org/wgbh/pages/frontline/shows/iraq/interviews/gellman.html
18. Chris J. Dolan, "Foreign Policy on the Offensive," in Betty Glad and Chris J. Dolan, *Striking First: Preemptive and Preventive War Doctrines and the Reshaping of US Foreign Policy* (New York: Palgrave-Macmillan, 2004).
19. Office of the Secretary of Defense, *Quadrennial Defense Review 2001* (Washington DC: 30 September 2001). See the QDR, other US planning and strategy documents, and analyses at the website of the Center for Defense Information at: http://www.cdi.org/issues/qdr/
20. U.S. Department of Defense, *Quadrennial Defense Review Report* (Washington DC: Office of the Secretary of Defense, 30 September 2001).

21. Edward Gargan, "Taliban Hang On; U.S. finds they are not so easy to defeat," *Newsday* (New York), (26 October 2001), A30; "Taliban Halts Opposition Advance on Key Northern Afghanistan City; Battle: Regime rushes 1,000 fighters to Mazar- i- Sharif. U.S. airstrikes shift focus to troops," *Los Angeles Times*, (18 October 2001), 1.

22. Michael R. Gordon, "A Month in a Difficult Battlefield: Assessing U.S. War Strategy," *New York Times*, (8 November 2001); Wright and Doyle Mcmanus, "U.S. Shifts Gears After a Week of Setbacks; Policy: Administration acknowledges short-term problems while insisting overall plan is working," *Los Angeles Times*, (28 October 2001), 1.

23. Cheney is quoted in Dana Milbank, "Upbeat Tone Ended with War," *Washington Post*, (29 March 2003), 1.

24. See Evan Thomas and mark Hosenball, "The Rise and Fall of Ahmad Chalabi," *Newsweek*, (31 May 2004), 21.

25. Dana Priest and Dafna Linzer , Panel Condemns Iraq Prewar Intelligence," *Washington Post*, (10 July 2004), 1. Also see: Select Committee on Intelligence, United States Senate, "Report on the U.S. Intelligence Community's Prewar Intelligence Assessments on Iraq," (9 July 2004), http://intelligence.senate.gov/iraqreport2.pdf

26. Bush is quoted in Evan Thomas, Richard Wolffe, and Michael Isikoff, "(Over)selling the World on War," *Newsweek*, (9 June 2003), 24.

27. "The Weapons That Weren't – Intelligence Failures," *Economist*, (17 July 2004), 34.

28. Mark Mezzetti, "An Enemy in the Shadows," *US News and World Report*, August 11, 2003, 18.

29. James Fallows, "Blind Into Baghdad," *Atlantic Monthly*, January/February 2004.

30. Todd S. Purdum, *A Time of Our Choosing* (New York: Henry Holt and Company, 2003).

31. Thomas E. Ricks, "The Invasion of Iraq,"
    http://www.pbs.org/wgbh/pages/frontline/shows/invasion/interviews/ricks.html

32. Mike Allen and Amy Goldstein, "Security Funding Tops New Budget; Bush's Plan Marks Return to Deficits," *Washington Post* , (20 January 2002), Richard W. Stevenson and Elisabeth Bumiller, "President To Seek $48 Billion More For The Military," *New York Times*, (24 January 2002).

33. Congressional Budget Office, *Estimated Costs of a Potential Conflict with Iraq*. (Washington DC: Congressional Budget Office, 30 September 2002): ftp://ftp.cbo.gov/38xx/doc3822/09-30-Iraq.pdf

34. Steven M. Kosiak, "Funding for Defense, Military Operations, Homeland Security, and Related Activities Since 9/11," Center for Strategic and Budgetary Assessments, (21 January2004), http://csbaonline.org
    /4Publications/Archive/B.20040121.Post_9.11_Funding /B.200401
    21.Post_9.11_Funding.pdf; Steven M. Kosiak, "One Year Later: The Cost of Military Operations in Iraq," Center for Strategic and Budgetary Assessments 18 March 2003: http://csbaonline.org/4Publications/Archive/U.20040318.OIFSpending/U.20040318.OI FSpending.pdf; David Moniz, "Monthly Costs of Afghan, Iraq Wars Approach That of Vietnam," *USA Today*, (7 September 2003), 1; Steve Schifferes, "The Costs of the Iraq War, One Year on," *BBC News* (8 April 2004),:
    http://news.bbc.co.uk/2/hi/business/3603923.stm

35. Sarah Anderson, Phyllis Bennis, and John Cavanaugh, "A Coalition of the Willing or a Coalition of the Coerced?" (Washington DC: Institute for Policy Studies, 26 February 2003); Eric Leaver and Sara Johnson, "A Coalition of Weakness," (Washington DC:

Foreign Policy in Focus, April 2003); Richard Norton-Taylor and Ewen MacAskill, "3000 More UK Troops for Iraq," *The Guardian*, June 19, 2004, 1; Robin Wright and Bradley Graham, "US Works to Sustain Iraq Coalition," *Washington Post*, (15 July 2004), A1.

36. Wright and Graham, "US Works to Sustain Iraq Coalition," A1.
37. Koizumi is quoted in Cory Oldweiler, "Allied Farces," *American Prospect* (3 March 2003), 3.
38. See Fallows, "Blind Into Baghdad"; Ricks, "The Invasion of Iraq," http://www.pbs.org/wgbh/pages/frontline/shows/invasion/interviews/ricks.html
39. See Matthew Engel, "Scorned General's Tactics Proved Right," *The Guardian*, (29 March 2003), 1.
40. See Michael Gordon, "US Puts Off Cutting Troops in Iraq," *New York Times*, (29 March 2003, 1.
41. See Fallows, "Blind Into Baghdad."
42. Thomas White, "The Invasion of Iraq," http://www.pbs.org/wgbh/pages/frontline/shows/invasion/interviews/white.html
43. Polling data is revealed in Richard L. Berke and Janet Elder, "Poll: Americans Willing to Accept Casualties," *New York Times* (24 September 2001), 1.
44. Pew Center for the People and the Press, "Bush Engages and Persuades Public on Iraq," 19 September 2002: http://people-press.org/reports/display.php3?ReportID=161
45. David Johnston and David E. Sanger, "New Generation of Leaders is Emerging for Al Qaeda," *New York Times*, (10 August 2004), 1.
46. Charles Hagel, "History's Lessons," *The Washington Quarterly* 24, no. 2 (Spring 2001): 93.
47. Stanley Hoffmann, "America Goes Backward," *New York Review of Books* 50, no. 12 (12 June 2003).
48. See David Sanger, "Diplomacy Fails to Slow Advance of Nuclear Arms," *Washington Post*, (8 August 2004), 1.

Chapter 8

Proportionality

Minimizing Destruction

Once war is underway as a *jus in bello* principle, we are required to assess the moral costs of waging offensive warfare against the moral benefits. Within this context, proportionality deals mainly with total summation of good and evil associated with preemptive and preventive strategies and other tactical methods utilized during the fighting. In this chapter, we are concerned with making an effective assessment of the consequences and penalties resulting from the use of particular forms of violence. Our examination will focus on specific military targets, weapons, combatant casualties, and military and civilian decision-makers in order to determine the actual use of force is made in proportion to America's primary objectives of preventing future terrorist attacks, obviating the spread of WMD among rogue states, and overcoming challengers and rivals. In doing so, it is essential that we make a clear distinction between proportionality and the equally important just war principle of non-combatant immunity (discrimination), which holds that non-combatants cannot be targeted by military forces.

Key to understanding how proportionality applies to America's use of offensive military force in the wake of 9/11 is Article 51 ("Protection of the Civilian Population") of Protocol I of the Geneva Conventions of 12 August 1949 and the Protection of Victims of International Armed Conflict of 8 June 1977 forbids using indiscriminate weapons (see Figure 8.1). Provisions 5, 7, and 8 of Article 51 are most important.

Figure 8.1 Key Portions in Article 51 on Proportionality

Provision 5: Among others, the following types of attacks are to be considered as indiscriminate: (a) an attack by bombardment by any methods or means which treats as a single military objective a number of clearly separated and distinct military objectives located in a city, town, village or other area containing a similar concentration of civilians or civilian objects; and (b) an attack which may be expected to cause incidental loss of civilian life, injury to civilians, damage to civilian objects, or a combination thereof, which would be excessive in relation to the concrete and direct military advantage anticipated;

Provision 7: The presence or movements of the civilian population or individual civilians shall not be used to render certain points or areas immune from military operations, in particular in attempts to shield military objectives from attacks or to shield, favour or impede military operations. The Parties to the conflict shall not direct the movement of the civilian population or individual civilians in order to attempt to shield military objectives from attacks or to shield military operations;

Provision 8: Any violation of these prohibitions shall not release the Parties to the conflict from their legal obligations with respect to the civilian population and civilians, including the obligation to take the precautionary measures provided for in Article 57.[1]

Indiscriminate attacks are those conducted with inaccurate weapons in which there exists a great degree of difficulty when utilized by warring parties. Examples include biological and chemical weapons in which the spread of toxins cannot be controlled (See Figure 8.2). Currently, states with known chemical and biological weapons programs include: China, France, India, Israel, Libya, North Korea, Pakistan, Russia, Syria, United Kingdom, and the United States.[2]

Figure 8.2 Chemical and Biological Weapons/Agents

Lethal Chemical Agents:

Choking Agents:
1. Chlorine;
2. Phosgene.

Blister Agents:
1. Mustard gas;
2. Lewisite.

Nerve Agents:
1. Taubun;
2. Sarin;
3. Soman;
4. GF;
5. VX.

Lethal Biological Agents:

1. Anthrax;
2. Cholera;
3. Plague Bacteria;
4. Botulism;
5. Tularemia;
6. Smallpox;
7. Ricin;
8. Q Fever;
9. Stsphylococcal Enterotoxin;
10. Brucellosis;
11. Equine Encephalitis;
12. Tricothecene.

Also, consider the use of cluster bomb units (CBU), or bombs that dispense an array of submunitions. Although characterized as indiscriminate by many, the US position, one correct as a matter of law, is that because CBUs can, in many circumstances, be directed with great effectiveness against specific targets, they are not indiscriminate.[3] For instance, CBUs could be used discriminately against fielded forces located far from the civilian population, as in those deployed in a desert or mountainous region.[4] A second, very politically charged example is the use anti-personal mines.[5] The United States, again correctly, urges that a mine is not an indiscriminate weapon, for it could be used, as an example, in a marked area or designed so that it self-neutralizes after a set period. As with the CBUs, the issue is whether weapons are being used indiscriminately.

There are also several dilemmas we should address. First, the US military has made efforts to conduct warfare in a manner that minimizes casualties and obviates the need for fighting broader wars. Such an approach represents a military advantage for the US, particularly in an era of high technology warfare. It is this military advantage, combined with destruction or damage to the objective, which must be weighed against the damage and injury. War fighters have always sought to minimize casualties to their forces. The extent of casualties is simply one of several military advantage components weighed in the proportionality balancing.

Second, there is the dilemma of ripple effects. It has most frequently surfaced in the context of attacks on electrical grids serving both military and civilian facilities. Notable examples include the attacks on Iraqi and Yugoslavian targets during Operations Desert Storm and Allied Force. Should the adverse effects of an attack on a military target be considered when calculating proportionality? Yes, and this will be explored in the next chapter. Nowhere does the law distinguish between the direct and indirect, or short and long term, consequences of an attack. Yet, the more interconnected and interdependent societies become, the greater the ripple effects of many attacks. Despite this, collateral damage must be included in the proportionality calculation.

Another potential alteration in the proportionality equation could be caused by the decision by the Bush Administration to reverse the twenty-year trend of relegating nuclear weapons to the category of weapons of last resort.[6] In its 2002 *Nuclear Posture Review* (NPR), the US planned to restructure US nuclear policy against potential targets in Afghanistan, Iraq, Iran, North Korea, Syria, and Libya by adopting a strategy that combined the utilization of possible offensive nuclear strikes with defensive nuclear capabilities and new delivery systems.[7] Although the NPR stressed the need to develop earth-penetrating nuclear weapons, it also called for improving systems needed for nuclear strikes and argued that the US may resume nuclear testing.[8] The NPR states that such a policy alteration was designed to deter and prevent "an Iraqi attack on Israel or its neighbors, or a North Korean attack on South Korea or a military confrontation over the status of Taiwan."[9] States in current possession of nuclear weapons programs include: China, France, India, Israel, North Korea, Pakistan, Russia, United Kingdom, and United States.[10]

Moreover, the Bush Administration did not exclude the use of tactical nuclear weapons for penetrating caves or bunker-busting in Afghanistan and beyond.[11] Although is the US is prevented from designing new nuclear weapons with a yield below 5 kilotons, the Department of Energy has focused on modifying existing nuclear warheads, most likely the stockpile of roughly 1,200 operational B61 bombs.[12] The B61 operates much the same way as the conventional BLU-113, triggering an underground explosion and can be dropped as a free-fall airburst, a delayed airburst, a free-fall surface burst, or dropped from low-level aircraft. Tactical versions, with lower yield options, have been deployed on a variety of US and NATO aircraft, namely F-15E, F-16, and the F-117 stealth bomber; the strategic version can be delivered by B-52, FB-111, B-1, and B-2 bombers.[13] It was believed that the B61 would be considered if bin Laden was located in a deep cave and the only way to get him was with a small nuclear weapon designed for deep underground targets.[14]

Some might see the use of tactical nuclear weapons as a proportional response to the 9/11 attacks. However, it would have negative political ramifications for the overall mission in Afghanistan, American geo-strategic interests and intentions in Central Asia, legitimately claiming a case for just cause, building a positive American perception in the Muslim world, and for efforts on nuclear arms control and non-proliferation. Still, the Bush Administration hinted that tactical nuclear bunker busters could be a legitimate component in an offensive against terrorism, due to Al-Qaida's perceived WMD intentions. The State Department maintained,

> the possibility of terrorist attacks using chemical, biological, radiological, nuclear or large explosive weapons 'remains real.' Most terrorists continued to rely on conventional tactics, such as bombing, shooting, and kidnapping, but some terrorists – such as Osama bin Laden and his associates – continue to seek chemical, biological, radiological and nuclear capabilities.[15]

The alteration in nuclear policy brings up the question of whether or not the US was deliberately seeking to use disproportionate force. The Principle of Proportionality holds that the level of applied force must be proportional to a state's war objectives. Assessing proportionality is clearly a concept open to debate and suggestion. When considering the use of nuclear weapons, the debate becomes heated as such weapons may directly impact the Principle of Non-Combatant Immunity.

Target #1: Afghanistan

With the initiation of Operation Enduring Freedom on 7 October 2001, it became possible to perceive how specific military actions were conducted by assessing the value of the Taliban and Al-Qaida targets attacked by American and British military forces. Moreover, we are able to make particular assessments with a thorough examination of the weapons used against those targets. Land-based bombers either originated from air craft carriers in the Arabian sea or Persian Gulf, or were launched from land-bases in the US (for ex: US B-2 Stealth Bombers from Whitman Air Force Base in Missouri), Kuwait, and Uzbekistan. Precision weapons were also launched from submarines destroyers deployed in the Arabian Sea and Gulf of Oman. Air attacks by the US and UK were conducted with precision-guided air to ground missiles against Taliban military installations and civilian targets in which military equipment was emplaced and personnel encamped in and around Kabul, Kandahar, and Mazar-i-Sharif.

The aerial bombing campaign had been intensified during the second week of the operation as daily sorties rose from about roughly 20 to 90 after the Taliban proved more resilient than initially expected and the Northern Alliance had failed in its initial effort to take the strategic city of Mazar-i-Sharif. Specific military targets included, communications towers, the palace of Mullah Mohammed Omar, the ministries of Vice and Virtue and Interior, and Al-Qaida training camps. All of this was legitimately consistent with the goal of dividing and then overthrowing the Taliban. US air weaponry included but was not limited to 15,000 pound slurry bombs (the BLU-82 "Big Blue" or "daisy-cutters"), cluster bombers (CBU-87), and hard target penetrating 1,000 and 2,000 pound joint direct attack munitions (J-DAM: GBU-31 or GBU-32).[16]

America's use of cluster bombs drew sharp rebukes from human rights and de-mining groups. Cluster bombs had been used near civilian areas, leaving submunitions scattered among residences. Unexploded components were even discovered inside Pakistan, apparently the result of accidental bomb releases in Tora Bora. Also contributing to civilian concerns about cluster bombs was that their submunitions were the same color and approximate size of the humanitarian food packets being dropped by the US Air Force. Moreover, the difficulties of getting accurate figures of impact deaths from aerial bombing need not detract from attempting to carry out such a study.[17]

The use by the US Air Force of such weapons of enormous destructive capability brings up the discussion of whether or not the US was unnecessarily escalating the devastation caused by the bombing. On 31 October, B-52's began carpet-bombing the Bagram and Mazar-i-Sharif front-line areas.[18] According to one observer: "a B-52 bomber made its debut in the war, sending up a wall of orange flame and clouds of dust along Taliban positions overlooking opposition-held Bagram airbase north of Kabul."[19] On 4 November, the US stepped up its effort and began dropping BLU-82 bombs on Taliban positions in northern Afghanistan.[20] The bombs destroyed everything in a 600 yard radius, producing a mushroom cloud and a nerve-effect on the targeted troops. On 23 November, a third BLU-82 was dropped near Kandahar and, later, a fourth in the Tora Bora campaign. A nightmarish progression has quietly taken place:

> It's nightmarish to see that the US is slowly desensitizing the public to the level of destruction taking place in Afghanistan. They have progressed from medium-sized missiles to Tomahawk and cruise missiles, to bunker-busting 2,000 lb bombs, then to [B-52] carpet-bombing using cluster bombs, and now the devastating daisy cutter bombs that annihilate everything in a 600-meter radius.[21]

In addition to engaging in a massive bombing campaign, intelligence collection and analysis were among the most important weapons in the US arsenal. An effective intelligence process would be absolutely essential in the manhunt for capturing or killing Osama bin Laden and his comrades. While the US military was prepared to kill high-ranking Al-Qaida terrorists with its advanced weaponry, the US intelligence community, namely the Central Intelligence Agency, Defense Intelligence Agency, and the National Security Agency, had to track his movements. Both technical intelligence (e.g. satellites, unmanned aerial vehicles) and human intelligence could be useful to locate bin Laden or elements of his network. Human intelligence was required to confirm identities of people or targets located by aerial technical intelligence gathering. Human intelligence was also needed to understand changing political conditions in Afghanistan and the entire Central Asian region.

The US and the Northern Alliance

A significant shift in the war effort was the Bush Administration's decision to quickly link up US ground force and other ground force with the Northern Alliance military effort. This gained substance during the last week of October 2001 when US B-52 bombers began a pulverizing carpet-bombing campaign against Taliban military positions opposite the Northern Alliance and when US Special Operations soldiers and military intelligence officers assumed a larger role in guiding both the air attacks and the alliance's efforts. Throughout the first ten days of November US air and ground support for the Northern Alliance grew in proportion with criticism of the war's slow progress and news of mounting civilian costs.[22]

America's new strategy of open support for the Northern Alliance was a decision made after weeks of alliance pressure on the Bush Administration and demands an investigation of whether or not force was applied in terms of proportionality. The alliance had criticized initial US air strikes for not bombing the Taliban frontline where most of the ruling movement's soldiers were now dug in after leaving the cities. The complaint came amid reports that opposition fighters have suffered a big setback in their attempt to capture the strategic northern city of Mazar-i-Sharif from the Taliban. [23]

Before the link up with the alliance, US planes had been making episodic attacks on the front north of Kabul but not the massive raids opening the road to the Afghan capital the Northern Alliance had hoped for. The alliance had not launched any ground attacks or even brought up reinforcements. The only alliance offensive that was underway was its push towards Mazar-i-Sharif, the largest city in northern Afghanistan. But the attack initially faltered after heavy Taliban resistance.[24] By 1 November 2001, the US bombing has clearly had an impact on the Taliban, but did not transform the military balance in Afghanistan. The Northern Alliance was still greatly outnumbered and unwilling to commit its small forces until the US has softened up its enemy.

It should be reiterated that the move by the US to throw its strategic military effort behind the Northern Alliance had the potential of incurring significant costs in terms of command and control. The contradiction inherent in fully supporting the Northern Alliance military effort was two-fold: first, as detailed in previous chapters, Northern Alliance Alliance's goals – beyond defeating the Taliban – were not the same as America's; and second, American influence over the Northern Alliance would likely decrease as its troops closed in Kabul, which was made possible by devastating US power.[25] In other words, fully supporting the Alliance meant losing a measure of control over it.

Despite the decision, the combination of US air power, American Special Forces, and Northern Alliance troops quickly produced one of the most significant victories when on 8 November, Taliban forces were ejected from the strategic city of Mazar-i-Sharif.[26] The victory set the stage for a de facto partition of

Afghanistan into a northern arc controlled by the US/anti-Taliban alliance and a southern rump controlled by the Taliban. The newly won territory offered a tremendous opportunity for the US to intensify its campaign all over Afghanistan. The Pentagon's first priority may be to establish new air bases inside this zone, which can be used not only to re-supply the Alliance and any expanded US troop presence, but also to further intensify up the air war. Before the fall of Mazar-i-Sharif, US bombers fad to fly over Pakistan from carriers in the Arabian sea or other land-bases in Central Asia, mostly from Uzbekistan, a distance that had limited sorties and necessitated by the heavier fuel load.[27] Basing the same fighters at bases around Mazar would allow them to fly three sorties a day and carry a heavier payload to the Taliban frontlines.[28]

Interestingly, while the bombing clearly played a vital role in enabling the Alliance victory, there may have been other factors weighing on the Taliban's decision to retreat. Many of the Taliban's fighters were reportedly not Afghan, but Pakistani, Chechen, and Arab. That, and the history of bloody massacres each time Mazar-i-Sharif changed hands precluded the possibility of surrender, and the overwhelming hostility of the local population to the Taliban left them little chance of victory.

Taliban lines north of Kabul broke in the afternoon of 12 November following repeated air strikes by US Air Force B-52H Stratofortress strategic bombers throughout the morning, combined with a two hour-long artillery barrage from Northern Alliance forces and small arms exchanges between US Special Forces and Taliban militias. By that time, armored Northern Alliance under the protection of US bombers advanced south along the Old Road as lines of infantry units swept through Taliban positions. However, by that time Taliban forces appeared to be pulling back in something close to a rout leaving behind their fatalities and large quantities of equipment. By nightfall, several thousand Northern Alliance troops advancing across the Shomali Plain had reached Qarabagh. The first hours of daylight revealed a power-vacuum in the city. In some quarters looting broke out immediately, while in others armed groups sympathetic to Northern Alliance forces, using arms that had earlier been hidden, moved in to take control. A small number of Pakistanis and Arabs who had failed to escape during the night were hunted down and killed. By the evening of 13 November, 6,000 Northern Alliance fighters marched into Kabul virtually unopposed.[29]

But the fighting did not stop there. On 24 November roughly 600 Taliban soldiers who had fled the US bombing of Kunduz, the last Taliban stronghold in the north of Afghanistan, laid down their weapons in the desert a few miles to the north of Mazar-i-Sharif. The Taliban fighters, many of whom were foreigners, were transported to a fortress in Qala-i-Jangi, a sprawling prison to the west of Mazar. The next morning, two Americans, among them CIA officer Johnny "Mike" Spann, went to meet the prisoners at Qala-i-Jangi to identify any potential Al-Qaida fighters among the prisoners. According to a German television crew who were later trapped in the fort with Dave, several fighters attack Spann and grabbed rifles from Northern Alliance guards and opened fire. He was the first American to die in combat in Afghanistan.[30] A few hundred yards to the south, in the prison block, the Taliban freed its comrades. The Taliban fighters, trapped in the southwestern quarter of the fort, stormed a nearby armory, making off with small arms, mines, rocket launchers, mortars and ammunition.

On 26 November, US Special Forces and CIA officers convened with Northern Alliance leaders and agreed to an air assault on the fortress with JDAM missiles guided by satellite communications. If properly placed, the entire prison revolt would be ended. Although the first missile struck the northern wall of the fortress, another slammed into an area of densely concentrated US Special Forces and Northern Alliance troops, killing three Americans and thirty alliance soldiers. Following the deadly friendly-fire incident, a US AC-130 gunship attacked the fortress with a stream of ammunition. Later a massive ball of flame lifted up from the fort and explosions sounded through the night. The massive blast could even be felt 10 miles away. By 27 November, surviving Taliban troops surrendered; of the original 600 prisoners, 50 survivors were accounted for.[31]

The attack on the fortress in Qala-i-Jangi was overwhelmingly violent, deadly, but a necessary and proportional attack on Taliban and suspected Al-Qaida fighters. In fact, it was a key exercise in the overall campaign of "decisive warfare" meant to overthrow the Taliban regime and to reduce the number of Al-Qaida terrorists in Afghanistan. Anything less would conform to Bush's determination to not just "pound sand."[32] Operation Enduring Freedom required overwhelming air power and the deployment of special operating ground forces and US intelligence personnel to aid the Northern Alliance.

Targeting bin Laden

What sort of force would be considered proportional to capture Osama bin Laden, who along with his closest associates was determined to elude American forces? In the last public speech given at a center for Islamic studies in Jalalabad on 10 November 2001, bin Laden painted the battle lines black and white: "The Americans had a plan to invade, but if we are united and believe in Allah, we'll teach them a lesson, the same one we taught the Russians."[33] With that speech, bin Laden was laying his plans to stay a step ahead of the US campaign. This led him to his favored fortified and mountainous region of Tora Bora, as the US expected.

Until the fall of Kabul on 13 November, the US-led war in Afghanistan was going well as the Taliban had been pushed from the northern half of the country and Kabul. It was a war like no other. In an evolutionary leap powered by technology, US ground soldiers were mainly employed as observers, liaisons, and spotters for air power, not as direct combatants. The success of US Special Forces was quite dazzling, except at Tora Bora, which may have been this unconventional Operation Enduring Freedom's most important battle. What was to come at Tora Bora was not about raiding caves or destroying fortifications, it was about seizing the world's most wanted terrorist "dead or alive."[34]

On 16 November, three days after Al-Qaida and Taliban forces fled the capital to the mountains, US air assaults intensified to keep bin Laden on the run. It was at this very moment, in retrospect, that the story of Operation Enduring Freedom would illustrate how poor intelligence, questionable allies, and a hastily applied and potentially disproportionate use of military force would foil a golden opportunity to capture or bin Laden and other senior Al-Qaida leaders at Tora Bora. As the US intensified its air strikes on Tora Bora, US helicopters began relieving Afghani fighters who had cornered bin Laden. Also as was its pattern elsewhere in Afghanistan, the US began enlisting the support of local warlords, namely Hazret Ali and Haji Zaman Ghamsharik who would become in the battle for Tora Bora and for capturing bin Laden. Both Ali and Ghamsharik were contacted by US intelligence officials in mid-November and asked to take part in an attack on the Tora Bora stronghold. As an anti-Taliban fighter allied to former Northern Alliance commander Ahmed Shah Masood, who was assassinated just two days before 9/11, Ali and his band of fighters fought against the Taliban in the north for six years. The US chose the powerful regional warlord Ghamsharik as a counterbalance to Ali. Known primarily for his participation in the trafficking of opium and regional smuggling, Ghamsharik was installed by the US as the Jalalabad commander of the Eastern Shura.[35]

US intelligence officials have assembled what they believe to be decisive evidence, from contemporary and subsequent interrogations and intercepted communications that bin Laden began the battle of Tora Bora inside a sophisticated cave complex.[36] Though there remains a remote chance that he died there, the intelligence community is persuaded that bin Laden slipped away sometime in the first tens days of the battle. A common view among those outside the US Central Command is that General Tommy Franks, the war's operational commander, misjudged the interests of putative Afghan allies, failed to adequately use available force, and let pass the best chance to capture or kill Al-Qaida's leader.

The cold, hard lesson of Tora Bora was: know which local leaders to trust; know how much force needs to be applied; and know when to go alone. In the fight for Tora Bora, corrupt local militias, led mainly by Ali and Ghamsharik, did not make an attempt to close off mountain escapes and some conspired to aid Al-Qaida fighters. Franks did not perceive the setbacks soon enough, because he ran the war from Tampa, Florida with no commander in Afghanistan above the rank of lieutenant colonel and the first American Special Forces units did not arrive until three days into the fighting.

The Bush Administration has never acknowledged that bin Laden slipped through the cordon placed around Tora Bora as US aircraft began bombing on 30 November.[37] The government of President Pervez Musharraf moved thousands of troops to his border with Afghanistan and captured roughly 400 of the estimated 1,000 Al-Qaida fighters who escaped from Tora Bora.[38] Roughly half of those are now detainees being held at the US base at Guantanamo Bay, Cuba, were turned over by the Pakistani government. Those successes included none of the top Al-Qaida leaders at Tora Bora. Of the dozen senior leaders identified by the US, two are now accounted for; Muhammad Atef, believed dead in a US air strike outside Kabul and Abu Zubayda, taken into US custody in late November 2001.

One view is that bin Laden is alive; however, the possibility cannot be ruled out that he died at Tora Bora or in subsequent raids or air strikes. Some believe bin Laden is suffering from Marfan syndrome, a congenital disorder that puts him at increased risk of heart attack or stroke and placed him in close proximity to his chief adviser and physician Ayman Zawahiri.[39] Those who believe bin Laden is dead note that years have passed since any credible trace of him has surfaced in intelligence collection. Those who argue that he is probably alive note that monitoring bin Laden's contacts has turned up no evidence of reaction to his death. If he is indeed dead, surely there would be some available information.[40]

In public, the Bush Administration acknowledged no regret about its prosecution of Tora Bora. However, some policymakers and operational officers were quite frustrated with the administration. According to anonymous counter-terrorism officials, "We [messed] up by not getting into Tora Bora sooner and letting the Afghans do all the work. Clearly a decision point came when we started bombing Tora Bora and we decided just to bomb, because that is when he escaped... We didn't put US forces on the ground, despite all the brave talk, and that is what we have had to change since then."[41] In subsequent battles at Shahikot in early March 2002, known as Operation Anaconda, President Bush stopped proclaiming the goal of taking bin Laden "dead or alive" and avoided referring to him as public enemy number one.[42]

In the end, most Al-Qaida associates were able to escape from Afghanistan because of a series of avoidable strategic blunders by US intelligence officials and US and Pakistani military commanders.[43] Of the 3,000 to 4,000 foreign militants trapped in Afghanistan after the collapse of the Taliban, most got away. Several high-profile military operations to capture them most notably last December in the mountainous region of Tora Bora failed because Britain and the US sent in too few troops of their own. Overall, US commanders placed too much confidence in unreliable local anti-Taliban warlords who had other interests in mind.[44]

Despite the failed attempt to capture or kill bin Laden at Tora Bora, the analysis here reveals that the intensity of the air attacks and ground assaults throughout the campaign was quite high and the elimination of particular targets contributed to America's goal of displacing the Taliban from governing power in Kabul and to disrupt Al-Qaida operations. As a result, proportionality appears to have been met, as such devastating force was required if the US was really serious about breaking apart the deeply entrenched positions of Taliban military forces and pave an open road to Kabul for the combined Northern Alliance and US ground forces. Degrading the Taliban's military capabilities and destroying Al-Qaida terrorist training camps could not have been possible, most likely, with simply employing surgical or limited air strikes against particular targets.

Target #2: Iraq

On the whole, US-led coalition forces took precautions to spare civilians and, for the most part, made efforts to uphold their legal obligations. According to

President Bush's National Security Council director of Near East Affair Eliot Abrams, the US-led invasion of Iraq fits the definition of "a proportional use of force." He claimed, "We don't want to destroy the infrastructure (schools, hospitals, historic and religious sites), and not because we don't want to pay to rebuild them."[45] In this section, we will examine the period between the commencement of Operation Iraqi Freedom on 19 March and the termination of major hostilities on 2 May 2003, the day on which, President Bush, standing on the deck of the USS Abraham Lincoln and against the backdrop of a banner proclaiming "Mission Accomplished," declared an end to major combat in Iraq. According to the Project for Defense Alternatives roughly 7,800 to 10,700 military combatants died.[46]

Total Force Applied

According to Human Rights Watch (HRW), US Central Command (CENTCOM) reported that US military forces used roughly 110,000 cluster bombs containing some 1.8 million submunitions. In addition, the British military used air-launched and 2,100 ground-launched cluster bombs, containing roughly 114,000 submunitions. An undisclosed number of BLU-82 bunker penetrating bombs and hard target penetrating 1,000 and 2,000 pound joint direct attack munitions were also employed (J-DAM: GBU-31 or GBU-32).[47]

The most intense application of force by US ground units came in the form of artillery.[48] The 3rd Infantry and 101st Airborne divisions fired more than 17,500 shells, roughly 1000 Multiple Launch Rocket System (MLRS) rockets, and almost 400 Army Tactical Missiles. The Marine Corps believes it fired an additional 20,000 artillery shells.[49] The total amount of artillery was estimated to have caused between 1,500 and 3,000 combatant fatalities.[50]

American and British aircraft also conducted roughly 20,700 sorties and struck more than 19,000 targets. Roughly 29,900 munitions were delivered, of which 68 per cent were precision guided weapons.[51] However, the bombing intensity was quite low; in fact, more sorties were flown and more targets were struck in the 1991 air campaign against targets in Iraq and Kuwait. Since Republican Guard divisions did not easily relent, the US launched cruise missile strikes and B-52 attacks with unguided bombs and other precision weapons.

Most of the total air and ground force applied concentrated on the Special Republican Guard, Republican Guard units, and the Fedayeen Saddam ("Saddam's men of sacrifice") militia units comprising a total of 120,000 Iraqi troops and paramilitaries.[52] The Iraqi high command, however, did not deploy its defensive forces in preparation for the invasion until February 2003.[53] Once the ground invasion began, air and ground attacks on Iraqi ground units rapidly intensified.

Emerging High Value Targets

Emerging targets develop as a war progresses instead of being planned prior to the initiation of hostilities. They include fleeting, time-sensitive targets (TST), such as leadership targets, senior military officers operating in the field, mobile targets, and other targets of opportunity.[54] An unclassified Air Force report issued in April 2003 categorized fifty attacks from 19 March to 18 April as having been time-sensitive strikes on high value emerging targets that included Iraqi political and military leaders.[55]

Designed to intimidate the Iraqi leadership, the strikes used precision-guided weapons against the fifty-five most senior Iraqi's, a group known as the "black list." According to former Defense Intelligence Agency (DIA) targeting analyst Marc Garlasco, "The thought is that if we attack and kill some of the folks on the top fifty-five list the war is going to be shortened or stopped altogether."[56] Among the most sought after targets were Saddam Hussein, his second in command General Izzat Ibrahim, Saddam's sons Uday and Qusay, former head of the Directorate of General Security Major General Rafi Abd al-Latif Tilfah, Sadaam's senior bodyguard and personal secretary General Abid Hamid Mahmud, senior adviser and Sadaam's half brother Watban Ibrahim Barzan, and General Ali Hasan al-Majid (Chemical Ali) who was known for his role in carrying out chemical attacks against Iranians and Kurds in 1988. In order to eliminate these targets, the US would have to launch air strikes in densely populated neighborhoods.

In Iraq, only four of the fifty air strikes against emerging high value targets have been described in public. All were unsuccessful, and many, including the raids on Saddam and his sons, were undercut by poor intelligence. It is believed that Ibrahim and Tilfah, who were reportedly targeted in several of the high value targets, have successfully eluded capture and are playing leadership roles in the anti-American insurgency. The poor record in the strikes raised questions about the intelligence they were based on, including whether that intelligence reflected deception on the part of Iraqis.

The most significant amount of force that was applied at any one time to a high value target during major combat was the US "decapitation" strike on 19 March that was intended to kill Saddam at the al-Dura compound (Dora Farms) near Baghdad. This was a major gamble, given that the decision was suggested by CIA Director George Tenet who was provided a tip from an Iraqi source on the ground that Saddam and his sons were in a suspected underground bunker at the site.[57] The Dora Farms strike would also prompt President Bush to accelerate the timetable for the beginning of the war, which was scheduled to commence on 21 March. However, the intelligence community placed significance confidence in the source. According to Garlasco, "we were told that the CIA source was beyond reproach and that sometimes you have to take that at face value."[58]

Strictly in terms of the force that would be used, the Dora Farms strike was actually the largest assassination attempt in history. The strike included four 2,000-pound satellite-guided bunker penetrating GBU bombs dropped by two F-117A stealth aircraft, followed moments later by forty cruise missiles. George Tenet was certain Saddam had been killed in the raid, citing a report relayed by satellite phone to CIA headquarters by the Iraqi source at the scene.[59] Garlasco states, "There was a belief at the highest levels of the Pentagon and White House that we had successfully killed Saddam. We got him that is it. War is over."[60]

The strike, however, was a complete failure. Since his capture by US forces on 13 December, Saddam has not answered whether or not even was even at Dora Farms. Put simply, the source of the information at Dora Farms proved to be unreliable. US Air Force Lieutenant Colonel David Toomey even claimed, "we did not know who it was."[61] In describing the failure at Dora Farms, Garlasco explained, "What happened? I am as puzzled as you are."[62] He claimed that the strategy against the Iraqi leadership after Dora Farms became "the war is on, you have got to hit you're your best stuff. And here is the best list that we have got, so were going to go town on it."[63]

The US Air Force made another attempt to kill Saddam and his sons at Al-Mansur in Baghdad. On 7 April a US Air Force B-1B aircraft dropped four 2,000-pound satellite-guided JDAM bombs on a house where it thought they were located.[64] The information was reportedly based on a communications intercept of a Thuraya satellite phone. However, Saddam and his sons were not present at the time of the strike.[65]

Another highly publicized strike came on 5 April at al-Tuwaisi in Basra against General Ali Hasan al-Majid (Chemical Ali), who was widely know for his utilization of chemical weapons against the Kurds in the Anfal genocide of 1988. Immediately following the strikes, top American officials expressed confidence that the strikes had been successful.[66] On 7 April, Defense Secretary Rumsfeld declared, "We believe that the reign of terror of Chemical Ali has come to an end." However, General Majid survived that raid and others, and was not captured until August 2003.[67]

Although the US eventually assumed custody of or killed forty-three of the top fifty-five targeted Iraqi leaders, none were eliminated in the high value air strikes.[68] General Majid was not captured until August 2003 and Saddam until 13 December. His sons, Uday and Qusay, remained at large until they were killed on 22 July. Several observers have even gone so far as to suggest that Ibrahim and Tilfah have assumed the leadership of the anti-American insurgency following the capture of Saddam.

In an August 2003 report, the US Air Force criticized its own use of time-sensitive attacks against emerging leadership targets. The report found that a "single authoritative TST process doctrine does not exist" and that "[t]here is no mechanism to measure performance of TST processes."[69] It called on the Air Force to: "develop meaningful metrics to assess the performance of the TST processes, and develop procedures to measure TST process performance during combat operations," and "study the relationship between TST doctrine and TST technology to determine the extent to which technology drives TST doctrine.[70] In Iraq, the Air Force acknowledged that technology should not be the driving factor behind the air strikes against emerging high value targets; just because a capability exists does not mean it should be used. It also recognized that the targeting process required an ability to measure effectiveness. In retrospect, the failures indicated significant shortcomings in US intelligence on targets in Iraq and on Saddam's inner circle. According to one senior military commander, "It was all just guesswork on where they were."[71]

Dependence on Technology

The United States identified and targeted the Iraqi leadership based on GPS coordinates derived from intercepts of Thuraya satellite phones.[72] Thuraya satellite phones were used throughout the Iraq campaign. They have an internal GPS chip that enabled American intelligence to track the phones. The phone coordinates were used as the locations for attacks on Iraqi leadership. However, targeting based on satellite phone-derived geo-coordinates turned a precision weapon into a potentially indiscriminate weapon, since the Thuraya global positioning system is accurate only within a one-hundred-meter radius. Thus, the United States could not determine from where a call was originating to a degree of accuracy greater than one-hundred meters radius; a caller could have been anywhere within a 31,400-square-meter area.[73] This begs the question, how does CENTCOM know where to direct the strike if the target area is so large? In essence, imprecise target coordinates were used to program precision-guided munitions.

However, in attacking leadership targets in Iraq, the United States used an unsound targeting methodology largely reliant on imprecise coordinates obtained from satellite phones. Leadership targeting was consistently based on unreliable intelligence. It is also likely that Iraqi leaders engaged in successful deception techniques. This combination of factors led directly to dozens of civilian casualties. The fascination with the ability to track targets via satellite phone and the inadequacies of the battle damage assessment process contributed to the failure of leadership targeting. Furthermore, it is not clear how CENTCOM connected a specific phone to a specific user; phones were being tracked, not individuals. It is plausible that CENTCOM developed a database of voices that could be computer matched to a phone user.[74]

The Iraqis may have even employed deception techniques to thwart the Americans. CENTCOM was so concerned about the possibility of the Iraqis turning the Thuraya intercept capability against US forces that it ordered its troops to discontinue using Thuraya phones in early April 2003. It announced, "Recent intelligence reporting indicates Thuraya satellite phone services may have been compromised. For this reason, Thuraya phone use has been discontinued on the battlefields of Iraq. The phones now represent a security risk to units and personnel on the battlefield."[75] It is highly likely the Iraqi leaders assumed that the United States was attempting to track them through the Thuraya phones and therefore possible that they were spoofing American intelligence.

The US undoubtedly attempted to use corroborating sources for satellite phone coordinates. Based on the results, however, accurate corroborating information must have been difficult if not impossible to come by and additional methods of tracking the Iraqi leadership just as unreliable as satellite phones. Satellite imagery and signals intelligence (communications intercepts) apparently yielded little to no useful information in terms of targeting leadership. Detection of conventional movements, namely by automobiles at key targets, was far from significant. Human sources of information were likely the main means of corroborating the satellite phone information in tracking the Iraqi leadership. Although human intelligence sources were used, for example, to verify the Thuraya data acquired in the attack on Saddam and his sons at al-Mansur, they were wrong.[76]

Without reliable human intelligence to identify the location of the Iraqi leadership, it seems as though the US relied on highly inaccurate information with no guarantee of the identity of the user. Leadership targets developed by inaccurate data should have never been attacked. Given the occurrence of non-combatants casualties, air assaults on high value targets most likely should have been abandoned until the intelligence and targeting failures were addressed.

Proportional Action and Discrimination

In a war between legitimate combatants, the utilization of proportionate military force can only be understood in a descriptive sense, since combatants are allowed to overwhelm their enemies in order to attain victory. If combatants use means that deliberately harm non-combatants, they fail the moral requirement of Non-Combatant Immunity or Discrimination, not proportionality. Note that this conception of proportionality coincides well with our considered judgments about just war and the purpose of the laws of war. Proportionality permits us to perceive our use of force not as a tradeoff of good for evil, but the inherent evil in some actions.

As will be discussed in the next chapter, although more care is taken to limit civilian casualties, there remains a growing inability to distinguish between combatants and non-combatants. One difficulty is that given the increase in surveillance and reconnaissance capabilities employed by cryptologists at the National Security Agency and officials at the National Reconnaissance Office, as well as other advances that render the battle space increasingly transparent, combatants have strong incentives conceal their identities. But on the whole, precision-guided weapons make it easier to surgically strike targets and use less explosive force to destroy a target. Technology has the potential of maximizing the positive effect of proportionality, although without completely eliminating errors.

Notes

1. See the United Nations Office of the High Commissioner for Human Rights (UNHCR), "Protocol Additional to Geneva Conventions of 12 August 1949, and Relating to the Protection of Victims of Non-International Armed Conflicts (Protocol 1): Geneva, 8 June 1977," Article 51: http://www.unhchr.ch/html/menu3/b/93.htm
2. Joseph S. Bermudez, Jr., *The Deterrence Series, Case Study 5: North Korea*, (Alexandria, VA: Chemical and Biological Arms Control Institute, 1998), 5; Avner Cohen, "Israel and Chemical/Biological Weapons: History, Deterrence, and Arms Control," *Nonproliferation Review*, Vol. 8, No. 3 (Fall-Winter), 27-53; Anthony

Cordesman, "Weapons of Mass Destruction in the Middle East: Regional Trends, National Forces, (4 October 1999), "Warfighting Capabilities, Delivery Options, and Weapons Effects,14, http://www.csis.org/mideast/reports/WMDinMETrends.pdf; M. Zuhair Diab, "Syria's Chemical and Biological Weapons: Assessing Capabilities and Motivations," *Nonproliferation Review*, 5, (Fall, 1997), 104-111; Clifford Krauss, "U.S. Urges Russia To End Production of Nerve Gas," *New York Times*, (6 February 1997; Russian Federation Foreign Intelligence Service, *A New Challenge After the Cold War: Proliferation of Weapons of Mass Destruction*, 1993, 100; U.S. Department of Defense, "Proliferation: Threat and Response 2001," http://www.defenselink.mil/pubs/ptr20010110.pdf, 14; Frank Von Hippel, "Russian whistleblower faces jail," *The Bulletin of Atomic Scientists*, 49, (March, 1993), http://www.bullatomsci.org/issues/1993/m93/m93vonhippel.html.

3. Eric Prokosch, *The Technology of Killing: A Military and Political History of Cluster Weapons*. (London: Zed Books, 1995).

4. Virgil Wiebe and Titus Peachey, "War's Insidious Litter: Cluster Bombs," *Christian Science Monitor*, (9 June 1999).

5. Bryan McDonald, Richard Anthony Matthew and Kenneth R. Rutherford, *Landmines and Human Security: International Politics and War's Hidden Legacy*, (Albany, NY: SUNY Press, 2004).

6. Michael R. Gordon, "US Nuclear Plan Sees New Weapons and New Targets," *New York Times*, (10 March 2002), 22; Paul Richter, "U.S. Works Up Plan for Using Nuclear Arms," *Los Angeles Times*, (9 March 2002).

7. Philipp C. Bleek, "Report Says U.S. Studying New Nuclear Capabilities," *Arms Control Today*, January/February 2002; Philipp C. Bleek, "Energy Department to Study Modifying Nuclear Weapons," *Arms Control Today*, April 2002; "United States: What's New?: The Nuclear Posture Review," *The Economist*, (16 March 2002), 35; Keith B. Payne, *The Fallacies of Cold War Deterrence and a New Direction* (Lexington, Kentucky: The University of Kentucky Press, 2001); James M. Smith, *Nuclear Deterrence and Defense: Strategic Considerations* (Colorado: U.S. Air Force Institute for National Security Studies Book Series, February 2001).

8. John H. Kushman, "Rattling New Sabers," *New York Times*, (10 March 2002), 23.

9. US Department of Defense, "Nuclear Posture Review [Excerpts]," January 8, 2002: http://www.globalsecurity.org/wmd/library/policy/dod/npr.htm; For more on policy reversal with the NPR, see: Gordon, "US Nuclear Plan Sees New Weapons and New Targets," 22; Walter Pincus, "US Nuclear Arms Stance Modified by Policy Study," *Washington Post*, (23 March 2002), 1; and Richter, "U.S. Works Up Plan for Using Nuclear Arms."

10. Avner Cohen, *Israel and the Bomb* (New York: Columbia University Press, 1998); Siegfried S. Hecker, Los Alamos National Laboratory, "Visit to the Yongbyon Nuclear Scientific Research Center in North Korea," Testimony before the Senate Foreign Relations Committee, (21 January 2004: http://www.fas.org/irp/congress/2004_hr/012104hecker.pdf; "French and British Nuclear Forces, 2000," *Bulletin of Atomic Scientists*, Vol. 56, No. 5, September/October 2000: http://www.bullatomsci.org/issues/nukenotes/so00nukenote.html; Andrew Koch and Jennifer Topping, "Pakistan's Nuclear Weapons Program: A Status Report," *Non Proliferation Review*, Vol. 4, No. 3, Spring/Summer 1997; Larry A. Nikisch,

"North Korea's Nuclear Weapons Program," *Congressional Research Service Issue Brief*, August 27, 2003: http://fas.org/spp/starwars/crs/IB91141.pdf; George Perkovich, *India's Nuclear Bomb* (Berkley: University of California Press, 2001); "Russian Nuclear Forces, 2000," *Bulletin of Atomic Scientists*, Vol. 56, No 4, July/August 2000:
http://www.bullatomsci.org/issues/nukenotes/ja00nukenote.html; "US Nuclear
"Forces, 2000," *Bulletin of Atomic Scientists*, Vol. 56, No. 3, May/June 2000: http://www.bullatomsci.org/issues/nukenotes/mj00nukenote.html

11. Nicholas Kralev, "U.S. Drops Pledge on Nukes; Won't Rule out Hitting Any States," *The Washington Times*, February 22, 2002; Paul Richter, "U.S. Works Up Plan for Using Nuclear Arms" *Los Angeles Times*, (9 March 2002), 1.

12. Robert Nelson, "Low-Yield Earth Penetrating Nuclear Weapons," *Journal of the Federation of American Scientists*, January/February, 2002; Stephen Younger,, (7 June 2000), "Nuclear Weapons in the Twenty-First Century," *Los Alamos National Laboratory*.

13. The full report and analysis of the B61 can be found at "The B61 Family of Bombs," *Bulletin of Atomic Scientists*, vol. 59, no. 1, January/February 2003, 74-76.

14. "Time to Use the Nuclear Option," *Washington Times*, September 14, 2001, 1.

15. Bill Gertz, "Bin Laden cohorts said in arms quest," *Washington Times*, (15 September 2001), 2.

16. See the weapons systems section of the website of the Federation of American Scientists: http://www.fas.org/man/dod-101/sys/index.html (accessed August 23, 2004). The CBU-87 is a 1,000-pound, Combined Effects Munition (CEM) for attacking soft target areas with detonating bomblets. The CBU-87 CEM, an all-purpose, air-delivered cluster weapons system, consists of a SW-65 Tactical Munitions Dispenser (TMD) with an optional FZU-39 proximity sensor. The bomblet case is made of scored steel designed to break into approximately 300 preformed ingrain fragments for defeating light armor and personnel. A total of 202 of these bomblets are loaded in each dispenser enabling a single payload attack against a variety and wide area coverage. The BLU-82B/C-130 weapon system, nicknamed Commando Vault in Vietnam and Daisy Cutter in Afghanistan, is a high altitude delivery of 15,000 pound conventional bomb, delivered from an MC-130 since it is far too heavy for the bomb racks on any bomber or attack aircraft. Originally designed to create an instant clearing in the jungle, it has been used in Afghanistan as an anti-personnel weapon and as an intimidation weapon because of its very large lethal radius (variously reported as 300-900 feet) combined with flash and sound visible at long distances. It is the largest conventional bomb in existence but is less than one thousandth the power of the atomic weapon detonated over Hiroshima in August 1945. The J-DAM or GBU-31 weapon is intended to be a high accuracy, all-weather, autonomous, conventional weapons upgraded from the existing US arsenal of penetrator bombs. The J-DAM can be launched from approximately 15 miles from a potential.

17. Laura King, "In Bomb Battered Afghanistan, An Accurate Account Nearly Impossible to Come By," *AP World Stream*, (19 October 2001).

18. Richard Norton-Taylor, "The Return of the B-52's," *The Guardian*, November 2, 2001, 1.

19. "US Carpet Bombs Kabul, 13 Killed in Kandahar," *Dawn*, (1 November 2001).

20. Richard Norton-Taylor, "Taliban Hit By Bombs Used in Vietnam," *The Guardian*, (7 November 2001),1.
21. "The Evils of Bombing," *The Guardian*, (8 November 2001).
22. Christian Caryl and John Barry, "Facing a long, cold war; The White House is casting its lot with the Northern Alliance," *Newsweek*, (12 November 2001); Patrick Cockburn, "Opposition Force Demands Stepping up of Air Strikes," *The Independent*, (26 October 2001), 4; ; Michael R. Gordon, "U.S. Adjusts Battle Plans as Strategy Goes Awry," *New York Times*, (9 November 2001); David Rohde, "Rebel Alliance Is Frustrated By U.S. Raids," *New York Times*, (29 October 2001), 1; Alan Sipress and Vernon Loeb, "US Uncouples Military, Political Efforts. Officials decide to step up bombing without a postwar government arranged," *Washington Post*, (1 November 2001).
23. Rohde, "Rebel Alliance Is Frustrated By U.S. Raids," 1.
24. Patrick Cockburn, "Northern Alliance Assails US Bombing Strategy," *The Independent*, (26 October 2001), 1.
25. Norimitsu Onishi, "Afghan Warlords and Bandits Are Back in Business," *New York Times*, (28 December 2001), 1; Catherine Philp, "Lawless tribes vie for abandoned territory," *The Times* (London), (29 November 2001); Paul Watson, "Rivalries and Lawlessness Thwart Efforts to Deliver Aid to Afghans," *Los Angeles Times*, (5 December 2001), 3.
26. Michael R. Gordon, "A Month in a Difficult Battlefield: Assessing U.S. War Strategy," *New York Times*, (8 November 2001); Steve Kosiak, *Estimated Cost of Operation Enduring Freedom: The First Two Months*, CSBA Backgrounder (Washington DC: Center for Strategic and Budgetary Assessments, 7 December 2001): http://www.csbaonline.org
27. Thomas E. Ricks and Susan Glaser, "US Operated Secret Alliance with Uzbekistan," *Washington Post*, (14 October 2001),1
28. Tony Karon, "Rebels: Mazar-i-Sharif is Ours," *Time*, (9 November 2001), 23.
29. Anthony Davis, "Fall of Kabul," *Jane's Defence Weekly*, (13 November 2001); Scott Peterson, "Despite US, Rebels Approach Kabul," *Christian Science Monitor*, (13 November 2001); John Simpson, "Eyewitness: the Liberation of Kabul," *The Guardian*, (13 November 2001), 1.
30. Alex Perry, "Inside the Battle at Qala-I-Jangi," *Time*, December 1, 2001, 14.
31. "Taliban Prison Revolt Over," *The Guardian*, (27 November 2001), 1.
32. Bob Woodward and Dan Balz, "We Will Rally the World," *Washington Post*, (28 January 2002), 1.
33. Quote is found in Philip Smucker, "How bin Laden Got Away," *Christian Science Monitor*, (4 March 2002), 3.
34. Charles Babington, "'Dead or Alive': Bush Unveils Wild West Rhetoric," *Washington Post*, (17 September 2001), 1.
35. Philip Smucker, "Tora Bora Falls, but No bin Laden," *Christian Science Monitor*, (17 December 2001), 2; Scott Baldauf and Philip Smucker, "A Post Taliban Scramble for Power," *Christian Science Monitor*, (19 November 2001), 3.
36. Smucker, "How bin Laden Got Away," 3.
37. "Escape from Tora Bora," *The Guardian*, (4 September 2002), 1; Matthew Forney, "Letter from Tora Bora," *Time*, (22 December 2001); Barton Gellman and Thomas E. Ricks, "US Concludes bin Laden Escaped at Tora Bora Fight," *Washington Post*, (17

April 2002), 1; Michael E. O'Hanlon, "Did the Military Misstep? Let bin Laden Escape," *Baltimore Sun,* (28 April 2002).

38. Rahmullah Yusufzai, "How bin Laden Got Away," *Time,* (17 July 2002).
39. Barton Gellman and Thomas E. Ricks, "US Concludes bin Laden Escaped at Tora Bora Fight," *Washington Post,* (17 April 2002), 1.
40. Ibid; Liz Shy, "Bin Laden, Dead or Alive, Eludes US," *Chicago Tribune,* (11 September 2002), 1.
41. Gellman and Ricks, "US Concludes bin Laden Escaped at Tora Bora Fight," 1.
42. Vincent Cannistrarro, "The War on Terror Enters Phase 2," *New York Times,* (2 May 2002), 27.
43. Ibid.
44. "Escape from Tora Bora," 1.
45. Abrams is quoted in: Michael Flach, "Administration Officials Defense Operation Iraqi Freedom," *Catholic Herald,* (10 April 2003).
46. Carl Conetta, "The Wages of War: Iraqi Combatant and Non-Combatant Fatalities in 2003 Conflict," Project on Defense Alternatives *Research Monograph* #8, (20 October 2003),
    http://www.comw.org/pda/0310rm8.html#4.%20Iraqi%20combatant%20fatalities%20i n%20the%202003
47. Human Rights Watch, *Off Target: The Conduct of the War and Civilian Casualties in Iraq* (2003): http://hrw.org/reports/2003/usa1203/usa1203.pdf
48. Jim Dwyer, "Under Blizzard of Bullets, a Battle Inches On," *New York Times,* (1 April 2003), 1; Dexter Filkins, "Little Resistance Encountered as Troops Reach Baghdad," *New York Times,* (5 April 2003), 3; Scott Bernard Nelson, "Little Slows Marines in Roll to Baghdad," *Boston Globe,* (5 April 2003), 17; and, Michael Wilson, "Marines Meet Potent Enemy In Deadly Fight," *New York Times,* (24 March 2003), 1.
49. Jose E. Guillen, "Barbara's trusty big gun: It's slated for replacement, but it was 'the right weapon' for OIF," *Scout Newsletter,* Camp Pendelton, California.
50. Conetta, "The Wages of War: Iraqi Combatant and Non-Combatant Fatalities in 2003 Conflict."
51. *Operation Iraqi Freedom: By the Numbers* (Shaw AFB, South Carolina: CENTAF, Assessment and Analysis Division, 30 April 2003).
52. Bradley Graham, "US Air Attacks Turn More Aggressive; Risk of Civilian Casualties Higher as Range of Targets Is Broadened, Officials Say," *Washington Post,* (2 April 2003), 24; Bradley Graham and Vernon Loeb, "An Air War of Might, Coordination and Risks," *Washington Post,* (27 April 2003), 1 Paul Richter, "Bombing Is Tool of Choice to Clear a Path to Baghdad; Heavy strikes are meant to grind down top-level forces before an assault," *Los Angeles Times,* (1 April 2003),1.
53. Scott Peterson, "Iraq prepares for its Defense," *Christian Science Monitor,* (28 February 2003),1; Robert Collier, "Scale of Iraqi Strength is a Mystery," *San Francisco Chronicle,* (20 January 2003), 1.
54. Ibid, 134
55. Ibid., 22-24, 38.
56. Marc Garlasco, "Transcript: The Invasion of Iraq," http://www.pbs.org/wgbh/pages/frontline/shows/invasion/etc/script.html
57. Human Rights Watch, *Off Target: The Conduct of the War and Civilian Casualties in Iraq,* 28 and 38.

58. Garlasco, "Transcript: The Invasion of Iraq."
59. Peter Boyer, "The New War Machine," *The New Yorker*, (30 June 2003), 23.
60. Ibid.
61. David Toomey, "Transcript: The Invasion of Iraq," http://www.pbs.org/wgbh/pages/frontline/shows/invasion/etc/script.html
62. Marc Garlasco, "Transcript: The Invasion of Iraq," http://www.pbs.org/wgbh/pages/frontline/shows/invasion/etc/script.html
63. Ibid.
64. David Blair, "Smart Bombs Aimed at Saddam Killed Families," *Daily Telegraph*, (21 April 2003), 11.
65. Human Rights Watch, *Off Target: The Conduct of the War and Civilian Casualties in Iraq*, 37-38.
66. Ibid., 28-31; Peter Baker, "Fate of Chemical Ali Remains in Question," *Washington Post*, (8 April 2003), 23.
67. Anthony Shahid, "American Forces Nab Brutal 'Chemical Ali,'" *Washington Post*, (22 August 2003), 1.
68. Douglas Jehl and Eric Schmitt, "Precision Strikes were Wide off the Mark," *International Herald Tribune*, (14 June 2004), 1; Scott Ritter, "Saddam's People are Winning the War," *International Herald Tribune*, (22 July 2004), 1.
69. Leonard LaVella, (25 August 2003) "Operation Enduring Freedom Time-Sensitive Targeting Process Study," Air Combat Command Analysis Division, Directorate of Requirements.
70. Ibid.
71. For quote, see: Douglas Jehl and Eric Schmitt, "Air Strikes on Iraqi Leaders 'Abject Failure," *New York Times*, (13 June 2004), 1.
72. Michael Knights, "U.S.A. Learns Lessons in Time-Critical Targeting," *Jane's Intelligence Review*, (1 July 2003); Brian Ross, Rhonda Schwartz, and Jill Rackmill, "Missed Opportunity? U.S. Attack May Have Ended Saddam Surrender Attempt," ABC News.com, (21 April 2003), http://abcnews.go.com/sections/wnt/World/iraq030421_missed_deal.html
73. Human Rights Watch, *Off Target: The Conduct of the War and Civilian Casualties in Iraq*, 24-25.
74. Ibid.; .US CENTCOM, Headquarters, "Use of Thuraya Phones Discontinued," News Release, (3 April 2003).
75. US CENTCOM, Headquarters, "Use of Thuraya Phones Discontinued"; Jason Burke, "Bin Laden Still Alive, Reveals Spy Satellite," *The Observer*, (6 October 2002).
76. John Donnelly, "War in Iraq/Targeting the Leadership; After Air Strike, U.S. Seeks Clues on Fate of Hussein and Sons," *Boston Globe*, (9 April 2003), 21.

Chapter 9

Non-Combatant Immunity

The discussion of using appropriate and proportional levels of force against military targets in relation to the attainment of America's military objectives leads us to an examination of the role of non-combatants in war. While significant attention was placed on targets of destruction, weapons, and methods in the previous chapter, warring parties must agree that deliberately targeting non-combatants and civilian properties violates just war theory. The principle of Non-Combatant Immunity (Discriminating between combatants and non-combatants) is a necessary distinction that must be delineated in order to prosecute a just war. According to James Turner Johnson, the "just war tradition... is a moral tradition of justifiable and limited war."[1] This is especially the case when deterrence and containment are abandoned and preemptive force against an ongoing threat and preventive war against what is perceived to be a future threat are invoked.[2]

Specifically, according to Provisions 1-3 in Article 51 ("Protection of the Civilian Population") of Protocol I of the Geneva Conventions of 12 August 1949 and the Protection of Victims of International Armed Conflict of 8 June 1977, non-combatants cannot be subjected to the destructive effects of war (see Figure 9.1).

Figure 9.1 Article 51 and Civilian Immunity

Provision 1: The civilian population and individual civilians shall enjoy general protection against dangers arising from military operations. To give effect to this protection, the following rules, which are additional to other applicable rules of international law, shall be observed in all circumstances;

Provision 2: The civilian population as such, as well as individual civilians, shall not be the object of attack. Acts or threats of violence the primary purpose of which is to spread terror among the civilian population are prohibited;

Provision 3: Civilians shall enjoy the protection afforded by this Section, unless and for such time as they take a direct part in hostilities.[3]

Most important is prohibiting indiscriminate attacks against non-combatants. Provisions 4 and 6 of Article 51 are clear on this prohibition (see Figure 9.2).

Figure 9.2 Article 51 and Indiscriminate Attacks

Provision 4: Indiscriminate attacks are prohibited. Indiscriminate Attacks are: (a) those which are not directed at a specific military objective; (b) those which employ a method or means of combat which cannot be directed at specific military objective; or

(c) those which employ a method or means of combat the effects of which cannot be limited as required by this Protocol; and consequently, in each such case, are of a nature to strike military objectives and civilians or civilian objects without distinction;

Provision 6: Attacks against the civilian population or civilians by way of reprisals are prohibited.[4]

Provisions 1-5 in Article 57 specify the precautions a state must assume during war (see Figure 9.3).

Figure 9.3 Article 57 and Required Precautions in Attacks

Provision 1: In the conduct of military operations, constant care shall be taken to spare the civilian population, civilians and civilian objects;

Provision 2: With respect to attacks, the following precautions shall be taken: (a) those who plan or decide upon an attack shall: (i) do everything feasible to verify that the objectives to be attacked are neither civilians nor civilian objects and are not subject to special protection but are military objectives within the meaning of paragraph 2 of Article 52 and that it is not prohibited by the provisions of this Protocol to attack them; (ii) take all feasible precautions in the choice of means and methods of attack with a view to avoiding, and in any event to minimizing, incidental loss of civilian life, injury to civilians and damage to civilian objects; (iii) refrain from deciding to launch any attack which may be expected to cause incidental loss of civilian life, injury to civilians, damage to civilian objects, or a combination thereof, which would be excessive in relation to the concrete and direct military advantage anticipated; (b) an attack shall be cancelled or suspended if it becomes apparent that the objective is not a military one or is subject to special protection or that the attack   may be expected to cause incidental loss of civilian life, injury to civilians, damage to civilian objects, or a combination thereof, which would be excessive in relation to the concrete and direct military advantage anticipated; (c) effective advance warning shall be given of attacks which may affect the civilian population, unless circumstances do not permit.

Provision 3: When a choice is possible between several military objectives for obtaining a similar military advantage, the objective to be selected shall be that the attack on which may be expected to cause the least danger to civilian lives and to civilian objects;

Provision 4: In the conduct of military operations at sea or in the air, each Party to the conflict shall, in conformity with its rights and duties under the rules of international law applicable in armed conflict, take all reasonable precautions to avoid losses of civilian lives and damage to civilian objects;

Provision 5: No provision of this Article may be construed as authorizing any attacks against the civilian population, civilians or civilian objects.[5]

What is the legal status of a non-combatant? Article 3 common to the Geneva Conventions of 12 August 1949 and the Protection of Victims of International

Armed Conflict of 8 June 1977 (Protocol 2) supplies clear standards for identifying non-combatants (see Figure 9.4).

Figure 9.4 Legal Status of Non-Combatants

1. Persons taking no active part in the hostilities, including members of armed forces who have laid down their arms and those placed hors de combat by sickness, wounds, detention, or any other cause, shall in all circumstances be treated humanely, without any adverse distinction founded on race, dolor, religion or faith, sex, birth or wealth, or any other similar criteria. To this end, the following acts are and shall remain prohibited at any time and in any place whatsoever with respect to the above-mentioned persons:

   (a) violence to life and person, in particular murder of all kinds, mutilation, cruel treatment and torture;

   (b) taking of hostages;

   (c) outrages upon personal dignity, in particular humiliating and degrading treatment;

   (d) the passing of sentences and the carrying out of executions without previous judgment pronounced by a regularly constituted court, affording all the judicial guarantees which are recognized as indispensable by civilized peoples.

2. The wounded and sick shall be collected and cared for.[6]

These principles apply to all parties to the conflict, both government and guerrillas. This includes civilians living in a war zone and international humanitarian workers, namely personnel from the Red Cross, Red Crescent, or the United Nations.

Within the realm of combatant status, a distinction needs to be between lawful and unlawful combatants. Article IV (see Figure 9.5) of the Geneva Convention (Protocol 3) specifies that lawful combatants must be considered Prisoners of War (POW).

Figure 9.5 Lawful Combatant Status

Members of the armed forces of a Party to the conflict as well as members of militias or volunteer corps forming part of such armed forces;

Members of other militias and members of other volunteer corps, including those of organized resistance movements, belonging to a Party to the conflict and operating in or outside their own territory, even if this territory is occupied, provided that such militias or volunteer corps, including such organized resistance movements, fulfill the following conditions: (a) that of being commanded by a person responsible for his subordinates; (b) that of having a fixed distinctive sign recognizable at a distance; (c) that of carrying arms openly; [and] (d) that of conducting their operations in accordance with the laws and customs of war.[7]

If any one of these provisions is not met, then lawful combatant or POW status cannot be granted and belligerent are designated as unlawful combatants or those who have not been legitimized by a state authority to take part in hostilities.[8]

One of the most significant problems is the utilization of terror attacks by disaffected groups that lack the resources to use force against a state's military. Any attack on non-combatant civilians or civilian objects is a violation of the constraint imposed by the Principle of Non-Combatant Immunity. In order to promote their views and acquire an audience, terrorists deliberately hope to violate the principle of non-combatant immunity and conventional rules of war by assaulting civilian non-combatants.[9] This problem is exacerbated by America's a fear-based anticipation that the next attack by terrorists or rogues states will not only be around the corner, it will more socially, politically, and economically devastating than the 11 September 2001 attacks.[10] The most frustrating element is that America's military, intelligence, and police forces are expected to adhere to non-combatant immunity even though its non-combatant citizens have been targeted by terrorists. The temptation to engage in reprisals against non-combatants who may or may not aid terrorists could lead a state to violate non-combatant immunity out of frustration.

Wars Against the Taliban and Al-Qaida

This chapter argues that to understand efforts made by the US to limit or minimize non-combatant casualties in offensive wars, we must understand and appreciate the meaning of combatant status in the war on terrorism. Put simply, the status of an individual determines whether or not he or she can be deemed a justifiable target. It should be made clear that the argument put forth in this chapter is that both lawful and unlawful combatants may be directly and indirectly attacked and targeted for attack. A person's status is a driving force behind the actions and behavior he or she can engage in during the prosecution of an armed conflict.

Legal Status of Taliban and Al-Qaida Forces

What is the combat status of Taliban and forces and Al-Qaida fighters killed or captured in a foreign combat zone, namely Afghanistan? As discussed in previous chapters, the Taliban was the governing authority in Afghanistan, that is, until they were overthrown as a result of Operation Enduring Freedom. Although the Taliban did not actually carry out the attacks themselves, it did do through its sponsorship of the Al-Qaida leadership. The question whether detained Taliban members qualify as prisoners of war under the Geneva Convention's test is a difficult one indeed. Taliban soldiers resemble a traditionally organized army. Despite the fact that the Taliban was never recognized as a legitimate government by the UN and the US, and given that only Saudi Arabia, Pakistan, and the United Arab Emirates established diplomatic relations with it, the Taliban would have to be granted protections afforded by the Geneva Convention if it satisfied the four conditions set forth in Article IV.

To begin with, the Taliban held a slightly more distinguishable command structure than Al-Qaida, suggesting it might satisfy the first criterion of "being commanded by a person responsible for his subordinates." However, Taliban members did not satisfy the second and third criteria, for they did not wear uniforms that bore a "fixed distinctive sign recognizable at a distance," nor did they invariably "carry arms openly."[11] A technical contention holds that they should not be faulted since Taliban troops did not wear distinctive uniforms. This argument is weak because international laws of armed conflict hold that warring parties must be able to distinguish combatants from non-combatants in order to minimize civilian casualties. The Taliban was clear in its efforts to attack and brutalize non-combatants. For example, prior to the fall of Kabul, the Taliban concealed much of its military equipment in the civilian population. Complicating matters was that as the war progressed, it became increasingly difficult to distinguish the Taliban from Al-Qaida. Taliban forces would therefore be considered unlawful enemy combatants.[12]

As an instrument of the Taliban, Al-Qaida fighters detained in Afghanistan who carried out the attacks are properly deemed unlawful enemy combatants. Al-Qaida fighters were engaged in armed conflict in support of Taliban military forces in resistance to the American invasion. Since Al-Qaida and Taliban forces are so intimately tied, the relationship is reciprocal, especially in a foreign combat zone such as Afghanistan. Al-Qaida fighters were not considered formal members of the armed forces of Afghanistan and not otherwise complying with the requirements of combatant status but nevertheless participating in an international armed conflict, merits this status. Most important, Al-Qaida fighters captured or killed in a foreign theatre of war, namely Afghanistan, do not meet the four conditions set forth in Article IV of the Geneva Convention. It could be argued that Osama bin Laden is responsible for subordinates in his terrorist network. However, as it has been contended in Chapter 7, the cell structure of Al-Qaida places it beyond the conception of a formal chain of command traditionally akin to a state. However, Al-Qaida fighters seek to blend in with the non-combatant civilian population, do not wear emblems, and openly possess arms and munitions. Moreover, Al-Qaida operatives target non-combatants, which violates both the Geneva Conventions and the United Nations Charter.[13]

However, unlawful enemy combatants associated with Al-Qaida and the Taliban still qualify for "humane treatment" under the "Body of Principles for the Protection of All Persons under Any Form of Detention or Imprisonment."[14] Under President Bush's military order of November 13, Al-Qaida members and those who harbored them can be tried by military tribunals.[15] The Supreme Court approved the use of such tribunals for unlawful combatants in *Ex Parte Quirin*.[16]

The treatment of unlawful combatants has been the subject of criticism by other nations and international human rights institutions.   The International

Committee of the Red Cross contends that the legal status of captured and unlawful enemy combatants who have been detained in US military prisons, remains ambiguous:

> Whereas the terms "combatant" "prisoner of war" and "civilian" are generally used and defined in the treaties of international humanitarian law, the terms "unlawful combatant," "unprivileged combatants/belligerents" do not appear in them. They have, however, been frequently used at least since the beginning of the last century in legal literature, military manuals and case law. The connotations given to these terms and their consequences for the applicable protection regime are not always very clear. The legal situation of unlawful/unprivileged combatants.[17]

The US Supreme Court has sought to clarify the inherent legal status of Al-Qaida and Taliban fighters captured and designated as unlawful enemy combatants in Afghanistan. In *Hamdi v. Rumsfeld* (2004), the Court ruled that since the US Congress had authorized the detention of enemy combatants under circumstances in which Yasser Esam Hamdi, a Saudi national born in the US, was captured, he must be given the "meaningful opportunity to contest the factual basis for that detention before a neutral decision[-]maker."[18] Furthermore, the decision required that all captured Al-Qaida and Taliban operatives in US custody be granted the right to challenge the factual basis of their classification as enemy combatants.[19] The Bush Administration was eventually forced to release Hamdi in October 2004, because no formal criminal charges were filed against him in the US. Since Hamdi was barred from seeing an attorney until after two years in captivity and kept in solitary confinement, the majority opinion of the Court stated that the war in Afghanistan was not "a blank check" for the president and that "an unchecked system of detention carries the potential to become a means for oppression and abuse of others who do not present that sort of threat."[20] To overcome legal constraints, the US has adopted the term "fighters" to describe enemy forces during the US military presence in Afghanistan. A fighter is a member of the armed forces of a party to the conflict or one otherwise taking part directly in the hostilities.

Bombs Away

With non-combatant immunity as our backdrop, the strategic US bombing of Afghanistan has been guided by two prevailing goals. First the Bush Administration wanted to limit the number of American casualties. Second, it sought to limit non-combatant civilian deaths and injuries. To accomplish both, it initially pursued a hi-tech bombing campaign at high altitudes where Taliban anti-aircraft guns, Stinger missiles, and Al-Qaida guns could not reach. Once the US threw its support behind the Northern Alliance in late October 2001, the bombing campaign widened and threatened to heighten civilian casualties.[21]

Overall, the level of civilian casualties, which due to tight information control and difficulties making estimations, was largely the result of the decision by US military strategists bomb heavily populated areas where Taliban and Al-Qaida forces were firmly embedded. Moreover, years of civil war and resistance against the Soviet military during the 1980s resulted in the emplacement of military garrisons and facilities in urban areas where the Soviet-backed government. Subsequent Afghan governments continued the trend of installing anti-aircraft batteries close to government officer buildings and communications facilities. A heavy American bombing campaign would necessarily result in substantial numbers of non-combatant civilian casualties, due in large part to the close proximity of civilians to military targets. Non-combatant immunity was further reduced by poor targeting, human error, equipment malfunction, and general irresponsibility. Most important, enemy Taliban and Al-Qaida forces deliberately hid military hardware in civilian areas [the human shield argument].[22]

Initial reports of non-combatant casualties described the extensive use of 2,000 pound cluster bombs dropped by B-52 bombers. According to one US Navy commander, "A 2,000 pound bomb, no matter where you drop it, is a significant emotional event for anyone within a square mile."[23] Defense Secretary Donald Rumsfeld argued that the US had gone to great lengths to limit damage caused by US bombs to non-combatants and civilian objects. On 29 October, for instance, Rumsfeld told reporters that, "War is ugly. It causes misery and suffering and death, and we see that every day. But let's be clear: no nation in human history has done more to avoid civilian casualties than the United States has in this conflict."[24] This did not prevent several unavoidable cases of significant non-combatant deaths. On 9 October, the *Pakistan Observer* reported that on the first night of the US bombing thirty-seven non-combatants had been killed.[25] The next day, *The Guardian* reported seventy-six non-combatant deaths and by 15 October the *Times of India* reported over three hundred civilian deaths.[26] In late October, US planes bombed the electrical grid in Kandahar and generation facilities in Helmand, eliminating all power supplies used by both combatants and non-combatants in both cities.[27] On 12 November, a guided bomb struck the Kabul office of the Al Jazeera news agency.[28]

In many instances, American bombs fell on areas with little to no military value. On 25 October, US bombers destroyed a city bus filled with non-combatants in Kandahar, killing 20 non-combatant civilians.[29] On 18 November, US fighter-bombers struck Gluco on the Khyber Pass, killing seven villagers. It was deemed later that the village contained no military resources and had been vacated by Taliban soldiers.[30] On 11 October, the village Karam, located west of Jalalabad, was repeatedly struck by US bombers, destroying forty-five homes and killing roughly 160 non-combatant civilians.[31] On 21 October, American bombers dropped cluster bombs on a military hospital and mosque in Herat, killing up to 100 non-combatants.[32] Two days later, on 23 October, US AC-130 gunships strafed Bori Chokar and Chowkar-Karez, killing 93 non-combatants.[33] Also, on 18 November, B-52 carpet-bombing of Taliban lines near Khanabad killed at least 100 non-combatants.[34]

In addition, the bombardment of Afghanistan caused millions of non-combatants to flee their country.[35] Ever since the Soviet invasion in 1979 and during the subsequent occupation, Afghan refugees have suffered from disease, poverty, and hunger. The American invasion exacerbated the human tragedy. However, UN agencies, Doctors Without Borders, Christian Aid, Action Aid, OXFAM, Feed the Children, Islamic Relief, Caritas International/Catholic Relief Services have waged courageous and sometimes effective actions. After the Soviet invasion and the ensuing bitter civil war, close to four million Afghans flooded into Iran and Pakistan. In the late 1990s, another one million Afghans were uprooted by the lasting drought and the civil war between the Taliban and Northern Alliance. But since 9/11, the United Nations High Commission for Refugees has reported that another four million non-combatant Afghans have fled the violence.[36]

Iraq

President George W. Bush has referred to the ongoing war in Iraq as "one of the swiftest and most humane military campaigns in history."[37] Presidential adviser Jay Lefkowitz even contended "We are waging the most humanitarian war that has ever been waged."[38] Despite these comments, thousands of Iraqi civilians have been killed or injured ever since the US invaded Iraq on 19 March 2003. It should be emphasized, however, that it is impossible to make accurate assessments of non-combatant casualties in Iraq. The Department of Defense monitors civilian casualties but does not report figures. Though US forces do not publish non-combatant casualties (nor does international law require them to), they do make cash payments – usually several thousand dollars – to civilians injured or to the families of those killed.[39] However, the US was confident that it would not have to destroy Iraq in order to save it.

A lead independent organization responsible for assessing the level of non-combatant casualties during major combat was Human Rights Watch (HRW). HRW workers traveled to many of the hospitals and interviewed hospital directors and other medical personnel who had been working in these facilities during combat.[40] According to HRW, statistics drawn from hospital records indicate that the ground war caused the vast majority of civilian deaths. For example, more than 400 non-combatants died in al-Nasiriyya, including at least 72 women and 169 children; more than 700 additional women and children were injured.[41] The preponderance of these casualties was due to small arms fire as the battle raged in a densely populated neighborhood of the city. In al-Hilla, US surface-to-surface cluster munitions resulted in roughly 90 per cent of all non-combatant casualties in the city.[42] The Project on Defense Alternatives also tracked Iraqi non-combatant casualties through hospital surveys and demographic analysis. The group estimated that the number of non-combatants killed during major hostilities (19 March to 2 May 2003) combat was between 3,200 and 4,300.[43]

The use of cluster munitions in populated areas caused more civilian casualties than any other factor in the coalition's conduct of major military operations in March and April, according to HRW. America and British forces used almost 13,000 cluster munitions, containing nearly 2 million submunitions that killed or wounded more than 1,000 civilians.[44]   For Kenneth Roth, executive director of HRW, although "Coalition forces generally tried to avoid killing Iraqis who weren´t taking part in combat, the deaths of hundreds of civilians still could have been prevented."[45]   International humanitarian law, or the laws of war, does not outlaw non-combatant casualties in wartime. But armed forces are obliged to take all feasible precautions for avoiding civilian losses, and to refrain from attacks that are indiscriminate or where the expected civilian harm exceeds the military gain. The term "casualty" refers to both dead and wounded.

HRW observers and the Project on Defense Alternatives inspected bombsites, as well as fields and neighborhoods littered with unexploded cluster submunitions. They evaluated ballistics evidence and hospital records. The researchers also obtained limited US Department of Defense data that enabled them to pinpoint the locations of cluster-munition strikes. HRW estimated that cluster munitions killed or injured more than 1,000 civilians.[46] The total number of civilians killed in the war is much higher, since it would include people who died as a result of collateral damage from small arms fire and other factors.

Confronting Irregular Forces

While an approximate number of non-combatant casualties would help us to appreciate the real impact of the war on the Iraqi population, it is more essential that we discern key realities in the context of the war that contributed to the breakdown of non-combatant immunity between 19 March and 2 May 2003.   A key element in our examination has to do with a failure on the part of US military forces to prepare for the tactics of irregular combatants. According to retired Air Force Colonel Sam Gardiner, "In our war games, the bad guys gave up fighting us directly. They moved into cities. They attacked our supply lines with explosives. They wore civilian clothes. They took hostages." As a result, Gardiner claimed, "They responded to our new weapons by forcing on us the dilemma of killing civilians and of their killing of civilians."[47]

The likelihood of non-combatant deaths became highly probable when US soldiers confronted Iraq's irregular non-uniformed forces, such as the paramilitary Fedayeen Saddam (Saddam's 'Men of Sacrifice'). Founded by Saddam Hussein's son Uday in 1995, the Fedayeen, with a total strength estimated between 18,000 and 40,000 troops, is comprised of young soldiers recruited from Sunni regions in and around Fallujah, Baghdad, and Tikrit. The group reported directly to Saddam rather than to Republican Guard officers or though a formal chain of command and before.[48]

The Fedayeen deliberately targeted Iraqi non-combatants, especially Shiites, to keep them from aiding the invasion and often wore civilian clothes to confuse the US and UK forces. Other tactics were the use of false surrenders and forcing woman and children as decoys in the hope of ambushing US and UK soldiers.[49] Although the fall of Baghdad ended the Fedayeen as a paramilitary force, a large number survived and merged into disparate bands that would later comprise the Iraqi insurgency following the termination of hostilities on 2 May. Overall, the goal of the Fedayeen was to maximize the number of non-combatant casualties in order to sway American war efforts.[50]

Iraqi regular forces also committed an array of violations against civilians, which contributed in large measure to the overall number of non-combatant casualties committed by both Iraqis and Americans. This included the use of non-combatants as human shields, red cross and red crescent emblems, antipersonnel landmines, military objects in mosques, hospitals, and cultural property, and a the failure to evacuate non-combatants from the dangers of military operations. The Iraqi military's practice of wearing civilian clothes tended to erode the distinction between combatants and civilians, putting the latter at risk, although it did not relieve US and UK forces of their obligation to distinguish at all times between combatants and civilians and to target only combatants.[51]

Revisiting the High Value Targets

While the ground war caused significantly more casualties, the air war, especially failed attacks targeting Iraqi leadership, contributed to the total number of civilian deaths and injuries. The fifty "decapitation" strikes on top Iraqi leaders during major combat failed to kill any of the intended targets, but instead killed dozens of civilians. In targeting the Iraqi leadership, the strategy relied on intercepts of senior Iraqi leaders satellite phone calls along with corroborating intelligence that proved inadequate. As a result, the US military could only locate targets within a 100-meter radius.[52] According to HRW, the high value targeting strategy ...failed on human rights grounds. It's no good using a precise weapon if the target has not been located precisely."[53]

The aerial strikes on the Iraqi leadership constituted one of the most disturbing aspects of the war in Iraq for several reasons. First, many of the civilian casualties from the air war occurred during US attacks on senior Iraqi leadership officials. Second, the intelligence and targeting methodologies used to identify potential leadership targets were inherently flawed and led to preventable civilian deaths. Finally, every single attack on leadership failed. None of the targeted individuals was killed, and in the cases examined by HRW, local Iraqis repeatedly stated that they believed the intended targets were not even present at the time of the strike. However, according to US Army General Stanley McChrystal, strikes against emerging targets received review although the process was done much more quickly: "There tends to be a careful process where there is plenty of time to review that [the targets]... [T]hen we put together certain processes like time-sensitive targeting. And those are when you talk about the crush of an emerging target that might come up, that doesn't have time to go through a complicated vetting process... [T]here still is a legal review, but it is all at a much accelerated process because there are some fleeting targets that require a very time-sensitive engagement, but they all fit into pre-thought out criteria."[54]

General Moseley, the top Air Force commander during the war who is now the Air Force vice chief of staff contended US Air Force and Navy commanders were required to obtain advance approval from Rumsfeld if any planned airstrike was likely to result in the deaths of 30 more civilians. More than 50 such raids were proposed, and all were approved.   But raids considered time-sensitive, which included all of those on the high-value targets, were not subject to that constraint, according to current and former military officials.   For that reason, HRW concluded, "attacks on leadership likely resulted in the largest number of civilian deaths from the air war."[55]

HRW studied non-combatant casualties in the four air attacks against time-sensitive, high value targets examined in the previous chapter. The war opened on 19 March with an air strike on Saddam who was thought to be in a bunker at Dora Farms. According to US Air Force General Michael Moseley, "This was a direct shot at the Saddam Hussein regime and a direct shot at the Baathist regime and a direct shot at a oppressive regime, not the Iraqi people nor their infrastructure."[56] The strike, however, killed one and injured fourteen non-combatants including nine women and a child.[57]   DIA analyst Marc Garlasco argued that the controversial decision to strike at Dora Farms prematurely launched the war and, as a result, "the Iraq leadership new the war was on. They then moved to civilian areas."[58]

Following the Dora Farms strike, on 5 April, at Al-Tuwaisi in Basra, the US sought to kill General Ali Hassan al-Majid (Chemical Ali). Although US cruise missiles hit the targeted building in a densely populated section of the city, the buildings surrounding the bomb strike – densely packed with non-combatants – were also struck. According to HRW, seventeen non-combatants were killed in the attack and Majid eluded US military forces until his capture in August 2003.[59] The failed attempt to kill Majid was worst losses of civilian life in southern Iraq. Three days later, US missiles struck a target in Baghdad where it was believed Hussein's half brother and presidential adviser Watban Ibrahim Barzan was being protected, resulting six non-combatants deaths with no sign of Barzan. On 7 April, US intelligence indicated that Saddam and perhaps one or both of his sons were meeting in Baghdad at Al-Mansur.[60] The attack killed eighteen non-combatants.[82] Garlasco contends that the overall strategy "failed to kill the HVT's and instead killed civilians and engendered hatred and discontent in some of the population."[61]

The Impact of Collateral Damage

Collateral damage to non-combatants and civilian objects are a standard element in the US military's official targeting process and serve as a way for the military to fulfill its obligations under international humanitarian law.[62]   The Geneva Conventions require that an attack must be cancelled or suspended if it is expected to cause non-combatant casualties that are "…excessive in relation to the concrete and direct military advantage anticipated."[63] Collateral damage estimates factor into target and weapon selection and the timing of an attack, it is the military's best means of minimizing civilian casualties and other losses in air strikes. The US Air Force carries out collateral damage estimations using computer models to determine the weapon, fuse, and time of day that will ensure maximum effect on a military target and minimum impact on non-combatants.   According to

CENTCOM senior U.S. Central Command official responded, "with excruciating pain."[64] Defense Secretary Rumsfeld reportedly had to authorize personally all targets that had a collateral damage estimate of more than thirty civilian casualties.[65]

For the most part, the collateral damage assessment process for the air war in worked well, especially with respect to preplanned targets. HRW's month-long investigation in Iraq found that, in most cases, aerial bombardment resulted in minimal adverse effects to the civilian population. Major General McChrystal of the Joint Chiefs of Staff stressed the degree to which the United States is concerned about collateral damage and effective battle damage assessment:

> [O]ne of the things I would highlight at the beginning, that we have proven already in this operation, as we said we would, every time we have a case where there is a real or even potential case of unintended civilian injury or death or collateral damage to structures, we've investigated it. And we go back and we look at the targeting; we account for every munition that, in fact, was suspended; we look for whether the aim points that we intended to hit were hit, to determine if, in fact, there was the result of our targeting unintended civilian damage – or casualties, or damage, and then we correct the errors as we go.[66]

The major exception was emerging targets, especially leadership targets. A Department of Defense source told HRW that CENTCOM did not perform adequate collateral damage estimates for all of the leadership strikes due to perceived time constraints.[67] While the US military hailed the quick turnaround time between the acquisition of intelligence and the air strikes on leadership targets, it appears the haste contributed to excessive civilian casualties because it prevented adequate collateral damage estimates. In the four publicly acknowledged air strikes against emerging high value targets, forty-two civilians were killed and dozens more were injured.[68]

For example, at the strike on 7 April in Al-Mansur, forty-five minutes, including the approximately twelve minutes it took the B-1B to fly the mission, was little time to take the raw data of the time and location of the meeting, interpret it, prepare and target the mission, and pass it up the chain in CENTCOM for the decision to make the strike.[69] The effects of the strike were stark, a huge crater surrounded by damaged homes. Interviews with residents of the area and press reports indicated approximately eighteen non-combatants died in the strike. Pentagon officials admitted that they did not know precisely who was at the targeted location. According to McChrystal, "What we have for battle damage assessment right now is essentially a hole in the ground, a site of destruction where we wanted it to be, where we believe high-value targets were. We do not have a hard and fast assessment of what individual or individuals were on site."[70]

This strike shows that targeting based on satellite phones is seriously flawed. Even if the targeted individual is actually determined to be on the phone, the person could be far from the impact point. The GBU-31s dropped on al-Mansur have a published accuracy of thirteen meters (forty-three feet) circular error probable (CEP), while the phone coordinates are accurate only to a one-hundred-meter (328-foot) radius.[71] The weapon was inherently more accurate than the information used to determine its target, which led to substantial civilian casualties with no military advantages. US military leaders defended the attacks even after revelations that the strikes resulted in civilian deaths instead of the deaths of the intended targets. One has steadfastly maintained that the strikes "demonstrated US resolve and capabilities."[72]

The Power of Intentions

The analysis presented here indicates that invaders and defenders must assume some risk in order to protect noncombatants and make an honest effort not to harm them. The application of military force must be conducted in a measured and disciplined fashion and direct violent tactics only at combatants. Therefore, as was demonstrated on the part of the US, American military forces were openly willing to accept greater costs associated with fighting wars in both Afghanistan and Iraq with discriminatory and proportional tools. This does not mean that full non-combatant immunity is assumed; however, it strongly suggests that the US military did not deliberately target or harm non-combatants in a manner that is inconsistent with the principle of Non-Combatant Immunity.

It is not enough to justify noncombatant deaths incurred during an attack on a military target by simply examining the tactical options available to commanders. While the actions of military commanders can be legitimated with respect to the tools, training, and intelligence they have been supplied, the overall provisioning and training of troops, as well as intelligence operations, can be criticized from a moral perspective if such provisioning fails to provide warring parties with as wide a sphere of tactical options as possible. In order for the killing of noncombatants to be considered discriminatory in a just war, deliberate lethal force against non-combatants and civilian objects has to further a valuable military goal.

Although US military commanders announced their intention to reduce non-combatant casualties, they also refused to discuss the actual number of civilians killed and injured. This reluctance questions whether or not the US military really assumed responsibility for non-combatant casualties that occurred. In a time when the military seeks to wage major war and minimize military casualties, just war theory should be no less aggressive about the protection of non-combatants.

Notes

1.   James T. Johnson, "Threats, Values, and Defense: Does the Defense of Values by Force Remain a Moral Responsibility?" in *Just War Theory*, ed. Jean Bethke Elstain (New York: New York University Press, 1992), 56.

2. David Fisher, "Priorities in Just Deterrence," in *Just Deterrence: Morality and Deterrence into the 21st Century*, ed. Malcolm McCall and Olver Ramsbotham (London: Brassey's, 1990).

3. United Nations Office of the High Commissioner for Human Rights (UNHCR), "Protocol Additional to Geneva Conventions of 12 August 1949, and Relating to the Protection of Victims of Non-International Armed Conflicts (Protocol 1): Geneva, 8 June 1977," Article 51: http://www.unhchr.ch/html/menu3/b/93.htm

4. United Nations Office of the High Commissioner for Human Rights (UNHCR), "Protocol Additional to Geneva Conventions of 12 August 1949, and Relating to the Protection of Victims of Non-International Armed Conflicts (Protocol 1): Geneva, 8 June 1977," Article 51: http://www.unhchr.ch/html/menu3/b/93.htm

5. UNHCR, "Protocol Additional to Geneva Conventions of 12 August 1949, and Relating to the Protection of Victims of Non-International Armed Conflicts (Protocol 1): Geneva, 8 June 1977," Article 57: http://www.unhchr.ch/html/menu3/b/93.htm

6. UNHCR, "Geneva Convention relative to the Protection of Civilian Persons in Time of War. Adopted on 12 August 1949 by the Diplomatic Conference for the Establishment of International Conventions for the Protection of Victims of War, held in Geneva from 21 April to 12 August, 1949," Article 3: http://www.unhchr.ch/html/menu3/b/92.htm

7. UNHCR, "Geneva Convention relative to the Treatment of Prisoners of War Adopted on 12 August 1949 by the Diplomatic Conference for the Establishment of International Conventions for the Protection of Victims of War, held in Geneva from 21 April to 12 August, 1949," Article 4: http://193.194.138.190/html/menu3/b/91.htm

8. Detter, *The Law of War* (Cambridge: Cambridge University Press, 2000).

9. Rich Mkhondo, "Terrorism," in *Crimes of War*, ed., Roy Gutman and David Rieff (New York: WW Norton, 1999).

10. Rohan Gunaratna, *Inside Al-Qaida: Global Network of Terror*, (New York: Columbia University Press, 2002); David Teather, "Al-Qaida 'has regrouped,'" *The Guardian*, (18 October 2002).

11. UNHCR, "Geneva Convention relative to the Treatment of Prisoners of War Adopted on 12 August 1949 by the Diplomatic Conference for the Establishment of International Conventions for the Protection of Victims of War, held in Geneva from 21 April to 12 August, 1949," Article 4: http://193.194.138.190/html/menu3/b/91.htm

12. Aldrich, "The Taliban, Al-Qaida, and the Determination of Illegal Combatants"; Michael Rubin, "Who Is Responsible for the Taliban?" *Middle East Review of International Affairs*, (March 2002).

13. Frances Williams, "Combatants Accssed of Breaking Geneva Conventions," *Financial Times*, December 5, 2001, 2; Gwen Robinson, "US Prepares Cuban Jail for Al-Qaida," *Financial Times*, (8 January 2002).

14. United Nations General Assembly, "Body of Principles for the Protection of All Persons under Any Form of Detention or Imprisonment Adopted by General Assembly Resolution 43/173 of 9 December 1988." See the entire document at: http://www.unhchr.ch/html/menu3/b/h_comp36.htm

15. George W. Bush, "Military Order of November 13, 2001: Detention, Treatment and Trial of Certain Non-Citizens in the War Against Terrorism," *Federal Register* 66, no. 222 (2001): 57833-57836.

16. *Ex parte Quirin*, 317 U.S. 1 (1945).

17. Knut Dormann, "The Legal Situation of Unlawful/Unprivileged Combatants," *IRRC* Vol. 85, No. 849 (March 2003): 45-74.
18. See *Hamdi v. Rumsfeld*, 316 F.3d 450 (4th Cir. 2003).
19. Ibid; David B. Rivkin and Lee Casey, "Bush's Good Day in Court," *Washington Post*, (4 August 2004), 22.
20. *Hamdi v. Rumsfeld*, 316 F.3d 450 (4th Cir. 2003).
21. Fareed Zakaria, "Face the Facts: Bombing Works," *Newsweek*, (13 October 2001).
22. John Nichol, "The Myth of Precision," *The Guardian*, October 29, 2001.
23. Richard Norton-Taylor, "The Return of the B-52s," *The Guardian*, (2 November 2001).
24. Donald Rumsfeld, US Department of Defense, "Press Conference Secretary of Defense Donald Rumsfeld and Chairman of the Joint Chiefs of Staff Richard Myers," (28 October 2001, http://www.washingtonpost.com/wp-srv/nation/specials/attacked/transcripts/rumsfeldtext_102901.html
25. "37 Killed, 81 Injured in Sunday's Strikes," *Pakistan Observer*, (9 October 2001).
26. "Raids Restart with 76 Reported Dead," The *Guardian*, October 10, 2001. Siddarth Varadarajan, "An Ignoble War," *Times of India*, (15 October 2001).
27. "Bombing Alters Afghans Views of U.S.," *Pakistan News Service-PNS*, (7 November 2001).
28. "U.S Targeting Journalists Not Portraying Her Viewpoint," *The Frontier Post*, (20 November 2001).
29. Owen Brown, "'Bus Hit' Claim as War of Words Hots Up," *The Guardian*, (26 October 2001).
30. Phillip Smucker, "Village of Death Casts Doubts over U.S Intelligence," *The Telegraph*, (21 November 2001).
31. Richard Lloyd Parry, "Witnesses Confirm That Dozens Were Killed in the Bombing," *The Independent*, (13 October 2001).
32. "UN Confirms Destruction of Afghan Hospital," The *Guardian* (23 October 2001).
33. Noreen S. Ahmed-Ullah [Quetta], "Afghan Survivors Recount Bombings: Civilian Deaths Turn Them Against U.S.," *Chicago Tribune*, (27 October 2001).
34. Justin Huggler, "Carpet Bombing 'Kills 150 Civilians' in Frontline Town," *The Independent*, (19 November 2001).
35. "Afghan Refugee Crisis," *The Guardian*, (29 September 2001); Jonathan Steele, "Bombing Brings Flood of Refugees. Camps Set up as Thousands Flee US Attacks," *The Guardian*, (21 November 2001).
36. Visit the UNHCR website on Afghan Refugee statistics at: http://www.un.org.pk/latest-dev/Afstats1-mainpopu.htm. Also see: 3 James E. Jennings, "U.S Wages Overkill in Afghanistan," *Newsday*, (11 December 2001).
37. George W. Bush, "President Addresses the Nation," (7 September 2003), http://www.whitehouse.gov/news/releases/2003/09/20030907-1.html
38. Lefkowitz is quoted in: Michael Flach, "Administration Officials Defense Operation Iraqi Freedom," *Catholic Herald*, (10 April 2003).
39. Jeffery Gettleman, "For Iraqi's in Harm's Way, $5000 and I'm Sorry," *New York Times*, (17 March 2004), 23.
40. Human Rights Watch, *Off Target: The Conduct of the War and Civilian Casualties in Iraq* (2003): http://hrw.org/reports/2003/usa1203/usa1203.pdf. See also: Laura King, "Baghdad's Death Toll Assessed," *Los Angeles Times*, (18 May 2003).

41. Human Rights Watch, *Off Target: The Conduct of the War and Civilian Casualties in Iraq* (2003):
   http://hrw.org/reports/2003/usa1203/usa1203.pdf
42. Ibid.
43. Carl Conetta, "The Wages of War: Iraqi Combatant and Non-Combatant Fatalities in 2003 Conflict," Project on Defense Alternatives, *Research Monograph* #8, 20 October, 2003,
   http://www.comw.org/pda/0310rm8.html#4.%20Iraqi%20combatant%20fatalities%20in%20the%202003 (accessed September 2, 2004); Suzanne Goldenberg, "Up to 15,000 People Killed in Invasion, Claims Think Tank," *The Guardian*, (29 October 2003, 1).
44. Human Rights Watch, *Off Target: The Conduct of the War and Civilian Casualties in Iraq* (2003): http://hrw.org/reports/2003/usa1203/usa1203.pdf
45. Ibid.
46. Ibid; Carl Conetta, "The Wages of War: Iraqi Combatant and Non-Combatant Fatalities in 2003 Conflict," Project on Defense Alternatives *Research Monograph* #8, (20 October 2003),
   http://www.comw.org/pda/0310rm8.html#4.%20Iraqi%20combatant%20fatalities%20in%20the%202003
47. Quoted in Brad Knickerbocker, "Who Counts the Civilian Casualties?," *Christian Science Monitor*, (31 March 2004), 2.
48. David Rose, "Death Squads the CIA Ignored," *The Observer*, (30 March 2003).
49. Barbara Slavin and Vivienne Walt, "Allies' Prewar Assumptions Fall Short as Iraqi Resistance Stiffens," *USA Today*, (25 March 2003), 1.
50. Jack Gruber and Steven Komarrow, "Allied Officials: Iraqi Troops Coerced to Fight," *USA Today*, (28 March 2003), 22.
51. Ibid; Terry McCarthy, "Enveloped in Smoke and Fear," *Time*, (6 April 2003), 23.
52. Michael Knights, "U.S.A. Learns Lessons in Time-Critical Targeting," *Jane's Intelligence Review*, (1 July 2003); Brian Ross, Rhonda Schwartz, and Jill Rackmill, "Missed Opportunity? U.S. Attack May Have Ended Saddam Surrender Attempt," ABC News.com, (21 April 2003)
   http://abcnews.go.com/sections/wnt/World/iraq030421_missed_deal.html
53. Human Rights Watch, *Off Target: The Conduct of the War and Civilian Casualties in Iraq*, 24-25.
54. Major General Stanley McChrystal, "Coalition Targeting Procedures," Foreign Press Center Briefing, (3 April 2003).
55. Human Rights Watch, *Off Target: The Conduct of the War and Civilian Casualties in Iraq*, 27.
56. Michael Moseley, "Transcript: The Invasion of Iraq,"
   http://www.pbs.org/wgbh/pages/frontline/shows/invasion/etc/script.html
57. Marian Wilkinson, "Decapitation Attempt Was Worth a Try, George," *Sydney Morning Herald*, (22 March 2003).
58. Marc Garlasco, "Transcript: The Invasion of Iraq,"
   http://www.pbs.org/wgbh/pages/frontline/shows/invasion/etc/script.html
59. Human Rights Watch, *Off Target: The Conduct of the War and Civilian Casualties in Iraq*, 28
60. Ibid., 37.
61. Garlasco, "Transcript: The Invasion of Iraq,"

http://www.pbs.org/wgbh/pages/frontline/shows/invasion/etc/script.html

62. Targeting and Collateral Damage," U.S. CENTCOM Briefing, (5 March 2003).
63. UNHCR, "Protocol Additional to Geneva Conventions of 12 August 1949, and Relating to the Protection of Victims of Non-International Armed Conflicts (Protocol 1): Geneva, 8 June 1977," Article 57: http://www.unhchr.ch/html/menu3/b/93.htm
64. Human Rights Watch, *Off Target: The Conduct of the War and Civilian Casualties in Iraq*, 19.
65. Bradley Graham, "U.S. Moved Early for Air Supremacy," *Washington Post*, (20 July 2003), 26.
66. Human Rights Watch, *Off Target: The Conduct of the War and Civilian Casualties in Iraq*, 27.
67. Ibid., 26-27.
68. Ibid., 6, 22-23.
69. Mark Thompson and Timothy J. Burger, "How to Attack a Dictator, Part II," *Time*, (21 April 2003).
70. Rowan Scarborough, "Saddam Seen at Site," *Washington Times*, (9 April 2003).
71. Human Rights Watch, *Off Target: The Conduct of the War and Civilian Casualties in Iraq*, 6, 24, 38.
72. Graham, "U.S. Moved Early for Air Supremacy," 26; Human Rights Watch, *Off Target: The Conduct of the War and Civilian Casualties in Iraq*, 38.

Chapter 10

Just Peace

Just Cause for Termination

Afghanistan

Although there was no formal proclamation of an end to major hostilities in Afghanistan, the overthrow of the Taliban by US and Northern Alliance military forces is a good starting point for our *jus post bellum* analysis. The collapse of the Taliban forever changed America's strategic interests in a number of ways, which over the long run, may impede a realistic chance for a just peace in Afghanistan.[1] In the short term, the quick victory of the US and the Northern Alliance gave rise to regional warlords, banditry, opium production, and exacerbated Afghanistan's humanitarian catastrophe.[2]

The long-term prospects for a just peace in Afghanistan proved even more troubling. The fast paced victory called into question the ability of the US and post-Taliban authority to construct a unified political system and national military force under a central command. Among the most potentially destabilizing factors was the rapid ascent of Tajik and Uzbek interests, which came at the expense of the largely Pashtun (most of which were pro-Taliban) majority. Instead of the primary cleavage being Taliban versus anti-Taliban, the emerging new conflict appeared to be Pashtun versus non-Pashtun. The redefinition of Afghan politics along a most ethnic line would likely change the political implications of US military operations in the country. As a result, the prospects of enhanced regional conflicts between warlords seemed more of a reality.[3] These outcomes were mostly the political result of the Bush Administration's hasty decision to throw its full support behind the Northern Alliance prior to the fall of Kabul in November 2001.

Once the Taliban was driven from Kabul, between 2002 and 2004, political remnants of the Northern Alliance sought to bring stability and order to Afghanistan. They failed almost immediately. Tajik and Uzbek warlords sought reprisals against former Taliban enemies and against one another. Without the Taliban to oppose, the Northern Alliance simply lost its coherence and ability to set aside internal squabbling. The Alliance collapsed itself into four bases: the largely Tajik northeast under the control of Masoud's allies; the mostly Uzbek area of the north and northwest controlled by Abdul Rashid Dostum; the provinces around Heart, a mostly a Pashtun zone controlled by Tajik warlord Ismail Khan; and, the Hazara area of central Afghanistan, controlled by the Shiite leader

Mohammad Karim Khalili.[4] Violent conflicts among the groups are common and the potential for another widespread civil war is quite high, since none of the areas is under absolute ethnic control and the lack of a modern infrastructure and technological impediments make it almost impossible for any warlord to exercise clear authority.

The construction of the national government of US-backed Interim President Hamid Karzai is quite different from the actual balance of power and economic resources within the country.[5] The possibility of an adjustment to these realities is virtually certain. The post-Taliban balance between former Northern Alliance leaders and civilian authority does not favor Karzai. No central military authority is able to exercise control over the provinces, which look like a loose association of medieval fiefdoms and chaotic areas. These features imply a significant potential for future conflict and terrorism. Two steps that might have mitigated this potential were an initial creation of a well-balanced government of national unity and the deployment of a large-contingent of United Nations or international peacekeepers. Although the 2001 Bonn meeting produced both a new government and a peacekeeping force for Afghanistan, neither of these really fill the bill, for several reasons.[6]

The successful formation of a new Afghan government in Bonn was a step in the right direction, seeing as how it was only formed in early December 2001. But the agreement generated substantial dissent among Northern Alliance warlords who had fought the Taliban for a number of years. Karzai's interim government was a basic compromise among the Tajik minority, which installed fellow Tajiks to high positions in the ministries of defense, interior, and foreign affairs.[7] But neither Karzai nor the other (much weaker) Pashtun members of the administration can reliably command the loyalty of all the Pashtun factions.[8]

Moreover, Karzai lacks significant military power that he can reliably call his own. Karzai is politically dependent on US military power, which has made him unpopular among the former US-backed Northern Alliance. Karzai's dependence on the US may restrain his ability to build a national governing political base. Also, Karzai is also dependent on individual warlord militias, which can be easily bought off by anyone with enough money or opium. In fact, at present there are several clusters of military power, most of which are beyond Karzai's control. The first is the central government located in Kabul. The Tajik ministers have local Tajik militias at their disposal, but these number roughly 12,000 soldiers and the overwhelming majority is Tajik. The second cluster is led by Uzbek General Abdul Rashid Dostum, who operates out of Mazar-i-Sharif and controls five Afghan provinces and between 5,000 to 8,000 fighters. The third is Tajik warlord Ismail Khan controls Heart and has 5,000 armed fighters under his command. Fourth, Mohammad Karim Khalili, leader of the Shiite Hazara coalition based in the Bamiyan province, controls roughly 8,000 fighters. The fifth is former Afghan President and Northern Alliance political leader Burrhanuddin Rabban is allied with Abdul Rassoul Sayyaf, a Pashtun leader of the Saudi-backed Ittihad-i-Islami party. The sixth power cluster is a loose alliance of known as the Peshawar Group led by Pir Syed Gailani who controls the Logar province. A seventh cluster is Haji

Abdul Qadir, former Northern Alliance council member and head of the Pashtun Eastern Council, who controls Nangarhar province and incorporates three other warlords: Mohammad Zaman, Hazarat Ali, and Younis Khalis. Another power cluster is the remnants of the Taliban, led by its reclusive leader Mullah Mohammed Omar and Khuddamul Furqan the eastern provinces.[9]

In addition to overthrowing the Taliban and dispersing the Al-Qaida leadership, America also sought to work with local warlords to capture and imprison as many Taliban and Al-Qaida fighters as possible. The US was primarily interested in rank-and-file Afghan Taliban and Al-Qaida and other foreign fighters and terrorists who did not defect after the US launched Operation Enduring Freedom. Given the calamitous 11 September 2001 attacks, the US contended there was no acceptable alternative to these goals, which meant a willingness to prosecute them to the death. For the increasingly decentralized Northern Alliance, the disintegration of the Taliban and the defection of Al-Qaida meant the end of the war and the beginning of a postwar period governed by its own interests.

In Pashtun areas, Afghan militias were not concerned with capturing or detaining Taliban and Al-Qaida leaders, a viewpoint and practice that angered the US. For Pashtun groups in the Northern Alliance, the reason for pursuing the Taliban and their leaders was to reintegrate them into governing factions, not to punish, imprison, or eliminate them.[10] There was a tacit recognition that engaging in reprisals was a waste of resources and even risked a protracted civil war.

Although the Karzai government also even sought to reconcile with the Taliban, it did support the US in capturing and arresting the Al-Qaida leadership but not with the ferocity exhibited by the US. Instead, they gave priority to the tasks of building government legitimacy, averting communal violence, and relieving the nation's humanitarian crisis. Afghan cooperation with America's overall intention of pursuing the Taliban and Al-Qaida was mostly partial and was often characterized as highly contentious. This included the release of Taliban prisoners by a number of Afghan militias opposition to America's ongoing bombing campaigns and use of Special Forces manipulation of target areas by ethnic minorities to eliminate internal dissent.[11]

The divergence of priorities within the US-Afghan coalition has been especially disruptive to the US campaign since it was originally premised on cooperation between the US and the Northern Alliance. This dependency virtually guaranteed that, should priorities diverge, US mission capabilities would be seriously compromised. The problem lies not with the concept of "cooperation", *per se*, but rather with the expectation that a strong basis for cooperation, trust, and joint operations can be established overnight.

The chaotic state of post-Taliban Afghan politics is a major challenge to the US and the interim government. Karzai can tap US military and political support when he needs to; however, US interests are not always identical to those expressed by the interim government. Currently the US cares mostly about locating, capturing, or killing Osama bin Laden, not nation-building. Thus, the long-term stability of Afghanistan, the authority of its government, the relief of its humanitarian crisis, and the country's prospects for reconstruction and recovery all depend on managing the power clusters.[12]

Iraq

Three weeks after the fall of Baghdad, the White House staged its own spectacular to celebrate the victory in Iraq, arranging for President Bush to land on the deck of the USS Abraham Lincoln off the coast of California.[13] On 2 May 2003, under a banner that proclaimed "Mission Accomplished," the commander-in-chief congratulated his troops on a job well done. For Bush, victory was obtained with the fall of Baghdad and the overthrow of Saddam Hussein: "And tonight I have a special word for Secretary Rumsfeld, for General Franks, and for all the men and women who wear the uniform of the United States: America is grateful for a job well done."[14] According to James Fallows, "I would have thought that the people who cared most about making Iraq an example of democracy to the Arab Islamic world would have been the most insistent on taking the long view, on making sure that the whole campaign was a success, not just the military campaign to take over Baghdad."[15]

The war, said Bush, had been carried out "with a combination of precision and speed and boldness the enemy did not expect, and the world had not seen before."[16] But the mission wasn't accomplished then, and it still is not. The reconstruction of Iraq has proved far more difficult than any official assumed it would be. Since 2 May, total US combat deaths in Iraq have surpassed 1100 in the face of more frequent violent attacks.[17] Two potential leaders of the new Iraq – Ayatollah Mohammed Baqir al-Hakim and Akila al-Hashimi, a member of the US-appointed Governing Council in Iraq – have been assassinated. Also dead is Sergio Vieira de Mello, the UN chief representative in Iraq, who was killed when a bomb exploded at UN headquarters last month. After a second bombing last week near the building, UN Secretary General Kofi Annan ordered a reduction in the size of the organization's mission for reasons of safety.[18]

What the Bush Administration now faces in Iraq is far different from what it had planned for. In the two years since the invasion, the insurgency has grown in size, and its strength has not been diminished. In the Sunni triangle around Baghdad, remnants of the Fedayeen, the Baath Party, foreign jihadi fighters and even ordinary Iraqis began waging a guerrilla war. Former Bush Army Secretary Thomas White states, "I think it's enormously frustrating because the signs were all there that this could, in fact, be enormously difficult. We just underwhelmed it, and we are paying the price for that. And the price is both in lives and in treasury is going to be quite high."[19]

When will the job be considered complete? Was it completed when the government of Saddam was toppled, when he was captured, or when every insurgent and foreign terrorist is killed or lays down his or her weapon? Even though Iraq may have achieved some level of sovereignty following the handover of authority on 28 June 2004, US military commanders have correctly predicted that the insurgency will has become more deadly and widespread. The violence is even expected to continue well after the January 2005 national election. US General John Abizaid recently announced, "I would predict... that the situation will become more violent even after sovereignty because it will remain unclear what's going to happen between the interim government and elections. So moving through the election period will be violent and it could very well be more violent than we're seeing today."[20]

The problem is most likely due to the premature end of major hostilities, which had a direct impact on its ability to manage subsequent phases of the war. Frequent disruptions in power made civilian life unbearable, while the flow of oil, which the Bush Administration had hoped would fund Iraq's reconstruction, was, on some days, less than half what it had been before the war. Moreover, despite five months of searching, the WMD, whose possession by Saddam had been the principal reason advanced by Bush for the war, are nowhere to be found. The Bush Administration's budget request of $87 billion for military operations and reconstruction in Iraq and Afghanistan is staggering.[21] As it becomes clear that there will not be a sudden influx of international troops or UN peacekeepers, the US has been forced to extend tours of duty of regular soldiers and to even tap into the Reserves and several National Guard units.

Those consequences flow from a series of flawed assumptions and naïve presuppositions, which produced an array of unintended consequences. According to Democratic Senator Joseph Biden last week, the president "believed we would find an oil-rich, functioning country, that we'd be met by cheering crowds, that all we had to do was sweep out the top Baathist layers, implant our favorite exiles and watch democracy take root as the bulk of the troops returned home by Christmas."[22] Bureaucratic infighting, wishful thinking and influence in Congress and the Department of Defense exerted by former Iraqi National Congress leader Ahmed Chalabi exacerbated the adverse effects.[23]

The most significant miscalculation, which had the most detrimental effect on the prospects for a just peace, was and is America's inability and failure to find real evidence of a banned WMD program under Saddam. Dr. David Kay's Iraq Survey Group never found stockpiles of deadly chemical, biological or nuclear weapons.[24] A senior Bush Administration official has stated, "they have come across only parts and pieces and things and that's about the best they are going to come up with." US policymakers "are as surprised as anyone, they really thought that it would be a lot easier to find, identify and show the world everything that was there."[25] Iraqi sources insisted that there was nothing to find; all weapons, they say, were destroyed long ago. The failure to find WMD has been a source of domestic political embarrassment for Bush and of international contempt on the part of the international community.

Why were so many convinced that Saddam had WMD? Well, in part, because he did once have them, and until challenged by UN inspectors after the first Gulf War had tried to conceal them.[26] Saddam may have engaged in the world's most famous deception by fooling everyone into thinking that he had something, when in fact he had nothing. The question now is: does America's inability to locate a banned WMD program operated by Saddam directly hamper its effort to establish a just peace given that the primary justification for going to war in the first place has been lost, or more importantly, never existed?

Right Intention

Afghanistan

Preventing a total breakdown in authority in Afghanistan was among America's most pressing intentions. Afghan president Hamid Karzai, UN Secretary General Kofi Annan, former UN Envoy to Afghanistan Lakhdar Brahimi, and a number of nongovernmental aid organizations have all called for a larger operation that would protect the delivery of humanitarian assistance throughout the country and deter fighting among regional warlords. Although the war effort is not nearly as intensive today as it was in 2001 and 2002, US forces are now more focused on search and destroy missions than engaged in major battles. This in no way should imply that Afghanistan is more stable today, since internal strife among former Northern Alliance militias and attacks from foreign fighters and remnants of the Taliban still occur. In essence, while there may not be an actual war, Afghanistan is not at peace.

American long term intention is to safeguard a governing system, which empowers President Karzai with the necessary tools so the new national government can be responsible for its own security in the long run. This begins with promoting stable and effective national security institutions, namely local and provincial police forces that can rival and manage the warlords, a border patrol that could prevent terrorist infiltration, and the construction of a national army powerful enough to quell internal chaos and respond to regional threats with US support. At present, US Special Operating Forces along with the Central Intelligence Agency are working with the Karzai government to train and equip these new security institutions. Conflicts remain over how to set new policies in place and with what means new institutions will depend on.

The Bush Administration is intent on such an approach in order to prevent against a more large-scale peacekeeping effort that could be passed by a United Nations Security Council resolution. Defense Secretary Rumsfeld contended that Afghanistan should be made independent enough to care for itself: "Should we spend the time and money and effort in training now to expand the international security force, which ultimately will leave and create an unstable situation when they leave, unless there's something to take their place? Or should the time and money and effort and training be spent now to create that national army?"[27] If Afghanistan's stability deteriorates, the opportunity for those institutions to accomplish anything could be lost, particularly if Karzai fails to extend his national authority into the regional provinces. More importantly, Afghans, who traditionally fear and distrust any central government, have to be convinced that new national and provincial security institutions can ensure their safety and promote their interests.[28]   Otherwise, the security forces will be swallowed up by the warlords who themselves fear the emergence of any rival power.

America's effort to support the new government and its institutions is certainly an uphill battle, especially given several contingent factors. Not only will political and military institutions have to be built and maintained, Afghanistan is in dire need of economic help.   Alternative to opium poppy production, which has skyrocketed since the overthrow of the Taliban, still have yet to be established.[29] Corruption is a regular practice among the police forces and border guards and extortion is a considered a normal social and economic practice. As a result, humanitarian aid cannot reach the areas in most desperate need due to banditry and violence.

While violent conflicts have emerged between rival warlords and different ethnic groups, the US has succeeded in preventing ethnic cleansing in Afghanistan or skirmishes over particular landmarks or areas of religious significance. Although Afghanistan seems immune from suffering from widespread property destruction or reprisal killing, the rapid increase in opium poppy production and mass chaos are real and actual threats to peace and could unravel America's primary intention of promoting national order and stability.

Furthermore, while the Bush Administration has avoided the intervention of UN peacekeepers, US Special Forces are already carrying out various kinds of peacekeeping activities in scattered local areas throughout the Afghan countryside. From almost the very start of the war, US soldiers have been performing humanitarian needs assessments in Afghan villages and coordinating the delivery of aid. This effort was enhanced between 2002 and 2004 resulting in the completion of several humanitarian aid missions, including rebuilding residential and commercial structures and clothing and feeding the most impoverished.[30] Moreover, the US Army has dispatched forces to negotiate between warring factions, mingled with the population to gain intelligence, seized weapons caches and large reserves of opium, and provided personal security to Karzai and his cabinet.   While such operations and missions resemble a peacekeeping effort, there are not enough military and intelligence personnel to make it more of a far-reaching national effort.

For the most part, Afghans have not expressed fear about US intentions in their country and the Bush Administration is overly sensitive about appearing as an occupying force in Afghanistan. Deputy Defense Secretary Paul Wolfowitz has emphasized, "We have been very mindful of [the] historical Afghan animosity to foreign armies and foreign occupiers. ... We have made it clear, and we need to continue to do so, [that] we have no intent of colonizing Afghanistan."[31] However, the US is keenly aware of the historical trend that when governments fall, anarchy is likely to follow.   In Afghanistan, America's fear is that should Karzai's government collapse, its security interests within the country and in Central Asia are likely to fail, especially given that terrorists will probably exploit the mayhem to reassert their goals.   In the absence of UN peacekeepers, the US must demonstrate its will to remain in Afghanistan over the long run. Current US policies are adequate in the short run; however, if the US is really seeking to prevail against terrorism, the Bush Administration must be willing to engage in more widespread peacekeeping operations designed to avert additional human suffering, aimed at preventing anarchy and to seek broad multilateral support for these missions.[32]

Iraq

A key element in establishing just intentions in Iraq was America's urgent effort at "de-Baathification," that is, identifying and arresting senior figures responsible for the political crimes of Saddam's regime, including leading figures of his Sunni-dominated Baath Party, and banning his allies from post-war governance. Under Order Number One, which was issued by former US Administrator L. Paul Bremer who along with the Iraqi Governing Council ruled Iraq before sovereignty was transferred to the Iraqi Interim Government of Prime Minister Iyad Allawi on 28 June 2004, all senior military and civilian Baathist officials would be stripped of their positions and replaced by the American-led governing council.[33]

Among the most important elements in building a post-Saddam Iraq would be the completion of the trial of Saddam. The trial, which was set to occur in an Iraqi criminal court, would contend with the following charges against Saddam: the Anfal campaign against Kurds, the use of chemical weapons in Halabja in 1988, massacring members of Kurdish Barzani tribe, crushing Kurdish and Shia rebellions after the Gulf War in 1991, killing political activists, orchestrating the killing of Shiite religious leaders in 1974, and invading Kuwait in 1990.[34] The challenge for the US was ensuring that Saddam would not be subjected to an American-run "show trial" and that Iraqi civilian authorities would be in control of his sentencing. The decision to give ultimate control over the trial to Iraqi civilian prosecutors as opposed to the International Criminal Court or US judicial officials was morally right: Slobodan Milosevic's disastrous trial in The Hague has been far too easily dismissed in Serbia as "foreigners' justice" and has actually helped rehabilitate the Serbian dictator. But the investigations may fall into American hands, since Iraqis lack the necessary tools to conduct a forensic examination of the hundreds of people buried in mass graves.

While the trial was the symbol of de-Baathification, America's more substantive efforts have not produced the desired outcome. Bremer's disastrous decision to disband the Iraqi army put thousands of armed men on the streets with no pay and no reason to support the US-led Iraqi Governing Council.[35] Interim Prime Minister Iyad Allawi, who was a key Shiite representative on the council, even recommended that the US keep the Iraqi army and police force intact in order to obviate potential Sunni resistance.[36]

A major challenge to America's case for right intentions in promoting a just peace rested on the fact that the US placed former Iraqi National Congress Chair Ahmad Chalabi in charge of Bremer's de-Baathification initiatives. Prior to his downfall, Chalabi's efforts were tumultuous for Iraq and the US following the cessation of major hostilities on 2 May 2003. Soon after Chalabi returned to Iraq, allegations of corruption and criminal behavior surfaced. Chalabi's militia, the

Free Iraqi Fighters, had also been accused of looting and stealing as the US approached Baghdad in April 2003.[37]

Other problems have surfaced as a result of the Bush Administration's support of Chalabi. Following the fall of Saddam, Chalabi was named by Bremer to head the finance committee of the Iraqi Governing Council and, as a result, was able to install his friends as oil, finance, and trade ministers, as well as governors of Iraq's Central Bank. Several were awarded lucrative reconstruction contracts.[38] Chalabi's embrace of the Shiite faction of Iraq has also fed the speculation that he gave intelligence secrets to the Shiite-led government of Iran. His aide, Aras Habib, was even accused of spying for Iran. Chalabi himself has been openly collegial with reformist leaders in Iran, such as President Mohammad Khatami, and has acknowledged meeting with officials of Iranian Ministry of Intelligence and Security.[39] By May 2004, the US had enough of Chalabi and launched a raided of his home in Baghdad, which uncovered evidence of his illicit behavior.[40]

On the whole, the Bush Administration was insistent that US forces were welcomed by Iraq's as liberators and that there was gratitude for their presence now. While popular sentiment is certainly difficult to measure, Iraq has struggled with the transition to a post-Saddam society. The reality of the present situation in Iraq can be summarized along the following lines: whatever horrors Iraqis suffered under Saddam, they are more horrified at the presence of the US military forces in their country. However, resentment and anti-Americanism is growing.

A strong challenge to the case for America's justifiable intentions in establishing a just peace involves the use of torture and humiliation by the US military and intelligence community to extract information from detained Iraqi POWs. During an inspection of the infamous Abu Ghraib prison in October 2003, inspectors with the International Committee of the Red Cross were deeply disturbed by what they observed at the facility and demand an immediate explanation from the military prison authorities. According to the Red Cross, prisoners were being held "completely naked in totally empty concrete cells and in total darkness," for days. The inspectors also documented the type of behavior that would explode onto the American mass media in April and May 2004, namely: "acts of humiliation such as being made to stand naked against the wall of the cell with arms raised or with women's underwear over the heads for prolonged periods while being laughed at by guards, including female guards, and sometimes photographed in this position."[41] The report also referred to military intelligence officers who had confirmed Red Cross reports that those "methods of physical and psychological coercion used by the interrogators appeared to be part of the standard operating procedures by military intelligence personnel to obtain confessions and extract information."[42]

Even more, the US Army and the CIA kept dozens of detainees at Abu Ghraib prison and other detention facilities off official rosters to hide them from Red Cross inspectors. According to General Paul Stern, "The number is in the dozens, to perhaps up to 100."[43] Although the Geneva Conventions allow for the temporary failure to disclose the identities of prisoners to the Red Cross under an exemption for military necessity, US Army commanders were certain that such practices used by the CIA in Iraq went far beyond that. The disclosure added to questions about CIA practices in Iraq, including why the agency took custody of certain Iraqi prisoners, what interrogation techniques it used and what became of the ghost detainees, including whether they were ever returned to military custody.[44] Defense Secretary Donald H. Rumsfeld has acknowledged that in one case, acting at the request of former CIA Director George J. Tenet, he ordered military officials in Iraq in November to hold a man at Camp Cropper, a high-level detention center, but not to register him.[45] The White House and the US Senate issued different responses to the Iraqi prisoner abuse scandal. While the Senate adopted a resolution condemning the prisoner abuse by 92 to 0, President Bush praised Donald Rumsfeld by stating, "You are doing a superb job. You are a strong secretary of defense, and our nation owes you a debt of gratitude."[46]

As events throughout 2004 demonstrated, the US intervention in Iraq may have caused more problems than it solved them. As the US occupation gave way to a UN-recognized sovereign Iraqi interim government, the prospects for a stable, democratic future were in serious peril due in large measure to the failure of US occupation leaders to fulfill their stated goals and the inability to subdue a rising national insurgency and to calm a growing separatist movement in the autonomous Kurdish region. The US occupation evolved from an optimistic relationship in April 2003 into one characterized by bitterness and disappointment as illustrated by the open strife between the Bush White House and the once favored Ahmad Chalabi and Iraqi National Congress. Moreover, the insurgency has not only threatened US goals in Iraq, it has endangered the fragile state of Iraqi sovereignty. The combined effects of the Sunni/Baathist resistance, the Shiite Mahdi Army of Moqtada Sadr, and foreign terrorist infiltration have succeeded in destabilizing the interim government and killed scores of American and Iraqi soldiers. According to former US occupation authority adviser Larry Diamond, "We blatantly failed to get it right. When you look at the record, it's impossible to escape the conclusion that we squandered an unprecedented opportunity."[47]

Discrimination

Afghanistan

America's inability to effectively adjust to a post-Taliban Afghanistan most likely contributed to is failure to capture bin Laden and destroy the Al-Qaida leadership by the end of December 2001. It also led to high non-combatant casualties and humanitarian costs on civilians in Afghanistan following the fall of Kabul. In post-Taliban Afghanistan, the US military sought to continue the practice of furthering a new style of warfare, which promises minimal collateral damage and civilian casualties. President Bush summarized the essentials of this proposition in a speech before workers at a Boeing aircraft plant in April, 2003: "By a combination of creative strategies and advanced technologies, we are redefining war on our terms. In this new era of warfare, we can target a regime, not a nation."[48]

The human cost of the war has questioned the legitimate imposition of a just peace and has resulted in long term repercussions for the American military presence in Afghanistan. As illustrated by Defense Secretary Rumsfeld,

> [I]f you kill a lot of civilians, the people inside Afghanistan will believe you're not discriminating and that you are against the people of Afghanistan ... [I]nstead of defecting and leaving Taliban and leaving Al-Qaida, they're going to be more supportive and they're going to be against the United States and the coalition forces. And we don't want that ... [T]here are a lot of Muslims in the world. To the extent you behave in a way that suggests that you don't really care about whether or not you're killing soldiers and people that are terrorists or civilians ... it makes life difficult for countries that are supporting us that have large Muslim populations.[49]

The primary concern for the US is that significant non-combatant casualties could much of the civilian population into enhancing their support of local warlords at the expense of the emerging national government, in which the US has placed significance confidence. Another potentially fatal result could be a massive embrace of the Taliban and Al-Qaida as a result of a rise in anti-Americanism. A cycle of violence could also be emerge as the number of revenge attacks against Karzai's allies and US military personnel and civilians increase.

What constitutes "acceptable casualties" from the vantage point of containing such effects depends on whether or not peace can really be attained. America's support for the Northern Alliance and its more extensive bombing campaign against Taliban and Al-Qaida forces in the post-Taliban phase of the war have hampered its efforts to win the peace over the long run. Northern Alliance militias were not only unreliable, they engaged in reprisals against both combatants and non-combatants, mostly Pashtuns who supported the Taliban. The bombing was far too broad and inevitably, although inadvertently, produced non-combatant casualties. The result was a combatant to non-combatant casualty ratio during the post-Taliban phase of the war that was close to one-to-one. High non-combatant casualties led to a popular suspicion of the purpose of the new national government and caused friction between civilian Afghans and the US.[50]

If the US really wanted to demonstrate its support for the national government and avert non-combatant casualties, the US military should have placed a greater emphasis on the use of Special Forces soldiers and other smaller ground force units. Large scale air attacks must be an exceptional practice. Although it is difficult to cite a specific number of non-combatant deaths in the post-Taliban phase of the war, one report estimates between 8,000-18,000 Afghani deaths occurred resulting from starvation, exposure, associated illnesses, or injury sustained while in flight from war zones. Roughly forty per cent of the deaths were the result of Northern Alliance reprisals and US bombing (Internally Displaced Persons). International aid organizations have estimated that 1.5 million civilians have suffered from starvation caused by the violence.[51]

On the whole, US bombing missions in 2002 and 2003 exacerbated the Afghan humanitarian crisis in increasing the number of refugees, disrupting and at times inadvertently destroying relief efforts, handicapping the ability of farmers in planting crops, and degrading the country's already battered infrastructure. The general result was a greater demonstrated need to increase food production, medical supplies, and refugee camps.

Iraq

Immediately prior to the invasion of Iraq in March 2003, President Bush maintained that "If war is forced upon us, we will fight in a just cause and by just means, sparing, in every way we can, the innocent."[52] Bush was mainly concerned with averting additional suffering for innocent Iraqis who lived for years under the yoke of Saddam. During the ensuing US occupation, that is the period following the declaration of an end to major combat on 2 May 2003, US defense personnel reiterated that "even one innocent person injured or killed is something we sincerely regret."[53] To avert higher non-combatant casualties, the US military even abandoned the utilization of cluster munitions and relied on precision guided weapons as an added protection for non-combatants.

However, it has been extraordinarily difficult to distinguish between civilian non-combatants and guerrilla forces or common criminals. Not all casualties are taken to hospitals where records are kept, and Muslim practice is to bury victims the same day they die, which makes recordkeeping even more challenging. The death toll resulting from criminal and politically-motivated violence was also dramatically higher than violent deaths before the invasion. These figures do not include non-combatant casualties from the most violent cities that have been at the center of the national insurgency, in particular the holy Shiite city of Najaf that has seen a massive increase in violence since early April 2004 between US military forces and the Mahdi Army of Moqtada Sadr.[54] It should be emphasized again that there is no precise count for non-combatant casualties in Iraq, nor is there a breakdown of deaths caused by the different sorts of attacks. The US military, the occupation authority and Iraqi government agencies do not track civilian deaths.

According to a report issued by the *Associated Press*, more than 5,500 non-combatants died in Iraq's major cities in the first 12 months of the occupation. In Baghdad, roughly 4,300 people were recorded killed between May 2003 and April 2004. The figure does not include most people killed in big terrorist bombings and foreign citizens who have been executed by insurgents or terrorists. The death toll was an average of 357 violent deaths over the twelve month period, a stark contrast compared to the average of 14 per month in 2002. In comparison, New York City had about 7.5 per 100,000 in 2002.[55]

Other cities have also experienced high non-combatant casualties between May 2003 and April 2004. In Karbala, 663 non-combatants were killed, which is much higher from the 2002 total when there was an average of 1 violent death per month. In Tikrit, 205 non-combatants have been killed or an average of 17 a month. No one was killed as a result of violence in 2002 in Tikrit. In Kirkuk, 401 non-combatants have been killed, an average of thirty four per month. The city averaged three violent deaths a month in 2002. In Fallujah, after US Marines launched offensives into the city following an attack on US contractors in April 2004 and before insurgents regained control of Fallujah during the summer and fall of 2004, 731 non-combatants were reported killed.[56]

US forces have records for the numbers of claims for compensation from Iraqis for personal injuries, deaths, and damages to civilian homes and businesses caused by US military action in "non-combat" situations. In total, roughly $3 million has been paid to a total of 3,000 with about 8,000 having been rejected as frivolous by the US-led Coalition Provisional Authority. No US soldier has been prosecuted for illegally killing an Iraqi civilian. Before sovereignty was transferred to the Iraqi Interim government of Prime Minister Iyad Allawi, an order issued by the US-led authority in Baghdad in June 2003 prohibited judicial cases from being initiated by Iraqi non-combatants against US soldiers or any other foreign troops or civilians in Iraq. In effect, US soldiers operated with relative immunity from US or international prosecution.[57]

These figures, which remain incomplete at the time of this publication, do not mean to suggest that Iraq is a more dangerous place than during Saddam's regime. Recall that well over a half-million civilians were murdered by Iraq's security forces and buried in mass graves during Saddam's rule.[58]

Likelihood of a Lasting Peace

Afghanistan

The most widespread and positive accomplishment of Operation Enduring Freedom was the use of military power to eject the Taliban from governing power. However, while Al-Qaida has been reduced as a force in Afghanistan, it has not been eliminated as a terrorist threat. As a result, the future hope of a lasting just peace is uncertain for the people of Afghanistan. On the national level, despite the change of government in Kabul, Afghanistan may be less stable today than it was during the reign of the Taliban. At the sub-national level, the Taliban-Al-Qaida axis has been replaced by regional conflicts between rival warlords once united in their common struggle against the Taliban.

Another significant bright spot was the October 2004 presidential election, which resulted in the victory of Interim President Hamid Karzai. This was an extraordinary event, since it occurred in spite of efforts by the Taliban and Al-Qaida to prevent it. The turnout, which included registered women voters, rivaled that of the US presidential election in November 2004. However, it should be noted that fifteen of the presidential candidates who campaigned against Karzai abruptly announced a boycott because of a mixup at some polling stations about the type of ink used to mark voters' fingers. Their protest did cast doubt on the legitimacy of the election results.

Although the removal of the Taliban, the dispersal of Al-Qaida, and the Afghani presidential elections are hopeful indicators, the fact remains that Afghanistan is located in a region of the world where violence and instability are present-day realities. Years of chaos, the Soviet invasion and occupation, civil wars, the Taliban, warlords, and the American invasion have led Afghanistan's neighbors to build up their defenses. Iran has quickened its pace towards a strong WMD program and a potential nuclear weapons initiative. Pakistan, already a nuclear power, and its President Pervez Musharrev, are in a highly tenuous position as its northwestern frontier rapidly grows into a haven for terrorists and displaced Afghan refugees. Finally, the US bombing campaign has resulted in high non-combatant casualties and the post-war treatment of combat detainees has fanned the flames of anti-American sentiment throughout the Muslim world.[59] While America's influence in Central Asia has been quietly growing for a number of years, its future in Afghanistan is really a secret. A more enhanced and visible presence has a strong likelihood of preventing the establishment of a just peace, especially given that the stationing of the US military makes Afghanistan an object of geo-strategic interest for Russia and China, as well as for Central Asia's Islamist movement.[60]

The US has also indicated that it would like to deploy thousands more US troops and military equipment to an unspecified number of other countries in order to replicate its perceived success against terrorists operating in Afghanistan.[61] However, the exercise of additional US military power is bound to challenge its hope for a just peace, which the Bush Administration believes can be attained with military might and political influence. Consistent with this anti-terrorism strategy is the Bush Administration's reduced emphasis on humanitarian interests, international legal mechanisms, and nation-building. A key element in that strategy is an overwhelming emphasis on regime change against rogue states that sponsor terrorist activity and pursue WMD, which could fall into the hands of terrorists.[62]

Thus, according to the Bush Administration, the problem of terrorism should be met with what it sees as a fairly straightforward solution currently being applied to Afghanistan: a quick and decisive application of preemptive or preventive military force designed to eliminate rogue states that consort with or tolerate terrorists. Although the US aim is to "drain the swamp" and repair holes in the dyke, such a strategy has broad implications and could impose significant adverse effects, namely destabilizing new regimes, non-combatant casualties, and anti-Americanism.[63] The application of offensive force and its supposed long-term deterrent-effect are seen as sufficient enough to eliminate terrorist threats and to establish a longstanding just peace.

The idea that transnational terrorist organizations need states in order to survive and prosper is misleading. None of Al-Qaida's capabilities on 9/11 required a large state-supported infrastructure or cooperation. In fact, the 9/11 terrorists relied more on flight schools in Florida and facilities in Hamburg than on camps in Afghanistan to carry out their operations. Of course, the Taliban's open support of Al-Qaida was crucial to its success. However, most important to the evolution of Al-Qaida and its operational strength was the actual direction of US foreign policy, which was structured around the American military presence in Saudi Arabia following the first Gulf War, dependence on Middle Eastern oil, militarization of the Central Asia and the Middle East, and support for Israel.

American foreign policy towards Central Asia is reflective of a peripheral vision that makes additional military action more likely in years to come and the hope of a just peace all the more difficult to achieve. Operation Enduring Freedom correctly targeted the Taliban for extinction and minimized the effects of pursuing this course. However, with regard to the war's strategy, it led the US to overestimate its capacity to quickly and reliably bend Pakistan to its purposes. It also led the US to minimize the risks of unleashing the Northern Alliance. In addition, it depreciated the negative side effects of the strategic bombing campaign, the potential for post-war chaos, and the importance of economic measures to rehabilitate Afghan society from decades of deterioration and international isolation.

Effective action to promote a lasting just peace in Afghanistan depends on a combination of military and non-military measures, including diplomatic, humanitarian, financial, peace-building, and law-enforcement efforts. Military force should be used to guarantee the success of non-military initiatives and to build the necessary conditions in which a just peace over the long run can be attained. It is also essential that the US combat terrorism in ways that do not contribute to interstate instability. A failure to do this would simply exchange one type of problem for another and undermine the basis for attending to either. This requires that military force be constrained. It is only through the integration and balance of military and nonmilitary measures and global and regional cooperative initiatives that a lasting peace can be established.

But is the US interested in mixing military and non-military measures to promote a real and lasting just peace? Richard Haas, the Bush Administration's former Director of Policy Planning at the State Department, has argued that the US would limit its participation in the post-war reconstruction of Afghanistan. Since, according to Haas, the US performed applied the "lion's share of the world's work" in terms of military operations, he believed other countries would help in rebuilding the country.[64] Although the US was asserting itself as the world preeminent global power, it was not seeking to place significant attention on issues unrelated to promoting political stability and security in Afghanistan.

Iraq

There are several urgent challenges that must be addressed in order for a real lasting just peace to occur in Iraq. First, the most pressing short term need is for the US and the Iraqi Interim government to deliver food and medical supplies to citizens in need, to meet protect and safeguard Iraqi refugees, and to restore power and water to cities and towns that experienced major disruptions. Supplies must be distributed and services restored with an intense, comprehensive, and focused effort that draws on the broadest possible range of relief agencies, both American and international. Second, in order for economic reconstruction to take place, the US and the Iraqi Interim government must create a comprehensive and supportive economic environment. This includes repairing and developing the physical infrastructure of the country and the promoting a stable national political order in Baghdad. The problem is that unemployment rate is in excess of 40 per cent and the crime rate is much higher than it was during Saddam's final years in power.[65] While conditions have improved somewhat since 2 May 2003, the reality is that the high rate of unemployment and crime are a dangerous combination that could motivate ordinary Iraqis with nothing to lose to aid or take part in the insurgency.

Similar to its goals in Afghanistan, for the US, the future of Iraq and the hope for a lasting peace resides firmly on building national political institutions. The prospects for building a central state authority on a democratic foundation seemed more hopeful in Iraq, since there has been a long, although bloody, history of strong national political institutions. To reassert a governing authority in Iraq, the US immediately sought to prevent against too much devolution of political power to the three competing ethnic groups in the country: the majority Shiites, the minority Sunnis, and the Kurds. After major combat was declared over on 2 May 2003, the US created a US-led authority named the Iraq Governing Council, which was led by US Administrator L. Paul Bremer and included several top Iraqis, namely Ahmad Chalabi and would be Interim Prime Minister Iyad Allawi.

Following the transfer of sovereignty on 28 June 2004, the Iraqi Interim government sought to establish and maintain national and to control the emerging national insurgency. However, the interim government, which was endorsed by the United Nations as the sovereign government of Iraq, is almost completely dependent on the US military and to some extent UK forces for policing the cities.[66] While a new Iraqi police force is slowly being trained; however, its legitimacy has been questioned because of its close association with the American military.

Moreover, Interim Prime Minister Allawi has relied on the American military to fight the national insurgency and patrol Iraq's porous eastern and western borders to prevent against foreign terrorist infiltration. The insurgency is organized, far-reaching, and has the potential for preventing any lasting peace in Iraq on terms set by the US and the Iraqi Interim government. The key elements that comprise the insurgency include an array of loosely aligned forces. Initially, it was thought that some of those suspected of being behind attacks against the US were Iraqi criminals. Prior to the invasion, Saddam released thousands of criminals from jail before the war, allowing these once detained criminals to roam the streets and command strikes against Coalition Forces. The insurgents also appear to include a mix of mostly Sunni former regime loyalists and Baath Party hardliners, Shiite militias, Kurdish groups, outside Arab volunteers, and foreign terrorists suspected of being tied to Al-Qaida.[67] Currently a few hundred of the roughly 10,000 detainees in US custody are foreign nationals, suggesting that most of the violent attacks have been conducted by Iraqis.

Among the most deadly and organized of these insurgent groups are Sunnis loyal to Saddam and other Baath Party hardliners. This contingent has deliberately targeted Iraqi civilians, Iraqi government forces, US military personnel, and other coalition forces. Any hope for a peaceful and prosperous future for Iraq hinges on America's ability to destroy this group. Paul Bremer may have actually helped to unleash these insurgents via his de-Baathification policies and by dismantling Republican Guard and Special Republican Guard units.[68] Following the termination of major combat on 2 May 2003, Bremer denied former Baathist officers and soldiers their incomes. Most were never compelled to give up their weapons and munitions and all were denied positions in the new interim government.[69] This dangerous combination contributed to many of the attacks against Iraqi civilians and US soldiers in largely Sunni areas of Baghdad, Fallujah, and Saddam's home city of Tikrit.[70] Former Baathists are also suspected of fomenting ties with Ansar al Islam (Supporters of Islam), which is itself thought to have links with Al-Qaida.[71] Formed in December 2001, Ansar al Islam is a Sunni Islamic group composed primarily of Kurds and located in northeastern Iraq.

Fallujah was the symbol of a greater struggle for Sunni and Baathist insurgents. For the US, Fallujah became the primary focus for stabilizing Iraq since insurgents assumed control of the city following the April 2004 attacks on US contractors. The objective guiding the strategy of US and Iraqi government forces was to retake Fallujah before the January 2005 national elections and to ensure Sunni participation in the post-Saddam political order. However, the US risked creating a backlash that may keep Sunnis away from the polls.[72]

Even more problematic was the fact that Sunni and Baathist insurgents have escalated their attacks throughout the Sunni triangle and in Baghdad. Their goal has been to demonstrate that creating new fronts away from Fallujah might ease pressure on the city and signal that after an inevitable US attack, the resistance would continue.[73] Although US and Iraqi military forces launched a successful military offensive on 8 November 2004 that resulted in the retaking of Fallujah, most of the insurgents, including former Baathist military officer loyal to Saddam, dispersed and attacked new targets in Mosul, Ramadi, Samarrah, Baquba, Tal Afar and Baghdad.[74]

Another key group involved in the national insurgency is the Shiite al-Sadr family, which calls itself "The Active Religious Seminary." Until recently it was headed by Grand Ayatollah Muhammad Sadiq al-Sadr, who was assassinated along with two of his sons by presumed agents of Saddam in Al-Najaf in 1999. Control of the seminary then passed on to Muqtada al-Sadr, a mid-level cleric The seminary's role in the insurgency is absolutely consequential to America's role in promoting peace in Iraq because of al-Sadr suspected working relationship with the government of Iran.[75] The seminary's militant wing is called the "Mahdi Army," which may have several thousand armed combatants.[76]

The al-Sadr group has drawn charges of involvement in attacks and intimidation in Najaf that have highlighted political differences among Shi'a political organizations. The most notable of those attacks was a mob killing of a pro-US cleric, Abd al-Majid al-Khoi, shortly after his return from exile in London in early April.[77] Immediately after al-Khoi's murder, supporters of al-Sadr have sought the open support of Iraqi's Shiite Grand Ayatollah Ali Sistani. Although

Sistani has at times indicated his support of Sadr and at other times has called on him to remove himself from the insurgency, US and coalition troops have fought several violent battles with the Mahdi Army in Basra, Kirkuk, Al-Nassiriya, Amara, and Kut. Deadly clashes have also been concentrated in Sadr city in the south of Baghdad and in the old city of Najaf near the Imam Mosque.

In early June 2004, Prime Minister Allawi called on the Mahdi to disarm and offered them the opportunity to join state-controlled security services or return to civilian life. The offer was followed by sporadic periods of violent clashes and failed truces. Then on 7 August 2004, Allawi granted a general amnesty to pardon insurgents who have committed minor crimes and ordered the Mahdi Army to disband, essentially giving Sadr the chance to distance himself from his followers and peacefully assume a role in the political process.[78] Militiamen loyal to Sadr did eventually surrender their weapons in what was thought to be an encouraging response to a deal struck between the Iraqi interim government and the US military. However, reigning in Sadr's Mahdi Army was less of an illustration of US influence or Allawi's diplomatic skill and more of a reflection of the authority of Grand Ayatollah Ali Sistani, who marched hundreds of thousands of his Shiite supporters through the city of Najaf in September 2004 as a demonstration of who the real power is among Iraqi Shiites.[79]

The foreign terrorist group known as Jamaat al-Tawhid wa'l-Jihad (Unity and Jihad Group) is directed by Jordanian-born Sunni terrorist Abu Musab al-Zarqawi , who is associated with Osama bin Laden and enjoys the support of Al-Qaida.[80] Evidence of al-Zarqawi's allegiance to bin Laden came in the form of a 17 October 2004 website posting, in which al-Zarqawi claimed, "We deliver to the nation the news that both Jama'at Al-Tawhid wa Al-Jihad's Amir and soldiers have pledged allegiance to the sheikh of the mujahedin, Osama bin Laden, and that they will follow his orders in jihad for the sake of God so there will be no more tumult or oppression, and justice and faith in God will prevail."[81] He is wanted by the US on suspicion of organizing terrorist attacks in Iraq and, prior to the November 2004 offensive, was thought to be operating out of Fallujah.[82] Al-Zarqawi, who was once reviled for beheading civilians, has gained support among Iraqis outraged over the US presence in Iraq. According to Baghdad University Professor Salman al-Jumaili, Iraqis now "welcome anyone who is anti-American. The public trend is toward extremism because their houses and towns are under bombardment. They don't support Zarqawi himself, they support the resistance he represents."[83]

America's own prospects for establishing a lasting peace are quite grim. The US Army has even conceded that it lacks control over large portions of key Iraqi cities.[84] The reason for such a loss of control maybe that American military commanders did not foresee the possibility of an insurgency in the first place. According to General Tommy Franks, "We just didn't know (about the insurgency). I think there was not a full appreciation of the realities in Iraq at least of the psychology of the Iraqis. On the one hand, I think we all believed that they hated the regime of Saddam Hussein... On the other hand, the psychology of the people, the mix of the Sunnis, the Shiites, the tribal elements and the Kurds and what they would expect and tolerate in terms of coalition forces, their numbers, where they are and what they're doing in Iraq, I don't know that we made willful assumptions with respect to that."[85]

Franks initially projected that troop strength in Iraq required 250,000 American combat soldiers to meet all of its objectives in the post-invasion component of the war. However, total combat troop strength never got higher than 150,000, with 130,000 American troops comprising the total. Franks also maintained that "the wild card in this was the expectation for much greater international involvement. I never cared whether the international community came by way of NATO or the United Nations or directly ... We started the operation believing that nations would provide us with an awful lot of support."[86] Instead, coalition troops in the invasion totaled roughly 22,000 and many of those, except for the United Kingdom, have been withdrawn.

Furthermore, a classified National Intelligence Estimate prepared for President Bush in late July 2004 spelled out a bleak future for Iraq. The estimate outlined several possibilities for Iraq through the end of 2005, with the worst case being an all-out civil war. The most favorable outcome is an Iraq whose political, economic, and social stability would remain tenuous over the long run. The intelligence estimate was prepared by the National Intelligence Council and approved by the National Foreign Intelligence Board under Acting CIA Director John McLaughlin. Senator Richard G. Lugar of Indiana, chairman of the Foreign Relations Committee, called it "exasperating for anybody to look at this from any vantage point," and Senator Chuck Hagel, Republican of Nebraska, said of the overall lack of spending: "It's beyond pitiful, it's beyond embarrassing. It is now in the zone of dangerous."[87] The most telling illustration of the deteriorating situation in Iraq may have been provided by President Bush's former Secretary of the Army Thomas White:

> I suppose, looking back on it, it is hard to believe that rational people, looking at that situation before the combat operation, could have thought it was going to come out in any other way than it, in fact, did. Is the world a better place because Saddam is gone? Certainly. Will Iraq eventually become a better place for the average Iraqi? Certainly, we hope it will. But it isn't yet, and we've got a long ways to go.[88]

The dismal situation in Iraq has prompted harsh criticism from both Republicans and Democrats for the Bush Administration's apparent shift of spending priorities from reconstruction to security in order to confront the insurgency and enhance support for the interim government. Republicans on the Senate Foreign Relations Committee issued warnings about the American campaign in Iraq, saying the administration's request to divert more than $3 billion to security from the $18.4 billion aid package of last November was a sign of trouble. "Although we recognize these funds must not be spent unwisely," Committee Chairman Lugar argued that "the slow pace of reconstruction spending means that we are failing to fully take advantage of one of our most potent tools to influence the direction of Iraq." Less than $1 billion has been spent so far on economic revitalization programs in Iraq. Ranking Democrat, Senator Joseph

Biden stated "The president has frequently described Iraq as, quote, 'the central front of the war on terror. Well by that definition, success in Iraq is a key standard by which to measure the war on terror. And by that measure, I think the war on terror is in trouble."[89]

On the whole, the Bush Administration's emphasis on states as opposed to terrorists fits well with conventional and traditional notions of American military power. This includes applying overwhelming military force in order to attain the overall goal of deterring so-called rogue states from challenging American global preeminence. The reduction in attention to non-state entities, transnational dynamics, and cultural and economic realities, reflects an ignorance of the actual conditions that give birth to terrorism. Terrorists and Islamic movements motivated by hatred of the West cannot simply be deterred with applications of military power and political solutions. Yes, the Cold War demonstrated that states possessing WMD can be contained, deterred, and dealt with to a limited extent. However, the major drawback is that rogue states are but one problem in the threat equation.

Notes

1. Peter Baker and John Pomfret, "A Patchwork of 20 Rival Fiefdoms," *International Herald Tribune,* (30 November 2001); Scott Baldauf, "Power shift in Afghanistan," *Christian Science Monitor,* (10 December 2001), 8; Stephen Farrell and Zahid Hussain, "Cities fall to chiefs with divided loyalties," *The Times* (London), (15 November 2001); Norimitsu Onishi, "Afghan Warlords and Bandits Are Back in Business," *New York Times,* (28 December 2001), 1.
2. Pamela Constable, "Two Rebel Groups Vie for Control of Key City; Rival Guerrillas Move Into Power Vacuum Left Taliban Flight From Jalalabad," *Washington Post,* (16 November 2001), 26; Beth Daley, "Warlord Rivalries Gunfight shows peril facing many Afghans," *Boston Globe,* (10 January 2002); David Filipov, "Warlords, Bandits Rule Most Terrain," *Boston Globe,* (17 December 2001), 1; Carlotta Gall, "Anti-Taliban Factions Clash in North," *New York Times,* (13 December 2001), 2; Paul Harris, "After the Taliban: Decent into Anarchy: Warlords bring new terrors," *The Observer* (London), (2 December 2001), 18; Richard Lloyd Parry, "Opium Farmers Rejoice at Defeat of the Taliban," *The Independent* (London), (21 November 2001); Rone Tempest, "Opium growers rejoice at Taliban loss Poor farmers till land to plant crop that brings cash," *Chicago Tribune,* (2 December 2001); Paul Watson, "Rivalries and Lawlessness Thwart Efforts to Deliver Aid to Afghans," *Los Angeles Times,* (5 December 2001), 3; Tim Weiner, "A Bazaar Is Newly Abuzz and the Talk Is of a New Era: After the Taliban, What?", *New York Times,* (29 November 2001), B5; and Tim Weiner, "With Taliban Gone, Opium Farmers Return to Their Only Cash Crop," *New York Times,* (26 November 2001), B1.
3. Pamela Constable, "US Plans Greater Security Role to Help Curb Regional Fighting," *Washington Post,* (25 February 2002), 16; David D. Laitin and Ronald Grigor Suny, "Thinking a Way Out of Karabakh," *Middle East Policy,* Vol. 7, No. 1 (October 1999), 145-176.

4. "Afghanistan: Peace Elusive for New Government," *Stratford*, (19 December 2001), http://www.stratfor.com; Onishi, "Afghan Warlords and Bandits Are Back in Business," B1.

5. Peter Finn, "Afghan Factions Sign Accord," *Washington Post*, (6 December 2001), 1; Michael R. Gordon, "A Nation Challenged," *New York Times*, (4 December 2001), 2; Steven Mufson, "U.N. Security Council Backs Afghan Pact," *Washington Post*, (7 December 2001), 31.

6. Peter Baker, "Quietly, in Dark, Karzai Arrives in Kabul," *Washington Post*, (14 December 2001), 29; Ilene R. Prusher, "Rebuilding amid Afghan Disorder," *Christian Science Monitor*, (22 January 2002), 1.

7. Rod Nordland, "Warlord Nation," *Newsweek*, (3 December 2001), 47; James S. Robbins, "Triangulation, Afghan-Style," *National Review*, (4 December 2001). Benjamin Soskis, "Why All Pashtuns Are Not Alike," *New Republic*, (3 December 2001), 14

8. Christian Caryl, "The Ways of a Warlord," *Newsweek*, (11 February 2002), 20; Pete Engardio, Manjeet Kripalani, and Christian Otton, "Can Karzai Pull Afghanistan Together?," *Business Week*, (17 June 2002), 51; Ann Marlowe, "'Warlords' and 'Leaders,'" *National Review*, (18 February 2002); Ron Moreau And Sami Yousafzai, "Striking a Bargin," *Newsweek*, (30 August 2004), 34; Michael E. O'Hanlon, "A Flawed Masterpiece," *Foreign Affairs*, May/June 2002, 47; Kevin Whitelaw; Philip Smucker; Lucian Kim, "Meet the New Boss," *US News and World Report*, 11 February 2002), 21

9. James D. Fearon and David D. Laitin, "NeoTrusteeship and the Problem of Weak States," *International Security* (Spring 2004): 5; Carlotta Gall, "In Afghanistan, Violence Stalls Renewal Effort," *New York Times*, (26 April 2003), 1; Robert O. Keohane, "Political Authority after Intervention: Gradations in Sovereignty," in J.L. Holzgrefe and Keohane, eds., *Humanitarian Intervention: Ethical, Legal, and Political Dilemmas* (Cambridge: Cambridge University Press, 2003); Stephen D. Krasner, "Troubled Societies, Outlaw States, and Gradations of Sovereignty," Stanford University, (20 July 2002); Sebastian Mallaby, "The Reluctant Imperialist: Terrorism, Failed States, and the Case for American Empire," *Foreign Affairs*, (March/April 2002), 2-7.

10. Kathy Gallon, "Afghanistan Unbound," *Foreign Affairs* (May/June 2004); Kevin Whitelaw; Mark Mazzetti, "War in the Shadows," *US News and World Report*, (11 November 2002), 48; Seth G. Jones, "A Dangerous Peace," *Newsweek*, (9 August 2004), 28.

11. Peter Baker and Kamran Khan, "Deal-Making Let Many Leaders of Taliban Escape," *Washington Post*, (17 December 2001), 1; Mark Landler, "Seven Taliban Officials Surrender to a Governor and Go Free," *New York Times*, (10 January 2002); Amy Waldman, "Afghan Warlord's Rivals Link Him to U.S. Attacks," *New York Times*, (3 January 2002), 15.

12. Michael Ignatieff, "Nation-Building Lite," *New York Times Magazine*, (28 July 2002; Max Boot, *The Savage Wars of Peace: Small Wars and the Rise of American Power* (New York: Basic Books, 2002); Roland Paris, "International Peacebuilding and the 'Mission Civilisatrice,'" *Review of International Studies*, Vol. 28 (2002), 637-656.

13. Jonathan Chait, "Mad About You," *The New Republic*, (29 September 2003), 20; Ryna Lizza, "Mo' Better," *The New Republic*, (2 February 2004), 15.

14. See Bush's entire speech at: http://www.washingtonpost.com/ac2/wp-dyn/A2627-2003May1

15. James Fallows, "Transcript: The Invasion of Iraq," http://www.pbs.org/wgbh/pages/frontline/shows/invasion/interviews/fallows.html

16. Bush's quote is cited in: Michael Elliot, "So, What Went Wrong?," *Time*, (6 October 2003), 32.

17. Eric Schmitt and Steven Weisman, "The Conflict in Iraq," *New York Times*, (8 September 2004), 1.

18. Richard C. Holbrooke, "The UN's Day of Reckoning," *Newsweek*, (8 September 2003), 22; George Packer, "War After the War," *The New Yorker*, (24 November 2003), 59.

19. Thomas White, "Transcript: The Invasion of Iraq,"http://www.pbs.org/wgbh/pages/frontline/shows/invasion/etc/script.html

20. Abizaid is quoted in: Alec Russell, "We Are Looking Into the Abyss, Admits General," *The Telegraph*, (21 May 2004), 1.

21. Matthew Continetti, "Brother, Can You Spare $87 Billion?," *The Weekly Standard*, (27 October 2003); David Gergen, "Toughing it Out in Iraq," *US News and World Report*, (10 November 2003), 72; Fareed Zakaria, "Guns, Butter And the Deficit," *Newsweek*, (16 February 2004), 35.

22. Joseph Biden, "Opening Statement, Iraq- Next Steps," (24 September 2003), http://foreign.senate.gov/testimony/2003/BidenStatement030924.pdf

23. Spencer Ackerman and Franklin Foer, "The Radical," *The New Republic*, (1 December 2003), 17.

24. Ackerman and Foer, "The Radical," 17. John Barry and Mark Hosenball, "What Went Wrong," *Newsweek*, (9 February 2004), 24;

25. Both quotes can be found in Elliot, "So What Went Wrong?"

26. Chaim Kaufmann, "Threat Inflation and the Failure of the Marketplace of Ideas: The Selling of the Iraq War," *International Security* (Summer 2004).

27. Donald Rumsfeld, "Secretary Rumseld on NBC Meet the Press," (24 February 2004), http://www.defense.gov/transcripts/2002/t02242002_t0224nbc.html

28. Max Boot, "The False Allure of 'Stability,'" *The Weekly Standard*, (3 December 2002); Chester Crocker, "Bridges, Bombs, or Bluster?" *Foreign Affairs* (September/October 2003), 32; Rod Norland, "War Without End," *Newsweek*, (2 May 2003).

29. Seymour Hersh, "The Other War," *The New Yorker*, (12 April 2004), 40; Ron Moreau And Sami Yousafzai, "Flowers of Destruction," *Newsweek*, (14 July 2003), 33; Samantha Power, "Force Full," *The New Republic*, (3 March 2003), 28.

30. Eliot Cohen, "A Revolution in Warfare," *Foreign Affairs*,(March/April 1996), 37-54; Melinda Liu, "Occupational Hazards," *Newsweek*, (6 April 2004), 30; Thomas G. Mahnken and James R. FitzSimonds, "Revolutionary Ambivalence: Understanding Officer Attitudes toward Transformation," *International Security* (Fall 2003): 112-117; Barry R. Posen, "Command of the Commons; The Military Foundation of U.S. Hegemony," *International Security* (Summer 2003): 7-10.

31. Paul Wolfowitz, "Testimony as Delivered to the Senate Committee on Foreign Relations: the Situation in Afghanistan," Dirksen Senate Office Building, Washington, DC, (26 June 2002), http://www.defenselink.mil/speeches/2002/s20020626-depsecdef2.html

32. "The Rebirth of a Nation," *Economist*, January 11, 2003; Fareed Zakaria, "How to Wage War," *Newsweek*, (21 April 2003), 38.
33. Stephen F. Hayes, "New Sheriff in Town," *The Weekly Standard*, (26 May 2003); Scott Johnson and Colin Soloway, "And They Shall Lead," *Newsweek*, (28 July 2003), 21; Robert Kuttner, "All the President's Handouts," *The American Prospect*, June 2004, 44.
34. Robert Alt, "Trying the Tyrant," *National Review*, June 30, 2004; Christian Caryl and Christopher Dickey, "Trying Iraq's War Crimes," *Newsweek*, (29 December 2003), 52.
35. Reuel Marc Gerecht, "Iraqification." *The Weekly Standard*, (22 September 2003); Lawrence Kaplan, "Flashback," *The New Republic*, (1 December 2003), 15; Evan Thomas, Rod Nordland and Christian Caryl, "Operation Hearts and Minds," *Newsweek*, (29 December 2003), 34.
36. "Doomed or Still Recoverable?" *Economist*, (6 December 2003).
37. Jane Mayer, "The Manipulator," *The New Yorker*, (7 June 2004), 58; Paul Richter and Mary Curtius, "From Ally to Outcast in U.S. Eyes," *Los Angeles Times*, (21 May 2004); Evan Thomas and Mark Hosenball, "Rise and Fall of Chalabi: Bush's Mr. Wrong," *Newsweek*, (31 May 2004), 22.
38. Thomas and Hosenball, "Rise and Fall of Chalabi," 22.
39. Brian Whitaker, "Friend of US and Iran has too Many Enemies," *The Guardian*, (25 May 2004), 5.
40. Scott Wilson, "U.S. Aids Raid on Home of Chalabi," *Washington Post*, (21 May 2004), 1.
41. See "Red Cross Found Abuses at Abu Ghraib Last Year," *New York Times*, (11 May 2004), 23.
42. Ibid.
43. Eric Schmitt and Douglas Jehl, "Army Says C.I.A. Hid More Iraqi's Than it Claimed," *New York Times*, (10 September 2004), 1.
44. Ibid.
45. Eric Schmitt and Thom Skanker, "Rumsfeld Issued and Order to Hide Detainee in Iraq," *New York Times*, (17 June 2004), 22.
46. Richard W. Stevenson and Carl Hulse, "President Backs His Defense Chief in Show of Unity," *New York Times*, (11 May 2004), 22.
47. Quoted in Rajiv Chandrasekaran, "As Handover Nears, US Mistakes Loom Large," *Washington Post*, (20 June 2004), A01.
48. Bush is quoted in Linda Diebel, "US Military Muscle 'Redefining War," *Toronto Star*, (17 April 2003), 1.
49. *News Hour With Jim Lehr*, Online Transcript, "Ronald Rumsfeld Part II," (7 November 2001),
http://www.pbs.org/newshour/bb/military/july-dec01/rumsfeld2_11-7.html
50. Rory Carroll, "Bloody Evidence of US Blunder," *The Guardian*, (7 January 2002); Kim Sengupta, "Americans 'duped' into attack on convoy," *The Independent*, (24 December 2001); Anthony Shadid, "Bombed Village Is Testimony to Risks to Civilians," *Boston Globe*, (10 January 2002), 1; Amy Waldman, "Afghan Warlord's Rivals Link Him to U.S. Attacks," *New York Times*, (3 January 2002), 15.
51. Marc Herold, "Dossier on Civilian Casualties of United States' Aerial Bombing," March 2002: http://www.cursor.org/stories/civilian_deaths.htm
52. George Bush, "State of the Union," (28 January 2003),

http://www.whitehouse.gov/news/releases/2003/01/20030128-19.html

53. Brad Knickerbocker, "Who Counts the Civilian Casualties?," *Christian Science Monitor*, (31 March 2004).

54. "Still a Qualdron, Not a Quagmire," *The Economist*, (1 May 2004).

55. Assid Jabbar, Zeki Hamad, Yahya Barzanji, "Morgue Records Show 5,500 Iraqis Killed," *Associated Press*:
http://www.abcnews.go.com/wire/World/ap20040524_103.html?CMP=OTC-RSSFeeds0312

56. Ibid.

57. Amnesty International, "Iraq: One Year on the Human Rights Situations Remains Dire," (18 March 2004),: http://web.amnesty.org/library/Index/ENGMDE140062004

58. Christopher Dickey, "Shadowland: War by the Numbers," *Newsweek*, (3 October 2003), 21.

59. "OIC Says it Demanded Probe into Killing of Prisoners in Afghanistan," *AP Worldstream*, (9 January 2002).

60. William M. Arkin, "US Air Bases Forge Double-edged Sword; Deployment: Presence in Nine Countries Ringing Afghanistan Enhances Capability but Also Fuels Islamic Extremism," *Los Angeles Times*, (6 January 2002), 1; Ian Traynor, "Russia Edgy at America's Military Buildup in the Region," *The Guardian* (London), (10 January 2002),14; Syed Saleem Shahzad, "Iran takes center stage," *Asia Times*, (22 January 2002).

61. Bryan Bender, "Terror War Remaps US Troop Deployments," *Boston Globe*, (17 January 2002), 1.

62. Elisabeth Bumiller and Jane Perlez, "Bush and Top Aides Proclaim Policy of 'Ending' States That Back Terror," *New York Times*, (14 September 2001), 1.

63. David Brooks, "Dreams And Glory," *New York Times*, (16 December 2003), 35; Merrill Goozner, "Bioterror Brain Drain," *The American Prospect*, October 2003, 30; Joseph Lieberman, "The Theological Iron Curtain: A Foreign Policy Strategy for Engaging the Muslim World," *The National Interest*, (Fall 2003).

64. Jonathan Wright, "US outlines limited role in rebuilding," *Houston Chronicle* (from *Reuters*), (7 December 2001), 28; Justin Huggler, "Campaign Against Terrorism: Legacy of Civilian Casualties in Ruins of Shattered Town," *The Independent*, (27 November 2001), 5.

65. Michael E. O'Hanlon, "Iraq- By the Numbers," *Los Angeles Times*, (3 September 2004, 1.

66. Laura Rozen, "Building a Better UN," *The American Prospect*, July 2004, 17; Kevin Whitelaw, Julian E. Barnes, Kenneth T. Walsh, Bay Fang, and Ilana Ozernoy, "Staring into the Abyss," *US News and World Report*, (20 September 2004), 18.

67. John Lee Anderson, "The Uprising," *The New Yorker*, (3 May 2004), 63.

68. "Barely Ready, Not Yet Steady," *Economist*, (26 June 2004).

69. Reuel Marc Gerecht, "What Is To Be Done in Iraq?," *The Weekly Standard*, (3 May 2004); Fareed Zakaria, "Reach out to the Insurgents," *Newsweek*, (5 July 2004), 31.

70. John O'Sullivan, "Unacceptable Paralysis," *The Weekly Standard*, (27 April 2004).

71. Alexis Debat, "Vivisecting the Jihad," *The National Interest* (Summer 2004).

72. Tony Karon, "The Grim Calculations of Retaking Fallujah," *Time*, (8 November 2004), 22.

73. Richard A. Oppel and Robert Worth, "Invasion of Fallujah Begins," *New York Times*, (7 November 2004), 1; Jackie Spinner and Karl Vick, "US and Iraqi Troops Push Into Fallujah," *Washington Post*, (9 November 2004), 1.
74. Tony Karon, "After Fallujah," *Time*, (16 November 2004), 23.
75. Robert Collier, "Democracy How?," *The American Prospect*, March 2004, 23; Steven Vincent, "The Ungovernable Shiites," *The National Review*, (8 April 2004).
76. Bay Fang, "The Call of the Imams," *US News and World Report*, (10 May 2004), 20; Michael Rubin, "Losing the Shia," *The National Review*, (19 August 2004).
77. Babak Dehghanpisheh, Melinda Liu, and Rod Nordland, "'We Are Your Martyrs," *Newsweek*, (19 April 2004), 36.
78. "Can Muqtada al-Sadr now Become a Peaceful Politician?," *The Economist*, (4 September 2004.
79. Dexter Filkins and Edward Wong, "Al-Sadr Loyalists Start Deal, Give up Dangerous Weapons," *New York Times*, (12 October 2004), 1.
80. Michael Isikoff and Mark Hosenball, "Terror Watch: Friends of Al Qaeda," *Newsweek*, (16 June 2004), 10; Jonathan Schanzer, "Inside the Zarqawi Network," *The Weekly Standard*, (23 August 2004).
81. Al-Zarqawi's pledge of allegiance to Osama bin Laden can be found at: http://www.globalsecurity.org/military/world/para/zarqawi.htm
82. "Al-Zarqawi has Likely Left Fallujah, US Says," *Dallas Morning News*, (10 November 2004), 1; Andrew Gilligan, "The Sound of Rockets in the Morning," *The Spectator*, (17 April 2004), 12-13.
83. Hannah Allam, "Sympathy for al-Zarqawi Grows Among Iraqis Amid US Air Strikes," *Knight-Ridder*, (6 October 2004).
84. Steve Fainaru, "US Warplanes Strike Two Iraqi Cities," *Washington Post*, (10 September 2004, 1; Howard LaFranchi, "Coalition Holds off Efforts to Take Rebel-Run Cities," *Christian Science Monitor*, (13 September 2004), 1; Eric Schmitt and Steven Weisman, "The Conflict in Iraq: Confronting Insurgents," *New York Times*, (9 September 2004); George Wright, "US Loses Control of Two Cities," *The Guardian*, (8 April 2004), 1.
85. Franks is quoted in "Insurgency Not Anticipated," *Chicago Tribune*, (3 August 2004), 1. See also, Tommy Franks, *American Soldier* (New York: Harper Collins, 2004).
86. Ibid.
87. See: Douglas Jehl, "US Intelligence Shows Pessimism on Iraq's Future," *New York Times*, (15 September 2004), 1.
88. White, "Transcript: The Invasion of Iraq," http://www.pbs.org/wgbh/pages/frontline/shows/invasion/etc/script.html
89. All quotes can be found in: Jehl, "US Intelligence Shows Pessimism on Iraq's Future," 1.

Chapter 11

Conclusion

Just war theory provides a lens through which we can assess the moral dimensions and political implications of the Bush Doctrine. Just war theory's emphasis on the importance of international law supplies a strong foundation upon which international relations and foreign policy scholars can assess the impact of America's preemptive and preventive war strategies on the post-9/11 global system. We also know that just war theory is not naïve to the realities of America's security dilemma, which the Bush Doctrine claims has been heightened by terrorism and WMD proliferation. Therefore, the goal of this book has been to assess the nexus between America's global commitments and its national interests, as well as to analyze the Bush Administration's interpretation of that nexus.

Given the specific observations drawn in this book along the *jus ad bellum, just in bello,* and *jus post bellum* lines, for some, it is possible for some to conclude that much of the Bush Doctrine is beyond the parameters of key just war principles. This is especially the case with respect to America's invasion, occupation, and ongoing military presence in Iraq. Others may conclude that the 9/11 attacks sparked a re-definition of US national interests that demanded a more expansive interpretation of security threats. Those who fall into this category contend that the American invasion and enduring presence in Afghanistan represented an incomplete response to 9/11 and justified a foreign policy grounded on the notions of American global hegemony and preemptive and preventive force.

Ethical Dimensions

To effectively explain the exercise of preemptive and preventive use of force, decision makers and attentive international publics must have an interest in promoting an ethical and moral understanding, as well as a political interest, in exercising offensive force. Based on the empirical observations in this book, legitimate offensive force must be exercised within a set of parameters that establishes specific criteria for self defense, puts forth a threshold of credible fear from attacks, and engages in plausible threat assessments.

Afghanistan: A Strong Case of Just War

It can be plausibly concluded that America's invasion and subsequent offensive military operations in Afghanistan are largely ethical, legitimate, and strongly defensible from a just war perspective. Just cause was met when the US sought to punish those responsible for carrying out the 9/11 attacks, as well as to prevent additional terrorist attacks from being directed from the Al-Qaida leadership, which was closely guarded by the Taliban. Moreover, America's case against Al-Qaida and the Taliban was strong, which resulted in overwhelming global support against the global terror network. While there were some lingering issues, such as economic intentions, the difficulty of promoting democratic change, and other humanitarian challenges, the objective of eliminating Afghanistan as a safe haven for terrorist activity was the top priority.

Other factors have strengthened the American case in Afghanistan. In basing its claim on Legitimate Authority, the US assertion of a moral and political right of self-defense was highly consistent with Article 51 of the United Nations Charter as a legitimate response to 9/11 and to obviate additional attacks that had the strong potential of being waged against American civilian and military targets at home and abroad. From a Last Resort perspective, we could not expect the US to use non-military options against the Taliban and Al-Qaida leadership, since they were largely recognized as being of little utility given the calamitous nature of the 9/11 attacks. However, the Likelihood of Success in prevailing against terrorism was certainly a lofty one to realistically attain. Part of the problem is America's narrow definition and perception of the global terror network. Moreover, America has largely promoted military solutions to address the conditions that give rise to terrorism. Of course, the US succeeded in overthrowing the Taliban and in capturing and killing a significant portion of Al-Qaida terrorist operatives. Military success on the battlefield in the short term was much more likely than prevailing against terrorism over the long run.

The *jus in bello* principles were largely met respected with Operation Enduring Freedom. In terms of proportionality, while a significant amount of military force was applied, it was required to defeat elusive enemy forces. Besides, much of the force, represented by special operating forces, precision-guided weapons, and high value military targets, was necessary to attain America's broader objectives of preventing additional terrorist attacks from being planned and funded from Afghanistan. The balance of the weapons used and targets selected was largely consistent with proportionality, since the US focused on overthrowing the Taliban by supporting the Northern Alliance and focusing on capturing or killing bin Laden. Although a large number of non-combatants were killed and injured during Operation Enduring Freedom as a result of cluster munitions, this was not the result of deliberate targeting by US military commanders, since the Taliban and Al-Qaida intentionally merged their identities into the civilian non-combatant population in order to maximize non-combatant casualties. It must be stressed, however, that proportionality and non-combatant immunity were difficult to measure given the covert nature of US military operations.

As was demonstrated to a great extent by the US in Afghanistan, the conduct of preemptive actions must be limited in purpose to reducing or eliminating the immediate threat. Therefore, offensive security policies must not only be judged on grounds of legality and morality, but also on forethought. However, should preemption evolve into a regular practice, the exercise may become indistinguishable from preventive war and could increase instability and insecurity. While capability may not be in dispute, the motives and right intentions of a potential adversary may be misinterpreted. Specifically, states may mobilize in what appear to be aggressive ways because they are fearful or because they are aggressive.

Iraq: Falling Short of Just War

The American invasion, occupation, and military presence in Iraq demonstrates that preventive war against potential threats that could materialize sometime in the future may not adhere to several just war principles. Just cause was certainly difficult to promote because America's case was largely grounded on allegations of Iraqi failure to comply with its international disarmament commitments represented a threat to US national security interests. Just cause was also weakened by poor intelligence estimates that Iraq conspired with Al-Qaida against the US and aggressively pursued extensive WMD programs when previous multilateral efforts to disarm the Iraqi regime were to a great extent successful. America's intentions should also be questioned. Its history of supporting Saddam's brutal repression of the Kurds and the Shiites, its participation in arming Iraq with WMD during the Cold War, and its economic intentions greatly weaken any argument on humanitarian grounds. Moreover, America lacked legitimate international legal authority to wage offensive warfare against Iraq in bypassing the United Nations Security Council. This relates to the principle of Last Resort, in which the US may have prematurely gone to war when other non-lethal choices remained available to overthrow Saddam.

On the principle of Likelihood of Success, the US attack on Iraq could eventually lead to more fearful and aggressive behavior on the part of rogue states. Remember, there is a clear distinction between short term military success and long term goals. While the Bush Administration can point to Libya as evidence of a potentially positive long term deterrent effect of offensive warfare, Iran's demonstrated nuclear intentions, North Korea's deliberate failure to abide by international restrictions on its WMD programs, and the extensive clandestine efforts of Pakistan to promote its nuclear technology on the black market are evidence that proliferation may in fact be on the rise. In response, other states may defensively arm because they are afraid of a state's preemptive or preventive war doctrine or policy; others may arm offensively now that a precedent for preventive war has been set. In other words, instability and mutual fears are the likely byproducts of America's offensive war doctrine.

Unlike *jus ad bellum* principles, *jus in bello* requirements were to a great degree consistent with the prosecution of a just war. In terms of proportionality, while the total force applied was quite considerable, the US military went to great lengths to focus on targeting the Iraqi political and military leadership, although the high value targeting approach greatly failed. As was the case in Afghanistan, the number of non-combatant casualties was high, although the US never sought to deliberately target non-combatants. However, the use of significant military force resulted in two relatively quick cases of major combat that prevented high loss of non-combatant life.

However, the preventive war against Iraq undermines morality, international law, and diplomacy because it is inconsistent with the legitimate bounds of self-defense and rushes to eliminate deterrence, containment, and economic means of solving problems. More important, the line between preemptive military force and preventive war has been blurred by the invasion itself. If all states reacted to adversaries as if they faced a clear and present danger of imminent or future attack at any time, global tensions would escalate, just cause could be invoked in any circumstance, and the principle of Last Resort would become non-existent. Moreover, America's long support of Article 51 of the UN Charter would also lose its legitimacy. In sum, preventive war moves states away from the constraints of international law.

Preventive wars are imprudent because they bring about violent conflicts that may not be necessary and have a strong likelihood of fostering resentment. They are also unjust because they assume complete assessments of an adversary's future motivations and intentions and are based on a presumption of guilt. By contrast, preemption can be justified if it is undertaken against an immediate and imminent threat, when diplomacy cannot be attempted, and where the violent action is limited to reducing that threat. There is a great temptation, however, to step over the line from preemptive to preventive war, since the line is vague and because the stress of living under a possible threat is great.

Offensive warfare may seem to be a legitimate method for dealing with terrorism. Terrorists are extremely flexible and, unlike conventional militaries, they can project power with great efficiency: they do not have to develop weapons and delivery vehicles; they may live among their target populations; and they require comparatively little in the way of logistical support. In other words, terrorists act beyond the legitimate constraints of just war, whereas states are expected to wage just wars, even against terrorists. It is the refusal to accept and acknowledge the reality of vulnerability. And though the US was open to serious threats in the past, Americans are perhaps more emotionally aware of that exposure today since, as Condoleezza Rice says, "9/11 crystallized our vulnerability."[1]

However, the dual threats of terrorism and the spread of WMD do not mean that offensive warfare is the only solution. For example, terrorists' sources of funding, often tied to illicit transactions and black market economies, are vulnerable to disruption through determined law enforcement. And while terrorists can piggyback on the infrastructure of their targets, they are also vulnerable to detection via that same infrastructure as they use phones, faxes, the Internet, and other electronic media. Finally, many WMD are still relatively expensive to acquire and difficult to produce and reproduce in any quantity. Still, if we imagine all possible scenarios, the potential for devastation seems limitless and it ostensibly makes great sense to get them before they get us.

On the whole, the just war analysis presented here allows us to clearly differentiate between how the Bush Doctrine perceives intentions and actual capabilities. In estimating potential threats, the intentions of a likely adversary are much more important than capabilities that "might" be employed by someone. So the assertion that the US faces rogue enemies who "hate everything" about it must be carefully evaluated. While there is certainly compelling evidence that Al-Qaida seeks to kill all American citizens, the *National Security Strategy* makes a questionable leap when it assumes that "rogue states" also desire to harm the US and pose as imminent military threats. Moreover, the administration blurs the distinction between "rogue states" and terrorists, thereby erasing the difference between terrorists and those states where they reside: "We make no distinction between terrorists and those who knowingly harbor or provide aid to them."[2] Our just war interpretation demonstrates that these distinctions make a difference when a country is deciding whether to initiate offensive force.

To see how the Bush Administration has blurred the distinctions between intentions and actual capabilities, consider the arguments about the threat posed by Iraq's potential to acquire WMD. Vice President Cheney has argued that Iraq posed a threat to the US: "Many of us are convinced that Saddam Hussein will acquire nuclear weapons fairly soon. . . . Deliverable weapons of mass destruction in the hands of a terror network or murderous dictator or the two working together constitutes as grave a threat as can be imagined. The risks of inaction are far greater than the risks of action."[3] But was Iraq really in possession of actual WMD programs or did Saddam simply fool the US into believing that his cat-and-mouse game with UN weapons inspectors meant that he did possess WMD programs, when in reality he did not? Cheney, indeed the entire Bush Administration, seems confused by the two. In the end, the US launched a preventive war against Saddam's Iraq simply to bring an end to the confusion.

Political Consequences

This just war analysis demonstrates that what is at stake is nothing less than a fundamental shift in America's political and moral leadership of the post-9/11 world. America's invasion of Afghanistan was largely supported by most of the world as a justified response to the Taliban's sponsorship of the Al-Qaida global terrorist network. Following President Bush's designation of an axis of evil of rogue states that support terrorism and seek WMD, this intense level of global support began to wane.

Rather than continuing to serve as a first among equals as it attempted to do during the Cold War via containment and deterrence strategies, America's belligerence towards Iraq greatly weakened international support. This is especially the case in terms of *jus ad bellum* and *jus post bellum* principles on the specific issues of WMD possession, circumvention of the UN, the abandonment of weapons inspection, no-fly zones, and sanctions, the inability to anticipate the Iraqi insurgency, the largely American effort to topple Saddam, and a deteriorating post-invasion peace has weakened the case for claiming that America's war policy toward Iraq is just. The US now appears to be taking international law into its own hands, creating new rules and standards of military engagement in the absence of multilateral consent.

Moreover, opposition to the US from the UN and Europe reveals a credible global fear of a world in which there is no state powerful enough to counterbalance American power in much in the same fashion as the USSR served as ballast to the US during the Cold War. With 9/11, the Bush Administration has made the claim that policy change was inevitable after years of continuity and relative policy tinkering during the Cold War. In the immediate aftermath of 9/11, hardly anyone in Congress or the public debated the overall consequences of the Bush Doctrine. Even fewer raised the more fundamental point: A global strategy based on a first strike doctrine could signify a sustained period in which the very same international institutions, laws, and norms the US built and strengthened during the Cold War are now being challenged by America itself. President Bush's desire to make his doctrine a highly public declaration and his claim that the wars against terrorists and WMD are just render these questions legitimate.

The Invasion of Iraq: Contributing to the Problem?

Events throughout 2004 demonstrated, the US intervention in Iraq may have caused more problems than it solved them. As the US occupation gave way to a UN-recognized sovereign Iraqi interim government, the prospects for a stable, democratic future were in serious peril due in large measure to the failure of US occupation leaders to fulfill their stated goals and the inability to subdue a rising national insurgency and to calm a growing separatist movement in the autonomous Kurdish region. The US occupation evolved from an optimistic relationship in April into one characterized by bitterness and disappointment as illustrated by the open strife between the Bush White House and the once favored Ahmad Chalabi and Iraqi National Congress. Moreover, the national insurgency has not only threatened American goals in Iraq, it has endangered the very fragile state of Iraqi sovereignty. Sunni and Baathist insurgents, Al-Qaida terrorists and foreign fighters, and the Mahdi Army of Shiite cleric Moqtada Sadr have challenged the stability of the interim government and killed scores of US and Iraqi soldiers. According to US occupation authority adviser Larry Diamond, "We blatantly failed to get it right. When you look at the record, it's impossible to escape the conclusion that we squandered an unprecedented opportunity."[4]

American policy towards Iraq may have actually reduced American global power. According to the Pew Research Center, "In most countries, opinions of the US are markedly lower [2003] than they were a year ago [2002]. The war [on Iraq] has widened the rift between Americans and Western Europeans, further inflamed the Muslim world, softened support for the war on terrorism, and significantly weakened global public support for ... the UN and the North Atlantic alliance."[5] As PRC Director Andrew Kohut has noted, the latest survey results show, "The bottom has fallen out" in Muslim countries. "Very unfavorable" or "somewhat unfavorable" views of the US were expressed this spring by ninety-nine per cent of the respondents in Jordan, ninety-eight per cent in Palestine, eighty-three per cent in Turkey and Indonesia, eighty-one per cent in Pakistan, seventy-one per cent in Lebanon, and sixty-six per cent in Morocco. As Kohut concluded, "Anti-Americanism has deepened, but it has also widened ... People see America as a real threat. They think we're going to invade them."[6]

More important, in an international environment in which there is an absence of a counterweight to American global power (as opposed to the Cold War), can offensive US war measures be seen as moral, ethical, and just? The Bush Administration is correct in demanding that the threat of non-state terrorism requires a more forward-leaning response. However, the invasion of Iraq was a different ethical matter altogether. The US may have been able to successfully contain Saddam, deter him and bring him down the way the US in part forced a peaceful end to the USSR; that is, by applying a combination of multilateral economic, diplomatic, political, military, and moral pressure.

In addition, overall, the presence of US military forces in both Afghanistan and Iraq represent highly significant yet controversial deployments of US power that have arguably stretched America's global resources. For example, the Bush Administration's decision in June 2004 to withdraw an army brigade of approximately 3,600 soldiers from South Korea in order to redeploy it in Iraq is a reflection of the strain on the US military caused by the Bush administration's March 2003 decision to invade and occupy Iraq. The redeployment will largely make little tactical difference to America's ability to defend South Korea from a North Korean attack; nevertheless, the decision has symbolic importance since it demonstrates the Bush Administration's continued difficulty in stabilizing Iraq in addition to highlighting the strain placed on US military forces in Afghanistan and Iraq.

While it was expected that contingents of US troops would remain in Afghanistan and Iraq for years, civilian leaders in the Department of Defense did not expect that over 100,000 troops would be necessary for these missions, especially in Iraq. The US military, an all-volunteer force, is not suited to handle large-scale missions for long periods of time. Since active duty US troops are being pressed to their capacity, the Bush Administration has been forced to rely on Reserve and National Guard soldiers for combat missions, rather than for their traditional combat support roles. Indeed, US troops are spread so thin that the Pentagon announced on 2 June 2004 that the Army would expand its "stop-loss" program, meaning thousands of soldiers who planned on retiring will now be forced to extend their terms of service and join their units in combat in Iraq or Afghanistan. The controversial decision raises broad implications since it challenges the validity of an all-volunteer military force.

The stretching of US military resources has also prevented the Iraqi interim government from stabilizing and securing Iraq. On 8 September 2004, the Defense Department revealed that Shiite and Sunni insurgents wield significant influence in the so-called Sunni triangle, where Saddam remains popular and many forces loyal to him have gathered strength. Other areas where the US has been unable to manage have been in the Shiite stronghold of Najaf and Sadr City in Baghdad.

The explanation for why there is such a strain on US forces lies in the Bush Administration's miscalculation of how straightforward it would be to manage the occupation and continued deployment of military forces in Iraq. From the start of the invasion there were a number of similar miscalculations, such as the failure to anticipate the extensive looting that took place after the fall of Saddam, the level of support US soldiers would receive from the Iraqi population, and the ferocity and diversity of the insurgency.

Permanent War Against Terrorists and Rogue States?

The Bush Administration's post-9/11 national security policy has set the US on a seemingly permanent course of promoting a significant military expansion of US global interests. The US appears determined to maintain access to the rapidly growing network of military facilities it has built or refurbished in Central Asia, the Middle East, and East Asia for years. This contradicts Bush's criticism of the Clinton Administration for sending US troops off on "aimless and endless deployments" that allegedly detracted from their core mission of fighting and winning wars. Although Bush was primarily referring to humanitarian interventions in Kosovo and Somalia, he gave the impression that he was planning to reduce the overall global US military presence and avoid "nation building."

Since September 2001 US forces have built, upgraded or expanded military facilities in Bahrain, Qatar, Kuwait, Saudi Arabia, Oman, Turkey, Bulgaria, Pakistan, Afghanistan, Iraq, Uzbekistan and Kyrgyzstan; authorized extended training missions or open-ended troop deployments in Djibouti, the Philippines and the former Soviet republic of Georgia; negotiated access to airfields in Kazakhstan; and engaged in major military exercises, involving thousands of US personnel, in Jordan, Kuwait and India. Additional funding is primarily going to support US Uzbekistan, Pakistan, and India, which had previously been under restrictions on what they could receive from the US because of records of systematic human rights abuses, antidemocratic practices, or development of nuclear weapons. Military equipment has been added to key Middle Eastern and Persian Gulf states, including Israel, Jordan, Kuwait and Qatar. There are also plans to possibly send US forces to Yemen and build an intelligence-gathering installation aimed at monitoring activities in Sudan and Somalia.

Budgetary funds in support of these and other American defense programs have drained US financial resources. The US defense budget for fiscal year 2005 is $401.7 billion, which represents an annual increase of seven per cent and a total increase in defense spending of thirty-five per cent since fiscal year 2002 when the US government spent $296.8 billion.[7] As a result, the US budget deficit expanded to $521 billion in fiscal 2004.[8] The new global military buildup represents not so much a return to the Cold War, when the US had many more troops stationed overseas than it does today, but rather an elaboration of a new policy for intervening in the Middle East, the Caucasus, and East Asia.

Given the devastating effects of the 9/11 attacks, the reader may understand why the Bush Administration would favor an offensive war doctrine in principle and practice. The primary drawback of this line of thinking is that it is easy to be tempted by what is arguably the Bush Doctrine's promise of a guarantee of invulnerability. Such presuppositions are inconsistent with just war requirements and do not appreciate the flow and management of power and resources in the international system. Moreover, the reassurance promised by the Bush Doctrine is deceptive and the effort to attain it may be counterproductive.

Notes

1. Condoleezza Rice, "Remarks by National Security Advisor Dr. Condoleezza Rice to the National Legal Center for the Public Interest," (31 October 2003), http://www.whitehouse.gov/news/releases/2003/10/20031031-5.html
2. *The National Security Strategy of the United States*, Chapter III, http://www.whitehouse.gov/nsc/nss.html.
3. Richard Cheney, "Vice President Speaks at VFW 103rd National Convention," August 26, 2002, http://www.whitehouse.gov/news/releases/2002/08/20020826.html
4. Quoted in Rajiv Chandrasekaran, "As Handover Nears, US Mistakes Loom Large," *Washington Post*, (20 June 2004), A1.
5. Pew Center for the People and the Press, "Views of a Changing World 2003," 3 June 2003: http://people-press.org/reports/display.php3?ReportID=185
6. Ibid.
7. For an overview of US Department of Defense budget expenditures, see the Office of Management and Budget website: http://www.whitehouse.gov/omb/budget/fy2005/defense.html
8. See the online version of the *Budget of the United States* at the website of the White House Office of Management and Budget: http://www.whitehouse.gov/omb/budget/fy2005/budget.html

Bibliography

Official Sources and Other Documents

International Atomic Energy Agency (IAEA) (27 January 2003), "The Status of Nuclear Inspections in Iraq, January 27, 2003 with February 14, 2003 update," (available online:
http://www.iaea.org/NewsCenter/Statements/2003/ebsp2003n005.shtml).
(7 March 2003), "The Status of Nuclear Inspections in Iraq: An Update," (available online: http://www.un.org/News/dh/iraq/elbaradei-7mar03.pdf).
International Criminal Court (ICC) (27 June 1986), *Nicaragua v USA* (1986) (available online: http://www.icj-cij.org/icjwww/icases/inus/inusframe.htm).
The National Commission on Terrorist Attacks on the United States (2004), *The 9/11 Report*. New York: St. Martins Press.
Russian Federation (1993), *A New Challenge After the Cold War: Proliferation of Weapons of Mass Destruction*, Russian Federation Foreign Intelligence Service.
United Kingdom (UK) (24 September 2002), Prime Minister Tony Blair, "Iraq's Weapons of Mass Destruction - The assessment of the British Government," (available online: http://www.number10.gov.uk/output/Page271.asp).
United Nations Chapter VII, Article 51, *Charter of the United Nations* (available online: http://www.un.org/aboutun/charter/chapter7.htm).
U.N. Chapter I, Article 2, *Charter of the United Nations* (available online: http://www.un.org/aboutun/charter/chapter1.htm).
U.N. Food and Agriculture Organization of the United Nations (FAO) (1995), *Technical Cooperation Programme: Evaluation of Food and Nutrition Situation in Iraq*, New York: United Nations, September.
(21 January 2002), "Peace and Stability in Afghanistan Depend on Productive Agriculture- Appeal for US $39 million Launched," (available online:
http://www.fao.org/WAICENT/OIS/PRESS_NE/english/2002/2180-en.html).
U.N. Children's Fund (UNICEF) (August 1994), *Proposal for War and Environmental Sanitation Project*, New York: United Nations.
U.N. Development Programme (2002), *Human Development Report 2002: Deepening Democracy in a Fragmented World*, New York: Oxford University Press. (available online: http://hdr.undp.org/reports/global/2002/en/pdf/complete.pdf).
U.N. General Assembly (9 December 1988), "Body of Principles for the Protection of All Persons under Any Form of Detention or Imprisonment Adopted by General Assembly Resolution 43/173 of 9 December 1988," (available online: http://www.unhchr.ch/html/menu3/b/h_comp36.htm).
United Nations General Assembly Report, A/RES/46/134, New York: United Nations (available online:
http://www.un.org/documents/ga/res/46/a46r134.htm).
U.N. Office of the High Commissioner for Human Rights (UNHCR), "Protocol Additional to Geneva Conventions of 12 August 1949, and Relating to the Protection of Victims of Non-International Armed Conflicts (Protocol 1): Geneva, 8 June 1977," (available online: http://www.unhchr.ch/html/menu3/b/93.htm).

U.N. Security Council (U.N.S.C.) (August 1998), "The Implementation of United Nations Security Council Resolutions Relation to Iraq, Report by the Director-General."

U.N.S.C. Resolution 660 (2 August 1990) (available: http://ods-dds-ny.un.org/doc/RESOLUTION/GEN/NR0/575/10/IMG/NR057510.pdf?OpenElement).

    661 (6 August 1990) (available online at: http://ods-dds-ny.un.org/doc/RESOLUTION/GEN/NR0/575/11/IMG/NR057511.pdf?Openelement).

    678 (29 November 1990) (available online: http://ods-dds-ny.un.org/doc/RESOLUTION/GEN/NR0/575/28/IMG/NR057528.pdf?OpenElement).

    688 (5 April 1991) (available online: http://ods-dds-ny.un.org/doc/RESOLUTION/GEN/NR0/596/24/IMG/NR059624.pdf?OpenElement

    706 (15 August 1991) (available online: http://ods-dds ny.un.org/doc/RESOLUTION/GEN/NR0/596/42/IMG/NR059642.pdf?OpenElement).

    712 (19 September 1991) (available online: http://ods-dds-ny.un.org/doc/RESOLUTION/GEN/NR0/596/48/IMG/NR059648.pdf?OpenElement).

    715 (11 October 1991) (available online: http://ods-dds-ny.un.org/doc/RESOLUTION/GEN/NR0/596/51/IMG/NR059651.pdf?OpenElement

    986 (14 April 1995) (available online: http://ods-dds-ny.un.org/doc/UNDOC/GEN/N95/109/88/PDF/N9510988.pdf?OpenElement).

    1115 (21 June 1997) (available online: http://ods-dds-ny.un.org/doc/UNDOC/GEN/N97/168/32/PDF/N9716832.pdf?OpenElement

    1154 (2 March 1998) (available online: http://www.un.org/Depts/unscom/Keyresolutions/sres98-1154.htm).

    1368 (12 September 2001) (available online: http://ods-dds-ny.un.org/doc/UNDOC/GEN/N01/533/82/PDF/N0153382.pdf?OpenElement).

    1373 (28 September 2001) (available online: http://ods-dds-ny.un.org/doc/UNDOC/GEN/N01/557/43/PDF/N0155743.pdf?OpenElement).

    1377 (12 November 2001) (available online: http://ods-dds-ny.un.org/doc/UNDOC/GEN/N01/633/01/PDF/N0163301.pdf?OpenElement).

    1378 (14 November 2001) (available online: http://ods-dds ny.un.org/doc/UNDOC/GEN/N01/638/57/PDF/N0163857.pdf?OpenElement).

United Nations Special Commission, Iraq (UNSCOM) (25 January 1999), "Report to the Security Council." (available online: http://www.fas.org/news/un/iraq/s/990125/index.html).

United States Congress, Congressional Budget Office (30 September 2002), *Estimated Costs of a Potential Conflict with Iraq*, Washington DC: Congressional Budget Office (available online: ftp://ftp.cbo.gov/38xx/doc3822/09-30-Iraq.pdf

    House Committee on Foreign Relations (1975), *Background Information on the Use of US Armed Forces in Foreign Countries, 1975 Revision*, Committee Print, 94th Congress, 1st Session.

    Senate, Select Committee on Intelligence (9 July 2004), "Report on the U.S. Intelligence Community's Prewar Intelligence Assessments on Iraq," (available online: http://intelligence.senate.gov/iraqreport2.pdf

U.S. Department of Defense, (30 September 2001), *Quadrennial Defense Review Report*, Washington DC: Office of the Secretary of Defense.

    Office of the Secretary of Defense *Quadrennial Defense Review 2001* (30 September 2001), Washington DC (available online at the Center for Defense Information at: http://www.cdi.org/issues/qdr/).

Secretary of Defense Donald Rumsfeld (28 October 2001). "Press Conference Secretary of Defense Donald Rumsfeld and Chairman of the Joint Chiefs of Staff Richard Myers," (available online: http://www.washingtonpost.com/wp-srv/nation/specials/attacked/transcripts/rumsfeldtext_102901.html).

Deputy Secretary of Defense Paul Wolfowitz (26 June 2002), "Testimony as Delivered to the Senate Committee on Foreign Relations: the Situation in Afghanistan," Dirksen Senate Office Building, Washington, DC (available online: http://www.defenselink.mil/speeches/2002/s20020626-depsecdef2.html).

U.S. Department of State (2000-2003), *Patterns of Global Terrorism,* Counterterrorism Office, Annual Reports: 2000-2003 (available online: http://www.state.gov/s/ct/rls/pgtrpt/
(September 1999), "Saddam Hussein's Iraq," Washington DC.

U.S. Secretary of State, Colin Powell (13 September 2001), "Powell Very Pleased with Coalition-Building Results" (available online: usinfo.state.gov/topical/pol/terror/01091366.htm).
(5 February 2003), "Remarks to the United Nations Security Council" (available online: http://www.state.gov/secretary/rm/2003/17300.htm).

U.S. Department of Energy, Energy Information Administration (EIA), "Annual Energy Outlook 2004 with Projections to 2025, Market Trends- Energy Demand" (available online: http://www.eia.doe.gov/oiaf/aeo/demand.html#trans
"Annual Energy Outlook 2004 with Projections to 2025.Market Trends-Oil and Natural Gas" (available online: http://www.eia.doe.gov/oiaf/aeo/gas.html).

U.S. President, George W. Bush (11 September 2001), "Statement by the President in Address to the Nation" (available online: http://www.whitehouse.gov/news/releases/2001/09/20010911-16.html).
(14 September 2001), "President's Remarks at National Day of Prayer and Remembrance" (available online: http://www.whitehouse.gov/news/releases/2001/09/20010914-2.html
(20 September 2001), "Address to a Joint Session of Congress and the American People" (available online: http://www.whitehouse.gov/news/releases/2001/09/20010920-8.html).
(13 November 2001), "Military Order of November 13, 2001: Detention, Treatment and Trial of Certain Non-Citizens in the War Against Terrorism," *Federal Register* 66, no. 222, 57833-57836.
(7 October 2001), "Presidential Address to the Nation" (available online: http://www.whitehouse.gov/news/releases/2001/10/20011007-8.html).
(29 January 2002), "State of the Union" (available online: http://www.whitehouse.gov/news/releases/2002/01/20020129-11.html).
(1 June 2002), "Graduation Speech at West Point" (available online: http://www.whitehouse.gov/news/releases/2002/06/20020601-3.html).
(12 September 2002), "President's Remarks at the United Nations General Assembly" (available online: http://www.whitehouse.gov/news/releases/2002/09/20020912-1.html).
(17 September 2002), "The National Security Strategy of the United States of America" (available online: http://www.whitehouse.gov/nsc/nss.html).
(25 September 2002), "President Bush, Colombia President Uribe Discuss Terrorism" (available online: http://www.whitehouse.gov/news/releases/2002/09/20020925-1.html).

(28 January 2003), "State of the Union" (available online:
http://www.whitehouse.gov/news/releases/2003/01/20030128-19.html).
(7 September 2003), "President Addresses the Nation" (available online:
http://www.whitehouse.gov/news/releases/2003/09/20030907-1.html).
U.S. Supreme Court (1945), *Ex parte Quirin,* 317 U.S. 1.
(2003), *Hamdi v. Rumsfeld,* 316 F.3d 450 (4th Cir).
U.S. Vice President, Richard B. Cheney (26 August 2002), "Vice President Speaks at VFW
103rd National Convention" (available online:
http://www.whitehouse.gov/news/releases/2002/08/20020826.html).

Newspapers, Magazines and Other Sources

Arms Control Today
Asia Times
Associated Press
Atlantic Monthly
The American Prospect
Baltimore Sun
Boston Globe
Bulletin of the Atomic Scientists
Business Week
Chicago Tribune
Christian Science Monitor
Daily Telegraph
Dallas Morning News
The Economist
Financial Times
The Guardian
The Independent
International Herald Tribune
Jane's Defence Weekly
Jane's Intelligence Review,
Los Alamos National Laboratory
Los Angeles Times
National Review
Newsweek
New York Times
The New York Times Magazine
The New Yorker
The New Republic
The Observer
PBS: Behind Closed Doors
Pew Center for the People and the Press
Program on International Policy Attitudes
San Francisco Chronicle
Times of India
Time
US News and World Report
Wall Street Journal

Washington Post
Washington Times
The Weekly Standard

Monographs

Aburish, Said K. (2000), *Saddam Hussein: The Politics of Revenge*, New York: Bloomsbury Publishing.

Ambrose, Stephen E. (1997), *Rise to Globalism*, Middlesex: Penguin Books.

Bass, Warren (2004), *Support Any Friend: Kennedy's Middle East Policy and the Making of the US-Israeli Alliance*, Oxford: Oxford University Press.

Bathelemey, J. (1904), *The Founding Fathers of International Law*, Paris: V. Giard & E. Briere.

Betts, Richard K. (1982), *Surprise Attack: Lessons for Defense Planning*, Washington, DC: Brookings Institution.

Blix, Hans (2004), *Disarming Iraq*, New York: Pantheon Books.

Boot, Max (2002), *The Savage Wars of Peace: Small Wars and the Rise of American Power*, New York: Basic Books.

Brilmayer, Lea (1994), *American Hegemony: Political Morality in a One-Superpower World*, New Haven: Yale University Press.

Brown, Chris (1992), *International Relations Theory: New Normative Approaches*, New York: Columbia University Press.

Burchill, Scott, ed (1996), *Theories of International Relations*, London: Macmillan Press.

Carr, Edward Hallett (1945), *Nationalism and After*, London: Macmillan.

——— (1951), *The Twenty Years' Crisis 1919-1939*, London: Macmillan.

Coates, AJ (1997), *The Ethics of War*, Manchester: Manchester University Press.

Cohen, Avner (2004), *Israel and the Bomb*, New York: Columbia University Press.

Collin, Richard H (1990), *Theodore Roosevelt's Caribbean: The Panama Canal, The Monroe Doctrine, and the Latin American Context*, Baton Rouge: Louisiana State University Press.

Coppieters, Bruno (2001), *Federalism and Conflict in the Caucuses*, London: Royal Institute for International Affairs.

Coppieters, Bruno and Nick Fotion (2002), *Moral Constraints on War: Principles and Cases*, Lanham: Lexington Books.

Daadler, Ivo and James Lindsay (2003), *America Unbound: The Bush Revolution in Foreign Policy*, Washington DC: Brookings Institution Press.

Detter, I (2000), *The Law of War*, Cambridge: Cambridge University Press.

de Vattel, Emmerich (1863), *The Law of Nations or the Principles of Natural Law*, Paris: Guillaumin.

Doyle, Michael (1997), *Ways of War and Peace: Realism, Liberalism, and Socialism*, New York: WW Norton.

Elstain, Jean Bethke, ed (1991), *Just War Theory*, New York: New York University Press.

Franks, Tommy Franks (2004), *American Soldier*, New York: Harper Collins.

Gilpin, Robert (1981), *War and Change in World Politics*, Cambridge: Cambridge University Press.

Glad, Betty and Chris J. Dolan, eds (2004), *Striking First: The Preventive War Doctrine and the Reshaping of US Foreign Policy*, New York: Palgrave-Macmillan.

Glover, Jonathan (2001), *Humanity: A Moral History of the Twentieth Century,* London: Pimlico.

Goodwin, Geoffrey (1982), *Ethics and Nuclear Deterrence,* New York: St. Martins Press.

Green, Leslie C. (1993), *The Contemporary Law of Armed Conflict,* Manchester: Manchester University Press.

Gregor, Mary (1998), *Groundwork of the Metaphysics of Morals,* Cambridge University Press: Cambridge.

Grose, Peter (1983), *Israel in the Mind of America,* New York: Knopf.

Grotius, Hugo (1901), *The Rights of War and Peace,* Washington, DC: M. Walter Dunne.

Gunaratna, Rohan (2002), *Inside Al-Qaida: Global Network of Terror,* New York: Columbia University Press.

Guzzini, Stefano (1998), *Realism in International Relations and International Political Economy: The Continuing Story of a Death Foretold,* New York: Routledge.

Harris, Sheldon H. (1995), *Factories of Death,* London: Routledge.

Herrick, Christopher and Patricia B. McRae (2003), *Issues in American Foreign Policy,* New York: Addison Wesley Longman.

Hoffman, Stanley (1968), *Gulliver's Troubles, or the Setting of American Foreign Policy* New York: McGraw-Hill.

Holzgrefe, JL and Robert Keohane, eds (2003), *Humanitarian Intervention: Ethical, Legal, and Political Dilemmas,* Cambridge: Cambridge University Press.

Homes, Robert (1989), *On War and Morality,* Princeton: Princeton University Press.

Hook, Steven W. and John Spanier (2000), *American Foreign Policy Since World War II,* Washington DC: Congressional Quarterly Press.

Hooper, Townsend and Douglas Brinkley (2000), *FDR and the Creation of the UN,* New Haven: Yale University Press.

Howard, Michael, George J. Andreopoulos, and Mark R. Shulman (1994), *The Laws of War: Constraints on Warfare in the Western World,* New Haven: Yale University Press.

Human Rights Watch (2003), *Off Target :The Conduct of the War and Civilian Casualties in Iraq,* New York: Human Rights Watch (available online: http://www.hrw.org/reports/2003/usa1203/usa1203.pdf
(1995), *Iraq's Crime of Genocide: The Anfal Campaign Against the Kurds.* New Haven: Yale University Press.

Ignatieff, Michael (2000), *Virtual War,* London: Chatto and Windus.

Jervis, Robert (1976), *Perception and Misperception in International Politics,* Princeton: Princeton University Press.

Johnson, James Turner (1993), *Can Modern War Be Just?,* New Haven: Yale University Press.
(1999), *Morality and Contemporary Warfare,* New Haven: Yale University Press.
(1981), *Just War Tradition and the Restraint of War,* Princeton: Princeton University Press.

Kant, Immanuel (1983), *Perpetual Peace and Other Essays on Politics, History and Morals,* New York; Hackett Publishing Co.

Karsh, Efraim and Inari Rautsi (1991), *Saddam Hussein: A Political Biography,* New York: The Free Press.

Katzenstein, Peter J. (1978), *Between Power and Plenty: Foreign Economic Policies of Advanced Industrial Countries,* Madison: University of Wisconsin Press.

(1996), *The Culture of National Security: Norms and Identity in World Politics*, New York: Columbia University Press.

Keohane, Robert, ed. (1986), *Neorealism and its Critiques*, New York: Columbia University Press.

Kosiak, Steve (2001), *Estimated Cost of Operation Enduring Freedom: The First Two Months, CSBA Backgrounder*, Washington DC: Center for Strategic and Budgetary Assessments.

Krasner, Stephen D. (1999), *Sovereignty: Organized Hypocrisy*, Princeton: Princeton University Press.

Lackey, Douglas (1988), *The Ethics of War and Peace*, New York: Prentice-Hall.

Lee, Steven P (1993), *Morality, Prudence, and Nuclear Weapons*, Cambridge University Press.

Malone, David M. and Yuen Foong Khong (2003), *Unilateralism & US Foreign Policy*, Boulder: Lynne Rienner Publishers, Inc.

McDonald, Bryan, Richard Anthony Matthew and Kenneth R. Rutherford (2004), *Landmines and Human Security: International Politics and War's Hidden Legacy*, Albany: SUNY Press, 2004.

Mead, Walter Russell (2002), *Special Providence: American Foreign Policy and How it Has Changed the World*, New York: Routledge.

Morgenthau, Hans J. (1948), *Politics Among Nations: The Struggle for Power and Peace*, 6d ed, New York: Knopf.

Morris, Edmund (2001), *Theodore Rex*, New York: Random House.

Nisbet, Robert (1988), *The Present Age: Progress and Anarchy in Modern America*, New York: Harper and Row.

Niebuhr, Reinhold and Alan Heimert (1963), *A Nation So Conceived*, New York: Charles Scribner's Sons.

Nye Jr., Joseph S. (2002), *The Paradox of American Power: Why the World's Only Superpower Can't Go it Alone*, New York: Oxford University Press.

Orend, Brian (2001), *War and International Conflict: A Kantian Perspective*, Toronto: Wilfrid Laurier University Press.

Patrick, Stewart and Shepard Foreman (2003), *Multilateralism & US Foreign Policy*, Boulder: Lynne Rienner Publishers, Inc.

Payne, Keith B. (2001), *The Fallacies of Cold War Deterrence and a New Direction*, Lexington: The University of Kentucky Press.

Phillips, Robert and Duane Cady (1996), *Humanitarian Intervention: Just War Versus Pacifism*. Lanham: Rowman & Littlefield.

Prokosch, Eric (1995), *The Technology of Killing: A Military and Political History of Cluster Weapons*, London: Zed Books.

Purdum, Todd S. (2003), *A Time of Our Choosing*. New York: Henry Holt and Company.

Ramsey, Paul (1968), *The Just War: Force and Political Responsibility*, New York: Scribner's.

Rashid, Ahmed (2001), *Taliban: Militant Islam, Oil and Fundamentalism in Central Asia*, New Haven: Yale University Press.

Rawls, John (1971), *A Theory of Justice*, Cambridge, MA: Belknap Press.

Regan, Richard J. (1996), *Just War: Principles and Cases*, Washington DC: Catholic University of America Press.

St. Augustine (1972), *City of God*, David Knowles, ed., New York: Penguin Classics.

St. Thomas Aquinas (1997), *Summa Theologica*, New York: Ave Maria Press.

Scott, James Brown (1944), *Classics of International Law*, 2d ed., Oxford: Clarendon Press.

Smith, James M. (2001), *Nuclear Deterrence and Defense: Strategic Considerations*, Colorado: U.S. Air Force Institute for National Security Studies Book Series.

Snyder, Glenn H. and Paul Diesing (1977), *Conflict Among Nations: Bargaining, Decision-making and System Structure in International Crises*, Princeton: Princeton University Press.

Stork, Joe (1975), *Middle East Oil and the Energy Crisis*, New York: Monthly Review Press.

Sulzberger, CL. (1973), *An Age of Mediocrity: Memoirs and Diaries, 1963-1972*, New York: Macmillan.

Trachtenberg, Marc (1991), *History and Strategy*, Princeton: Princeton University Press.

Waltz, Kenneth (1979), *Theory of International Politics*, Reading: Addison-Wesley.

Walzer, Michael (1992), *Just and Unjust Wars: A Moral Argument with Historical Illustrations*, 2d ed., New York: Basic Books.

Wells, Donald A. (1996), *An Encyclopedia of War and Ethics*, Westport: Greenwood Press.

Whicker, Marcia Lynn, James P. Pfiffner and Raymond A. Moore, eds. (1993), *The Presidency and the Persian Gulf War*, Westport, Connecticut: Praeger.

Wilson, Heather (1988), *International Law and the Use of Force by National Liberation Movements*, Oxford: Clarendon Press.

Articles

Ackerman, Spencer and Franklin Foer (1 December 2003), "The Radical," *The New Republic*, p. 17.

Aldrich, George (2002), "The Taliban, Al Qaeda, and the Determination of Illegal Combatants," *American Journal of International Law*, Vol. 96.

Baldwin, A (1999/2000), "The Sanctions Debate and the Logic of Choice," *International Security* Vol. 24, no. 3, pp. 87-92.

Barry, Tom (November 2002), "The US Power Complex: What's New," *World Policy Journal*).

Betts, Richard K. (September 1981), "Nuclear Proliferation After Osirak," *Arms Control Today*, Vol. 11, pp. 1-7.

(Spring 2002), "The Soft Underbelly of American Primacy: Tactical Advantages of Terror," *Political Science Quarterly* Vol. 117, no. 1, pp. 19–36.

Burr, William and Jeffrey T. Richelson (Winter 2000/2001), "Whether to 'Strangle the Baby in the Cradle': The United States and the Chinese Nuclear Program, 1960-64," *International Security*, Vol. 25.

Byman, Daniel (Summer 2003), "Scoring the War on Terrorism," *The National Interest*.

Chait, Jonathan (29 September 2003), "Mad About You," *The New Republic*, p. 20.

Cohen, Avner (Fall-Winter 2003), "Israel and Chemical/Biological Weapons: History, Deterrence, and Arms Control," *Nonproliferation Review*, Vol. 8, no. 3, pp. 27-53.

Collier, Robert (March 2004), "Democracy How?," *The American Prospect*, p. 23.

Continetti, Matthew (27 October 2003), "Brother, Can You Spare $87 Billion?," *The Weekly Standard*.

Cortright, David (3 December 2001), "A Hard Look at Iraq Sanctions," *The Nation*.

Crawford, Neta C. (March 2003), "Just War Theory and the US Counterterror War," *Perspectives on Politics*.

Crawford, Neta C. (2 March 2003), "The Slippery Slope to Preventive War," *Ethics and International Affairs*.

Danner, Mark (Fall 1997), "Marooned in the Cold War: America, the Alliance, and the Quest for a Vanished World," *World Policy Journal,* pp. 1-23.

Debat, Alexis (Summer 2004), "Vivisecting the Jihad," *The National Interest).*

Diab, M Zuhair (Fall 1997), "Syria's Chemical and Biological Weapons: Assessing Capabilities and Motivations," *Nonproliferation Review* Vol. 5, pp. 104-111.

Falk, Richard (15 July 2002), "The New Bush Doctrine," *The Nation.*

Fallows, James (January/February 2004), "Blind Into Baghdad," *Atlantic Monthly.*

Fearon, James. D. and David D. Laitin (Spring 2004), "NeoTrusteeship and the Problem of Weak States," *International Security,* pp. 5-12.

Fisher, David (Spring 1994), "The Ethics of Intervention," *Survival* Vol. 36, no. 1.

Gallon, Kathy (May/June 2004), "Afghanistan Unbound," *Foreign Affairs.*

Gardner, Richard N. (September 1990), "The Comeback of Liberal Internationalism," *Washington* Quarterly Vol. 13, no. 3, pp. 23-29.

Gerecht, Reuel Marc (May 2004), "What Is To Be Done in Iraq?" *The Weekly Standard.*
(22 September 2003), "Iraqification," *The Weekly Standard.*

Gholz, Eugene, Daryl G. Press, and Harvey M. Saplosky (Spring 1997), "Come Home America: The Strategy of Restraint in the Face of Temptation," *International Security* Vol. 21, no. 4, pp. 5-48.

Goozner, Merrill (October 2003), "Bioterror Brain Drain," *The American Prospect,* p. 30.

Hagel, Charles (Spring 2001), "History's Lessons," *The Washington Quarterly,* Vol. 24, no. 2, p. 93.

Heir, J Bryan (1995), "Intervention: From Theories to Cases," *Ethics and International Affairs,* Vol. 9, pp. 5-6.

Herz, John H (January 1950), "Idealist Internationalism and the Security Dilemma," *World Politics,* Vol. 2, no. 2, pp. 157-180.

Hoffmann, Stanley (12 June 2003), "America Goes Backward," *New York Review of Books,* 50, no. 12.

Holloway, Steven (July-September 2000), "US Unilateralism at the UN: Why Great Powers Do Not Make Great Multilateralists," *Global Governance,* Vol. 6, no. 3, pp. 361-381.

Ignatieff, Michael (28 July 2002), "Nation-Building Lite," *New York Times Magazine.*

Jervis, Robert (Summer 1999), "Realism, Neoliberalism, and Cooperation: Understanding the Debate," *International Security,* Vol. 24, no. 1, pp. 42-63.

Kagan, Robert (Summer 1998), "The Benevolent Empire," *Foreign Policy,* Vol. 111, pp. 34-35.
(June/July 2002), "Power and Weakness," *Policy Review.*

Kaplan, Lawrence (1 December 2003), "Flashback," *The New Republic,* p.15.

Kaufmann, Chaim (Summer 2004), "Threat Inflation and the Failure of the Marketplace of Ideas: The Selling of the Iraq War," *International Security.*

Kellogg, Davida E. (Autumn 2002), "Jus Post Bellum," *Parameters,* pp. 87-99.

Koch, Andrew and Jennifer Topping (Spring/Summer 1997), "Pakistan's Nuclear Weapons Program: A Status Report," *Nonproliferation Review,* Vol. 4, no. 3

Krauthammer, Charles (1990/1991), "The Unipolar Moment," *Foreign Affairs,* pp. 23-32.

Kristol William and Robert Kagan (July/August 1996), "Toward a Neo-Reaganite Foreign Policy," *Foreign Affairs,* pp. 18-32.

Laitin David D. and Ronald Grigor Suny (October 1999), "Thinking a Way Out of Karabakh," *Middle East Policy,* Vol. 7, no. 1, pp. 145-176.

Lawrence, Robert M. and William R. Van Cleave (10 September 1968), "Assertive Disarmament," *National Review,* pp. 898-905.

Layne, Christopher (Spring 1993), "The Unipolar Illusion: Why Great Powers Will Rise," *International Security,* Vol. 17, no.2, pp. 5-51.

Lemann, Nicholas (1 April 2002), "The Next World Order: The Bush Administration May Have a Brand-New Doctrine of Power," *The New Yorker*.

Lieberman, Joseph (Fall 2003), "The Theological Iron Curtain: A Foreign Policy Strategy for Engaging the Muslim World," *The National Interest*.

Litwak, Robert S. (Winter 2002/2003), "The New Calculus of Pre-emption," *Survival*, Vol. 44.

Lizza, Ryna (2 February 2004), "Mo' Better," *The New Republic*, 15.

Luban, David (Winter 1980), "Just War and Human Rights," *Philosophy and Public Affairs*, Vol. 9, no. 2, pp. 160-181.

Mahnken, Thomas G. and James R. Fitzsimonss (Fall 2003), "Revolutionary Ambivalence: Understanding Officer Attitudes toward Transformation," *International Security*, pp. 112-117.

Mallaby, Sebastian (March/April 2002), "The Reluctant Imperialist: Terrorism, Failed States, and the Case for American Empire," *Foreign Affairs*, pp. 2-7.

Marlowe, Ann (18 February 2002), "'Warlords' and 'Leaders,'" *National Review*.

Masek, Lawrence (April 2002), "All's Not Fair in War: How Kant's Just War Theory Refutes War Realism," *Public Affairs Quarterly*, Vol. 16, no. 2.

Mayer, Jane (7 June 2004), "The Manipulator," *The New Yorker*.

Mearshimer, John J. (Winter 1994/1995), "The False Promise of International Institutions," *International Security*, Vol. 19, no. 3, pp. 5-49.

Moravcsik, Andrew (Autumn 1997), "Taking Preferences Seriously: A liberal Theory of International Politics," *International Organization*, pp. 513-553.

Mueller, John and Karl Mueller (May/June 1999), "Sanctions of Mass Destruction," *Foreign Affairs*, Vol. 78, no. 3.

O'Hanlon, Michael E. (May/June 2002), "A Flawed Masterpiece," *Foreign Affairs*.

Paris, Roland (2002), "International Peacebuilding and the 'Mission Civilisatrice,'" *Review of International Studies*, Vol. 28, pp. 637-656.

Patrick, Stewart (Fall 2001), "Don't Fence Me In: A Restless America Seeks Room to Roam," *World Policy Journal*.

Posen, Barry R (Summer 2003), "Command of the Commons: The Military Foundation of U.S. Hegemony," *International Security*, pp. 7-10.

Rice, Condoleezza (January/February 2000), "Promoting the National Interest," *Foreign Affairs*, pp. 45-62.

Robbins, James S. (4 December 2001), "Triangulation, Afghan-Style," *National Review*.

Schwartz, Benjamin (Winter 1994-1994), "The Vision Thing: Sustaining the Unsustainable," *World Policy Journal*, pp. 101-121.

Soskis, Benjamin (3 December 2001), "Why All Pashtuns Are Not Alike," *New Republic*.

Tucker, Robert Tucker (November/December), "Alone or With Others," *Foreign Affairs*, Vol. 78, no. 6 , pp. 15-20.

Vincent, Steven (8 April 2004), "The Ungovernable Shiites," *The National Review*.

Wendt, Alexander (Spring 1992), "Anarchy is What States Make of It: The Social Construction of Power Politics," *International Organization*, Vol. 46, no.2, pp. 391-425.

Index

Abu-Ghraib 189
Abu Nidal 61, 109
Adams, John Quincy 9, 10
Afghanistan civil wars 66, 68, 75, 128,
    129, 131, 132, 133, 170, 171,
    control of by Taliban 48-50, 66, 67,
        68-69, 74-75, 79, 103, 104-106,
        129, 131-133, 139
    opium production in 75, 105, 152,
        181, 182, 187
    Soviet invasion of 68, 131-132,
        170, 171
Al-Jazeera 70
Al-Qaida
    attack on the Khobar Towers 47,
        123
    attacks in Somalia 47, 67, 123
    attacks against US embassies 47, 79
        124
    attack on the USS Cole 47, 123
    history and formation of 123-124
    operations 125-126
    perception in Muslim world 70-71
    relationship with the Taliban 48-50,
        66, 74-75, 87-91, 98, 103-106
        128-133, 151-153, 167-169,
        183, 190-191, 193-195, 207
Al-Sadr, Maqtada 138-139, 190, 192,
    197-198
Allawi, Iyad 188, 193, 196, 198,
Anfal genocide campaign 72, 73
Ansar al Islam 60, 197
Anti-Americanism 54, 70-71, 106-107,
    109, 113, 114, 125, 189, 191,
    194, 198
Arafat, Yasser 61
Atef, Mohammed 124, 152

Baath Party 135, 139, 174, 186, 187,
    188, 190, 196-197
Barry, Tom, 16
Betts, Richard 4, 9, 52
Bin Laden, Osama 48-49, 52, 60-61,
    103, 106, 118, 123-125, 129, 132,
    146-148, 168, 183, 190, 198, 207
Blair Tony 56, 58
Bremer, L. Paul 188-189, 196-197
Bush Doctrine 194
    anti-terrorism and 2-9, 12, 15-18,
        22, 24, 25, 30-33, 34, 36, 37, 38,
        47-49, 52-55, 58, 60-61, 66-74,
        76, 80-82, 86-91, 93, 98, 99, 102-
        103, 105, 106, 107, 109, 111,
        116, 118, 122-130, 132-135, 139,
        147-151, 153, 156, 167-169, 172-
        173, 182-184, 186, 187, 190-196,
        198, 200, 206, 207, 209-210,
        211-213
    consequences of 8-9, 12, 15, 16, 25,
        28-29, 31, 37, 53, 86, 90, 102,
        107, 117, 208, 208, 211, 213-214
    emphasis on self-defense in 2, 6-8,
        22, 24-25, 28, 47, 87-98, 105,
        207, 209
    expression of hegemony in 25,
        51, 206
    imminence and 5-8, 24-27, 29-30,
        68, 71, 86, 90, 92, 102, 209-
        210
    National Security Strategy of 2002
        6-8, 24, 47, 86, 103, 107,
    preemptive military force and 7, 9,
        15, 17, 23-26, 29, 30, 86, 89,
        90, 92, 94, 97, 102-103, 107,
        206-209
    preventive war and 2, 5-10, 15, 17,
        22-26, 29, 89-90, 92-94, 102-
        103, 107, 206, 208-210
    regime change and 32, 36, 50, 55,
        110, 122, 127, 194
    rogue states and 2-4, 7-9, 15, 18,
        24, 32, 48, 53, 96, 117, 122, 127-
        128, 129, 130, 131, 133, 139,
        140, 144, 167, 194, 200, 208,
        210, 213-214
    State of the Union (2002) 5